William Livingston's
American Revolution

William Livingston's American Revolution

JAMES J. GIGANTINO II

PENN

UNIVERSITY OF PENNSYLVANIA PRESS

PHILADELPHIA

Publication of this volume was aided by a gift from
Eric R. Papenfuse and Catherine A. Lawrence.

A volume in the Haney Foundation Series, established in 1961
with the generous support of Dr. John Louis Haney.

Published by
University of Pennsylvania Press
Philadelphia, Pennsylvania 19104-4112
www.upenn.edu/pennpress

Printed in the United States of America on acid-free paper

1 3 5 7 9 10 8 6 4 2

Library of Congress Cataloging-in-Publication Data
Names: Gigantino, James J., II, author.
Title: William Livingston's American Revolution / James J. Gigantino II.
Other titles: Haney Foundation series.
Description: 1st edition. | Philadelphia : University of Pennsylvania Press,
    [2018] | Series: Haney Foundation series | Includes bibliographical
    references and index.
Identifiers: LCCN 2018007652 | ISBN 978-0-8122-5064-0 (hardcover : alk.
    paper)
Subjects: LCSH: Livingston, William, 1723–1790. | New Jersey—History—
    Revolution, 1775–1783. | New Jersey—Politics and government—
    To 1775. | New Jersey—Politics and government—1775–1865. |
    Governors—New Jersey—Biography. | United States—History—
    Revolution, 1775–1783.
Classification: LCC E302.6.L75 G54 2018 | DDC 974.9/03092 [B]—dc23
    LC record available at https://lccn.loc.gov/2018007652

For Stephanie

CONTENTS

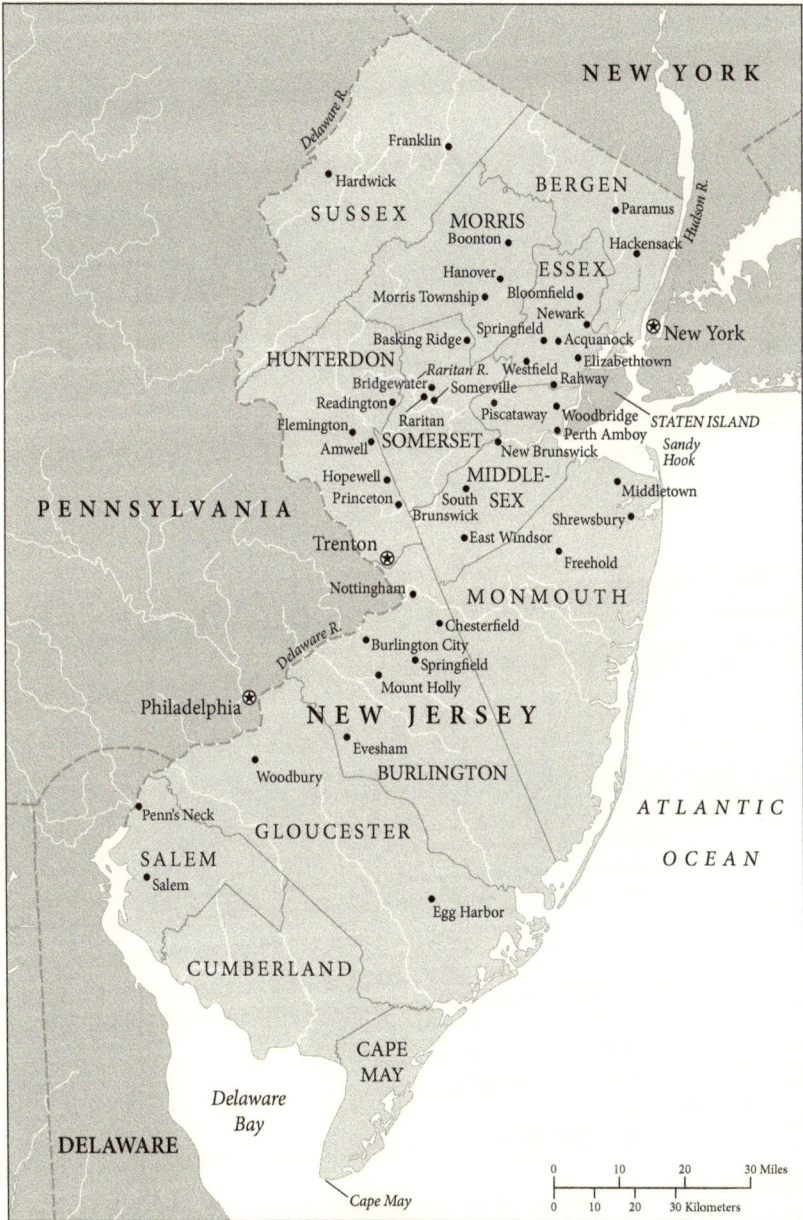

New Jersey, showing county lines, 1753–1824.

Introduction

In the fall of 1778, William Livingston lamented to his cousin John Henry Livingston that he had not seen his family for more than two weeks in the previous two years. The hardships of prosecuting the American Revolution—the "lodging & diet" and the "numerous stratagems laid for" him—had filled his days with "indisposition, weariness, or discouragement." Dodging kidnapping plots and raids on his home, he believed that "the Tories are ready to devour me, bones & all"; yet he also felt that "Providence supported" him and made him useful to his country.[1]

This book is about these types of hardships and discouragements that William Livingston, New Jersey's first governor, experienced during the American Revolution and, specifically, how he managed a state government on the war's front lines. Livingston, as a wartime bureaucrat, played a pivotal role in a pivotal place, prosecuting the war on a daily basis for eight years. Although few historians have paid serious attention to these state-level executive operations before, during, and after the Revolution, second-tier founding fathers like Livingston actually administered the war and guided the day-to-day operations of revolutionary-era governments, serving as the principal conduits between the local wartime situation and national demands placed on the states. *William Livingston's American Revolution* examines the complex nature of the conflict and the choice to wage it, the wartime bureaucrats charged with administering it, and the limits of that patriot governance under fire during and after the war.[2]

This book, then, is as much about the position Livingston filled as about the man himself. The reluctant patriot and his position as governor quickly became one, as Livingston's distinctive personality molded his office's status and reach. A tactful politician, successful lawyer, writer, satirist, political operative, gardener, soldier, and statesman, Livingston became the longest-serving patriot governor during a brutal war that he had not originally wanted to fight or believed could be won. His prewar experiences put him in a difficult position as a wartime bureaucrat but also helped him seize power from an increasingly hostile legislature. The battle between Livingston and the legislature over control of governmental operations created a power relationship that allows an exploration of the dynamic prosecution of the war on a range of important issues, including the role of finances, the battle against loyalism, and the creation of a new federal government that benefited from the lessons of the Revolution. In each area, Livingston contended for increased executive power, effectively arguing that the governor's office served as the primary guardian of state power, as opposed to the elected legislature or the militia, both of which he often criticized for bowing to the will of a fickle electorate. His vantage point on the war was much wider than most. He not only sat for the war's entirety in a central political position but also served in both the Continental Congress and the Constitutional Convention, holding high political office continuously from 1774 to 1790. As a founding father, Livingston not only saw it all but also contributed substantially to the new nation's making at every level.

Despite his efforts to improve the condition of New Jersey during the Revolution, Livingston remains one of the forgotten founders. No complete biography of him has appeared since 1833.[3] Some of this obscurity can be attributed to Livingston himself: while serving in the Continental Congress and the Constitutional Convention, he seldom voiced his opinion on the record. He was bookish, intimidated by oral debate, and far more at home participating on committees and penning elegant prose that could motivate or define the revolutionary movement. Decades of political activism in his native New York had seasoned many of those thoughts. There the Livingstons had become the predominant political family and, with William's help as a satirical writer and propagandist, had battled for control of the colony from the 1740s onward.[4] Indeed, part of Livingston's historical allure comes from his intense familial, social, political, and business networks, which enabled him to interact with almost every major revolutionary figure across the new nation and beyond. Some of these connections arose from his prewar career as a writer who railed against the establishment of an Anglican bishop in North America, decried the Stamp Act, and advocated war against France in the Seven Years' War. All who met Livingston in Philadelphia in 1774 and 1775 already knew him from these writings. Other connections came from family. Brothers, cousins, sons-in-law, nephews, and many others served in key posts in the Continental Congress, in New York state government, and as ambassadors abroad. Likewise, his Dutch upbringing in Albany made him well known as an American partisan in Holland, while his family's business dealings gave him contacts stretching from Vermont to the Caribbean to Africa.[5]

Figure 1. William Livingston. Portrait by John Wollaston (c. 1750).
Courtesy of Fraunces Tavern Museum, New York City.

Livingston's familial and business connections enabled him to see how his local prosecution of the war reverberated to national and international levels, particularly because New Jersey remained at the center of military and political affairs for the war's duration. Historian Leonard Lundin's 1940 observation that New Jersey was the "cockpit" of the American Revolution remains true: New Jerseyans experienced the war far more intimately than other Americans in terms of military operations and social and economic dislocations. The British occupation of New York in late 1776 placed New Jerseyans on the war's front lines, where they endured constant skirmishes and had to decide early on to support the patriots or to remain loyal to the king. Being on the front lines, though, was not new; the state's geographic position between Philadelphia and New York and its trading connections with the Caribbean and Europe provided its residents with a constant flow of ideas from around the Atlantic World before the Revolution. More important, the war's dramatic effects on the state confronted Livingston with unprecedented wartime and postwar issues to manage.[6]

An examination of this distinctive individual in a locale central to the revolutionary movement sheds new light on the Revolution's impact on politics, the economy, and common people while engaging several important historical questions. The first theme explored here is the choice to go to war. Livingston's struggles with independence as he served as a delegate to the Continental Congress from 1774 to 1776 reflect the same difficult choices faced by thousands of Americans. Moreover, Livingston epitomizes those founders who saw the revolutionary movement in royalist terms. Several founders believed that Parliament had usurped the prerogatives of the crown after the Glorious Revolution and inappropriately interfered with issues, including colonial affairs that should have been the sole province of the king. Livingston and others hoped George III would exert a stronger executive authority against Parliament, though popular Whig ideology that converted many to republicanism soon overtook this line of reasoning as the war began. This popular ideology—something Livingston never took comfort in—remade New Jersey's patriot government and led to Livingston's ejection from the Continental Congress in June 1776 for his continued opposition to immediate independence. Livingston never abandoned his royalist leanings and retained both a strong interest in greater executive authority and a healthy suspicion of legislators, beliefs that dramatically affected how he prosecuted the war in New Jersey.[7]

Livingston's moderation provides a model with which to explore the choice of independence, especially in the Middle Colonies, where feelings for democracy ran tepid. The dynamic battle over independence in New Jersey reveals previously underexplored class conflicts embedded in society that pressured the patriot leadership and challenges how historians have understood moderates and their decision for war. Social historians have argued for the necessity of understanding how common people forced the elite into war through crowd action, manipulation, and the threat of violence. Viewing this period through Livingston's eyes highlights something quite different: the patriot movement had already enfranchised common white men in New Jersey. They not only participated in the crowd but also, by late spring 1776, used their votes to elect leaders who supported war. These common Jersey whites then infused the popular Whig ideology directly into the political arena. Moderates like Livingston did not change their minds; rather, patriots cast them aside and replaced them with delegates willing to vote with the more radical majority.[8]

The second theme, and the heart of *William Livingston's American Revolution*, examines Livingston's role in prosecuting the war and illuminates governmental operations and relationships with soldiers and civilians in the midst of significant armed conflict. The British invasion and occupation of New Jersey in late 1776 briefly ended patriot rule there, forcing Livingston to reconstruct a government amid a constant foraging war in 1777. He did so by consolidating executive power in ways that the 1776 Whig constitution had rejected—that is, by creating agencies that not only exerted executive power but also exercised judicial and legislative power in this time of emergency. The governor's Privy Council and Council of Safety significantly elevated Livingston's power in the state and essentially allowed him to act as the entire government in the aftermath of the invasion. As in South Carolina after the fall of Charleston, Livingston became the focal point of New Jersey's patriot government and served as a conduit among Washington's army, state lawmakers, and local officials to advance the patriots' wartime agenda. Livingston's prosecution of the war could not have been possible without the strong support of the state's militia, though its use in New Jersey challenges its role in the historiography. Historians have championed the central role of the militia in the revolutionary movement; however, after roughly two years of fighting, Livingston realized that he could not rely on the militia to enforce patriot control. Instead, Livingston believed that only his own executive agencies, with himself as the chief arbiter for the government, could wage the revolution effectively. The interplay between Livingston and the militia looms large because of Livingston's continued frustrations with the militia's effectiveness. Too often, he saw the legislature act against the general good by making exemption from military service easy; such measures violated his belief in shared republican sacrifice and hit him hard personally because he felt he had given up much of his own livelihood to support the movement. This patriot failure reinforced Livingston's royalist leanings and encouraged his belief that a sound executive should wield more power than legislators willing to bend to the demands of their constituents. However, it also highlights the contradictions within his character. Though he remained committed to royalist ideals of executive control, he simultaneously exhibited republican tendencies by demanding shared sacrifice.[9]

Loyalty during the American Revolution is this volume's third theme. Livingston's experiences as governor of a state under siege by enemy forces placed him at the center of this vital concern of patriot governance, as he spent much of his time assessing the danger of and protecting the state from third-column attacks. Livingston's royalist leanings and interest in efficient government moved him to use his executive agencies, especially the Council of Safety, to investigate suspected loyalists and root out their threat. Personally, Livingston never fully understood the motivations of those who remained loyal to the crown, and he vilified them as traitors deserving death. In a state precariously balanced on the edge of obliteration, Livingston as governor demonstrated to thousands of Americans the critical importance of restricting loyalist ideology.

Livingston's dealings with loyalism expand historical understanding of who, exactly, was a loyalist and what effect loyalists had on revolutionary government. Loyalists could be found among all races, ethnicities, and economic standings. Discerning loyalty in a state bordered by occupied New York and Philadelphia, however, was complicated. Definitions of who fell under the term *loyalist* seemed to fluctuate on a daily basis, and New Jerseyans, to Livingston's chagrin, continually contested what actions deserved punishment. Personal concerns dictated understanding of loyalty in communities surrounding New York and prompted frequent social and economic interactions across the front lines, especially in East Jersey, where Livingston and the Council of Safety became increasingly involved in policing the illegal trade with British-occupied New York.[10] Livingston thought this London Trade represented the vilest type of disloyalty and deserved death. *William Livingston's American Revolution* examines the patriot side of this story, detailing how Livingston mobilized the state government to stymie these illegal border interactions by using his executive authority through organizations like the Council of Safety. As the war dragged on, however, Livingston lost the battle over the London Trade as patriot New Jerseyans began to see that trade as a necessary survival strategy. The British offered plenty of hard money for Jersey foodstuffs, and East Jersey residents became reluctant to prosecute their neighbors for illegal dealings when they had done the same themselves or would do so if the situation presented itself. In the last years of the war, Livingston's failure to deploy the militia effectively to halt this practice or to motivate the judicial system to punish these criminals illustrates the limits of patriot control. Instead of seeing a clear divide between themselves and British New Yorkers, most of the patriot public viewed loyalty as a far more complicated, disputed, and changeable status that many willingly embraced intermittently for survival on the war's front lines.[11]

The fourth and final theme of this book examines the limits of state government in revolutionary America in more detail, showing how Livingston's government responded to changes in the war over time and the interplay between patriot administration and the public's unwillingness to cooperate. For Livingston, the last half of the war was far more difficult to prosecute than the first, even though the primary theater of military operations shifted south to the Carolinas and Georgia after 1780. The lesser existential threat gave Livingston's enemies in the legislature reason to restrict the governor's growing executive power. Champions of the same Whig ideology that helped draft the 1776 state constitution eliminated Livingston's Council of Safety and returned legislative and judicial power to those respective branches of government. This major setback forced Livingston to refashion himself as a wartime politician. He brought his argument for greater executive authority and efficient government directly to the people through numerous editorials in Jersey papers that challenged the direction the legislature had taken and advocated for a reinvigoration of his own brand of political engagement.

Most New Jerseyans, however, had grown tired of war, especially the constant foraging raids, the threat of loyalist insurgents, and the physical and economic devastation. Moreover, by 1780, Congress and the states had made the nation's currency almost worthless as inflation enveloped everyone. New Jerseyans felt the currency crisis more acutely than others because the Continental Army had spread worthless quartermaster certificates across the state after seizing needed supplies. These certificates joined equally worthless Continental dollars to create a currency crisis that encouraged avoidance of military service and its depreciating pay. State legislators, who stood for election each year before almost all adult males, responded to the crisis by easing the path to militia exemptions, a decision that undermined Livingston's ability to organize a strong state defense. Without militiamen to stop them, New Jerseyans easily flocked to New York throughout the war.

Livingston looked at the legislature's easing of wartime burdens on the population with suspicion and attempted to mobilize his political allies to continue a strong prosecution of the war. He failed. The system that Whig ideology created stymied Livingston's actions and illustrates the limits of the patriots' ability to sway the population. In the critical period 1783–1787, the legislature refused to burden state residents with the realities of postwar life despite Livingston's cautioning. Debt and monetary policy again loomed large. In New Jersey and across the nation, voters elected pro–paper-money legislators who printed money with abandon to assist desperate farmers and artisans. Those states that demanded hard money from residents to meet their tax burden paid the price as yeoman rebelled. In the conventional historical interpretation, an "excess of democracy" and resistance to continued congressional taxation forced the new nation's political elite to think about reforming the Articles of Confederation to secure control from demagogues who invited legislators to act with reckless abandon, eventually culminating in the Constitution.[12]

New Jersey's experience in the critical period complicates such an easy interpretation. Instead, the unbridled power the state legislatures wielded in postwar New England that resulted in episodes like Shays' Rebellion had actually begun far earlier in New Jersey as the expanded electorate in prewar and wartime New Jersey had frequently forced legislators to bend to their will. Livingston and others who eventually became Federalists had seen these excesses of the legislature and the legislators' willingness to please the electorate through the war and its aftermath. With this in mind, they waged a wider battle over the role of the legislature in state government on both monetary and military issues, with Livingston always harkening back to his prewar royalist approach to independence. For Livingston and others at the helm of state government, the deficiencies of the legislature throughout the war had only strengthened their desire to create a strong national government with firm checks against legislative excess. Livingston's experience thus illustrates how the royalist underpinnings of the Constitution's birth combined with concerns over the excesses of the legislatures. As Livingston hoped to "tame the Revolution" and use the new Constitution to stop the democratization of the nation that state legislators had begun, he simultane-

ously wanted to ensure a stronger executive to make the government function more effectively, an idea he had supported during the initial independence
crisis. This need to enhance efficiency in government was of paramount importance to Livingston; his international viewpoint on the Revolution from
his many contacts abroad underscored the need to create a strong executive
authority that could readily and efficiently advocate for the nation in an increasingly dangerous world. Livingston therefore brought his long experience of legislative excess along with his royalist leanings and support of a
strong and efficient executive to Philadelphia as a representative to the Constitutional Convention, where he quickly became an ally of Alexander Hamilton, James Madison, and others who hoped to restrict the power of the
states and to reshape the nation.[13]

Exploration of these four themes takes priority in the pages that follow,
and therefore this study is not a traditional biography of a political leader. I
use Livingston's life and experiences to shape the book's narrative, but there is
much more to Livingston than is covered here. I diverge from him at times to
consider average Americans living in Livingston's world and leave out other
pieces of his life that do not advance the larger themes. Livingston's choice for
war, his prosecution of it, and his battle to define the limits of revolutionary
power reveal the fluid and contested world all Americans lived in from 1774
to 1790 and the role of middle-tier wartime administrators. One exception to
this general outline is the first chapter. Here, in more traditional biographical
fashion, I survey the first fifty years of Livingston's life in New York and place
his experiences as a political operative and propagandist for his family within
the larger context of late colonial events. Livingston's New York years are important to understanding him in New Jersey. His shifting identity from artist
to journalist to propagandist to lawyer to businessman in his early life served
him well as a wartime bureaucrat and affected the decisions he made as a
revolutionary political leader.[14]

In Chapter 2, I look at the state's choice to go to war through Livingston's
eyes after New Jersey elected him to the First Continental Congress in 1774.
The interplay among elite actors, the Sons of Liberty, and other allied com-
moners remains imperative here as Livingston, from his vantage point in Philadelphia, observed a gradually more radical New Jersey emerging over time.
Livingston agreed with the moderation expressed by John Dickinson of Pennsylvania; both raised concerns over the readiness of the colonies to wage war
with Britain, saw an alliance with France as unrealistic, and worked tirelessly
for reconciliation. Livingston's royalist leanings come out in this chapter,

though his actions in the Continental Congress illustrate that he was not opposed to independence but, like many others, doubted its necessity. As Whig ideology grew more powerful, his viewpoint became increasingly unpopular in New Jersey and led to his expulsion from Congress in June 1776.

Chapters 3–5 examine the war years and the key themes of loyalty and wartime governance, beginning after the legislature elected Livingston as governor in September 1776. The newly appointed wartime bureaucrat immediately faced the task of rebuilding the state's crippled government in the midst of economic destruction and dislocation after the British invasion in the winter of 1776–1777. These chapters also highlight the importance of discerning loyalty and the constant reinterpretation of that term. These real and perceived threats led Livingston to advance his plan to accumulate stronger executive power. The power he gained, however, proved insufficient to battle the crippling inflation and economic turmoil created and compounded by the Continental Congress and its constant printing of paper money to fuel the war. The limits of revolutionary government are explored, too, as New Jerseyans suffered from not only the repudiation of the dollar but also the reluctance of merchants and tax collectors to accept the devalued money or the even more worthless certificates issued by the army in exchange for confiscated supplies.

Paper money and the limits of state government in the postwar period continue as themes in Chapter 6. After years of economic troubles and uncooperative legislators, Livingston was largely sidelined and his power reduced even further as legislators debated congressional requisitions and their impact on struggling residents. Livingston's opposition to printing paper money placed him in firm opposition to most legislators, who approved of pro-debtor legislation like those in other states did. This battle influenced his procreditor position while sitting in the Constitutional Convention. In the end, few New Jerseyans opposed ratification, even though they would be hurt by the new Constitution's restrictions on money and state power. They understood that a stronger union that could pay its debts would not have to rely on local tax requisitions. Remaining in a confederation without the Constitution seemed worse than submitting to the new federal government.

In the end, this book is about the Revolution's effect on patriot government and the limits of that government's control in the wartime crisis and its aftermath. Livingston's experience helps frame these issues and can be seen as representative of the interplay among various actors in revolutionary America. Moreover, Livingston's life at the center of the war shows how New

Jerseyans and other revolutionary Americans struggled with defining themselves and their nation before, during, and after the American Revolution. Above all, Livingston illustrates the power of the individual to influence national trends and to contribute to the America that emerged from the revolutionary movement.

CHAPTER 1

Making a Revolutionary,

1723–1774

In William Livingston's first fifty years, his career as a New York lawyer, satirical writer, political spokesman, and powerbroker placed him at the center of colonial controversy in the budding trading mecca of New York City. A member of the third generation of a powerful New York political dynasty, Livingston played a central role in building his family's economic and political base and in its decline in the late 1760s after the Stamp Act controversy. Searching for relief from both politics and the economic downturn, Livingston retired from public life and retreated to New Jersey's rural tranquility to live in the stately home he had dreamed of building since his early twenties. Yet even there, he yearned for the political scene that he had participated in for most of his life.

Livingston's frustrations on becoming a lawyer, his deep interest in art and literature, and his status as propagandist for his family's political machine made him well known throughout the colonies and directly affected actions he later took as New Jersey's governor and during his service in the Continental Congress and Constitutional Convention. The variety of his experiences points to a general ambivalence of position that characterized Livingston for much of his life. Nevertheless, his flexibility and constantly changing status, due sometimes to his own wandering interests and sometimes to circumstance, made him better able to take on the ever-changing role of a governor at the center of revolution. Moreover, many of his early political experiences led him to embrace his role as a political commentator and a behind-the-scenes leader rather than a public orator or figurehead; these skills proved useful when New Jersey's weak wartime governorship frequently forced him to rely on surreptitious political maneuvering to prosecute the war. Further, through

his pen before the war, Livingston engaged some of New York's most important political issues, ranging from battles against the establishment of an
Anglican-sponsored college in New York City to a strong stance against
France in the Seven Years' War to a punishing attack against Parliament in
the Stamp Act crisis. In each episode, Livingston exposed his thoughts on the
role of constitutionalism, republicanism, religion, and democracy in the colonies, all issues he again confronted as a wartime governor.

These episodes informed Livingston's understanding of the colonial relationship with Great Britain and his perception of the late colonial political,
economic, and social situation. They also illustrate how his family's experiences with debt, tenant uprisings, and trade strongly influenced his political
beliefs. In sum, Livingston's ambivalent and flexible nature ensured that as he
left New York for New Jersey he had accumulated consequential lessons that
directed his response to the imperial crisis in his new home.

* * *

The Livingston family had deep roots in New York, starting with William's
grandfather Robert (1654–1728) in the late seventeenth century. Robert emi-
grated from Scotland after having lived in Rotterdam, where he had his first
introduction to the dynamic Atlantic World. Robert used his inheritance to
travel to Massachusetts and from there to New York in 1674, just as the territory reverted to English control at the end of the Third Anglo-Dutch War.
Robert positioned himself for success by settling in Albany to engage in the
lucrative fur trade, where he used his knowledge of English, French, and
Dutch to communicate easily with the diverse population. By 1675, he not
only had established himself as a merchant but also had become secretary of
the Board of Commissioners for Indian Affairs, leveraging his linguistic skills
in negotiations with Indians and Dutch traders.[1]

In 1679, Robert married Alida Schuyler Van Rensselaer, a widow with
connections to two of the most powerful New York families, which brought
him into the center of New York politics and allowed him to gain patents for
2,600 acres along the Hudson River. Robert soon expanded his economic
enterprises into New York City, where he became heavily involved in financ-
ing privateering operations and trading in furs, foodstuffs, and luxury goods
from Europe to the Caribbean, New York, and New England. Most important, Robert leveraged his political connections so that by 1715 he received a
patent for lands around his original estate—some purchased under dubious

circumstances from local Indians—totaling approximately 160,000 acres. Livingston Manor became the center of the family's power and conferred upon the family its own seat in the colonial Assembly, allowing Robert and his sons to build their political and economic base.[2]

Robert died in 1728, five years after William's birth. By then, he had solidified the position of his heir, William's father, by transferring to Philip Livingston (1686–1749) his lifetime political appointments. Philip inherited the manor and soon gained an appointment to the governor's council. He added these vast holdings to the already sizable estate acquired from his marriage to Catherine Van Brugh, daughter of Albany's mayor and member of a wealthy Dutch family. Philip never made Livingston Manor his home, instead opting to reside in Albany; there, from his position on the Board of Indian Affairs, he advocated strong intervention against the increased French influence on the fur trade. His connections with the Indians also allowed him to become one of the largest speculators in western New York; among several problematic land deals he signed was one agreed to by three supposedly intoxicated Mohawks for 8,000 acres.[3]

Philip, like his father, saw the future of his family's fortunes in the Atlantic World and increased investments in trade with the Caribbean and Europe, the African slave trade, and ironworks in New York. This mercantile expansion and diversification of his holdings increased as the colony grew and encouraged him to direct his sons into various professions as agents for the family across the Americas and Europe. William, the eighth child of Philip and Catherine, became immersed in the family business as he grew up in Albany, cared for mainly by his maternal grandmother, Sarah Van Brugh. Indians coming into Albany to trade furs and converse with his father were frequent sights, as were the ever-present Dutch traditions followed by his family and Albany itself. William grew up in the Dutch Reformed Church and heard Dutch spoken frequently by his parents. His young life in Albany afforded him rural surroundings that allowed him to fish, hunt, and ride horses, skills that he quickly mastered and that contributed to his later love for rural solitude. Albany, however, lacked educational choices, leading Philip to hire Henry Barclay, a recent graduate of Yale College, to tutor William. In 1735, at age twelve, William accompanied Barclay on a yearlong mission to the Mohawk under the auspices of the Society for the Propagation of the Gospel in Foreign Parts, during which he continued his classical education while also learning much about Indian customs and culture.[4]

Livingston's enrollment at Yale in 1737 at age thirteen exposed him to the major social undercurrents of the time, including the Great Awakening and Enlightenment political thought. At Yale, he developed a lifelong friendship with William Peartree Smith, who became important as a fellow revolutionary in Livingston's early New Jersey years. The Calvinist teachings at Yale proved off-putting to the young Livingston: he rejected all forms of rigid religious traditions. He heard both George Whitefield and William Tennent preach in New Haven, Connecticut, and observed the growing New Light movement adopted by many of his classmates. For Livingston, however, the Great Awakening proved less appealing; he had no emotional connection to the revival movement, nor could he appreciate its importance intellectually. Instead, Livingston developed a rational approach to the religious fervor at Yale, using John Locke and the Enlightenment to reinforce his rejection of rigid religious doctrine and to attack the extremism of some of the revivalists. In a letter to fellow classmate Noah Welles in 1742, Livingston remarked that he could "never persuade (himself) that such convulsions . . . agitations, swoons, fluctuations, trances, groanings, yellings . . . howling, crying, shrieking . . . are any sign that Christianity prevails amongst a people." These strong feelings on religion continued to develop after Yale.[5]

Livingston's graduation in 1741 sent him back to Albany, where he briefly worked with his father and quickly figured out that he had little interest in business. Of Philip's six sons, only William did not become a merchant. Instead, his father determined that law would be William's profession; the family's business interests certainly needed legal help, and few college-educated lawyers existed in New York. This decision had long-term ramifications: William would be the least affluent of all his brothers, and revolutionary depreciation diminished much of his wealth, making him economically vulnerable. Rebuffing an attempt by William to study law on a European tour, Philip instead arranged for an apprenticeship in the New York office of James Alexander, who had gained fame in 1735 for his part in the defense of printer Peter Zenger against an accusation of libel in the case celebrated for protecting freedom of the press. The four-year apprenticeship proved trying for Livingston, as most legal education rested on self-directed study or copying deeds, reference books, and other legal documents to service the master's practice. Livingston's already minimal interest in the law waned further as the doldrums of apprenticeship continued, abated only by free time spent in New York's taverns and by a friendship formed with Alexander's son William, who later married Livingston's sister Sarah and claimed the title Lord Stirling. In late 1744, James Alexander warned Philip of young William's lack of study. A reprimand from his father did not prevent William from publishing the first of the many anonymous pieces he wrote in his lifetime. This squib in the *New York Weekly Post Boy* criticized the lack of teaching and mentoring for apprentices, claiming specifically that apprenticeship was "servile Drudgery . . . fit only for a slave to submit to." The article resulted in no substantial changes in the system or in William's situation, even though Alexander suspected he had written the piece. The article is important, however, as evidence of Livingston's very early interest in using the press as an expressive tool and his adoption of elements of Enlightenment philosophy to make new arguments.[6]

Livingston's frustrations increased in the summer of 1744, when he met Susannah French (1723–1789), who quickly became the object of his affection. Although she had not "had the benefit of a college education," her intellect showed "either that you are endowed by nature with as great a share of understanding as men attain by a long series of studies" or that she had, without the benefit of a tutor, "enriched (her) mind with a curious variety of useful knowledge by indefatigable reading." French's family lived in New Jersey, but she was very much a part of the New York social scene. Her rural upbringing attracted Livingston; he felt she was "a country girl with all the distinguishing characteristics of a lady properly so called." Indeed, Livingston delighted in the "noble serenity and solitude" to which French could retreat, commenting to her that "a country life is more tranquil and agreeable than any other." This interest in French's New Jersey home eventually encouraged Livingston to move to the colony in the 1770s to find that same rural solitude.[7]

Rejecting any plans his father might have for his marriage prospects, Livingston embarked on his courtship very much in the name of love, especially as Susannah's family had recently suffered financial ruin and had little to offer any potential suitor. Livingston remarked in his letters to French on the "sparks of refined love which heaven has handled in my breast" and the "sacred principles of amity and beneficence" that "can never be extinguished" between the couple; he repeated her name "with rapture, while my soul almost relinquishes its prison to fly into your spotless bosom." He wholeheartedly believed that "there never was a couple whose dispositions did more accord and harmonize" to form "the happiness of married persons," which would lead them both to "be as happy as in this imperfect state [as] it is possible or even desirable to be."[8] At the same time, Livingston beseeched his father to approve the union, which Philip reluctantly did after almost a year. Susannah and William decided to delay their marriage until the end of

William's apprenticeship and the establishment of his own practice. French even implored her future husband to continue his studies, writing to him in late 1744 that "I am much concerned to hear that you neglect your study and are abroad most every night." Livingston calmed French's fears by relaying that he woke at five in the morning to read by candlelight.[9]

Livingston's ambivalent nature, though, diverted him in 1746 from those early morning study sessions to the composition of yet another inflammatory newspaper article, which criticized Alexander's wife and New York's elite social society. As a member of a leading New York family, Livingston had gained admittance to the city's highest circles, but he remained awkward and uncomfortable in most social settings. He mocked those who dressed extravagantly; he himself dressed rather plainly, something that would be remarked upon when he entered the Continental Congress. He never acquired a large number of friends and he frequently shunned the society that he was a part of. Though not physically unattractive, he famously sketched his own portrait and depicted himself as "a long-nosed, long-chinned, ugly-looking fellow" whose intellectual nature never seemed to fit into the growing mercantile center that New York increasingly became.[10]

In another article in the *New-York Weekly Post-Boy*, Livingston attacked the decision by Alexander's wife to forbid her daughter to accept the affections of a young man of lesser social status, the organist at Trinity Church. Though Livingston used satirical characters and an imagined setting to castigate "the haughtiest and most insolent woman" in New York, few readers could fail to discern the attack's true target. Alexander promptly terminated Livingston, who returned to Albany and petitioned his father to allow him to study art in Italy, a passion he maintained throughout his life. Philip instead quickly arranged for a new apprenticeship at the office of Alexander's partner, William Smith Sr.[11]

Livingston, displaying his general ambivalence to his future profession, abandoned his hopes of becoming an artist but soon found Smith to be a better teacher than Alexander, one whose interests spanned beyond law into science, mathematics, theology, and linguistics. This broader set of academic interests matched well with Livingston's eclectic learning pursuits, and the program Smith developed for his apprentices proved more wide ranging than mere copying of deeds and legal papers. Livingston also established a strong friendship with fellow apprentices William Smith Jr. and John Morin Scott. The three would later rise to prominence as the "New York Triumvirate," whose political writings informed a generation of learned men of the intricacies of Whig ideology and Enlightenment thought, making all three famous throughout North America.[12]

A year after Livingston returned to New York City, Susannah French became pregnant, and the couple secretly married in New Jersey. Dutch Reformed Minister Johannes Van Driessen, who had held ministerial posts around Albany and on Livingston Manor, agreed to marry them without the required parental consent, public announcement, or license. French retired to her uncle's house in New Brunswick while Livingston returned to New York to continue his apprenticeship, even though he had violated its terms by marrying without permission. The Livingstons successfully kept the pregnancy quiet, and later that year Susannah gave birth to their first child, named Philip in honor of William's father. Within a few months, though, the baby died, causing Livingston much unexpected grief. To a former Yale classmate, he remarked on the unfairness and the mysterious reasons why God would allow a child to arrive and depart the Earth so quickly. Four of the couple's thirteen children would suffer Philip's fate, dying before age five, with a fifth dying at age eight.[13]

Livingston completed his apprenticeship in 1748 and practiced law for less than a year before his father died. Of his eleven children, Philip probably understood William the least. The secret marriage and the birth of his first child strained William's relationship with his family, though his brothers quickly forgave him. Philip, however, never would. With five older living brothers, William would never inherit Livingston Manor—it went to his brother Robert, fifteen years his senior—but each of the other sons, save William, had already received a lump sum at maturity and then, upon their father's death, a house in either Albany or New York City. The remainder of Philip's lands and property outside of the manor passed to William's mother. Only upon her death in 1756 did William receive 20,000 acres from his father's estate.[14]

*　　*　　*

Livingston's law practice grew slowly before he collaborated with William Smith Jr. to secure a contract to create a digest of New York's laws. The transition from Dutch to English control and subsequent disputes over property rights based on previous colonial law and Indian patents required this first major compendium. The task, though tedious and time-consuming, instantly elevated Livingston's visibility when the first volume was published in 1752 to wide acclaim both in New York and in England. The same year also saw the addition of John Morin Scott to the practice, the third member of the New York Triumvirate.[15]

The trio's business boomed from 1753 to 1755, when the colony became the epicenter of the privateering trade and a military fulfillment center at the start of the Seven Years' War. Building on the infrastructure created during the economic boom of King George's War (1739–1745), New Yorkers expanded the reach of their trade and financial networks. More than 450 ships—up from 157 before the Seven Years' War—imported luxury goods, sold needed military supplies, and provisioned the Caribbean sugar islands. The Triumvirate, and Livingston especially, became preeminent practitioners of maritime law, operating within the Admiralty Courts as well as in debt suits caused by the trade imbalances during the war and lack of paper currency across the Mid-Atlantic colonies. The trio used their windfall profits to expand, hiring several apprentices and clerks whom Livingston educated much as Smith's father had educated him and his partners, providing a well-rounded and robust legal education that included literature, science, and mathematics along with case law and the ceaseless copying.[16]

At the same time that Livingston's legal practice began to flourish, he became more closely involved in his family's political fortunes, especially during New York's Assembly election of 1750, which saw the Livingston family develop a brief alliance with its major opponents, the De Lanceys. James De Lancey had risen to power by challenging Governor George Clinton over his support for King George's War and, by 1750, De Lancey had found common ground with the Livingstons. After Philip's death, Clinton had ensured that none of the father's lucrative government posts in Albany would pass to his heir Robert, who now represented the manor in the Assembly. Robert then endorsed De Lancey candidates, who had already successfully mobilized popular support within the colony against Clinton. Though ambivalent about law, Livingston's flexibility helped him find his passion in political writing. He scored multiple political victories with scathing polemics against Clinton, which brought him critical acclaim in political circles and gave him a public outlet for the type of writing that he had been privately practicing since his apprenticeship.[17] By 1751, though, William had ended his alliance with De Lancey over the politician's failure to support Robert in securing ownership of disputed Indian lands.

A rapid population increase—the highest growth rate anywhere in North America—had not only expanded the accessibility and availability of print media in New York City but also created new opportunities for crowd politics and public association. Throughout the 1740s, while an apprentice, Livingston undoubtedly saw the growth of fraternal and trade organizations among the city's artisanal community in his many sojourns to the taverns. These associations "fused defenses of custom and the common good with belligerent assertions of Protestant and English rights and liberties" that sometimes resulted in a "violent celebration of liberty" in otherwise bustling New York commercial spaces. Some of these men had helped propel the De Lancey faction to victory, something the Livingstons hoped to reverse, especially after James De Lancey became acting governor in 1753.[18]

While Robert led the family's break with De Lancey over land titles, William opposed the building of King's College, the episode that gained him notoriety across the colonies. Livingston challenged De Lancey on the college not only because it offered a political tool but also because it related to two subjects of great importance to him: education and religion. Livingston saw education as integral to social and economic mobility and advocated for it as a necessity to support good citizenship and membership in civil society. New York, however, lacked a college of its own. Many of the colony's brightest young men, Livingston among them, left for either the Presbyterian College of New Jersey (later Princeton University) or Congregationalist Yale in Connecticut. The creation of the College of New Jersey was especially concerning to New York Anglicans; it allowed Presbyterianism to anchor not far from the state and to create alliances with nonconformists, especially New England Congregationalists and Dutch Reformed members. These alliances altered the religious balance of power in the region just as the rise of new commercial networks spurred unprecedented growth. Many of New York's elites truly believed the colony needed its own publicly supported college. Livingston gained a seat on the board of trustees of this new endeavor.[19]

Livingston's concern over King's College also derived from its purported relationship with the Anglican Church, especially after Trinity Church donated land for the project. Livingston believed the college would solidify Anglicanism in New York, where it had always been in the minority. Moreover, using funds from a publicly sponsored lottery to support a church-related institution struck Livingston as compromising the college's independence to teach a broad spectrum of students using a civic, as opposed to a religious, model. This possibility was particularly dangerous, he believed, because colleges "are generally scenes of endless disputations" where students "only receive the dogmata of their teachers"; those "principles or doctrines implanted in the minds of youth, grow up and gather strength with them" and become "a second nature." Livingston feared hundreds of indoctrinated Anglican graduates would "appear on the Bench, at the Bar, in the Pulpit, and in the Senate, and unavoidably affect our civil and religious principles" by working to weaken the independence of nonconformist churches. Instead, he championed independent trustees to establish a truly nonsectarian college that would prohibit the teaching of divinity and mandatory prayer.[20]

Livingston and the Triumvirate used their newly founded literary magazine, the *Independent Reflector*, to wage war against Anglican control of the college and to gather support among New York's majority non-Anglican population to oppose De Lancey, who came under pressure as both an Anglican and a friend of the Archbishop of Canterbury. The *Reflector* became a critical voice in convincing New Yorkers of the dangers of an established church, with the Triumvirate inspiring numerous petitions to the Assembly in opposition to using public money to support private institutions.[21] The Assembly then became the battleground where Presbyterians and Dutch Reformed members, some of whom had been De Lancey's greatest allies, voiced concerns. After almost two years of agitation and the closing of the *Reflector*— De Lancey threatened to cut off its printer's lucrative contracts to print legislative news—Livingston successfully diverted half of the public funds away from the college.[22]

Beyond the political considerations, the King's College incident offended Livingston's own religious sensibilities because he personally abhorred many of the practices of the Anglican Church. Livingston's spirituality was grounded in enlightened rational thought. His four years at Yale had alienated him from most aspects of organized religion, and he developed an independent streak, creating a personal religious creed that, in thirty-nine points, melded biblical teachings and affirmed that individuals must create their own relationship with God. No one religion fully encapsulated his beliefs. He believed in the Old and New Testaments but categorically rejected "riches, ornaments, and ceremonies." An individual, he asserted, might still "be a good Christian though he be of no sect in Christendom."[23]

In addition to opposing the emotionalism he saw in the Great Awakening, Livingston, along with the New Light movement, decried the rigidity of clerically mediated worship and especially the Catholic Church, which bled over to his opposition of Anglicanism. Instead of linking faith to emotion, Livingston believed that each person could use his or her own rational mind to find divine salvation. His interest in Enlightenment rationalism informed his own religious conversion. Raised in the Dutch Reformed Church and then converting to Presbyterianism with most of his family, Livingston considered himself a Christian and a nonconformist above all else. Perhaps because he was a nonconformist within his own family, Livingston found support in the Presbyterianism practiced after the Great Awakening that remained "liberal in doctrine and interdenominational in character" and allowed him a flexible outlet for his Christian faith. To be sure, he never became a deist, describing its adherents in a 1786 editorial as "blockheads."[24]

The importance of the King's College controversy for Livingston's career lies in his engagement on a range of political issues covered by the *Independent Reflector*. His writings gave New Yorkers an investigative look at the controversy and provided Livingston with a wide, politically engaged, and interested audience. Modeled on the London magazines *Spectator* and *Gentleman's Magazine* of the 1720s, the *Reflector* hit hard on political affairs and reaffirmed satire as a powerful tool for Livingston. The Triumvirate successfully used the controversy to highlight religious liberty within the colonies, convincing many nonconformists to challenge the Anglican Church by "defining religious liberty as the independence of the church from the state." This call may have mobilized anti-Anglican sentiment to a greater degree in New Jersey than in New York; the College of New Jersey came to represent "liberty, piety, and prosperity" in opposition to the "backwardness and lethargy" of Anglicanism. To generate fear of Anglicanism, the Triumvirate adopted the successful methods of the English polemicists Thomas Gordon and John Trenchard, who had warned, in the *Independent Whig*, of the dangers of a Catholic revival. The *Reflector* even republished a 1720 essay by Gordon that utilized many of the same tropes Livingston employed against the Anglicans. In this way, Livingston portrayed British liberty as a Protestant one, always on guard against popery or the unbridled powers of religious authority. The fear and controversy became so important to New Yorkers that even after the *Reflector* stopped publication, the *New-York Mercury* published Livingston anonymously in a weekly column named the "Watchtower" for an additional year.[25]

For Livingston, both the *Reflector* and the "Watchtower" refined his nascent political ideas and reconciled his religious views with the political undertones of the time, specifically those related to Enlightenment concepts of liberty, and helped place him within the larger context of the late colonial experience. This ideology that attracted Livingston had been powerful in both Britain and the colonies, convincing many to support freedom in all arenas (the press, religion, and politics) and to stand against the further concentration of power, especially in the church or any institution that could subjugate the individual. Whig ideology taught Livingston to make the connection between civil and religious liberty and to perceive how a collapse of religious liberty would spell the downfall of natural rights and the imposition of arbitrary restraints on the population. Livingston's *Reflector* writings contained the same anticlericalism articulated by others of his generation; he personally believed that clergymen worked for their own self-interest and invented what they claimed as religious truth. In this belief, he was not unlike thousands of other colonists who rebelled against the centrality of the clergy in the Great Awakening, even though Livingston himself never held the same emotional connection to faith.[26]

Instead of promoting self-interest, Livingston hoped the *Reflector* would force the government to protect civil interests only and not interfere in the religious world or engage in any unreasonable restriction of the liberty of thought. Livingston championed the English constitution's "aptitude to promote the true ends of society" in that it would restrict "our rulers should they ever have attempted to arraign and try the consciousness of men," especially since "religion . . . consists in the inward persuasion of the mind" and "cannot fall within the province of our civil rulers." More than just a defense of the freedom of religion, Livingston's *Reflector* writings encapsulated his belief in the role of the colonial government in defending liberty. To him, liberty meant not only unfettered freedom of thought but also limitations on government, especially monarchy.[27] For example, in a 1753 edition of the *Reflector*, Livingston painted an ugly picture of a tyrannical absolute monarch and argued that the people maintained absolute control over their own destiny: they possessed a natural right to reassert their political power "whenever it is employed in their destruction." The monarch, according to Livingston, had to be "accountable to his constituents," and allegiance was not to the king but to the constitution that the king swore to uphold. In his writings from the early 1750s, Livingston supported limited government and the power of natural law, an important ideology for his future positions on critical constitutional questions in the colonial relationship with Great Britain.[28]

The outbreak of the Seven Years' War quickly smothered debate over the religious controversy and changed the subject to imperial power against the French threat. Drawing on his experiences among the Dutch families who interacted with the French through the fur trade, Livingston challenged De Lancey's lack of support for the war, arguing that the security of English liberty necessitated ridding North America of the French. Livingston believed

that the French "thirst of Domination and insatiable lust for aboundless ex-
tension of Empire" created "dangers too great to think of without horror"; the
French Canadians routinely "train their people with a particular eye to war"
and produce "almost as many soldiers as men." Likewise, he lashed out
against De Lancey's failure to prosecute the war more aggressively and played
up fears of Indian warfare. One "Watchtower" column warned that if De
Lancey continued as acting governor, New Yorkers could expect the "shrieks
of women, the wailing of children, the hideous shouts of savages . . . the reek-
ing scalp, stripped from the hoary head . . . the wife torn from the embraces
of the husband . . . our houses ransacked . . . woe, despair, and horror raging
in every quarter."[29]

The war caused many in the Middle Colonies to support closer integra-
tion within a larger British imperial society. Livingston himself had identified
the centrality of the British constitution in ensuring English liberty in New
York during the King's College debates. Securing that liberty in the face of the
French threat was even more critical. Therefore, intercolonial unity became
important for Livingston, who was in Albany when representatives from
seven colonial legislatures met there in June and July 1754 to discuss common
defense measures. Livingston interacted socially with members of the Albany
Congress and appeared before them with brother-in-law William Alexander
to surrender claims to Iroquois lands dubiously acquired by his father. Most
important, Livingston readily endorsed Benjamin Franklin's Albany Plan of
Union for the colonies, writing several months later that he hoped "by the
divine blessing" that Parliament would ratify the plan and "enable us to repel
the encroachment of an ambitious and barbarous foe."[30]

A year later, in July 1755, the defeat and death of British General Edward
Braddock in western Pennsylvania left Massachusetts Governor William Shirley in command of the northern expedition against the French and Indians.
Livingston used the "Watchtower" to promote Shirley's leadership, but James
De Lancey, envious of Shirley's rising fame, prevented the transport of equip-
ment and men to Shirley and instead supported William Johnson, New York's
Indian agent, who led a detachment against Crown Point. After Shirley's fail-
ure to capture Fort Niagara and Johnson's victory, De Lancey successfully
campaigned to have Shirley removed and investigations launched against the
Livingstons, who had been awarded supply contracts by Shirley.[31]

Livingston and Alexander defended Shirley in *A Review of Military Operations in North America* (London, 1757), an essay that reiterated the need for
intercolonial unity against France while challenging De Lancey's obstructive

behavior. The *Review* portrayed Shirley as a strong military leader foiled only by supply failures caused by those envious of his rising popularity within the empire.[32] The essay's enthusiastic reception in New York just a year before new elections provoked De Lancey to threaten Livingston with a suit for libel. The distrust Livingston had sown among New Yorkers both on the King's College controversy and during the war reversed the ascendency of De Lancey's faction in the Assembly. Livingston then capitalized on the changing demographics of New York; a newly ascended middling class embraced his arguments on both religion and the war centered on natural rights and a government responsive to the people. These voters, already dealing with threats to their status as agricultural commodity prices rose and currency shortages increased debt, shifted their support to the Livingstons in 1758.[33]

William's brother Philip and two cousins were elected to the Assembly, and for the first time in his life, William himself assumed a political post, representing Livingston Manor in the Assembly. The renewed energy from the Livingstons brought increased support for the war effort from New York and a string of victories both on the battlefield and in the legislature. An election in 1760 further solidified the Livingston family's strength, but William departed the Assembly, surrendering the manor seat to his nephew Peter. In another example of Livingston's ambivalence, he returned to his legal practice, which had continued to grow as rising agricultural prices and shortages of paper money caused consumer debt to skyrocket. By 1761, the colony faced an economic crisis that was the "worst in memory."[34]

*   *   *

The economic crisis did not stop Livingston from challenging the colonial leadership over the issue of liberty to curry favor with the electorate. In 1763, Livingston battled with Acting Governor Cadwallader Colden over the appeal of an assault and battery case brought by Thomas Forsey against Thomas Cunningham, who Livingston and William Smith Jr. represented in both civil and criminal suits. In the civil case, Forsey won £1,500, an award Cunningham challenged. His appeal to the governor and council cited both matters of fact and errors of law. The latter reason for appeal routinely occupied the governor and council; as Smith argued, allowing the governor and council to overrule a jury on the facts of a case would undermine the entire jury system. Colden attempted to use the Forsey case to challenge the Livingstons and subordinate the judiciary.[35]

The Triumvirate published a series of articles called *The Sentinel* to capitalize on the general weariness of British power as the rising prices of goods and the downturn in the Atlantic trade had caused food shortages and compelled the introduction of price controls by 1763. Even the landless used the rhetoric of liberty to challenge price controls and the state of the economy, which only became worse in the wake of the Proclamation Line (1763), the Currency Act (1764), and the Sugar Act (1764). Livingston used this rhetoric of liberty to persuade middling New Yorkers that the Forsey case represented a much larger attack against their personal liberty: the unbridled power of an executive bent on eliminating trial by jury and the unrestricted power that Britain had over local decisions. For Livingston, Forsey represented a chance to defend a system of governance that rewarded local control and limited intervention by Britain. For average New Yorkers in the midst of an economic downturn, Livingston's defense of liberty made sense in an ever increasingly difficult political and social situation.[36]

Ultimately, Colden lost the Forsey battle, and Livingston capitalized on the discontent that he had roused to make a larger argument in his *Sentinel* essays about freedom in the light of the Stamp Act (1765), which challenged his belief in the power of the English constitution to prevent overreach by any one branch of government. Using the same arguments that he had made in the King's College debates, Livingston affirmed the right of no taxation without representation, making a connection between the public funds given to private King's College and Parliament's usurpation of the colonial legislature's power to tax. Consent remained essential to the functioning of the English constitution, and he supported the resolutions of the Stamp Act Congress that aimed at limiting the interference of Parliament in local matters. He forcefully argued for repeal of legislation like the Stamp Act that subverted the natural rights of Englishmen in the colonies.[37]

For most of 1765, Livingston continued to galvanize the middling and lower classes with constitutional arguments against Parliament. Favoring boycotts and peaceful protests, he argued that the colonies could not afford additional taxes given the stringent restrictions on trading with the Caribbean and lack of access to paper money in the aftermath of the Seven Years' War. However, the boycott would also limit the spending habits of those affected by the 1760s debt crisis, a consequence that betrayed some of Livingston's true feelings toward the common people. The conservative lawyer had become increasingly uneasy about the mob violence that had become more commonplace in New York by the end of 1765. In late August, Livingston published his last *Sentinel* essay after the Stamp Act riots in Boston and the formation of mobs to destroy the stamps delivered to New York. Despite the efforts of Livingston's nephew James Duane and cousin Robert R. Livingston, mob action intensified. In late October, merchants in New York agreed to a boycott, and on November 1 more than two thousand men gathered to protest the Stamp Act, hanging Colden in effigy. Despite the fact that these protestors made up a sizeable number of the electorate, as most had paid the one-time fee to declare themselves freemen and therefore eligible to vote, Livingston and his family soured on such tactics and the wanton violence they witnessed in October and early November 1765. William Smith Jr. remarked that the violence had created "a state of anarchy" in the city and threatened a civil war, leading Livingston to join the conservative backlash against the democracy that the crowds represented.[38]

For Smith and Livingston, diffusing the mob violence remained paramount; both men feared the power of democracy, especially because about two-thirds of New York's adult male population could vote, compared with less than half in Boston and Philadelphia. Smith mediated the peaceful transfer of the colony's stamps from Colden's care to the mayor's office after the November 1 riot and even proposed a new American parliament that would represent American interests in London. The rise of the Sons of Liberty in November 1765, drawn from the masses of artisans who had suffrage rights, further concerned Livingston and Smith. The Sons became a powerful democratic force supporting violent seizure of the stamps from the mayor and a resumption of trade without the stamps.[39]

The culmination of the mobilization came during a public meeting on November 25, when the Sons officially proposed that the city "boldly defy the new law and resume business as usual without the stamps." The Triumvirate, trusted by many New Yorkers because of their recent battles against Colden, worked behind the scenes to foil the Sons' petitions to the Assembly. The trio "dominated the meeting and took charge of drafting instructions to the Assembly" that did not support a resumption of trade. This show of their conservative stance on the Stamp Act hurt their reputation with the city's working classes. Although the Sons continued to gain strength, Livingston no longer supported their cause; their violence influenced his understanding of the proper role of government and left him troubled about the power of democracy for the remainder of his life. In 1768, looking back on the Stamp Act riots, Livingston reaffirmed his allegiance to the English constitution, "knowing the consequences ever to be dreaded, of a rupture between the mother country and these plantations, which is an event never to be desired by those who are true friends to either." Though he continued to use his pen to rouse public support, he remained cautious of those like the Sons who he felt endangered the colony's relationship with Britain.[40]

New York's middling and lower classes were confirmed in their perception that Livingston had abandoned them after he and his family battled against the 1766 Hudson River Valley land rioters. The large manors established along the Hudson River had been sites of agrarian unrest since the 1750s, when disputed land titles had caused tenant uprisings on Livingston Manor and other estates. William's brother Robert crushed the uprising in 1766 and retained William as counsel to eject the rebellious tenants, based on William's prior experience representing tenants living near Elizabethtown, New Jersey, against their landlords on essentially the same type of land disputes. The 1766 uprisings again involved disputed land titles and began in Dutchess County, New York, spurred by the rhetoric of the Sons of Liberty during the Stamp Act crisis. These farmers, some of whom participated in the mob violence in New York City, adapted Lockean notions of property to justify their squatter rights against the land titles claimed by the manor lords. William Prendergast, leader of the Dutchess County uprising, even called the rioters "Sons of Liberty." On June 19, 1766, two hundred tenants marched on the Livingston manor house, demanding free leases; they were repulsed by a group of armed men led by William's nephew Walter, and British troops were dispatched to restore order to the estates.[41]

Along with his nephew James Duane, William represented several Hudson River property owners in more than fifty cases in 1766 concerning the ejection of rioting tenants. His fellow Triumvirate members, Scott and Smith, served on a judicial proceeding that sentenced Prendergast to death. The legal actions reveal Livingston's conservative nature. In his rejection of violence against the landed aristocracy and his resistance to any fundamental change to the colonial social order, he was not unlike many of his elite contemporaries, including most of his family. The uprisings terrified Robert, the lord of the manor, as they "were utterly alien to the world in which" his family lived. However, this should not have surprised many, as he had consistently opposed several of the lower class's most important issues. For example, as early as 1753 in the *Reflector*, Livingston railed against paper money, an expedient especially important to average New Yorkers in the 1760s debt crisis. The "grand evil" of paper money, as Livingston saw it, was "a spirit of Extravagance and a greater consumption of European goods" than New Yorkers could actually pay for. Livingston would repeat this challenge against consumption as he rejected paper money during and after the war, believing it to be a means for the lower classes to avoid paying their debts.[42]

The economic crisis that had taken hold of the colony, the increasing restrictions imposed by Parliament, and the Livingstons' abandonment of the Sons allowed the De Lancey faction to secure political power until the Revolution. The Livingstons responded by appealing for support among the radical elements still present in New York, a reversal of their alignment during the Stamp Act crisis. To cement an alliance with Sons of Liberty leader Alexander McDougall, Livingston and Smith reversed course and wrote several letters to the New-York Gazette that highlighted the dangers of British troops quartered in the colony. McDougall had condemned the De Lancey followers for supporting the military and rallied the lower sort against him and toward the Livingstons. Tensions between citizens and soldiers resulted in the Battle of Golden Hill on January 19, 1770, after which McDougall was arrested for libel and jailed. Although Livingston disapproved of such violence, he believed that by continuing to align with McDougall, he could perhaps propel the Livingstons back into power. Livingston and John Morin Scott defended McDougall during his trial, and through their visible support for him in 1770, the Livingstons managed to regain some of the allegiance they had earlier lost to De Lancey.[43]

*　*　*

With the Livingstons on the rise after the alliance with McDougall, William retired at age forty-nine to the countryside of Elizabethtown, New Jersey, in 1772. Even though he had been a major political actor and a successful lawyer, Livingston's ambivalent nature caused him to become increasingly disgruntled with politics.[44] More important, the depression of the 1760s hurt lawyers like him who had made their livelihoods from the Atlantic trade. At the same time, lowered admissions requirements for the New York bar had increased the number of lawyers competing for work in the colony and decreased the fees they charged, further convincing him of the need to retire.[45]

Livingston's desire to live in the idyllic countryside also contributed to his decision to dedicate his life to writing and study. This desire, expressed in his various newspaper articles, poems, and political writings, coincided with his search for academic purity. As a young man, in 1747, Livingston had penned "Philosophic Solitude: or, The Choice of a Rural Life," a poem that reiterated his scorn for the luxury and pretentiousness of the aristocratic circles into which he had been born (and inhabited as an elite lawyer) and championed the rural and pastoral as truly virtuous. This enthusiasm for rural solitude characterized Livingston throughout his life and pointed to his paradoxical nature: he thrived in an urban, affluent life, yet could be satisfied in the quiet countryside as well. Of course, Livingston's disdain for aristocratic social conventions never evolved into a rejection of classism; rather, it originated from his extreme discomfort in social situations, his disinterest in his own outward appearance, and his recognition of his somewhat unhandsome physical features.[46]

Elizabethtown was a perfect choice for Livingston and his family, both close to New York yet far enough away to bask in its rural character. Livingston had methodically built his estate, purchasing about 80 acres of land in 1760 and adding acreage each year until he had roughly 115 acres by his retirement. The land allowed him to engage for the rest of his life in his second great love after writing: horticulture. In the 1760s, he had planted an orchard of apple, pear, and plum trees that he painstakingly managed both before and after his retirement and for which he earned a national reputation in horticulture later in life. Settling in Elizabethtown also allowed Livingston to reconnect with Yale compatriot William Peartree Smith and brother-in-law William Alexander, Lord Stirling, now a resident of nearby Basking Ridge. Livingston quickly assimilated into their social networks, befriending Elias Boudinot, Smith's neighbor and future Continental Congress president, as well as the young Alexander Hamilton, who attended Elizabethtown Academy with Livingston's son Brockholst. Hamilton spent significant time with Livingston and lodged in Boudinot's home for much of his stay in New Jersey. He even developed a one-sided infatuation with Livingston's attractive daughter Kitty, though he ended up marrying her cousin Elizabeth Schuyler, whom he first met at Livingston's home. Hamilton's experience with this cast of political and social leaders as an impressionable young man likely affected him deeply; he shared many of the group's conservative values both during and after the Revolution.[47]

The retirement to Elizabethtown enabled Livingston to build the home of his dreams, a palatial fourteen-room residence he called Liberty Hall. Begun in 1771, it contained a library for him, a large parlor, six bedrooms, and servants' quarters, and had its own trout pond along the Elizabeth River. Livingston drew the plans himself, worked with builders to secure the necessary supplies, and implored them to examine the styles of other stately homes in order to help him create the final design.[48]

After its completion in late 1773, Liberty Hall came alive with Livingston's new social circle, one inhabited by close friends and confidants instead of the New York socialites he had longed to escape. Attesting to the attraction of Livingston's parlor, New York Mayor Whitehead Hicks remembered, "Your wine used to run through its proper channel," even though he had recently discovered that Livingston's "wine shelf has given way and the liquor is all spilt."[49] With four attractive daughters of marriageable age to make up for the spilt wine, young men came often to Liberty Hall. His fourth-oldest daughter, Sarah (called Sally), used the newly completed home as the setting for her marriage to John Jay in April 1774. Jay had studied law with Livingston in New York in the late 1760s and had become close friends with William's cousin Robert Livingston Jr., with whom he briefly practiced law. By the end of 1775, according to his eldest daughter Susannah, Livingston no longer enjoyed the noise that came along with "young company" and sought to restore the rural tranquility that had attracted him to Elizabethtown in the first place.[50]

True to his ambivalent nature, however, Livingston never was quite able to divorce himself from the political scene. He quickly became a member of Elizabethtown's town corporation and increased the frequency of his visits to the College of New Jersey, where he was appointed a trustee in the 1760s.[51] His most important foray into New Jersey politics occurred in 1773, when he commented on the controversy over the robbery of the East Jersey Treasury, the most divisive political event in late colonial New Jersey. In July 1768, an unknown person stole more than £6,500 from a strongbox in the home of Stephen Skinner, East Jersey's treasurer. Governor William Franklin launched an investigation, but no one was ever charged with the crime. A parallel investigation by the New Jersey Assembly focused on Skinner's actions in protecting the colony's revenues. In December 1770, the Assembly concluded that Skinner had been negligent in his duties and demanded restitution for those losses. The motive behind this determination was an attempt to secure power over this gubernatorial appointee as the assemblies in New York and Pennsylvania had previously done.[52]

The demands of the legislature continued even after Franklin brought forward known counterfeiter Samuel Ford as a reasonable suspect in the robbery. In December 1773, a legislative panel discounted the likelihood of his guilt. That same month, Skinner wrote twice to the Assembly asking to be charged officially with a crime so that he could prove his innocence at trial.

Figure 2. Sarah Livingston Jay (1756–1802). Image #52572.
Courtesy of the New-York Historical Society.

The Assembly countered by demanding that Skinner resign before facing charges. Franklin, interpreting the legislature's treatment of Skinner as an attack against him and the king, affirmed his support for Skinner to remain in office in the absence of a conviction.[53]

In the midst of the controversy, Livingston delivered his legal opinion at the request of the Assembly. Even though Livingston had lived in New Jersey for less than two years, the Assembly's leaders recognized his expertise in law and his reputation as an avid supporter of limiting the extent of British intervention in colonial affairs. After all, the Assembly's real dispute with Franklin concerned the power of royal officials to appoint the treasurer without its approval.[54]

In addition to his opinion endorsing the Assembly's position that it could require Skinner to put up a bond and could charge him with misconduct in court, Livingston authored a separate imagined conversation between Franklin and the Assembly over the possibility of Ford as a suspect and Skinner's role in the affair. Livingston's flair for the literary in the 1750s had made him known as one of the most experienced polemical writers in the colonies, and he continued to use that skill to negotiate between the retired and the political worlds. In his satire, Livingston not only challenged Franklin's obstinate attitude but also criticized the Assembly for concentrating on the robbery for almost four years for a political purpose that, in reality, held little to no importance.[55]

By early 1774, the controversy had enveloped the colony, and local meetings across New Jersey sent twenty-eight petitions, signed by more than 2,100 citizens, against Skinner. Among the far fewer petitions (558 signatures) in favor, one from Hunterdon County in February 1774 desired a quick resolution, as Livingston had argued in his satirical piece, to this "unhappy dispute which has too long obstructed the public business and greatly increased the expense of the province."[56] These public protests encouraged the Assembly to threaten to put on hold all government expenses, including the governor's salary, until Skinner was removed. In addition, the Assembly began drafting a petition to the king demanding Skinner's resignation. It was Franklin's worst nightmare: above all, he feared that his superiors in London would learn the truth about his inability to control his Assembly.[57] Skinner himself broke the impasse and resigned, leading Franklin to bow to the Assembly and appoint its handpicked successor, though making clear he retained the right to appoint anyone of his choosing.[58]

The debate over the East Jersey robbery revealed a complicated and divisive atmosphere over the rural oasis that William Livingston expected in 1772. Although the Stamp Act had had little impact on New Jerseyans, the changes in the Atlantic economy after the Seven Years' War had ravaged the colony's agricultural economy and deprived it of hard money. From its inception, the colony had been largely dependent on trade with New York and Philadelphia and on those ports' connections to the wider Atlantic World, especially the provisioning trade that supplied wheat and pork to the Caribbean sugar colonies. The colony's leadership imagined itself as part of a larger interconnected rural enclave that serviced New York and Philadelphia which simultaneously provided New Jerseyans a conduit for commerce, ideas, and people to the larger Atlantic World. The proliferation of print culture in New York and Philadelphia, especially newspapers, almanacs, and the mail service to distribute them, created an interconnected Mid-Atlantic, allowing New Jerseyans to participate in a cosmopolitan culture while their issues with the British Empire remained quite different from those of neighboring New York and Pennsylvania.[59]

For New Jerseyans, the most vexing issue in the 1760s was the ready access to hard currency, especially after the Currency Act of 1764 prohibited colonies from issuing their own paper money. The depression after the Seven Years' War had hit New Jersey particularly hard. Like other colonists, New Jerseyans had been avid consumers of European products in the 1730s and 1740s, racking up debts that reached £350,000—the most of any mainland colony—after the economic collapse in the late 1760s. Then they saw what little money they had, both paper and hard, migrate to repay debts owed to New York and Philadelphia merchants, thereby exacerbating the credit crunch already underway in the colony as legislators increased taxes to retire public debt.[60]

The colony had always been in a tough economic position when it came to paper money, experiencing shortages as early as the 1720s, when the colonial government established its first loan office in 1723. The land bank system was therefore crucial for the colony. Landholders borrowed money against their real estate holdings, and the currency printed by the land bank circulated as legal tender. The system brought relief to landholders and merchants, but troubled the British Board of Trade, which believed it to be injurious to British merchants, who might have to accept depreciated paper instead of specie.[61]

Not surprisingly, a majority of New Jersey Assembly members favored the creation of another land bank despite the Currency Act of 1764, setting the stage for the animosity between them and Governor Franklin that Livingston waded into several years later.[62] Franklin keenly understood the colony's need for paper money; unlike most other royal governors, he was almost entirely dependent on his government salary and almost always in personal financial straits.[63]

In 1768, the Assembly authorized the issuance of £100,000 of bills of credit as the colony's economic situation deteriorated. Debtors were auctioning off both real and personal property at roughly a third of its value. Franklin rejected this bill, explaining to the Earl of Hillsborough, the secretary of state for the colonies, that its contents were "contrary to the Act of Parliament" as it "made the money a legal tender" and did not include a so-called suspending clause, which required the king's approval before taking effect. Franklin did communicate, however, that the colony desperately needed paper money and asked for permission to approve a bill that did not include a suspending clause and did not make the money legal tender.[64] Hillsborough replied that he could not approve such a bill; the king would consider the action "most unwarrantable and disrespectful." Instead, the suspending clause would "preserve entire and inviolate the supreme authority of the Legislature of Great Britain over every part of the British Empire."[65] The Assembly's outrage at the royal government's response—even though Governor Franklin's father, Benjamin, had been employed as New Jersey's colonial agent to help gain approval of such bills—fueled the animosity over the East Jersey treasurer. However, the larger impact of the failure to secure debtor relief came from outside the legislative arena, as East Jersey erupted into violent rioting over the colony's debt crisis.[66]

Violence in colonial New Jersey was nothing new; agrarian protests over conflicting land claims had swept the colony in the 1730s, 1740s, and early 1750s. This same frustration over land ownership reignited in the economic decline after the Seven Years' War and touched off riots like those that had threatened Livingston Manor and resulted in the tenant cases litigated by William. In New Jersey, the gentry "adopted a refined lifestyle as part of a broader attempt to legitimate their authority over an unruly province." By means of stately homes (like Livingston's Georgian-style Liberty Hall), higher education, and imported luxury goods, they sought to create a division between commoner and elite and to link themselves to the larger imperial world in an effort to stabilize their power and elevate both their status and their claim to leadership.[67]

The economic elite in the colony had been firmly rooted since its founding as a proprietary colony. Charles II's brother, James, duke of York, had granted New Jersey to George Carteret and John, Lord Berkeley after his victory against the Dutch in 1664. Quickly, New England Puritans, Baptists, and Quakers settled in East Jersey along with the existing Dutch settlers. These settlers never fully acknowledged Carteret or Berkeley's claim. They ejected Carteret's cousin, who served as the governor, and formed their own Assembly. Fighting these rebels bankrupted Berkeley, who sold his share of the colony in 1674 to Quaker investors, including William Penn. They formed their own separate colony, West Jersey, leaving Carteret, who later sold to a group of Scottish investors, with the now independent East Jersey. Though this division lasted only from 1674 to 1702, when the colonies unified as a royal colony at the end of Queen Anne's War, the proprietors in East and West Jersey continued to yield significant political and economic power until the Revolution. They inculcated two very different economic, social, and cultural systems in one colony that caused the two halves to develop very differently and helps explain later revolutionary-era disagreements between the regions. Westerners, predominantly Quaker, gravitated toward Philadelphia both economically and religiously as they belonged to the Philadelphia Yearly Meeting. Less populated and developed than East Jersey, West Jersey developed more sizeable landholdings whereas the size of individual landholdings in East Jersey declined throughout the colonial period. Some of this came from the constant land riots that had occurred throughout the colonial period, motivated by unclear land divisions between purchases from Indians, proprietor grants, and royal patents. Some came from a higher population attuned to smaller-scale dairying and vegetable farming needed to feed the growing population in New York. Slavery took much stronger hold in East Jersey than in West Jersey, as Barbadian planters soon brought their slaves with them to settle in the fertile lands around New York. These Barbadians joined a polyglot of settlers and cultures ranging from Scottish Presbyterians to New England Puritans to the original Dutch settlers of New Netherland.[68]

In both halves of the colony, the proprietors and their allies in the gentry had successfully consolidated power by the 1760s, yet the larger economic conditions within the colony only increased yeoman resentment and further distanced the gentry from the debtor-creditor relationships that they had used to create the deference that had quieted the rebellious colony. The connections between the colony's elite and the imperial order that had just recently refused to assist a cash-starved economy became a lightning rod to thousands of economically frustrated yeoman by 1769.[69] These yeomen, infuriated as they saw their lands and property auctioned to pay taxes and debts, rioted at court-houses in Monmouth and Essex Counties in 1769 and 1770 to prevent the adjudication of debt suits. Courts heard hundreds of debt cases each month, as well as suits brought by wealthy landholders to collect rents from their cash-poor tenants. The proprietors quickly became a target of attack as well since most of the riots in 1770 involved disputes on land they owned, espe-cially in western Essex County. Many yeomen believed that the proprietors, their creditors, and the province's lawyers had created an "unholy alliance" to rob them of their livelihoods. In March 1770, Governor Franklin told the As-sembly that the Monmouth protestors, "armed with Clubs and other offen-sive Weapons," shut down the courthouse at Freehold because they believed "the Lawyers have oppress'd them with exorbitant Costs."[70] Some residents in Essex even fortified their homes to physically resist expulsion from their lands, challenging an elite they believed had become morally bankrupt. Liv-ingston, as a sizable Jersey landholder, participated in this crisis. In 1772 and 1773, for example, he bought and sold mortgages throughout New Jersey and threatened to file suit to evict tenants and foreclose on landholders in arrears.[71]

These radicalized common New Jerseyans linked themselves to a much broader imperial crisis going on around them. Although the colony had not suffered as much as others from the Navigation Acts and Townshend duties, it did not, as some earlier historians have argued, simply follow its neighbors into war. The riots of the late 1760s and early 1770s show a healthy anti-imperial attitude growing before revolution. The rioters used Lockean ideas of liberty and tyranny to reimagine the defense of property, even calling themselves "Sons of Liberty" and "liberty boys." They learned from the Whig pamphlet literature from neighboring New York to articulate their feelings of oppression by the king's apparent indifference to their economic plight and the gentry's link to the imperial government.[72]

The influence of crowd politics was key to the revolutionary movement in other colonies as well, motivating a wide variety of Americans to support a fundamental change to the status quo. Regulators in North Carolina, land riots along the Hudson River, and revolts by the Green Mountain Boys in Vermont all showed an intense interest in public affairs by average Ameri-cans, who believed themselves to be in a critical situation in the 1760s and early 1770s. The familiarity of the riot as a mechanism to organize and ex-press political strength took on new symbolism as the Sons of Liberty raised liberty poles during the Stamp Act crisis and afterward. These rioters became tied to the larger revolutionary undertaking and provided a way to center a decentralized movement that would eventually culminate in their participation on local committees of inspection.[73]

Even after the riots had been quelled, concerns over the lack of paper money grew. The situation became so dire in 1772 that New York City's Chamber of Commerce would accept New Jersey currency only at a depreciated price; boycotts finally forced New York merchants to relent and accept Jersey money at face value later that year. Jersey yeomen continued to express their discontent to the Assembly. One Evesham petition declared that the lack of currency would prove "unavoidable ruinous destructive consequences." They believed their "case to be deplorable," especially since the past few years had "taught us there is no relying on any other in this government" to protect the poor.[74] By 1773, after the replacement of Hillsborough with Lord Dartmouth as colonial secretary, Parliament passed modifications to the Currency Act of 1764 that allowed for colonial currency issued from loan offices to serve as de facto legal tender. The New Jersey Assembly promptly created a new land office that poured £100,000 worth of paper money into the economy. However, between 1769 and 1775, when the new currency entered circulation, animosity toward both Parliament and the gentry had developed into a proto-revolutionary movement; if not supportive of independence, its followers were definitely distrustful of Britain's authority and dissatisfied with its most recent colonial actions.[75]

Animosity toward the ruling elites also grew as the colony's gentry attempted to suppress the rioting and blamed the yeomen for the economic malaise that had enveloped the colony, much as Livingston had done in New York when writing about the evils of paper currency. After the early 1770s riots, Governor Franklin moved quickly to punish "with exemplary Severity, those who forcibly oppose the holding or proceeding in the Business of any Court of Justice, or forcibly hinder the Sale of any Lands or Goods" confiscated by court order.[76] Franklin and other members of the gentry believed that the rioters' claims had little basis and that debtors had brought about their own downfall by failing to control their spending. Lawyer William Paterson became one of the most ardent voices against the debtor protests, denouncing paper money and praising the colony's lawyers, who, he believed, righteously defended law-abiding creditors from spendthrifts who wanted to shirk their debts. Paterson preached a very conservative philosophy of governance that supported law and order and the maintenance of a stable and morally just society.[77]

Paterson's stance against the debtor protests is particularly important be-cause he became one of Livingston's closest confidants as governor, serving as the state's attorney general from 1776 to 1783. Livingston himself never com-mented on the protests, but his background and conservative leanings would have aligned him with Paterson. Although the Sons of Liberty had become important Livingston allies in the family's battles for political dominance in New York, William was never comfortable with the more violent measures they used. His preference for rhetorical and abstract constitutional argu-ments meant that he likely remained a tepid supporter of those in New Jersey who were dissatisfied with Britain in 1774.[78]

*   *   *

Livingston never found the rural solitude that he had hoped for in New Jer-sey. His dreams of writing and reading perhaps never truly represented the man he imagined himself to be, especially as his talents and ambitions redi-rected his attention multiple times. In New York, he had thrived on being at the center of political controversy, using his wit and rhetorical skills to pen dozens of essays on a variety of important colonial topics. The engagement and satisfaction he found as part of those conversations about the place of the colonies in the larger imperial world could never be replicated in his library at Liberty Hall, no doubt convincing him to become involved in New Jersey's political affairs almost immediately upon his arrival. Livingston therefore turned his intellect toward the achievement of specific goals instead of aca-demic pursuits for their own sake.

Livingston's wide variety of experiences in New York allowed him to de-velop a firm set of principles on the proper role of government, the imperial state, and religion that became part of his character and informed him throughout his time as a delegate from New Jersey and as governor during the Revolution. These principles likewise brought him great acclaim through-out the colonies; his stance against the establishment of the Anglican Church was cheered throughout New England especially. His relative celebrity and extensive political connections therefore allowed him to enter the world of New Jersey politics quickly and rise to lead the state.

CHAPTER 2

Reluctant Patriot,

1774–1776

In 1774, New Jersey was in the midst of a fundamental transformation, as popular protests against the economic crisis that residents had suffered from for roughly a decade fused with challenges to British authority. These local concerns collided with larger imperial questions that drew attention away from New Jersey—specifically, to Boston, where the Boston Tea Party in December 1773 had led Parliament to issue the Coercive Acts in 1774, closing Boston Harbor and ending independent rule.

William Livingston remained ideologically committed to the idea of colonial liberty that he had articulated during his New York years, but his enthusiasm for independence never matched that of others in New Jersey. Representing the colony at the Continental Congress in Philadelphia, Livingston feared, as he had after the Stamp Act crisis, the radical destabilization and egalitarianism that the end of monarchy would bring. Like other royalists, he accepted the necessity to battle against a corrupt Parliament that had usurped royal prerogatives.[1] These men sought to "rebalance the English Constitution in favor of the Crown" by challenging Parliament's right to govern outside Britain's borders; they believed the colonies to be under the sole jurisdiction of the king.[2]

This ideological struggle for liberty against Parliament merged with Livingston's questioning of the readiness of the colonial military to fight a war, especially after military losses mounted in late 1775 and early 1776. Livingston continued to seek reconciliation and believed it a possibility until late spring 1776. Only as spring turned to summer and the tide turned against accommodation did Livingston become a reluctant revolutionary.

Livingston is representative of thousands of moderates in the Mid-Atlantic and many more royalists across the colonies who hoped to delay independence until the colonies could better prepare for war. His reluctance to support the revolutionary movement illustrates the concern among many patriot leaders who saw their royalist arguments falter under the weight of Whig fervor and highlights the utilitarian concerns facing his adopted state. Many New Jerseyans and other colonists in the Mid-Atlantic remained neutral or offered only tepid support for independence until the very end, realizing that their homes would be on the war's front lines. The choice to make the commitment to the patriot side was an individual one and affected each New Jerseyan, Livingston included, differently. Though Livingston adopted independence later than most other patriot leaders, extralegal forces did not push him to embrace it. Yeomen and poor farmers in New Jersey, unlike those in other states, had already gained the right to vote, and this newly liberalized electorate produced a radical Provincial Congress that supported independence, a transition that left Livingston behind. This new Whig-aligned leadership ejected the moderate Livingston from Congress, illustrating just how central the nontraditional electorate had become in prewar New Jersey.[3]

*   *   *

The situation in Boston led the New Jersey Assembly to form a committee of correspondence in February 1774 to communicate with the other colonies concerning their relationships with Great Britain. This nine-member committee, chaired by James Kinsey, who had staunchly opposed Governor William Franklin on the East Jersey Treasury affair, at first took little action, leading Franklin to remark to his superiors that he could easily check any actions it took.[4] On May 31, the committee met in New Brunswick and drafted a response to a May 13 letter from the Boston Committee of Correspondence warning that Parliament's decision to blockade Boston Harbor was a threat to all the colonies. The New Jersey committee expressed solidarity with Boston, though it shied away from the call for an embargo on trade with Britain because New York and Pennsylvania merchants had already rejected such a strategy. Kinsey hoped that he could convince Franklin or Assembly Speaker Cortlandt Skinner to recall the Assembly to discuss appointing delegates to an intercolonial congress. Both, however, knew that such a congress would oppose Britain and refused to convene the legislature. In seeking advice from fellow Whig Assembly member Elias Boudinot, Kinsey wondered how Boudinot's close friend and neighbor William Livingston felt about the situation.

Aware of Livingston's long history of writings critical of Parliament's power, Kinsey boldly asked Boudinot "to tell him from Me that the little trifling disputes of the Colony of N. York were Capable of Rousing him and that I think the present times shou[l]d; and that it is his duty." Moreover, Kinsey believed that if he himself "had the same Abilities" as Livingston did with a pen and did not act, "I shou[l]d hold myself inexcusable."[5]

Unbeknownst to Kinsey, Livingston and Boudinot had already taken action. The first of the mass meetings called across the colony to discuss New Jersey's response to the Boston crisis occurred in Livingston's own Essex County on June 11, 1774, in Newark. The resolutions adopted "unanimously & cheerfully" by those present decried the "late extraordinary & unprecedented acts of Parliament" that "sapp[ed] that solid basis of our political Freedom" and left the colonies "most unreasonably & injuriously deprived of [their] original Priviledges & Immunities." Following the royalist interpretation that Livingston supported, the Essex Resolves reiterated loyalty to the king, yet challenged "every attempt for establishing a mode of internal Taxation contrary to the established & constitutional Usage of being taxed by our own provincial Assemblies" and called for a general boycott of British goods and for an intercolonial congress to plan a common response. Boudinot earned an appointment to Essex's Committee of Correspondence, which was chaired by his close friend and leading politician Stephen Crane. Livingston, along with William Peartree Smith, joined Boudinot on this committee, the center of New Jersey's early organized protest.[6]

For Livingston, service on the Essex County Committee of Correspondence represented a chance to reenter a pressing political debate. He had readily argued that any taxes levied on the colonists by Parliament were strictly unconstitutional, believing as early as 1752 that "no man shall be taxed, but with his own consent" and that no tax or law could be binding on colonists without proper representation. In an address to the House of Lords in response to the Sugar and Currency Acts, he had even argued that colonial taxation "represented a manifest inequality in treatment of his Majesty's subjects in England and America," and he advocated economic pressure on British merchants and lawful petitions and protests to end unconstitutional Parliamentary taxation.[7]

Essex County in 1774 was a hotbed of anti-imperial feelings that emanated not from rhetorical questions like Livingston's but from previous economic strife and disputes over land ownership, currency, and debt. Essex yeomen infused their local concerns over currency and debt with much larger and more abstract concepts of liberty to support the Essex Resolves strongly. Across the colony, yeomen who had experienced the same economic strife became receptive audiences for the Essex arguments. In planning a colony-wide meeting, the Essex committee argued that the measures "taken to deprive the inhabitants of the American colonies of their constitutional rights and privileges," as well as the actions in Boston, "intended to crush them without Mercy and thereby disunite and weaken the Colonies"; this threat must be discussed and united action taken.[8]

Other New Jersey counties soon formed their own committees of correspondence and agreed on a meeting in New Brunswick, safely distant from the seat of royal power at Perth Amboy. Seventy-two representatives attended the July 21 meeting and acknowledged their loyalty to the crown but challenged Parliament's revenue acts as overreaching, "unconstitutional, and oppressive." The convention judged the latest actions in Boston to be both "subversive of the undoubted rights of his Majesty's American subjects" and "repugnant to the common principles of humanity and justice." The delegates endorsed an intercolonial congress and recommended that it consider a non-importation and nonconsumption agreement. Livingston readily agreed with these measures, especially the argument that Parliament had exerted far too much authority over the colonies. To continue to coordinate with the other colonies, the delegates appointed a twelve-member standing correspondence committee and a slate of five representatives, including William Livingston, to represent New Jersey in the First Continental Congress at Philadelphia. Men from Essex County, including Livingston allies William Peartree Smith and Elias Boudinot, accounted for half of the correspondence committee, while Elizabethtown leaders Stephen Crane and John DeHart joined Livingston as congressional delegates.[9]

Through his Elizabethtown social network and his own past New York fame, Livingston had quickly risen to political power, and he participated in a fundamental shift in New Jersey politics as an extralegal governmental system began to take over after Franklin declined to allow the elected legislature to meet. Although many of the men elected to the county committees had been active in local politics, only sixteen simultaneously served in the Assembly. The creation and support of a provincial congress therefore encouraged those disaffected from the colonial government to embrace this new extralegal system, which signaled the beginning of a transfer of power from the royal government to a patriot-controlled one over the next two years.[10]

Debate in New Jersey over the Continental Congress began in earnest.

What demands should the delegates make, and how should they approach their disagreements with Great Britain: as supplicants or as citizens with rights and privileges? One commentator wondered if and how the colonies could block trade with Britain and how to convince Parliament that taxation should be left to the colonial legislatures. The writer also questioned the appropriateness of paying for the tea destroyed in Boston; if an unconstitutional act by Parliament brought the tea to Boston, the colonists should not be liable for its destruction. Livingston's opposition to any restitution for the lost tea aligned him with the Reverend John Witherspoon, a member of the Somerset Committee of Correspondence, who joined in trying to convince New Jersey's congressional delegates to oppose such restitution in August 1774. Witherspoon, president of the College of New Jersey, knew Livingston well from his service on the college's board of trustees, and collaboration with Witherspoon undoubtedly helped Livingston articulate his own position as he readied himself for Philadelphia. Witherspoon had advocated a strong anti-imperial stance in the summer of 1774 in his influential "Thoughts on American Liberty," arguing that the colonies should "never submit" to the "illegal and unconstitutional" actions of Parliament and instead choose "war with all its horrors, and even extermination itself, to slavery rivetted on us and our posterity." Witherspoon had made the College of New Jersey a hotbed of Enlightenment ideas that transferred easily from the religious world to the temporal. Though Witherspoon did not advocate independence until 1776, he certainly had been, like Livingston, strongly influenced by a decade of passionate arguments that opposed the seemingly tyrannical and unconstitutional practices of Parliament.[11]

When Livingston arrived in Philadelphia, he was very much among friends. His brother Philip represented New York, as did his nephew James Duane and his son-in-law John Jay. Like many other observers, John Adams described Livingston as "a plain Man, tall, black, wears his Hair—nothing elegant or genteel about him." He added, "They say he is no public Speaker, but very sensible, and learned, and a ready Writer."[12] Adams knew Livingston from his time in the New York Triumvirate and especially from his attacks against an Anglican episcopate, a cause on which Adams himself had polemicized. Moreover, while Adams traveled through New York en route to Philadelphia, he heard that Livingston was "said to be lazy," a rumor that resonated with some truth. Livingston, who had always been far more comfortable with a pen, seldom spoke during his service in the Continental Congress, perhaps giving the appearance of being disengaged. Adams's opinion of Livingston nearly forty years later, that "Billy, alias Governor Livingstone, and his Son in Law Mr

Figure 3. John Jay (1745–1829), William Livingston's son-in-law, by Joseph Wright, 1786, oil on linen, object #1817.5. Courtesy of the New-York Historical Society.

Jay" had been members of the "Aristocratical flock," seems to contradict his original assessment but was perhaps more accurate. Though very much an aristocrat, Livingston seldom felt comfortable around others of his social standing, much less the lower classes; without his brother and Jay present in Philadelphia, Livingston might have found the proceedings less tolerable.[13]

As Congress began its work, Livingston's long opposition to what he per-ceived as the unconstitutional acts of Parliament, his support for economic pressure to compel it to repeal the Coercive Acts, and his rejection of tea reparations placed him among the majority. In the first of his few statements, Livingston addressed one of the Congress's two main purposes: to define the basis of American rights: "It will not do for America to rest wholly on the Laws of England," he urged. The colonies must ground their arguments firmly in natural law. Agreeing with both conservatives like John Jay and radicals like John Adams, Livingston maintained that the king had granted rights to the American colonies through their charters and that those should govern the relationship between the two entities.[14]

The attempt to defend American rights both according to royal preroga-tives and English constitutional rights resulted in the "Address to the People of Great Britain," drafted by a committee that consisted of Jay, Livingston, and Richard Henry Lee of Virginia. The address called on Britons to give thoughtful consideration to the constitutional practices and charters for their American colonists, and also to reflect on older concepts of liberty and free-dom that had been present "in almost every age." The "great and glorious ancestors" shared by Britons and Americans had "maintained their indepen-dence and transmitted the rights of men and the blessings of liberty" to their posterity. The committee assigned Jay as the primary author of the address, though at the time some believed that Livingston had written it because he introduced the final version to Congress. However, Jay, writing in 1818, af-firmed his authorship, and John Adams confirmed that Livingston himself had stated that Jay was the author. It remains likely, however, that some of Livingston's ideas and arguments on these issues, not so different from Jay's, appeared in his son-in-law's final version.[15]

The debate over the inclusion of natural rights in the rhetoric against Britain represented a fundamental difference Livingston had with his nephew Duane, as well as with John Rutledge of South Carolina and Joseph Galloway of Pennsylvania. All refused to link opposition to taxation with natural law; Galloway even feared that such a direct association might lead inevitably to independence. Galloway continued his conservative and Quaker-influenced approach to Britain in discussions over nonimportation, designed to address Congress's second purpose: how to defend American rights. Galloway's Plan of Union rested on the creation of an elected colonial parliament to work jointly with Britain to craft colonial policy. The scheme required both the colonial parliament and the British Parliament to approve new laws. Duane and Jay strongly supported the plan, as did other moderates in Congress, who feared mob violence if the colonies moved away from reconciliation. Though no direct evidence remains to assess Livingston's feelings on Gallo-way's plan, he likely supported the measure because it would have equalized colonial power with Parliament's in making laws for the colonies, the original intent of the charters, though it did veer away from his royalist leanings.[16]

John Adams later remembered that the more conservative Jay "had differ-ent systems and belonged to different sects . . . in opposition to all measures which . . . had a tendency to independence."[17] Although Livingston and Jay had been more aligned with Adams on the natural rights arguments, both main-tained a greater hope for reconciliation than Adams did. In 1778, Livingston claimed that he had not "been in Congress a fortnight" before he "discovered that parties were forming" among those delegates less interested in reconcilia-tion. He believed that New Englanders especially were advancing an outcome "altogether different" from what most Americans wanted at that time.[18]

At the same time, Livingston did not believe in the same type of conser-vatism that Galloway did. Like every other delegate, he saw the need to im-pose economic sanctions on Britain and wholeheartedly supported the Suffolk Resolves proclaimed in Massachusetts in September 1774 and the Continental Association established by the Congress in October to coordi-nate and enforce nonimportation and nonconsumption measures through-out the colonies. At the end of November, Livingston and the other members of the Essex County Committee of Correspondence called a meeting to set up local committees of inspection in three districts within the county to en-force the Association. Livingston and his family strongly supported the boy-cott, believing it a necessary step to ending the crisis with Britain. His earliest biographer famously claimed that the family quickly grew accus-tomed to drinking "strawberry tea" instead of imported English tea. Living-ston's firmness in supporting the Association and its goals reinforced his own political position and would continue throughout the war years. On numerous occasions, Livingston opposed making any exception to laws for himself or his family and openly challenged politicians who did so. For Liv-ingston, maintaining a consistent personal stance on a public issue, much as he had done with his own writings in New York, was critical to his political reputation.[19]

Elizabethtown acted first, in early December, to appoint a local committee to enforce the Continental Association, and other Jersey communities followed over the next three months. The Elizabethtown meeting likewise reelected Livingston and the remainder of the previous slate of delegates to the Essex County Committee of Correspondence and supported the actions of the First Continental Congress.[20] These extralegal committees of correspondence, formed throughout New Jersey, increased the political power of yeomen who had previously been excluded from politics and therefore broadened the appeal of the patriot movement, especially among yeomen angry at the current land and currency systems. Across the colonies, thousands of men who had never held public office rose to power and helped control both the economic and the political life of the colonies. In Middlesex, for example, the Continental Association became so popular that the initial meeting of the county's committee of safety had to be moved to a larger venue; in Essex, the committee openly welcomed all who wanted to participate. More important, by opening membership to a broad audience, the committees solidified the latent radicalism present in New Jersey and, as historian T. H. Breen argues, "provided a framework for sustaining and strengthening the insurgency" of average Americans. In addition to attracting those who sought to increase their own power, the committees appealed to yeomen and elites anxious to slow their consumption of imported goods, especially amid New Jersey's increasingly perilous credit crisis.[21]

The support for the Continental Association shown in Elizabethtown was not universal across New Jersey; some localities weakly enforced the boycott while others vehemently opposed it. This dissent provoked vigorous debate about the role of the colony within the larger imperial system. Opponents who lived in communities that supported the Association risked, as Governor Franklin indicated, "the danger of becoming objects of popular resentment." This reality, Franklin believed, would cause most of the colonies to adhere to the Association. However, many in New Jersey opposed it, some specifically because it had granted extraordinary powers to local committees of correspondence to enforce an extralegal boycott. One Essex resident who had supported calling the First Continental Congress but opposed the Continental Association believed it had actually taken away liberty from the colonists and had made reconciliation that much more unlikely. This freeholder challenged the Essex committee to examine the constitutionality of its enforcement measures "by which men are to be cloathed with power to revenge themselves upon their neighbours without controul, and the poor victim of their mad zeal, malice or wrath, is to be exposed to infamy and disgrace, unheard, without the form of a trial, and against the laws of this country."[22] Likewise, an earlier essay in the same newspaper described the First Continental Congress's actions as "dangerous to the people." The delegates had "in the hurry of our zeal, departed from our constitution and entered a new mode of governing, as inconsistent with liberty." In a larger sense, the writer claimed that by abandoning monarchy, the colonies had "slid into a republic" led by men more interested in convincing "the world that they are scholars, than to show a disposition to settle our differences."[23] These conservatives believed the Continental Association to be an unproductive, if not dangerous, means to convince Britain to end the Coercive Acts.[24]

Nevertheless, the idea of using economic protest to express colonists' dissatisfaction with actions of the crown was well received in late 1774 in some corners of New Jersey, especially in Greenwich in Cumberland County, where on December 22 a group of young radicals burned a shipload of recently arrived tea. Tea, of course, had become a politicized commodity after the more famous Boston Tea Party, and rejection of tea served to unify colonists against Britain's perceived unconstitutional actions. As historian John Fea indicates, enlightened ideas of "political jealousy" helped to create a "unifying . . . ideology of resistance grounded in a common morality" that explains political actions like the Greenwich Tea Party. Instigated by a young cast of Presbyterians from the Bridge-Town Admonishing Society, a literary club devoted to discussing the latest in cosmopolitan thought, the destruction rocked the more conservative local establishment and highlighted the radical attitudes that some New Jerseyans had adopted after the First Continental Congress. This insurgent radicalism propelled average New Jerseyans into the larger movement, even if their more moderate leaders opposed it. The owners of the tea pursued suits against several of the rioters, as did Governor Franklin, though the local sheriff, Jonathan Elmer, the brother of a tea burner, ensured that local juries would acquit them. These Whig tea burners, defended by future governor Joseph Bloomfield, were linked to William Livingston through Elias Boudinot, who assisted Bloomfield in the cases. Given his abhorrence of popular protests in the past, Livingston probably did not endorse the action. Instead, he would have been more comfortable with the direction of the Cumberland Committee of Correspondence, which advocated peaceful approaches to enforcing the Association.[25]

*   *   *

The New Jersey Assembly met in January 1775, its first session since the previous March. During the time between meetings, the royal government had been overshadowed by the proliferation of extralegal meetings and organizations throughout the colony. Although he had not yet received instructions from London, Governor Franklin knew that he must prevent the Assembly from choosing delegates to the Second Continental Congress. Instead, Franklin hoped to convince the Assembly to petition the king independently, thereby severing New Jersey from the rest of the colonies and Congress's actions, demonstrating New Jersey's loyalty and Franklin's usefulness to the crown, and acknowledging the support for the crown versus Parliament among New Jersey's patriot leaders. Franklin therefore opened the Assembly with a strong address that highlighted the two roads open to the Assembly: one led to the Continental Congress and "Anarchy, Misery, and all the Horrors of a Civil War"; the other aimed toward the king and promised "Peace, Happiness, and Restoration of the publick Tranquility." Franklin retained some hope of prevailing upon the members to consider their duty to preserve the government they were elected to serve and to refrain from approving the actions of the Continental Congress. Despite the continued activism, at least some New Jerseyans were wary of the consequences of extralegal bodies that had already endorsed the Association. For instance, a petition from Nottingham, a Quaker-dominated town in Burlington County, asked legislators to think of the "horrors of a Civil War" as they debated the merits of the Continental Congress. The petitioners hoped the Assembly would recognize that "the real interests" of Britain and the colonies "are inseparable."[26]

Franklin quickly lost his gamble. As the Assembly met, Livingston, Elias Boudinot, and John DeHart joined fellow congressional delegates James Kinsey and Stephen Crane, already sitting in the Assembly, to urge approval of the actions of the first Congress and the appointment of delegates to the second. Approval, for them, gave official license to the extralegal activities that had led to Livingston's presence in Philadelphia and to continued actions against Britain by Congress. The Assembly not only endorsed Congress's actions but also reelected the five delegates, including Livingston, to represent the colony in Philadelphia later that year. Franklin placed the blame for these setbacks at the feet of James Kinsey. He believed Kinsey "was weak enough to suffer himself to be made a Tool of by Wm. Livingston, J. Dehart & Elias Boudinot," who had "caballed among the Members" and "hurried" them to approve of the Continental Congress and align with the other colonies. Therefore, without Livingston and his Elizabethtown allies, the moderates and conservatives in the Assembly might have derailed approval of both the Continental Association and the appointment of delegates to the next Congress.[27]

Nonetheless, moderates induced the Assembly to compose an independent petition of grievances to the king. Livingston, however, provided its content, thereby nullifying Franklin's intent to divorce New Jersey from the other colonies. The petition drafted by Livingston, DeHart, and Boudinot succeeded over versions authored by staunch conservative speaker Cortlandt Skinner and James Kinsey, who raised suspicions by including language deemed too conciliatory to the British position. The draft offered by the Elizabethtown cohort aligned the Assembly with the actions of the Continental Congress and challenged Britain on a host of issues, even though it admitted that most of the issues "do not immediately affect the People of this Colony." New Jerseyans, however, will be "deeply involved" in "their Consequences." The grievances included the standing army housed within the colonies, the lack of self-government in Massachusetts, the expanded powers of royal offices, the blockade of Boston Harbor, and the passage of the Quebec Act, all areas where Livingston and others thought Parliament had overreached. Only three issues directly affected New Jerseyans: debt from the Seven Years' War and its resulting economic calamity, large expenses for operations of various royal offices paid from the provincial treasury, and the inclusion of judges on the civil list. Governor Franklin claimed that the petition "fabricated by . . . Livingston & Dehart & the Junto at Elizth. Town" was "an Echo of that sent by the Congress & contains the same List of pretended Grievances." With this petition, Livingston and his allies successfully foiled the development of a legitimate opposition to the extralegal activities begun in New Jersey the year before and again asserted the idea that Parliament had intruded into areas where it had no right to be. This success was especially important to Livingston because his family had failed to convince the far more conservative New York Assembly to approve the work of Congress, elect delegates to the Second Congress, or stop a more conciliatory petition to the king from being approved by their rivals, the De Lanceys, at the same moment.[28]

Support for intercolonial unity in the face of Britain's unconstitutional acts stood as central to the agenda of Livingston and his cohort. By linking New Jersey to the actions of the Continental Congress, they outflanked the colony's conservatism, which could have pushed the Assembly closer to Franklin's position. Livingston and his allies had discussed the importance of unity often at the Continental Congress; many worried that without the British to unite them, the colonies would find little common ground, especially in the light of the failures of schemes like the Albany Plan of Union. Livingston's brother Philip even believed that independence from Britain would cause the colonies "instantly to go to civil wars"; he, along with many others from the Middle Colonies, distrusted New Englanders and southerners. According to John Adams, Philip seemed to "dread N. England," especially its "Levelling Spirit" and the past religious persecution of Quakers and others there. Of course, many New Englanders thought southerners had sunk themselves in "luxury and sloth" during recent years and harbored suspicions about colonists from the Middle Colonies as well.[29]

In New Jersey, the need for unity was made clear in a letter written in April by "Essex," possibly Livingston's friend Elias Boudinot. Essex explained the importance of "strengthening our union" by supporting the Continental Congress in its efforts to ensure the general welfare of all the colonies and to secure assurances that Parliament would act constitutionally. Boudinot expressed similar sentiments in an April 30 letter to the Morris County Committee of Correspondence, advising its members to refrain from forceful displays of patriotism and violence against opponents of the patriot movement. Speaking for the Essex County Committee, Boudinot argued that any actions that "may in the End deter every good Man from joining with us" should be avoided. The prevention of violence, according to Boudinot and likely supported wholeheartedly by Livingston, was a "Measure essentially necessary to our union & Success." The creation of a united coalition and unity within that coalition became key in rallying support in New Jersey and beyond as the colonies prepared to meet again in Philadelphia.[30]

On May 10, 1775, William Livingston, along with his same four New Jersey colleagues from the previous year, entered the Second Continental Congress, whose members had become galvanized even further by the recent battles at Lexington and Concord. The committees formed to enforce the Association in New Jersey quickly began to drill local militias in preparation for a possible confrontation. In reaction to the news from Massachusetts, the standing committee of New Jersey's first Provincial Congress, which included Elias Boudinot and William Peartree Smith, called a second Provincial Congress to assemble at Trenton on May 23. Meanwhile, Governor Franklin recalled the Assembly to Burlington to persuade its members to accept Lord

North's plan of reconciliation. In his opening address, Franklin again tried to separate New Jersey from Congress by imploring the Assembly to recognize that the king had done much to respond to the colonies' grievances and that the proposal from London ensured that the colonies "can never be required to tax themselves without Parliament taxing the subjects in Great Britain in a far greater proportion." Identifying taxation as "the principal source of the present disorders," Franklin hoped that resolution of the issue would pave the way to reconciliation.[31]

Instead, the Assembly rejected both reconciliation and independent action. In an address to the king, the Assembly registered its belief that the reconciliation plan failed to resolve colonial grievances. Moreover, since the Continental Congress had begun its deliberations in Philadelphia, the Assembly had "the least design to desert the common cause in which all America appears . . . firmly united . . . without the advice of a body in which all are represented."[32] The efforts of Livingston earlier in 1775 paid dividends for the patriot cause, as the Assembly had become increasingly committed to intercolonial unity and the outcome of the Continental Congress instead of seeking independent reconciliation.[33]

The Assembly's failure to act strongly in favor of reconciliation lessened the chance that it would become a rallying point in New Jersey against the patriot movement and made the creation and legitimacy of a Provincial Congress far easier to achieve. On May 23, the Provincial Congress convened in Trenton and, seeking direction from the Continental Congress, sent Elias Boudinot and William Peartree Smith to Philadelphia to meet with Livingston and the other Jersey delegates to request instructions "concerning the line of conduct in which we ought to act." Though the two returned on May 30 with no such directions, the Provincial Congress showed a strong predilection to align with the actions of the Philadelphia Congress. For example, the Provincial Congress approved a new state nonimportation program, to be adopted by communities that had not joined the Continental Association, and required every township to form a militia company. These actions, along with Congress's military preparations, immediately affected Jersey farmers. Inhabitants of Bridgewater complained that the initial encampments of May and June 1775 had destroyed their crops and laid waste to their farms.[34] Most important, the Provincial Congress approved the raising of £10,000 for colonial defense, an assumption of political power that further eroded the legitimacy of the royal government. As Governor Franklin reported to London, "All Government is nearly laid prostrate, and the public

Officers from the highest to the lowest are now only on Sufferance." Royally appointed treasurers could not raise revenue because local communities were redirecting taxes to the Provincial Congress and military defense. Likewise, militia officers who had received commissions from Franklin resigned en masse, preferring commissions from the Provincial Congress.[35]

While the Provincial Congress met in Trenton, Livingston participated in multiple discussions in the Continental Congress concerning military preparedness in the colonies and the raising of an army to be led by George Washington. However, Livingston's name rarely appears in the session's minutes, and few letters or other records of his participation remain. He continued to hope for reconciliation and likely understood military readiness to be a necessity that could apply additional pressure on Britain to relent. At the same time, Livingston likely agreed with Boudinot and other members of the Essex Committee of Correspondence that violence should be a last resort; its deployment would polarize anyone not already fully committed to either reconciliation or the patriot cause.[36]

Livingston's main contribution to this session of Congress came through his participation on a committee in June and July that drafted the Declaration of the Causes and Necessity of Taking up Arms. The committee, originally composed of Livingston, John Rutledge, Benjamin Franklin, John Jay, and Thomas Johnson of Maryland, assigned Rutledge to draft a declaration that Washington could publish when he arrived in Boston with the Continental Army. The full Congress deemed Rutledge's draft unacceptable and added both John Dickinson of Pennsylvania and Thomas Jefferson to the committee. Livingston objected to both the Rutledge and the Jefferson drafts; each had "the faults common to our Southern gentlemen . . . much fault-finding and declamation with little sense of dignity." They relied on "a reiteration of tyranny, despotism, bloody, etcetera" as the only arguments "needed to unite us at home and convince" Parliament of "the justice of our cause." This objection highlights Livingston's continuing attachment to the royalist cause: Parliament is the clear aggressor in the relationship with the colonies because of its interference with both colonial and royal prerogatives. Dickinson also found Jefferson's draft too harsh, and his objections, according to Jefferson, led the committee to assign Dickinson to edit it. Despite Dickinson's efforts to moderate the declaration and make it more conciliatory, the result remained a forceful statement of colonial grievances against Parliament.[37]

The final document explained to Americans and Parliament the necessity of moving toward a more militant stance against Britain. It invoked the same natural rights rhetoric that Livingston had supported in the first Congress and challenged the constitutionality of Parliament's actions, arguing that peaceful and moderate measures had been attempted without success. The "unprovoked assault" by British troops at Lexington and Concord and the burning of Charlestown forced Americans to stand in arms against "this cruel aggression." The declaration insisted that the armies raised in the colonies were not for "ambitious designs of separating from Great-Britain" but were necessary to repel attacks "by unprovoked enemies."[38]

This declaration, approved on July 6, joined two other documents, the Olive Branch Petition, also written by Dickinson, and the Address to the Inhabitants of Great Britain, adopted on July 8, in communicating the colonial mindset. The paragraph-by-paragraph debate on the declaration in Congress allowed all, including Livingston, to suggest changes before everyone endorsed its contents. John Adams believed the declaration "has Some Mercury in it" as it was "pretty frank, plain, and clear."[39] Likewise, Philadelphia publisher William Bradford told James Madison that the declaration and address were written "with a Spirit that will charm you" and thanked his Creator that he had been "born in an age & country capable of producing such Gallant spirit." In replying to Bradford, Madison thought he detected "traces of Livingstons pen," especially in the address, but deferred to Bradford, who was "a better Judge & better acquainted with his Genius and writings."[40] Livingston had taken no part in writing the address and very little, other than objecting to Jefferson's original draft, in the declaration. However, both Madison's letter and the fact that Jefferson heeded Livingston's objections indicate that Livingston commanded much greater respect among the members of the Second Congress than he probably deserved by his participation in the First Congress. Livingston left Congress for Liberty Hall in late July to attend his wife, who had been stricken with an unknown illness. Her situation kept Livingston away from Congress until late September.[41]

The New Jersey to which Livingston returned had continued to prepare its military defense and to enforce the Continental Association. In early July, the Earl of Dartmouth had communicated to William Franklin the king's "firm Resolution that the most vigorous Efforts should be made both by Sea and Land, to reduce His rebellious Subjects to Obedience." A month later, Franklin reported that Livingston's committee in the Congress had drafted a declaration that sanctioned war, placing the royal government, and specifically the officers of that government, in mortal danger. To prove his point, Franklin enclosed a copy of a letter written by Daniel Coxe, a member of the governor's Provincial Council, who warned that "those deemed Tories have every thing to fear from the political persecuting Spirit now prevailing." Coxe complained that "Friends to Government . . . are not even allowed to preserve a neutrality, and passiveness becomes a Crime."[42]

New Jersey's Provincial Congress reconvened in August and approved the continued mustering of the militia, established regulations for the collection of tax revenue to support the military, and set a date for a new colony-wide election for another Provincial Congress. By giving the electorate a voice in selecting its representatives as the crisis continued, the Congress could claim more authority over colonial governance. Most important, the Congress also approved the creation of a Committee of Safety to make decisions for the colony after the Congress adjourned. It became the archetype for a body Livingston used as governor to root out loyalism and prosecute the war. The continued growth of patriot sentiment, buttressed by the increased power of the Provincial Congress and the new Committee of Safety, allowed a sustained military buildup and more strident prosecution of those who refused to accept the strictures of the Continental Association, making life for men like Franklin and Daniel Coxe that much more dangerous as summer turned to fall.[43]

Livingston returned to Philadelphia in the last week of September and became active in mediating communications between the Continental Congress and New Jersey's Provincial Congress on raising troops for Continental service. This more dedicated involvement in military affairs won him an appointment as second brigadier general of the militia from the Provincial Congress in late October. Although the reasoning behind the appointment is unknown, Livingston had been keenly interested in military affairs since the Seven Years' War, when he had become quite the "militant imperialist," advocating for stronger military action against the French and supporting the Albany Plan of Union. He had never sought a military post before, but this ongoing interest could have inclined him to accept the appointment.[44]

The military preparations in New Jersey exacerbated tensions over the direction charted by the Continental Congress and the Provincial Congress since the beginning of the year, causing a conservative resurgence. Before leaving New Jersey to preach in the backcountry of Virginia, Philip Vickers Fithian remarked on the overall "melancholy State" of the colony: "Numbers who a few days ago were plain Countrymen have now clothed themselves in martial Forms . . . Resolved, in steady manly Firmness, to support & establish American Liberty, or die in Battle!" To men like Fithian, Enlightenment ideals of liberty and the actions of the Continental Congress had converged by the end of 1775. Reconciliation was becoming far less possible or acceptable.[45] For others, however, the extralegal powers appropriated by the Provincial Congress and the increasing militarization of the colony strained their already tenuous relationship to the patriot movement, causing many to reiterate their desire that New Jersey should seek reconciliation. In heavily Quaker Burlington County, freeholders petitioned the Assembly to take its place as the duly elected representative body of the colony and pursue reconciliation instead of surrendering that duty to the Continental Congress, as it had done earlier in the year.[46]

Governor Franklin, now one of only four royal governors still in place, capitalized on the colony's latent conservatism and recalled the Assembly to Burlington in November 1775 to urge members to reassert control from the Provincial Congress. In his opening speech, Franklin argued that the Continental Congress had failed to pursue accommodations with the crown; instead, it had engaged "in a rebellion which menaces to overthrow the Constitution." He warned that the king would do everything possible to crush rebellious subjects. Further, Franklin reminded the Assembly that Britain had just approved an act authorizing New Jersey to issue paper money, thereby eliminating one of the colony's most urgent complaints. Franklin reiterated his earlier plea, foiled by Livingston, that the Assembly petition the king directly.[47]

In some ways, Franklin succeeded in his quest to strengthen the Assembly and the moderate forces in the colony. The legislature passed a series of routine measures to keep the colony operating, appointed a colonial agent in London, and, most important, instructed Livingston and the other delegates in Congress to "reject any Propositions" for independence and instead work for reconciliation. With these actions, the Assembly reasserted itself as the legitimate colonial legislative power. The Continental Congress recognized that unity remained key to the patriot movement and therefore dispatched John Dickinson, George Wythe, and John Jay to convince the New Jersey Assembly not to petition the king separately. Dickinson argued that to achieve reconciliation, the colonies needed "to convince Britain that we would fight, and were not a Rope of Sand"; thus an army needed to be formed and deployed. Indeed, he argued that "a Country so united cannot be conquered" and that unity must be preserved in order to convince France and Spain to support the colonies.[48] The Assembly concluded that because the petition Livingston had cowritten in early 1775 had yet to illicit a response from the king, there was little point in petitioning again, thereby ending Franklin's hope of divorcing New Jersey from the Continental Congress. Many royalists like Franklin could not understand the appeal of the Continental Congress. Assembly speaker Cortlandt Skinner, for example, believed Congress would create a republic that would surely "deluge this country in blood," the result of "mad enthusiasm and designing men." This session would prove to be the last sitting of the royal Assembly; it and Franklin became irrelevant in mobilizing anti-patriot support. Skinner, his allies, and the remaining proprietors, would become loyalists who either fled the state or remained in New Jersey and became irrelevant under the new revolutionary government that stripped them of their remaining political influence once the war began.[49]

Back in Philadelphia, the actions of the Assembly had little effect on Livingston's support for readying the colonial military and for the patriot movement. He continued to work as an intermediary between the New Jersey Provincial Congress and the Continental Congress on military affairs and gained a strong understanding of the colony's current defenses and the limitations on Congress's ability to supply its soldiers.[50] This knowledge had yet to convince him that reconciliation was not a possibility. In November 1775, New England theologian Ezra Stiles wrote in his journal that he believed Livingston was very much in favor of independence, though Livingston himself still harbored concerns that the colonies would not be able to defeat Britain militarily. In December, Livingston visibly broke with his fellow New Jersey delegate Richard Smith and voted against ordering Washington to destroy the British forces in Boston "in any way he can . . . even if the town must be burnt." Livingston's view of the military was not unlike that of fellow moderate John Dickinson, who had consistently argued that the army, raised but not deployed, remained the biggest bargaining chip the colonies had to convince Britain of the need to negotiate.[51]

Livingston's simmering dissatisfaction with the patriot movement arose in part from the Provincial Congress's delay in replacing James Kinsey and John DeHart, both of whom had resigned from the Continental Congress by December. Only Livingston, Stephen Crane, and Richard Smith remained to represent New Jersey, and Crane had been absent during much of the session because he also served in the Provincial Congress. Livingston believed it highly improper for a single delegate to cast the colony's vote, and when he differed with Smith, as he did on the attack on Boston, he understood that New Jersey would in effect cast no vote. He likewise complained of the "ruinous consequences" to the personal lives of those required to sustain "such constant and

perpetual attendance"; only his "devotion to the public" had kept him in Philadelphia "this long." Livingston was not alone in this feeling. DeHart cited the
"peculiar Circumstances of my family" when tendering his resignation to the
Provincial Congress. By the end of 1775, Livingston, like so many citizens
across the colonies, "scorn[ed] to quit my colours thro' impatience or discouragement" but had yet to be convinced of the necessity of independence and
had become exhausted by the preparations for a possible war.[52]

*   *   *

In early 1776, many colonists remained unsure of the path the Continental
Congress had charted for the colonies. Governor Franklin believed at this
point that "the Majority of people" in both New Jersey and Pennsylvania "are
greatly averse to an Independency; and if they could be once convinced that
their present Leaders have such Intentions, would immediately unite to oppose them." But, he went on, "the Danger seems to be that the Design will be
carried on by such Degrees" that New Jerseyans will not discern the true intentions of the Continental Congress until too late, especially because the patriots had seized control of the newspapers and few opposition voices could be
heard.[53] In some places, such as Shrewsbury in Monmouth County, where
open opposition to the local committee of inspection existed, resistance to
Congress's actions gained traction. However, in other locales, especially in
Quaker West Jersey, most residents opposed military action but supported
strengthening the provisional government and favored reconciliation.[54]

Those moderates, however, lived in an increasingly polarized colony, with
more and more active committees of inspection vigorously enforcing the
boycott and advocating the patriot cause. At the same time, Continental
troops, on January 2, had started to seize arms and ammunition from Jersey
loyalists, further infuriating opponents of the patriots. The publication of the
Plain Dealer, a pro-patriot periodical produced in Cumberland County by
Boudinot ally Joseph Bloomfield among others, became an especially important way for local patriots to rally support for the insurgency. In one January
edition, the anonymous authors identified three classes of New Jerseyans: Tories, Whigs, and the Turn-coats. The last group deserved the most contempt.
These "ignorant thoughtless beings . . . are one day Tories, and the next day
Whigs; and the third day nothing at all"; like the "pendulum of a clock," they
"are perpetually changing sides." Too easily influenced by both sides, the
turncoats have "no fixed principles" and little understanding of the "nature of

Government, the principles of the English constitution, and the rights of Americans." Though Livingston was certainly not a turncoat, he shared some of their same predicaments and definitely had not yet come to support either full-scale military action or independence.[55]

The first month of 1776 brought Livingston more work in Congress on the military affairs of the colonies. His congressional committee agreed that New York would be a primary British target and needed additional reinforcement through the raising of a third Continental battalion from New Jersey. Further, Congress became convinced of the "defenseless condition" of New Jersey and its lack of supplies—something Livingston knew well from communicating with the Provincial Congress—and approved additional resources to reinforce the colony.[56]

Livingston also became embroiled in local affairs in New Jersey as the point of contact between Congress and Lord Stirling. In January 1776, Lord Stirling attempted to arrest Governor Franklin and send him to confinement in Elizabethtown. Livingston believed that Franklin's military arrest crossed a line that would have further alienated Jersey moderates and, most important, dangerously upset the colonial social order. This last point became especially critical to Livingston; he increasingly feared the radical transformation of American society that would arise from the termination of royal government. For an aristocrat with little tolerance for the mob rule of the Sons of Liberty, opposition to Franklin's arrest became critically important in the effort to uphold the social order, at least for the time being.[57]

By early February, reports of increased danger to New York and the East Jersey coastline forced Livingston to leave Congress to assume command of militia units around Elizabethtown. Hearing reports that almost two hundred British marines intended to attack Staten Island, Livingston dispatched Jersey militiamen to fortify the island. For the first time, Livingston assumed a field command, though neither he nor his troops saw any combat. This new role placed Livingston, who as a delegate to Congress was reluctant to sanction military force, in an awkward situation. What he would have done if he and his militia had encountered British forces remains unknown.[58]

Though ambivalent about the use of force, Livingston vehemently opposed the presence of loyalists. New York's Provincial Congress had learned that in late 1775 loyalists had begun to acquire arms from the British warship *Asia*; these loyalists both organized militias to oppose the patriots and refused to recognize the New York Congress. The Continental Congress ordered New Jersey militia colonel Nathaniel Heard to disarm the loyalists in Queens

County, New York, and to restore patriot control. Livingston met with Heard and lauded him for his "greatest prudence and zeal for the cause" and his success at capturing "some of the most dangerous Tories in the Country."[59] Livingston likely supported this type of military confrontation because he could not understand those who condoned the unconstitutional practices of Parliament. Indeed, he had recently praised the destruction of "a nest of rebels against American liberty" in New Jersey, likely referring to loyalists seized by militiamen throughout Sussex County in December 1775. The unconstitutionality of Parliament's actions led Livingston to support the patriot movement in the abstract and oppose loyalists, even though he could not yet bring himself to approve full-scale military intervention. His opposition to loyalism grew to the point that, as governor, Livingston displayed an almost pathological hatred of loyalists. Especially after the signing of the Declaration of Independence, opposition to the patriot cause became to him unimaginable.[60]

Livingston returned to Congress for roughly a month, from late February to mid-March. John Adams later recalled that Livingston had expressed his opposition to continued military armament. Though Adams successfully advocated for the creation of a Continental Navy, he remembered how hard it had been to convince the delegates to support it, with Livingston and other moderates ardently opposing a stronger military stance by the colonies.[61]

Livingston's return also coincided with discussions on the Lord Drummond Peace Proposal, the most important plan for reconciliation in which he participated. Lord Drummond was no stranger to the colonies or to Livingston. In 1768, Drummond moved to New York to claim lands in New Jersey acquired by his great-grandfather, an original East Jersey proprietor. Drummond had become enmeshed in Livingston's social circle, befriending not only him but also Lord Stirling, Elias Boudinot (who served as Drummond's lawyer), and especially former Triumvirate member William Smith Jr. Drummond, like Livingston, deplored the mob violence that had begun in the colonies, yet he grew increasingly concerned with the seemingly unconstitutional actions of Parliament. In late 1774, he returned to England determined to serve as an intermediary among Parliament, the crown, and the more moderate elements in the colonies to achieve reconciliation.[62]

Drummond worked with Lord North to create an accommodation plan that looked similar to North's own reconciliation plan passed by Parliament in February 1775. Drummond focused on the immediate causes of the rebellion, taxation and revenue collection, and provided greater authority for the colonial legislatures to control funds raised and to respond to local economic concerns. Drummond further believed that his unofficial status might increase the chances of success, especially after Parliament's rejection of the Olive Branch Petition and the battles of Lexington and Concord. In January 1776, Drummond arrived in Philadelphia and began to meet secretly with delegates. He quickly identified James Duane, Livingston's nephew, as someone who would be inclined to support him and used William Smith Jr. to make contact. Duane, disillusioned by the end of 1775 at the chances for reconciliation, believed that Drummond's proposals could appeal to a wide audience in the colonies.[63]

Duane quickly connected Drummond with Thomas Lynch Sr. of South Carolina as well as with John Jay and Livingston. At first, Drummond remained cautious with Jay. Although he had been elected by moderates to "prove some check to the violent measures" from the more radical New Englanders, his recent mission with John Dickinson to convince the New Jersey Assembly to abandon its independent petition to the king caused Drummond to question Jay's true intentions. In particular, Drummond wondered "how far his connection . . . with Mr. William Livingston might influence his conduct." Drummond clearly identified Livingston as a moderate who strongly favored reconciliation, and he believed that Livingston was "from religion, connections, and abilities . . . a character of great moment at this juncture." From his lack of connections to the radical New Englanders and "from the tenor of his conversation in his careless moments," Drummond believed Livingston very "much averse from Independency" because he "foresees that this species of government (which he had perhaps a natural bias to) would be attended with numberless immediate evils to that part of the continent where his property and everything connected with him lay."[64]

Livingston's engagement with Drummond began a metamorphosis in his thinking about revolution, which led toward understanding the possibilities of war in the utilitarian terms that had begun to fill his thoughts over the last several months. Livingston, who William Smith Jr. would later claim was one of Drummond's principal contacts and closely involved in all negotiations on reconciliation, understood from his work in Congress and his position in the militia that New York and New Jersey would become the epicenter of any future war with Britain. Fearing the destruction not only of his own land and property but also of his family's extensive New York holdings, Livingston realized the dangers of the war and the radical reorientation of the society in which he had lived and thrived.[65]

Throughout January, Livingston and his moderate allies negotiated with

Drummond on the content of the reconciliation message and the strategies to convince Congress to accept its provisions. Livingston believed the entire proposition would fail if they asked Congress to appoint a delegation to travel to London with a reconciliation plan. After receipt of the king's October 26, 1775, speech that declared the colonies to be engaged in a rebellious war for an independent empire, many delegates worked with Drummond and others who had hoped for reconciliation, such as John Dickinson, and openly sought avenues to convince Congress to make a rapprochement with the king. Lynch, along with Livingston and Duane, continued to negotiate with Drummond and brought John Hancock into their confidence, who readily endorsed the plan. On January 16, Lynch would have introduced the measure to Congress, but news of the January 1 burning of Norfolk and the defeat at Quebec convinced him to wait until a more opportune moment. The plan lay veiled until late February, when Washington revealed it, suspecting that Drummond's negotiations might lead "to consequences of a fatal and Injurious nature to the rights of this Country."[66]

In early March, after having rejected just weeks earlier an address drafted by Dickinson and Duane that supported reconciliation, Congress discussed the situation with Drummond at length. Livingston supported bringing Drummond to Congress as did Duane, who throughout the month continued to believe a restoration of harmony possible. In the end, Congress did little with the Drummond plan, likely because it had just received news of the Prohibitory Act, which cut off trade with the colonies and established a naval blockade, in effect, an act of war. The Drummond affair, however, reveals Livingston's belief in reconciliation and how he had become concerned with the dangers of war. The realities of a disruptive and destructive contest with Britain began to override some of the ideological sensibilities that had guided him for the last decade.[67]

In mid-March, the British evacuation of Boston convinced Washington that New York City would be the next target. Livingston promptly left Congress to take command of the East Jersey militia and to work with Lord Stirling, the ranking officer in the region, to begin fortifying New York. New Jerseyans (and Stirling himself) remained "very uneasy about the defense situation of Elizabethtown and Amboy." Stirling recommended the construction of additional fortifications on Bergen Neck, immediately across from Lower Manhattan, and the placement of batteries on Elizabethtown point, which looked out over Staten Island. Militiamen from Bergen, Essex, and Middlesex under Livingston's command fortified these areas and, in cooperation with the larger plans of the Committee of Safety, helped solidify the integrated communications network designed to deliver intelligence on possible British movements throughout the region. By April 1, Livingston's militia had fortified East Jersey but refused to seize the strategic heights on Staten Island; the site was outside the colony's borders, and no immediate threat existed. Washington arrived in mid-April and assumed command in New York, while Stirling's Continental forces took control of Staten Island. With enough Continental troops to defend the city, Washington relieved the New Jersey militia, and Livingston prepared to return to Philadelphia.[68]

At that moment, New Jersey was enmeshed in debates over independence. By the time the colony's Second Provincial Congress had adjourned in early March, it had assumed leadership in place of the royal Assembly. As many observers anticipated, the election of the Third Congress, set for May, became a referendum on independence. Whig firebrands like John Witherspoon argued against any further attempts at reconciliation. British actions had subverted the foundations of constitutionalism, and the empire had unleashed its army on the colonies and refused Congress's attempts at reconciliation. Witherspoon rested his justification for independence on the unconstitutional nature of British taxation and on Britain's inability to understand American affairs from afar. His arguments, infused with Lockean notions of moral philosophy, convinced many colonists to think seriously about independence.[69]

Many of Livingston's closest friends remained hesitant, especially Elias Boudinot and William Peartree Smith, who visited with Livingston at Liberty Hall after his militia duty. Boudinot worried about the dangers for the existing social order. He believed "limited monarchy is the form of government which is most favorable to liberty" and that the colonies were "too unwieldy for the feeble dilatory administration of democracy."[70] Others agreed. William Paterson, soon to become Livingston's attorney general, viewed the potential transition to a republican government with apprehension. Likewise, William's brother Robert feared that a post-independence government would operate "without that influence that is derived from respect to old families wealth age etc." Virginian Landon Carter warned that Congress would create a new nation "independent of the rich man [with] every man . . . able to do as he pleased." Edward Rutledge of South Carolina feared the spread of New England egalitarianism, which could embolden the economically and socially oppressed to seize power and redress their previous grievances.[71]

In the spring of 1776, the transition to republican government had already begun to destabilize the class structure that had sustained Boudinot, Livingston, and Paterson. By late 1775, the colony's most active patriot supporters consisted of the landless, tenants, and smallholders, while the middle class and elites still tended to favor reconciliation. This radicalization of the small landholders and the lower classes in New Jersey, ongoing since the land and currency disputes of the early 1770s and encouraged by their services on various committees of inspection that enforced the Continental Association in 1775 and early 1776, came to fruition after the elections for the Second Provincial Congress. Voters had been required to meet the same high property qualifications previously used to determine eligibility to vote for the royal Assembly. Smallholders then complained that many New Jerseyans were taxed by the Provincial Congress but had no vote, the same grievance lodged by the colonies against Great Britain. In a petition to the Provincial Congress, forty-five residents of Salem County attempted to use their militia service to gain admittance into the body politic, arguing "whilst we were expending our time and money . . . repelling the invaders of our liberties," the government had "deprived" them "of the privileges we contended for." The petitioners therefore used the same military-service argument the Philadelphia Associators had the previous year. Other petitioners argued that their status as taxpayers should allow them to participate in the political process. Ultimately, both arguments failed, though the cries of "no taxation without representation" convinced the Provincial Congress to lower the property qualification from 150 acres of property and £50 personal property to £50 either real or personal property. The ability to use personal property to qualify to vote greatly enlarged and effectively liberalized the electorate that cast ballots for the Third Provincial Congress in the May 1776 election.[72]

Nearly half of the winning delegates had never served in elected office, and this new, more radical Congress fundamentally shifted the direction of the colony. Livingston's fellow Continental Congress delegate, John DeHart, quickly realized this new reality when he left Philadelphia in early April. He had thought about running for the Provincial Congress because he considered it "a more important post" and because someone needed to "control the mad Fellows who now compose that Body." Those in New Jersey who were "preparing to make their last stand against the principle of levelling which prevails in it" needed his assistance to stop the destabilization of the colony. However, Jonathan Dickinson Sergeant, another New Jersey delegate to Philadelphia, successfully ran for the Provincial Congress, bent on stopping the "old level of unrighteousness" that would "strive hard to poison" the Provincial Congress "by pushing in every creature that can list against Independence."[73]

The ordinary New Jersey citizens elected to the Third Provincial Congress looked not unlike those in Massachusetts and elsewhere; they had staffed committees of inspection, routed out loyalists, and marched on courthouses to push average Americans closer to revolution. Those local committees became training grounds for the larger insurgency and, through various methods of coercion, convinced their unwilling neighbors to support the movement. Especially after Lexington and Concord and the publication of Thomas Paine's *Common Sense*, the radicalism of revolution had begun to infect thousands in the lower echelons, who used the mob as a political tool to push the more moderate leadership toward independence. As Eric Nelson argues, this "frenzied antimonarchism . . . led to a widespread resurgence of Whig principles" that decentralized the power of the elites and prompted the majority of early legislatures to reject executive authority by realigning the movement with empowered legislatures and an empowered population. The relatively late elections of the Provincial Congress, the ability of the majority of white males to participate in the political process, and the overwhelming victory of Whig candidates allowed for an easier political acceptance of independence in New Jersey as opposed to other colonies, where elites retained control of the legislatures and the disenfranchised could exert extralegal influence only from the streets. Livingston's New Jersey firmly embraced a radical republican revolution whereby yeomen and the lower classes made substantial and early political gains.[74]

The results of the election in May likely further confounded Livingston's position on independence, as the patriot movement abandoned the royalist position and instead adopted a Whig ideology that spoke to a radicalism that historically had made him deeply uncomfortable. Practically, even as he had adopted republican ideals like shared sacrifice himself, Livingston still felt that the change in government would be devastating, perhaps even permanently ceding power to lower-class elements. Moreover, his recent experience in the militia had intensified his doubts about the overall readiness of the colonial military. His firsthand knowledge of the deplorable state of defenses around New York led him to question the ability of the colonies to win the coming war and further eroded his enthusiasm for independence.[75]

From his return to Philadelphia in late April until his removal from the Continental Congress on June 22, Livingston became increasingly isolated as the choice for independence gained popularity. In mid-May, John Adams believed that only New York, Pennsylvania, New Jersey, Delaware, and Maryland had not yet accepted independence, a decision he hoped to accelerate by championing a resolution that called on each colony to establish a new government to protect American liberties.[76] In Burlington, the newly elected Provincial Congress finalized its control over New Jersey by absorbing the provincial treasury and nullifying Governor Franklin's recent call for the royal Assembly to convene. It also cut off Franklin's salary and, on June 16, declared him an enemy to liberty and ordered his arrest. The very same action that Livingston had opposed in January signaled the end of royal government, the crumbling of the established social and political order, and the dominance of radical Whig ideology.[77]

At the time of Franklin's arrest, Livingston served as the sole Jersey delegate in residence in Philadelphia and so controlled the colony's vote. On June 21, the leaders of the Provincial Congress, knowing of his reservations about independence, offered Livingston command of the provincial militia that would be soon dispatched to New York. The next day, they elected new delegates to the Continental Congress, all of whom supported independence. According to Abraham Clark, one of these new delegates, Livingston seemed "much chagrinned at his being left out of Congress." In fact, Livingston believed that Clark had orchestrated his removal to install himself, though Clark maintained that he had actually used his influence to support Livingston's reelection. Jonathan Dickinson Sergeant had a very different view. He believed that New Jerseyans "were quite in the dark as to the sentiments of the delegates" currently serving and that the new slate "will not deceive us."[78] Resentful, Livingston turned down the militia appointment and instead relied on his previous militia commission to assume command of the troops in East Jersey. His ire had not ebbed by July, when he recommended the appointment of Abraham Clark as a brigadier general in the militia simply because Clark concurrently served in Congress. At this point, Livingston believed, correctly, that the Provincial Congress had arranged his removal by using the invitation to command the militia "as a reason against my being eligible as a member of Congress," even after he had "plainly refused that command."[79]

Contemporaries clearly understood that New Jersey had recalled Livingston because of his failure to support independence and because of his animosity to the Whig radicalism engrossing the country. On June 28, John Adams wrote in his diary that Livingston "had hitherto resisted Independence." Three days later, he described how he himself, with "much the Air of exhibiting like an Actor or Gladiator for the Entertainment of the Audience," summed up the arguments he had made in favor of independence for the benefit of the newly seated Jersey delegates. Adams placed Livingston alongside Jay and Duane, also moderates who opposed independence, and acknowledged that "all acquiesced in the Declaration and steadily supported it afterwards." However, in recalling the Congress for Jefferson in the 1820s, Adams agreed that Jay, Dickinson, and Thomas Johnson of Maryland had frequently "contributed to retard many vigorous measures ... particularly the vote of Independence"; but he apparently felt that Jay's constituents would never have recalled him as Livingston's had.[80]

Two years later, Livingston explained his reasoning very differently. The colonies had every right to "renounce our allegiance to a King" who, in his opinion, "had forfeited it by his manifest design to deprive us of our Liberty." Livingston affirmed his long-standing ideological stance, yet firmly disagreed with delegates who, he believed, had always supported independence. Livingston and moderates like him became incensed at their radical sensibilities and their attempts to seize control of the proceedings and declare independence earlier. More important, however, Livingston's utilitarianism won out; he believed that "if we could not maintain our separation without the assistance of France," the Continental Congress should have secured such an alliance before declaring independence. Livingston's experience with military issues both in the Congress and in the militia likely convinced him that the colonies could not stand alone against Britain.[81]

In the final congressional debate on the Declaration of Independence, John Dickinson of Pennsylvania made clear his sentiments on the need to delay independence. He saw little possibility of an alliance between the united colonies and either Spain or France; neither country could be trusted not to support Britain if enticed with a greater reward or to abandon the alliance if revolution in America appeared likely to upset control of their own colonial possessions and subjects. Like Livingston, Dickinson believed that the war would be so destructive that only foreign aid could ensure success, that the colonies needed to assure Spain that they would never support independence for its colonies, and, most important, that they must await the results of Silas Deane's mission to France to measure the French response to independence. Too many questions about territorial disputes concerning Canada and Florida as well as trade relationships after independence needed to be worked out before the colonies could embark on such a foolhardy step.[82]

The realities of impending independence convinced even the most radical members of the Continental Congress to address Livingston's utilitarian concerns. In late 1775, Congress had begun exploring options to secure munitions from Europe and to gauge the attitudes of foreign powers to possible independence. In addition, Congress had supported opening colonial ports to international trade—a rejection of the Navigation Acts—and by June 1776 had appointed a committee to prepare foreign treaties. Adams, who served on that committee, advocated for support from the French, though he believed that developments were moving so rapidly that independence might precede such treaties. Similarly, Richard Henry Lee understood that the colonies were "unequal to a contest with [Britain] and her allies without any assistance" from other European powers; still, Lee believed the colonies needed to proceed with independence in order to secure those alliances. Edward Rutledge thought the opposite and sided with Livingston, Wilson, and Dickinson. Writing to John Jay, Livingston declared that any effort to send emissaries to France "before we had united with each other" by passing a declaration of independence would render "ourselves ridiculous in the eyes of foreign powers" and reveal to the British the colonies' true intentions. He cautioned independence largely on pragmatic grounds, believing alliances essential before independence.[83]

Livingston joined with Rutledge in favoring an alliance before independence. He was even more reticent than other delegates because he "place[d] no confidence in the studied ambiguity of the Court of Versailles" and had serious reservations as to what France would gain from an alliance with the United States, even after the French had begun negotiating with the colonies. He could not conceive of any monarch assisting in a revolt that would provide "a pernicious lesson to his own subjects." Despite the constant discussion of an inevitable alliance with France, he "sometimes wished the very word inevitable expunged from our language." Livingston's vehemently anti-French writings during the Seven Years' War undoubtedly echoed in his head as he continued to caution against an alliance with France as late as January 1778. Writing in the *New-Jersey Gazette*, he maintained that "we have begun, we have continued, and we can conclude the war without foreign succours. It is upon God and our Right and not upon Louis the XVI that we depend for deliverance."[84]

Livingston later made clear that, despite his stance on independence before his removal from Congress, he fully supported independence after it had been declared: "We have passed the Rubicon . . . we cannot recede nor should I wish it if we could. Great Britain must inevitably perish." In this way,

Livingston's later support aligned with that of Dickinson, who also shifted from "a position of dissent to one of tacit endorsement," though not withdrawing his overall disagreement with how the decision had come about. In terms of practicality as well as support for the ultimate direction of the country, Livingston and Dickinson wholeheartedly endorsed the creation of a strong American state after the war had begun.[85]

Livingston's reticence until the very end makes clear that many former leaders in the royal colonies had to reassess fundamental beliefs before they became reluctant revolutionaries. Most delegates to the Continental Congress came to Philadelphia uncommitted to independence, and their moderation allowed them to support the more radical agenda on certain issues, just as Livingston had done, but then swing back to a more conservative stance on others. Hard realities played a major role in convincing Livingston and many others to believe that the colonies were not ready to stand on their own, a belief that led moderates like Livingston to argue for a delayed, rather than an immediate, declaration of independence. Livingston never adamantly opposed independence; rather, he hoped it would come about through more judicious means or as the last option. Not unlike the rest of his family, Livingston harbored latent fears of the destabilization of the social order that tempered his move toward independence. Most Livingstons bitterly feared the corrupted power of the majority. Concerns over destabilization resurfaced many times throughout the remainder of his life, as revolution marked the beginning of a new world for Livingston and for thousands more throughout North America.[86]

CHAPTER 3

General to Governor,

1776–1777

Although Livingston no longer had a seat in the Continental Congress, his commission as a brigadier general in the New Jersey militia placed him at the center of colonial military operations. He never saw combat but became closely involved in Washington's preparations to defend New York against the anticipated British invasion. Livingston himself admitted that he was a lackluster general, but his service in this critical period redeemed him in the eyes of the state's patriot leadership and propelled him into the political spotlight. In his role as New Jersey's de facto leader, he interacted with Washington and mediated among the Continental Army, the Continental Congress, and the Provincial Congress. The political skills he had learned in New York enabled him to organize New Jersey's defense effectively and would become valuable later as he took the governor's chair. Most of the Provincial Congress's business during that summer of 1776 involved supplying Livingston's forces or supporting Washington's army in New York, allowing Livingston to take part in important political decisions and serve as a symbol of imperial resistance.[1]

After the state elected its first legislature under its new constitution, legislators understood Livingston's importance and installed him as New Jersey's first governor—a position he heartily accepted because it removed him from the military post in which he felt increasingly uncomfortable. In his new role, Livingston served at the center of the revolutionary movement as General William Howe's forces successfully captured New York and invaded New Jersey in November 1776. Livingston utilized his militia experience to rally the state's defense, though few New Jerseyans volunteered to stand in the face of the British onslaught. By early December, British and Hessian troops had chased Livingston and Washington's army into Pennsylvania.

The British invasion and the subsequent counterattacks by Washington resulted in significant economic devastation and social dislocation for thousands of New Jerseyans. Livingston's warnings to the Continental Congress early in 1776 as he worked toward reconciliation came true. The first several months after the signing of the Declaration of Independence taught New Jerseyans that the war would be bloody and long. Moreover, the presence of sizable numbers of loyalists and the proximity of the British in New York portended constant foraging raids, skirmishes, and loyalist uprisings. The destruction experienced by average New Jerseyans lowered their support for the war effort and led Livingston to accuse legislators of failing to support the militia properly and refusing to force their constituents to share the burdens of defending the nation. Without an effective militia, he believed, the state would never be safe.

Livingston understood militias to be the enforcement arm of the new patriot governments across the nation. They replaced the old royal authority by functioning at the lowest level of government, interacting with every single individual in a state, assimilating those who joined, and using violence to become the ultimate political authority in towns and counties. In New Jersey, the militia represented the state's main defense against increasingly dangerous British assaults from New York and maintained control of the state in the absence of Washington's army. Even the British saw the militia as an unpredictably troublesome part of the war; they exacted casualties for every foray into East Jersey and prevented any attempt at reinstalling a royal government in the state.[2]

Enthusiasm for the war subsided across the new nation by late 1776. Divisions between states stymied cooperation among them, and patriots had created no state institutions to compel military service and mobilize men effectively. The centrality of New Jersey in the war propelled Livingston into the role of wartime bureaucrat. He mediated among Washington, state legislators, national politicians, and the public, especially in securing men to fight and in responding to the war's intense destruction and the subversive loyalism in the state. The interplay of this wartime state-level administration among Livingston, the public, and other political actors reveals the difficulties faced by even the most seasoned politicians in prosecuting the war, especially after so many men refused to fight. By March 1777, Livingston realized that the legislature, empowered by strong Whig ideology in 1776, could not adequately fight the war. Viewing the legislature with disdain, he knew that the executive needed far greater power than the state constitution had provided for. Livingston's previous political experience and his general flexibility seen during his New York years made him the perfect candidate to carve out this greater power in a fraught revolutionary environment. This confrontation became the turning point in his political career, as Livingston positioned himself as a central political actor defending his beliefs against the legislature on how the government should operate, how to quash loyalism, and how to respond to economic destruction and social dislocation.[3]

*   *   *

As early as February 1776, during Livingston's first militia field command and while he simultaneously served in Congress, British military officials had begun to focus on an invasion of New York City as the central element of their renewed plan to crush the American rebellion after their defeat in Boston. General Howe's forces, which had evacuated Boston, would join Henry Clinton's army, just defeated at Charleston, along with reinforcements from Europe. Once occupied, New York City would become the major base of British military operations in North America, allowing Howe to move up the Hudson River and eventually connect with Guy Carleton's forces driving south from Canada. This strategy would isolate New England and render those colonies easier to occupy.[4]

Washington, knowing that the British would likely set their eyes on New York, moved his army there from Boston and by mid-April assumed command of the city's defense. Washington hoped to fight a defensive war to harass British forces but preserve his army. To amass enough troops to defend New York, he had to rely on the militias of the surrounding states, including 3,300 New Jerseyans. Washington also recognized the need to garrison New Jersey in order to prevent a British landing and the possibility of being outflanked and trapped on Manhattan Island. This so-called post strategy, which Washington favored early in the war, would preserve his army by forcing the British to engage in offensive operations while his forces defended fortified outposts.[5]

New Jersey's defense, and therefore Livingston's position, remained paramount to Washington's overall strategy for New York. However, New Jersey's failure, unlike most other colonies, to create a structured government by the spring of 1776 hampered the Provincial Congress's ability to assist Washington. The lack of a governor especially limited Washington's attempts to secure quick and decisive action, leading him to request authorization from the Provincial Congress to call directly on the militia in this time of emergency.

Washington complained to General Livingston, then headquartered at Elizabethtown with his neighbor and close friend Elias Boudinot serving as his chief aide, that the means to recruit the troops authorized by the Provincial Congress appeared to him "to be totally inadequate to the Necessity of the Case." Howe's forces had left Halifax and would arrive in New York at any moment. Washington ordered Livingston to activate militiamen in East Jersey and have them report immediately to New York City. He had already requested six militia regiments from Connecticut and, combined with his Continentals and various militiamen from New York, hoped he would be prepared for the impending attack.[6]

On June 29, the first transports of Howe's fleet arrived in New York Harbor, and Washington reiterated to Livingston the need to send additional forces to New York. Livingston, however, believed Washington's New Jersey contingent sufficient and instead requested an exact number of troops from Washington.[7] Livingston's reluctance to send most of his troops away became more important after Howe landed on the largely undefended Staten Island on July 2, separated from Elizabethtown and Perth Amboy by only the narrow Arthur Kill. Washington restated the importance of an aggressive plan of readiness: "The time is now near at hand which must probably determine, whether Americans are to be, Freemen or Slaves; . . . whether their Houses, and Farms, are to be pillaged and destroyed, and they consigned to a State of Wretchedness from which no human efforts will probably deliver them." The importance of Livingston and his militiamen was therefore not lost on Washington or on the people of East Jersey, who remained on the front lines of the Revolution from this moment until the war's end.[8]

Livingston reported the following day that British units had dismantled a drawbridge near Elizabethtown Point and posted guards at key access points to cut off Staten Island from New Jersey. He immediately ordered the militia under his command to positions at Elizabethtown Point, Newark, and Perth Amboy to prevent British incursions into New Jersey. However, the defensive situation remained grave, with only four to five hundred men and limited arms and supplies at Elizabethtown Point, closest to Staten Island, to defend New Jersey. More important, Livingston reported that residents in East Jersey "seem to be greatly dispirited" by the sight of their local militia units marching off to defend New York City "while they are absolutely at their Mercy." He requested that those units return to New Jersey to fortify positions from Perth Amboy to Elizabethtown Point.[9]

The alarm over New Jersey's defenselessness resounded throughout East

Jersey's local patriot committees. On July 3, the Elizabethtown Committee of Safety petitioned Washington for additional supplies and men because most of the local militia had left for New York; ammunition, especially for the cannon defending Elizabethtown Point, remained dangerously low. Likewise, the Newark Committee of Correspondence pleaded that Washington allow the quick return of the New Jersey militia to "our defenceless Country": "We cannot behold our alarming Situation without anticipating the most cruel Distress. Our Country destitute of Inhabitants, Our Wives & Children unprotected either from the Enemy without or the Tories & Negroes in the midst of us." Livingston himself saw the fear and confusion in Elizabethtown, which made him "believe that the Enemy's landing" was "a much more serious affair than I at first imagined." The Woodbridge Committee of Correspondence reinforced Livingston's impression by complaining of the "defenseless situation of our shore" and the deployment of the militia to New York.[10]

For Livingston, the situation seemed especially dire because Liberty Hall lay just a few miles from British lines. Abraham Clark, another Elizabethtown patriot leader and delegate to the Continental Congress, did not "feel quite reconciled at" being in Philadelphia with "the Enemy by my door at home"; he feared Elizabethtown would be "laid in ashes" and reported that even the Continental Congress believed "our province in great danger of being ravaged by the enemy." John Adams, writing the following month, summed up the situation to wife Abigail, claiming that the "middle states begin to taste the sweets of war," something few there had dealt with before. The Provincial Congress even had to suspend its quorum requirement on July 6 in order to continue to transact business because so many members had fled to protect their homes. Livingston arranged for his wife and daughters to stay at the home of his sister, the wife of Lord Stirling, in Basking Ridge, farther west from Liberty Hall.[11]

The fear of a possible British attack led Livingston to fortify the coast opposite Staten Island, especially as British troops sometimes fired on small militia units near Elizabethtown Point and Perth Amboy. At the same moment, Washington and Livingston heard complaints from the Jersey militia stationed in New York that "they are very desirous to be nearer their families to take some care of them." Washington doubted that an attack on Manhattan would occur before Howe's reinforcements from Europe arrived and so allowed most of the Jersey militiamen to transfer back to their state. He ordered Livingston to prepare for a possible invasion by cutting all communications with Staten Island to prevent disaffected New Jerseyans from fomenting rebellion and to resist British attempts to gather food and supplies. Most of the Jersey coast lay unprotected, and British deserters were already reporting food shortages on the island. The Provincial Congress authorized, with Livingston's blessing, Monmouth County militia units to stay within that county to protect its cattle and other foodstuffs and ordered all stock animals driven away from the coast. Rumors of foraging attacks during this critical time in early July led Livingston to redouble his efforts to reinforce the coast.[12]

Washington's decision to return most of the New Jersey militia units elevated Livingston's overall status within the colonial defense framework. Although Hugh Mercer commanded the limited Continental forces in New Jersey and assisted Livingston in the placement and fortification of the militia, Washington made clear that Livingston would be primarily in charge of fortifying East Jersey. As someone who had never held a military commission before, Livingston felt inadequate to the task. In his initial pleas for assistance from Washington on July 4, Livingston lamented, "As the department I now act in is to me entirely new, I must be desirous of every aid that can possibly be obtained." To better support New Jersey's defense, Livingston requested "a few experienced Officers"; because "Our Men are raw & inexperienced—our Officers mostly absent—want of Discipline is inevitable." Unfortunately for Livingston, Washington could spare no officers but Mercer.[13] Mercer's arrival, however, failed to relieve Livingston's misgivings. He reported to the Provincial Congress that he felt himself "unequal to the present important command."[14] Samuel Tucker, president of the Provincial Congress, expressed some amusement that Livingston had been "taken from the cabinet to the field[,] for the one you have ample faculties, for the other you complain you are unqualified." Tucker assured Livingston that he believed in his abilities, yet Livingston privately mocked his own status, writing that he would "really be astonished to see how grand I look" as a general, yet "I can assure you I was never more sensible . . . of my own *nothingness* in military affairs."[15]

Although Livingston's feelings of inadequacy in his military role continued to grow in July and August, most of his work actually had more to do with his previous life as a politician. In his roughly two months as head of the East Jersey militia, Livingston and most of his troops never saw combat. Rather, his service concerned organizing defensive positions and lobbying the legislature to provision troops, which his political shrewdness enabled him to do successfully.[16]

Livingston's political savviness became even more important when New Jersey's government completely changed. On July 2, the Provincial Congress approved a draft of a new constitution written by a committee of ten led by the Reverend Jacob Green. Although Green and his committee believed independence to be the likely conclusion in Philadelphia, they knew that many in the state, including Livingston, held out for reconciliation with Britain. The state constitution therefore, at the insistence of Samuel Tucker and other moderates who had grown increasingly frightened at the prospect of a war so close to home, contained a clause that declared the document void if the Continental Congress and Britain amicably settled their differences.[17]

The document gained support from many elites for the limits it placed on the possibilities of mob democracy, even as expanding Whig notions of power shifted control of the new state toward the legislature and away from an executive. Green remained adamant that the poor would not act with civic virtue and had become "too beholden to" their "betters to participate in the life of the polity." He saw limitations as especially important because the new constitution granted voting rights to individuals with £50 of real or personal property, the same requirement that had liberalized the electorate and ensured almost universal manhood suffrage in the last election for the Provincial Congress. The lower property requirement aligned with the new constitutions of other states, including New York, Maryland, and Georgia. However, unlike Pennsylvania's unicameral legislature and plural executive, New Jersey's system maintained a bicameral legislature, where the upper house (the Legislative Council) served as an effective check against unruly democracy in the General Assembly, since its members needed to be worth at least £1,000. The new constitution further decentralized state authority by increasing the power of the legislature but mandating yearly elections. The governor was elected by the legislature, held a one-year term, had no veto power, and commanded little authority besides leading the militia. Overall then, New Jersey's 1776 constitution confirmed much of the democratic expansion seen earlier in 1776 by empowering the legislature even as it implemented safeguards to prevent social upheaval.[18]

As news of the Continental Congress's declaration of independence spread throughout the former colonies, the first public celebrations broke out in Trenton and Princeton. Volleys of musket fire and "loud acclamations" greeted the resolve that "our enemies have left us no middle way between perfect freedom and abject slavery." The Provincial Congress passed a resolution supporting the Declaration of Independence on July 18 and renamed itself the Convention of the State of New Jersey. It scheduled elections for the first legislature and disbanded itself on August 21 after those elections. Sussex

County assemblyman Joseph Barton believed that declaring independence at last "gives a great turn to the minds of our people." Barton doubted that "there will be five Tories in our part of the country in ten days." The large number of moderates who "would do nothing until we were declared a free State" are now prepared to "spend their lives and fortunes in defence of our country." Therefore, by the time Admiral Lord Richard Howe arrived in New York and, in his role as a peace commissioner, proposed a plan for reconciliation to Benjamin Franklin in late July, most New Jerseyans had either chosen neutrality or cast their lot with the patriots.[19]

As Barton expected, many New Jerseyans came into the patriot camp, but they were motivated more by the military preparations overseen by Livingston than by the new state government and the Declaration. In mid-July, John Adams remarked to Jonathan Dickinson Sergeant that he was pleased that New Jersey had ratified the Declaration and that support for independence increased "everywhere as the war approaches near." According to Adams, the British Army "brings a great heat with it and warms all before it"; nothing "makes and spreads patriotism so fast."[20] At the same time, however, the nearness of the British and New Jersey's moderate attitude toward independence gave loyalists the opportunity to sabotage the new patriot government and exacerbated fears of enemy activities conducted behind the lines. After the British occupation of Staten Island, the Provincial Congress had quickly passed a law to ban seditious speech and to punish treason with the death penalty. Adams thought that the law "would make Whigs by the thousand" once New Jerseyans understood the real danger from the British army on Staten Island and that they would protect themselves and their property by becoming patriots. To Adams, the treason law "in politics, like the article for shooting upon the spot a soldier who shall turn his back . . . turns a man's cowardice and timidity into heroism because it places greater danger behind his back than before his face."[21]

New Jersey's government did not share Adams's confidence in loyalist conversions and became increasingly fearful of third-column activity, especially after the aborted conspiracy led by former royal Governor William Tryon in New York in late June. Tryon hoped to rally up to five hundred men on Long Island and Staten Island to set fire to New York City and assassinate George Washington. At the time, Adams feared that the "chain of Toryism extending from Canada through New York and New Jersey into Pennsylvania" would slow the patriot cause. William Ellery of Rhode Island advised that "a good lookout" must be kept in New Jersey on "a number of tories who will show themselves should Howe's Army be successful"; Ellery himself was "as much afraid of those villains as of the British troops." These fears led to the jailing and exile of hundreds of suspected loyalists during the summer of 1776, and eventually voters were required to take a loyalty oath to participate in the new elections.[22]

On the front lines, concern grew as intelligence from loyalists in Newark reached Howe's troops before they had even disembarked on Staten Island. By early July, as Livingston's subordinates reported the arrest of several loyalist leaders in Perth Amboy, the threat grew more apparent. Perth Amboy was of particular concern as the former seat of royal authority. Washington worried about the "known Disaffection of the People of Amboy . . . who have shewn themselves our inveterate Enemies" and ordered the relocation of any suspected dissident from the coast. Livingston, however, had few places to send them; the lack of sufficient militiamen in the state's interior would make it dangerous to move so many suspected loyalists to almost anywhere else.[23]

The New Jersey Convention had become concerned that the continued presence of loyalists would slow militia recruitment, critical for Washington's defense of New York, and allow the British to rally the state's slave population to overthrow the patriot government. Newark's Committee of Correspondence echoed these fears and encouraged Livingston to interdict communication with Staten Island. By early August, the Convention approved a law requiring a pass for anyone traveling to New York to prevent desertion. This action buttressed Livingston's own attempts to limit communication; in one instance, he used reports of a large number of loyalists headed down the Hackensack River to Staten Island to ensure that "these rascals may be taken" before they could share any important information with the British.[24]

The largest uprising of loyalists that Livingston dealt with occurred in Monmouth County, especially around Shrewsbury. There, in late June and early July, bands of loyalists organized themselves in the county's cedar swamps to frustrate patriot forces. New York lawyer Balthazar De Hart reported that "the greatest part of that place was inhabited or rather infested with Tories" and that "their disaffection has been greatly increased" by an influx of loyalists fleeing New York City. The bands remained in contact with British ships anchored off the county's coastline. The uprising led the Convention to dispatch not only the Monmouth militia but also elements from Burlington to secure the coast and eliminate the loyalists. By early August, Washington reported to the Convention that the loyalists in Monmouth had been contained, though he feared new uprisings in Hackensack and in other areas of Bergen County, as intelligence indicated a potential British thrust into those areas. These uprisings, though quelled by Livingston's militia and Continental forces, diverted significant resources from the effort to contain the British on Staten Island.[25]

Beyond the military dangers posed by a disaffected population, two of New Jersey's leading politicians believed that the real danger to the new nation came from a careless attitude toward choosing leaders of the new government. Jonathan Elmer, a future member of the Continental Congress, believed that "to entrust the affairs of our state, while the bayonet is pointed at our breasts, to persons whose conduct discovers them to be enemies to their country" would result in ruin. Instead, only those men who firmly believed in the cause and committed themselves fully to the defense of the new nation could adequately lead the new state. John Witherspoon, speaking to the Continental Congress, was more explicit, arguing that "one of the greatest dangers" facing the states was "treachery among themselves, augmented by bribery and corruption from our enemies." For Witherspoon, professed patriots who did not want a stronger confederacy between the now independent states were just as dangerous as loyalists seeking to divide the unity that the Continental Congress had built up for the last two years. These republican arguments would have appealed to Livingston, who daily saw the dangers of disaffected New Jerseyans crossing back and forth between patriot and British lines.[26]

Although the possibility of attacks by loyalists worried many patriots, including Livingston, the largest concern he had during his time in the service remained the ability to organize, supply, and maintain an effective militia force in East Jersey. This constant and pressing responsibility was the core of Livingston's wartime bureaucratic experience and did not end when he became governor. Congress and Washington had organized a Flying Camp in New Jersey that became a base of operations for Mercer and the militia units from other states as well as for some of Livingston's men. In July, Livingston battled two issues: the failure to secure reinforcements and the desertion of troops to attend to the harvest. Concerns over troop levels consumed most of Livingston's time. He complained to the Convention, "We have been deserted in this moment of common danger by our western brethren," meaning the counties of West Jersey. Only one detachment from the Hunterdon militia had arrived to defend against the British on Staten Island.[27] The western militiamen were needed not only to reinforce posts in East Jersey but also to relieve men who had been active for some time.[28]

Livingston believed he could not recruit enough militiamen because the

fine for failure to perform militia service, ten shillings, was "of but little consequence at this time"; the state should enact stronger punishments to convince men to serve. However, officers of the Gloucester County militia
believed that the inducement for recruits to join the Continental service, fifteen shillings a week, was not high enough. Militiamen would rather stay
home than report for duty, a conclusion echoed by Washington when new
levies to raise troops in New Jersey had not returned enough men. These
circumstances led some militia units, such as one stationed at Bergen in early
July, to abandon their post and head home without orders.[29]

The larger inducement to avoid military service came from the timing of
the campaign. Livingston himself could sympathize that "our harvests [are]
perishing for want of hands to cut it."[30] Militiamen sent to New York in June
became the first to complain, especially when some towns, like Newark, sent
almost complete quotas to New York while others, like Elizabethtown, returned very few. The Newark militia, having "scarcely left a man behind us to
take care of the harvest," balked at having to serve while other men tended
their crops. Likewise, the militia activated to serve under Livingston remained "greatly concerned about their harvest and think the more hard of
confinement to the service as they understand that a great part of the militia
from other counties are returning home." Other militia leaders spoke of their
men's worry that they would lose "what must support their children."[31] Even
though Livingston understood these concerns, he did not take kindly to requests to be relieved of duty and instead questioned the men's support of the
cause, a challenge he commonly deployed throughout the conflict but an im-
putation not appreciated by the common soldier. The Pennsylvania militiamen who served around New York with John Adlum, for instance, saw no
problem with excusing all married men to return home to tend to their families. In this and in later cases, Livingston minimized his constituents' practi-
cal and economic concerns and instead believed their failure to sacrifice
those interests came from a want of patriotism. He particularly became concerned over the lack of virtue that he saw among the general population. For
example, in responding to those men who hoped to leave to harvest their
crops, Livingston wrote, "It is a little extraordinary that your regiment who
have suffered the least are the most clamorous." Perhaps thinking better of
this admonishing introduction, he crossed out "It is a little extraordinary"
and substituted "I am sorry to say." In the end, Livingston realized that ideology could not keep the men under his command: they valued their families
at home more than their duty to the patriot cause.[32]

Throughout July and early August, the complement of British and Hessian forces on Staten Island continued to grow, reaching between 32,000 and 34,000. Alarmed, Washington asked Livingston to recall the state militia and begin preparations for an impending invasion.[33] New Jersey's defensive situation and lack of troops became so dire in August that Jonathan Dickinson Sergeant authored a plan to raise a unit of black troops to serve as a home guard. Owners would be paid £50 for each slave's enlistment and receive an exemption from service; the slaves would be encouraged to serve by a promise of freedom once they had earned back the original outlay through their militia salary. Sergeant's plan never materialized, in part because of fears of a slave revolt in the midst of the British presence. Moreover, John Adams concluded that southern states would never allow its execution.[34]

Washington became increasingly pessimistic about the military situation in and around New York. On August 17, he reported to the New York Convention that the city "will in all human probability very soon be the scene of a bloody conflict." He worried that the "Shrieks & Cries" of the "great Numbers of Women, Children and infirm persons" remaining in the city would "have an unhappy effect on the Ears & Minds of our Young & inexperienced Soldiery" and hoped that some plan could "be devised for their removal." That same day, Washington issued a proclamation recommending a general evacuation, a choice that many affluent New Yorkers had already made. As early as April, when Washington had first arrived in New York, Livingston reported that nearly all of his friends and family there had already abandoned the city for safe harbor elsewhere.[35]

Reinforced with more troops, Howe's army landed on Long Island on August 22. The ample farmland provided needed supplies, and the British enjoyed the support of a large loyalist population. Washington believed the landing on Long Island to be a feint—the real target would be Manhattan itself—and sent only 1,500 troops to Brooklyn. Livingston and Washington also thought that 15,000 British soldiers would cross into New Jersey.[36]

The Battle of Long Island on August 27 resulted in an American defeat and the retreat of 9,500 of Washington's forces to Manhattan. Hugh Mercer's Jersey Continentals left to reinforce New York, and Livingston's militia proceeded toward Paulus Hook to defend the more northerly approaches into New Jersey. The first major battle in the campaign against New York had left Livingston on the sidelines; he had heard only the "almost incessant" fire from skirmishes after the main battle.[37]

For Livingston, the Battle of Long Island represented relief: the main assault would not come through his command. But developments in the new state legislature had a far greater impact on him. New Jersey's first legislature met for its initial meeting at the College of New Jersey in Princeton to elect the state's first governor. On August 30, they debated between Livingston and Richard Stockton, who was then serving as a delegate to the Continental Congress. The first ballot ended in a tie. A member of the legislature, John Stevens, then visited Stockton and afterward communicated that he had no interest in the governorship. In fact, Stockton had earlier stated that he saw the position of chief justice as the more desirable post but would accept the governorship if called upon. Stevens's report, however, undermined Stockton's bid and led to Livingston's election on the second ballot. Ironically, after the legislature appointed him Chief Justice, Stockton declined the nomination because he had actually wanted to be governor.[38]

No documentary evidence remains to determine why legislators supported Livingston for the governorship, though his central role in organizing the state's defense not only gave him visibility but also made him the de facto leader of the state. His political savvy likely contributed as well. However, some in the revolutionary leadership hoped others would ascend to the post. John Adams, just after Livingston had been replaced in the Continental Congress, wanted Joseph Reed, an aide to Washington, to become the state's first governor; Adams believed Reed to be a "man of sense and principle" with a "coolness and candor and goodness of heart" that would make New Jerseyans "very happy." Jonathan Dickinson Sergeant, writing to Adams after Livingston's election, believed "from the Manner in which the great Offices have been disposed of" that too many leaders in the state still hoped for reconciliation. However, despite his reluctance to support independence while he was in Congress, Livingston had for the last two months been at the center of revolutionary activity in the colonies, and his performance had done much to repair his reputation. In a letter to Livingston, William Hooper, a delegate to the Continental Congress from North Carolina, congratulated the members of the legislature "upon the return of their reason, that they have found at length discernment enough to distinguish real merit, & virtue enough to reward it."[39]

The governorship represented a welcome opportunity for Livingston to make a graceful exit from his militia duties. His inexperience and uneasiness in military affairs continued to weigh on him. In a letter to his son Brockholst, he rejoiced in his election and confessed that he had been "prodigiously hurried and fatigued for this month past." Especially after the events leading to the Battle of Long Island, Livingston told Hugh Mercer, he felt "immense fatigue . . . both in mind and body"; the news of his election caused him to be "agreeably relieved . . . on that account more than any other."[40]

The last letter Livingston received in his capacity as a militia general, from his successor, Jacob Ford, congratulated him on his new post and fore-shadowed the most important issue that Livingston would deal with over the next two years as governor: rooting out loyalism within New Jersey. Ford told of officers and men within the militia who would "embrace the first opportu-nity to cut our throats" and highly recommended that Livingston institute loyalty oaths for militia officers who renewed their commissions. Ford's con-cerns were not unfounded. Some militiamen, such as George Taylor of Mon-mouth County, supported loyalists while serving the patriot government. In late July, Taylor had used his authority to issue passes to Shrewsbury loyalists to travel to New York, and he assisted Monmouth loyalists Samuel Wright and Daniel Van Mater in securing supplies for the British before he left the militia. In 1777, he began to operate as a loyalist partisan on Sandy Hook, raiding patriot targets across Monmouth County. His father, who had been a key figure in the Provincial Congress, also became a loyalist. The question of loyalty, explored by both Livingston and the Provincial Congress in a prelim-inary fashion, now became a top priority in Livingston's new position, along with defense of the state from the overwhelming British threat.[41]

* * *

Livingston's militia experience gave him vivid insight into the danger New Jersey faced in the fall of 1776. British forces remained entrenched around New York City, and New Jersey's defense was tenuous. In his inaugural speech to the legislature on September 13, Livingston, with characteristic rhetorical flourishes, reflected on the path the state had taken, contrasting indepen-dence against the "long . . . system of despotism concerted for our ruin . . . and . . . attempted to be enforced by the violence of war." More important, however, he recast his role in the decision for independence, claiming that only after "the decisive alternative of absolute submission or utter destruc-tion" brought by the British military "had extinguished all hope of obtaining justice . . . the whole continent, save a few self-interested individuals, were unanimous in the separation." Of course, Livingston and several other Conti-nental Congress delegates who opposed independence did so in recognition that the likelihood of a victory against Britain would be slim after the fighting began. However, by invoking his military service instead of his congressional service, Livingston reclaimed himself as a defender of liberty instead of a cowardly moderate ejected from Congress in disgrace. Even John Adams, who thought ill of Livingston for his moderation, wrote to Abigail that Livingston's address was "the most elegant and masterly, ever made in America."[42]

More practically, as the state's highest-level wartime bureaucrat, Livingston immediately identified two key areas for legislators to focus on in the coming months: better organization of and pay for the militia and more consistent provisioning of it through impressment of civilian property. Organizing and paying the militia took precedence, given that half of the state's militia remained active in defense of New York, stationed both in New York City and throughout Essex, Bergen, and Middlesex Counties. In his first two months as governor, Livingston witnessed Washington's continuing losses just across the Hudson River. On September 15, British troops crossed the East River and landed at Kip's Bay on Manhattan Island north of New York City. The withdrawal of the Connecticut militia units defending Kip's Bay forced Washington into defensive positions around Harlem Heights. Despite the continued need for militia from New Jersey and other surrounding states to augment his army, Washington complained that "the Dependence which the Congress has placed upon the Militia, has already greatly injured—&I fear will totally ruin, our Cause—Being subject to no controul themselves they introduce disorder among" the regular troops. Moreover, the "change in their living brings on sickness," which "makes them Impatient to get home, which spreads universally & introduces abominable Desertions."[43]

In New Jersey, the militia situation continued to deteriorate. Militia General Matthias Williamson complained in mid-September that the state had not paid those units on duty, and he believed that the other half of the militia, scheduled to take over soon, would never appear because of pay issues, leaving key outposts in East Jersey undefended. Livingston attempted to secure funds from Congress to pay those militiamen activated into Continental service. Though he was ultimately successful by mid-October, many of the men on duty or scheduled for duty in late September and October refused to serve because of previous pay issues. Since financial incentives became the primary way all patriot governments mobilized men for war, pay issues seriously hampered Livingston's ability to ensure an adequate defense.[44]

In late September, Livingston made a more forceful plea to the state legislature, describing "all the regulations respecting the militia of this state" as "greatly inadequate" and calling for a new militia bill to reinvigorate the state's defense. The reorganization and restructuring of the militia became the most important issue Livingston worked on during this period. He knew the militia's inadequacies from firsthand experience, and he also acknowledged the general lack of support it had among average New Jerseyans.[45] Directly related to the issue of pay was the major problem of supplying the militia. Merchants and farmers increasingly refused to exchange foodstuffs for Continental dollars, fearing these would soon become worthless. Clement Biddle, the deputy quartermaster of the Flying Camp, contacted Livingston in early September because his agents had tried to buy two thousand bushels of oats, corn, and rye in Bergen County, but no one would "sell it without gold and silver." Likewise, the lack of winter clothing compelled Colonel William Maxwell to report that "not one man [is] willing at present . . . to engage to stay at this place during the winter." Maxwell rightly believed that few militiamen would sign a contract for additional service without assurances of proper supplies. William Paterson, the state's new attorney general, reiterated this point; the state's soldiers were "in a most wretched situation for the want of clothing," especially those serving as part of the northern expedition in upstate New York, Livingston's son Brockholst among them. Desertions increased as lack of pay and supplies and the increasingly cold weather spurred many to return to their families.[46]

In addition to watching the military situation deteriorate around New York City, New Jerseyans battled a far more insidious enemy: the continued activities of loyalists. To counter the perceived threat from within, the state legislature passed a law requiring loyalty oaths of all new state officials, though these did little to prevent interaction between New Jerseyans and the British. Fears over loyalist activities grew after Washington's army retreated from Manhattan Island and suffered defeat at White Plains. By early November, Washington had withdrawn to New Jersey to prepare for Howe's next offensive.[47]

With invasion looking ever more likely, the Continental Congress, Washington, and state officials feared more subversion by loyalists in New Jersey, specifically their sharing of intelligence with the British on Staten Island and their sabotaging of facilities in New Jersey. Congress received reports that "a free and open communication and correspondence" had been allowed to continue between New Jersey and Staten Island, and John Hancock requested that Livingston take immediate steps to stop it. Lord Stirling's Continental troops, as well as militia units, captured loyalists across the state and confined them, along with British prisoners, in the far northern reaches of Sussex County.

Figure 4. Brockholst Livingston (1757–1823). Image #93147d.
Courtesy of the New-York Historical Society.

Although these roundups stopped some communication, Livingston identi-fied a far more devious way leaks had occurred: through the numerous women who crossed back and forth between patriot and British lines. Livingston in-formed Washington that, "tho' they appear to be Whigs," these women "have a Number of Stories to tell which tho' probably told with no ill Intention, yet have a natural Tendency to discourage the weaker part of our Inhabitants." These "Mistresses of infinite craft & Subtlety," according to Livingston, were easily employed by the British to deliver secret messages or secure vital intelli-gence about New Jersey's defenses. He therefore instituted a strict policy of not granting passes to women traveling to New York for the war's duration, even denying his own relatives.[48]

The defeat at White Plains and the decision by Howe to withdraw to Manhattan Island allowed Washington's forces some breathing room. Wash-ington told John Hancock that he believed Howe would "make a descent with a part of his Troops into Jersey . . . for the purpose of making a Winter Cam-paign." To Nathanael Greene, he added that "they can have no Capital object in view unless it is Philadelphia." New Jersey would then become a thorough-fare for Howe's campaign. Washington therefore recommended that Living-ston ready the militia and request New Jerseyans to move stock animals, foodstuffs, and other valuable property away from the potential British path, lest they suffer "calamities . . . [beyond] all description." Already in New York, the British "have treated all . . . without discrimination"; the difference between "Whig & Tory has been lost in one general scene of ravage and des-olation." Washington wanted to minimize British opportunities for forage in New Jersey, as any additional supplies the British procured could prolong the campaign and the state's misery.[49]

After almost three months of wrangling with the legislature over a militia bill and militia pay and supply issues, Livingston could not easily comply with Washington's call for readiness. He promised the commander that when the invasion occurred, he would call out the militia, "but whether they will obey the orders God only knows." Moreover, he knew from personal experi-ence "that they will be worth but little if they do." The situation soon became critical when Howe's army captured or killed almost three thousand militia-men at Fort Washington, the last patriot outpost on Manhattan Island, on November 16. Only a continually shrinking force under Washington stood between Howe and New Jersey.[50]

Livingston sensed the invasion approaching after the fall of Fort Wash-ington and arranged for the publication of a broadside designed to elevate the spirits of the New Jersey militia and to rally them to the defense. Livingston's reliance on rhetoric, just as in his New York days, remained his only tool to coax recruits, since the legislature had failed to mandate military service or adequately supply and pay those who voluntarily served. Addressing himself to New Jersey's militia colonels, Livingston declared that "the enemy, despairing of conquest, seems determined to plunder" and would soon invade New Jersey. In order to "save ourselves and posterity from the most ignominious slavery," Livingston called on "brave Americans . . . to maintain that independence which British injustice and British cruelty compelled them to adopt." He boldly stated that the "militia of New Jersey will not forfeit, by any unworthy conduct, the favorable sentiments entertained of their prowess" and show "a spirit becoming a people disdaining slavery and ready to risk their lives in the cause of freedom, of virtue, and posterity." Unfortunately for Livingston, militia recruitment continued to dwindle. Colonel Isaac Smith of the Hunterdon militia noted in late November that the militia had been called out so many times that few now willingly answered. Smith's own unit, called for duty six times since March 1776, could neither muster many men nor equip those who did show up. This reality led the loyalist-leaning *New-York Gazette, and Weekly Mercury* to publish Livingston's broadside to the militia with the scornful comment that its message "met with so much credit in New Jersey, as to raise FOUR volunteers in the whole province."[51]

The British invasion of New Jersey began on November 18, when General Charles Cornwallis crossed into Bergen County with roughly six thousand men, captured Fort Lee, the patriot installation opposite Fort Washington, and thereby opened the Hudson River to Howe's navy. Lord Stirling observed on November 21 that "a fright seems to have seized the whole country" and that the state militia needed to rally to reinforce Washington. By then, the Continental Army in New Jersey had dwindled to roughly three thousand men, reinforced by another five hundred militiamen with expiring enlistments. Few additional troops rallied, even though the entire state militia had been activated. General Williamson complained that "we have had nothing but murmuring and desertion," especially after the fall of Fort Washington, "immediately on which great many have deserted." The defeat at Fort Lee had "sunk all their spirits," and Williamson expected that he would very soon "have scarcely men sufficient to mount the common guards."[52] Livingston redoubled his efforts to rally militia units from West Jersey, and he ordered Williamson's militia to engage the British. At the same time, he used his political skills to persuade the legislature to provide incentives to any of the already exhausted and disgruntled militiamen who would immediately join Washington's army.[53]

These calls for additional support during the invasion came to naught just as Washington reported that desertions continued to increase. As the British approached New Brunswick, the additional militia units expected from northern New Jersey came "out slowly and reluctantly, whether owing to the want of Officers of Spirit to encourage them or your Summons not being regularly sent to them." Many of these men, by late November, had refused militia service for all of the reasons that Livingston had attempted to remedy and because of the recent patriot defeats. Many of them, General Williamson believed, had "borne the character of warm Whigs" but had quickly sought Howe's protection to defend their homes and families after the occupation began. The failure of the militia to rally led William Hooper of North Carolina to identify that while Pennsylvania "is in a lethargy . . . Jersey is little better" since "no person here seems more interested to oppose the enemy than if they existed in the moon." Samuel Adams of Massachusetts likewise asked in exasperation, "What will be said of Pennsylvania & the Jerseys? Have they not disgraced themselves by standing the idle Spectators while the Enemy overran a great Part of their Country?"[54]

Negative comments on the militia's performance also appeared in Washington's report to Congress from Trenton after he had abandoned New Brunswick and most of East Jersey to the British. He believed that "the causes of our late disgraces" could be found in "the frequent calls upon the Militia of this State—the want of exertion in the Principal Gentlemen of the Country—or a fatal supineness and insensibility of danger." To shift some of the blame from himself, Washington claimed that, had the New Jersey militia "stepped forth in Season . . . we might have prevented the Enemy's crossing the Heckenseck [River]" or, "with equal probability of success, have made a stand at Brunswic on the Rariton." To Connecticut governor Jonathan Trumbull, Washington wrote that his hopes for reinforcements in New Jersey had been "cruelly disappointed . . . the Inhabitants of this State, either from fear or disaffection, almost to a man, refused to turn out." From the Pennsylvania side of the Delaware River, he summed up for his brother Samuel: "In short the conduct of the Jersey has been most infamous—Instead of turning out to defend their Country and affording aid to our Army, they are making their Submissions as fast as they can . . . the few Militia that were in Arms disbanded themselves or slunk off." Washington believed, however, that Congress's refusal to authorize

and pay for a significant standing army was the true cause of the patriot setbacks. As he told John Hancock, "If 40,000 Men had been kept in constant
pay since the first commencement of Hostilities . . . the Continent would have
saved Money." Nothing would have been paid to the unreliable militia nor
would as much damage have been done to the nation because of the failure of
the smaller army to defend it.[55]

With British forces pursuing him across New Jersey and his numbers
dwindling, Washington abandoned the state and fled to Pennsylvania on December 8. Howe decided not to pursue the Continentals in favor of an expedition to occupy Rhode Island and secure a year-round port for the navy. In
the meantime, he set up outposts across New Jersey to control as much of the
state as he could to start its reintegration into the empire. For New Jerseyans,
the occupation could best be described by the opening line of Thomas Paine's
American Crisis: "These are the times that try men's souls." While serving in
Washington's army as the British gradually pushed it southward from Bergen
County, Paine began to write the first of the sixteen pamphlets near Newark
and completed a draft by the time the army evacuated to Pennsylvania. It
appeared in print on December 19, "in the depth of winter, when nothing but
hope and virtue could survive."[56]

The state's bleak outlook led American General Alexander McDougall to
declare that New Jersey "is totally deranged, without Government, or officers
civil or military in it that will act with any Spirit." Some had "gone to the
Enemy for Protection, others are out of the State, and the few that remain are
mostly indecisive in their Conduct." In a subsequent letter, McDougall reiterated that, with "the Governor being out of the State as well as many other
principal people and no Legislature in it," the state's affairs had been thrown
"into confusion." In fact, Livingston's whereabouts from mid-December to
early January remain unknown; not knowing even if he remained alive, John
Hancock addressed a late December letter to "Governor Livingston or the
present Executive power in New Jersey."[57]

The occupation encouraged many New Jerseyans to become loyalists in
an attempt to protect their property and families. Of course, some had been
reluctant to support the patriot cause even before the invasion, and those
who had opposed independence readily welcomed the British and Hessians
as liberators. For Howe, New Jersey became a testing ground to begin the
restoration of the empire. With most of the densely populated counties under
occupation, the British could effectively support loyalists and eventually install a new government loyal to the king. Howe issued a proclamation on

November 30 that granted amnesty to anyone who took a loyalty oath to the crown within sixty days. Thousands of residents flocked to British lines to take the oath and receive a "protection," a signed statement that they hoped would safeguard them and their families from harassment. For example, Middlesex farmer John Bray advised his uncle in Hunterdon County that he could "come down & receive Protection & return home without molestation" from the Hessian soldiers in control there, who were believed to be far more destructive than the British. The seeming hopelessness of the patriot cause encouraged loyalist uprisings in Monmouth County, leading General Adam Stephen to complain that with so many "disaffected and mischievous persons daily supplying the enemy . . . who are not willing to distinguish their Friends from their Foes," the continued prosecution of the war remained that much harder.[58]

The success at securing so many Americans for the crown led the British Commissioners for Restoring Peace in America to believe that royal control had been reestablished, especially when many men in occupied New York and New Jersey readily joined loyalist units. One such unit, the 4th Battalion of New Jersey Volunteers, was raised during the occupation around Hackensack, Paramus, and Ramapo, drawing men from as far north as Sussex County. Among its members were Joseph Barton, a former patriot leader from Sussex, and, most important, Abraham Van Buskirk, a former member of the Provincial Congress who opposed independence. These men rallied hundreds across North Jersey to the loyalist cause. Van Buskirk even claimed that he had been working for New York Governor Tryon as a loyalist informant during his entire time in the Provincial Congress; now, with the British in control of New Jersey, he could outwardly support the king. Two high-ranking New Jersey officials also swore loyalty to the crown. Richard Stockton, captured by loyalists in Monmouth, swore the oath to secure his release, the only signer of the Declaration to do so. Likewise, Samuel Tucker, the former leader of the Provincial Congress and a state supreme court justice, took the oath and afterward resigned from public life because of it. The strong support Howe saw across the region encouraged him to plan an attack against Philadelphia in early spring to crush the rebellion.[59]

Stockton's and Tucker's defections and the pervasiveness of loyalty in New Jersey after the invasion puts Livingston's disappearance in perspective. No documentary evidence remains detailing his location, his reason for leaving the state, or his activities between his last series of letters in early December in Burlington and those from Morristown in mid-January. Like Washington, he probably fled to Pennsylvania to escape Stockton's fate. However, Livingston as the political veteran, likely acutely understood the state's dire situation and the realities of Washington's consistent failures to ward off British assaults first around New York and now across New Jersey. The British had easily taken the ground that Livingston himself had fortified for months. If months of preparing for a battle the Patriots knew would come had been for naught, Livingston likely questioned the ultimate outcome of the war just as many Americans had in late 1776. Livingston's tepid support for independence in Congress and his consistent hope for reconciliation might have even played a part in his decision to wait out the invasion before reentering the political and military scene in mid-January after Washington had seemingly turned the immediate tide of the British advance. A quick defeat of Washington's forces in Pennsylvania might have even placed Livingston in a strong position to broker that reconciliation if he had reengaged with his former colleagues in Congress who would have remembered his and his family's role in the Drummond affair. Unfortunately, Livingston's thoughts and motivations during this particularly trying time remain his own.[60]

To prevent loyalism from securing an even stronger hold with Livingston incommunicado, Washington planned to retake portions of the state especially as the threat to Philadelphia grew by the end of December. To execute this plan, Congress granted Washington extraordinary war powers to control much of the war department without its oversight. Livingston approved of this measure, which allowed Washington to plan an attack using the limited forces under his command more efficiently. In perhaps the most famous campaign of the Revolution, Washington surprised the Hessian garrison at Trenton on the morning of December 26 and defeated the British at Princeton a week later. Lord Stirling reported to Livingston on December 28 that the British and Hessian troops had evacuated much of West Jersey and fled to South Amboy and New Brunswick. More important, Stirling rejoiced that "the spirit of that part of the country is roused, every part of New Jersey will take spirit if proper measures be adopted." Those "proper measures" were very much up to Livingston. Still in hiding in Pennsylvania, he would have to return to the state to rally both the legislature and the militia to support the renewed campaign against the British.[61]

Both the condition of his troops and the successful liberation of much of New Jersey from British control led Washington to decide to retire to winter quarters at Morristown. With Livingston still out of the state, Washington took the lead in rallying the militia by issuing a proclamation to New Jerseyans on December 31. He asked them to "Evince their love to their Country, by boldly stepping forth and defending the Cause of Freedom" and to join him in ridding the state of its invaders. Over the next week, the militia skirmished with British and Hessian units across East Jersey. Patriot militiamen defeated more than two hundred loyalists from strongholds in Monmouth County during the first week in January, and Continentals from Pennsylvania captured more than a hundred wagonloads of provisions that had been confiscated from patriots over the previous month by Monmouth loyalists. Washington believed "the many injuries they have received" during the occupation would produce more recruits: "To oppression, ravage and a deprivation of property, they have had the more mortifying circumstance of insult added." From Baltimore, congressional delegate William Whipple of New Hampshire offered a similar view: "The ravages committed by the enemy in Jersey has had a most excellent effect; the inhabitants now turn out with spirit and breathe vengeance against the ravagers of their Country." John Adams echoed this sentiment. New Jerseyans, he told his wife, had begun "to raise their Spirits exceedingly, and to be firmer than ever. They are actuated by Resentment now, and Resentment coinciding with Principle is a very powerfull Motive."[62]

Returning to New Jersey in mid-January without any explanation, Livingston quickly took over the rallying of the militia. He ordered West Jersey's commanding militia general, Philemon Dickinson, to activate his men and compel deserters who had not joined in his raids against the British to provide support for Washington until officially discharged by the state. He also attempted to organize four regiments of Continentals and additional militia units to assist Washington at Morristown, where he temporarily headquartered the state's executive branch. Ever the political mind, Livingston took the opportunity to discuss with the legislature and Washington the continued need for a new militia law. Washington agreed that a "well regulated Militia Law" was needed to repair the "irregular and disjointed State of the Militia of this province." The militia should replace the current officers, who were "generally of the lowest Class of people," with leaders who would set "a good Example to their Men" instead of "leading them into every kind of Mischeif," especially "plundering the Inhabitants under pretence of their being Tories." Washington also identified perhaps the most intractable problem with the state's existing militia regulations: the ease with which those who did not wish to serve could escape militia duty by paying a small sum. Livingston had complained about the same issue when he was a general. Washington wanted "Men and not Money."[63]

In late January and early February 1777, Livingston used the recent invasion to prod the legislature to craft a new militia bill. He repeated Washington's criticisms and focused on the need not only to ensure service but also to prevent the possibility of "lawless Rapine." The current law had actually helped to shape the militia as a breeding ground for the "lowest Class of people" by creating a ready market for substitutes for hire, usually the most vulnerable and lowest class of society. These men, who would have probably served in Washington's army, instead took multiple tours in the militia and received substitute pay from men who sought to avoid military service. In the end, they actually made more money serving as substitutes than they would have as irregularly paid Continental soldiers. These reforms, according to Livingston, were "so clearly founded in reason and have been so frequently verified by experience that they cannot fail" to improve the militia's response.[64]

In his efforts to reform the militia, Livingston faced more political hurdles than many other revolutionary governors because of New Jersey's constitution. In South Carolina, for example, where John Rutledge anticipated an invasion of Charleston, the state's constitution gave the governor veto power over legislative acts and authority to take almost any action necessary for the security of the state without consulting the legislature. The legislature had even provided Rutledge with more than £20,000 in a discretionary account and the power to create courts-martial and order troops into neighboring states to defend against both the Cherokee and the British. However, the South Carolina militia presented its own difficulties for Rutledge. Its prewar past as a slave patrol encouraged militiamen to rally but to remain at home to defend against potential slave revolts instead of fighting the British out of state. Rutledge demonstrated to the legislature the need to impose stiff penalties on those who failed to appear when the militia needed to travel any great distance.[65]

Like Connecticut governor Trumbull, Livingston overcame his weak constitutional position to become the center of the war effort. Trumbull had little direct control over the state, yet he successfully secured legislative support through his political connections to create a committee of safety to direct, supply, and organize the militia. As in New Jersey, militiamen in Connecticut could easily avoid service by enlisting substitutes or paying minor fines. Connecticut farmers would have made far more money supplying the Continental Army or illegally trading their foodstuffs to New York than serving in the army, just as Jersey farmers realized. Like Trumbull, Livingston rallied support for stricter enlistment rules while trying to increase militia enrollments and challenge the negative images of the state's response to the invasion, now consistently chronicled in publisher Hugh Gaine's loyalist-leaning *New-York Gazette, and Weekly Mercury*, which had recently begun publishing from Newark.[66]

Livingston had a particular vendetta against Gaine: two decades earlier he had published the principal opposition piece to Livingston's *Independent Reflector*. To counter Gaine's "lying Gazette," Livingston relied on his experience as a propagandist to paint the British forces as easy targets of attack if the militia could be motivated. On February 18, the *Pennsylvania Packet* published "The Impartial Chronicle," a satirical piece that highlighted Livingston's wit and attempted to convince the public of the follies of the crown. For example, the "Chronicle" reported that the British had contracted with Persia's emperor to dispatch 3,500 Korazan archers to America, trained in the ancient manners of fighting, along with 7,000 men to cut down all of America's trees so that patriots could not hide from British soldiers. Livingston also launched more personal attacks against the crown, publishing a report that both the king and the queen were pregnant, as well as a satirical version of a speech George III gave to the House of Commons in October 1776, fused with elements of *Gulliver's Travels* and retitled "The most gracious speech of his imperial Majesty the Emperor of Lilliput." A few New Jerseyans may have been persuaded that the balance of power had shifted by early 1777, but little significant support materialized from Livingston's challenge to the authority and power of the British government.[67]

By mid-February, Livingston believed the situation brighter, as the militia had begun to rally to Washington's aid and to protect the state from British foraging. Livingston hoped that they would "before long retrieve the Honour they have lost by their late Backwardness," though he admitted that past failures should "be imputed to their officers" instead of to the average soldier. His hope most desperately centered on controlling foraging and loyalist attacks. Since early 1777, New Jersey had been a marauding zone where military forces on both sides crisscrossed the state looking for food and other needed supplies. It remained "the ragged borderline between the two Americas, loyalist and Patriot," where bloody attacks occurred with alarming frequency and without warning. Some of the most brutal fighting of this partisan war occurred in early 1777 and convinced the British of the need to dig in defensively for the long winter. After several skirmishes around Elizabethtown in early January, for example, British and Hessian troops retreated to the more secure Perth Amboy. With Livingston's hometown now back in patriot hands, the East Jersey militia engaged in the same guerilla tactics that had helped liberate their homes. These units, only marginally linked to Washington's command structure, increased their attacks against British positions running roughly from New Brunswick to Perth Amboy along the Raritan River. These independent actions became the high point of the militia's service, protecting areas where Washington had no troops and repelling at least some British raiders.[68]

For the British, sustaining themselves in New Jersey became increasingly difficult. New Brunswick and Perth Amboy were crowded places, and some troops had to stay on transport ships on the Raritan River. Smallpox, dysentery, and cholera thrived in these deplorable conditions, and food stocks dwindled. Hessian chaplain Philipp Waldeck described the dire situation for troops along the Raritan: with "no quarters, no shelter . . . not a single piece of bread and butter to be had," he and his group waited four hours to get only "a bone from which all the meat had been scraped four days earlier." As the British improved their logistics, most troops in New Jersey had enough food to sustain themselves, though meat remained in short supply. Forays outside the cities to look for animals increasingly ran into Jersey militiamen. In one such skirmish near Connecticut Farms in January, seventy-one of one hundred Hessian soldiers were killed or captured at the hands of three hundred New Jersey militiamen. Washington, acknowledging the benefit of such raids, supported the militia by using his own forces to restrict the area where the British could forage. British raids now required much larger details and had to draw from troops stationed on Staten and Manhattan Islands as well as in Perth Amboy and New Brunswick. For the first time, New Jersey's militia proved to be useful against British domination, which aided Livingston's efforts to provide for its support and organization. By winter's end, even British commanders, such as Colonel William Harcourt of the Sixteenth Light Dragoons, claimed that the militia and the supporting American troops "possess some of the requisites for making good troops, such as extreme cunning, great industry." Therefore, when the militia mustered, it could be an effective tool, and Livingston guided the mechanics of government to ensure that it did muster when needed. With almost three thousand British and Hessian troops killed, captured, or seriously wounded from Christmas 1776 to the end of March 1777, the effectiveness of Howe's army plummeted. In addition to these losses in battle, almost 40 percent of his army proved ineffective by spring, mainly because of disease. Elias Boudinot remarked that New Brunswick was "almost entirely destroyed" and that it looked "more like a collection of deserted gaols than dwelling houses." This setback proved to be costly for Howe, and the British government began to realize just how difficult it would be to suppress the American rebellion.[69]

However, the New Jersey militia still suffered from some of the same problems that had plagued it at the start of the war, mostly due to legislators' fears of their constituents' reactions to the substantial changes that were key to Livingston's overall defense plan. In mid-February, the legislature still seemed favorable to allowing men to buy themselves out of military service, even though leaders such as Continental General Israel Putnam believed that, "at a time like this, no sum can be really equivalent" to men in the field. Likewise, paying the militia on time continued to be problematic, further frustrating Livingston. To Philemon Dickinson, he fumed that the legislature would "never mean to make it [the militia law] otherwise," though he thought better of it and crossed out the passage. Livingston was more open with John Jay, writing in early March that the Assembly had spent "as much time" on the militia bill "as Alexander would have required to subdue Persia." To Livingston, even after all the debate, the legislature still would "not to oblige a single man to turn out." To Livingston, the crux of the militia bill was the requirement that all citizens share the burdens of independence, a theme that he continually voiced as governor.[70]

By early March, British officials in New York had noticed that desertions from New Jersey had increased. At the same time, Livingston made one final attempt to convince the legislature to eliminate the possibility of exemption from militia service by paying a fine. He failed, in part because in his address to the Assembly he claimed that anyone who supported exemptions was "altogether incompetent and nugatory." He feared the current bill "will be our only chance of obliging some of the poorer sort to turn out at last" and encouraged the legislature, at the very least, to increase the fine from £3 to £20. Writing to John Hancock, Livingston admitted that "few of our militia will turn out in addition to those now in service." Livingston blamed the legislature for the failure to alter the law: they were "so unduly influenced by the fear of disobliging their constituents, that they dare not exert themselves with the requisite spirit of the exigencies of war." This accusation rang true, especially in Quaker West Jersey, but also applied to regions untouched by the conflict, where few wanted to wade into danger or, as Livingston claimed to the legislature, where farmers would lose significant time tending their crops for the coming season. In a state with elections every year, legislators feared that a vote to require dangerous militia duty and disrupt everyday life on multiple occasions would mean the end of their political careers. Similar fears caused the Connecticut legislature to reduce the fine for employing substitutes from £10 to £5. The *New-Jersey Gazette* cultivated that fear, reminding legislators of the watchful eye of their constituents on key issues. Fear became reality: from 1776 to 1782, voters returned a majority of legislators for the next term in only one election (1778), upending the results in the previous forty-six years of colonial government, when voters returned a majority of incumbents all but one time.[71]

In the end, the state legislature approved a bill on March 15 that increased Livingston's authority over the militia and allowed it to support the Continental Army in New Jersey and neighboring states. However, those who did not want to muster could still pay a fine, which remained an impediment to defensive preparations for an expected British assault on New Jersey after the spring thaw. Throughout late February and early March, Hancock and Washington communicated to Livingston that the British had reinforced New Brunswick in preparation for an offensive to secure additional forage toward Morristown. Little Continental protection could be provided. As Nathanael Greene remarked, "If there is not some separate measures taken to get out the militia . . . the enemy will be left in a great degree of liberty to range" in New Jersey. Livingston feared that the legislature's failure to support a stronger militia law imperiled the state's continued defense.[72]

* * *

The partisan fighting across East Jersey in early 1777 not only brought British and Hessian forces into battle but also highlighted the number of New Jerseyans who had supported the British during the occupation. Many of these men and women left their homes and headed for safety behind British lines in New York while others found themselves abandoned by their allies. Those who had taken Howe's loyalty oath now faced angry patriot militiamen who pillaged their property. More troublesome than those who had taken the oath were those who joined loyalist militias and British army units. Loyalist units in Bergen and Monmouth Counties were ambushed by patriots and suffered significant casualties; they either retreated to New York or hid in the sparsely populated Pine Barrens of South Jersey.[73]

After returning to New Jersey in mid-January, Livingston realized the need to protect the state from the large number of still-active loyalists recruited by the British in December. He encouraged militia operations against them, promising Governor George Clinton of New York that "we shall make rough work with them as soon as the state is reduced to a little more tranquility."[74] In early February, he demanded that local justices of the peace actively enforce one of the new state's first laws, the Act to Punish Traitors and Disaffected Persons, which imposed fines, imprisonment, or confiscation of property upon those who spoke or acted against the government. The law also required justices of the peace to force suspected loyalists to take oaths to the patriot government, which reinforced Washington's efforts in late January to offer amnesty to those who would take a new oath to the patriots in place of an earlier oath to the crown. Though some observers, like congressional delegate Abraham Clark, believed that Washington's offer illegally superseded state law, Livingston saw oaths administered by Washington or the state government as important tools to counter situational loyalty. They represented the first attempt to reestablish patriot control over outlying areas.[75]

Despite these efforts, loyalists continued to attack patriot targets throughout early 1777. Livingston conveyed to Washington his suspicion that "there is a constant Communication carried on between the County of Bergen & the City of New York, & that the latter are supplied with Provisions by the former." Cases of supplying the enemy became endemic in East Jersey in late 1776 and early 1777. For example, loyalist John Corles of Shrewsbury in Monmouth County helped send eight quarters of beef to British forces on Staten Island. The issue of loyalty in Monmouth was particularly difficult because its largely undefended coastline provided easy access by boat to Staten Island. Further, many patriot militia units there had surrendered and taken Howe's oaths themselves. During the British occupation, most of the militia's arms and munitions had been seized, preventing them from stopping the "very considerable proportion of the inhabitants" who were now "most notorious disaffected" and continued to provide the British with "all possible intelligence but also to join them in arms upon every possibility of success." A similar group of young men in Elizabethtown drew Washington's ire; they stayed in the area, without taking the oath of allegiance, "for no other purpose than to convey Intelligence to the Enemy & poison our people's Minds." Washington ordered them expelled with nothing but their clothing and furniture to take behind British lines.[76]

Throughout early 1777, loyalist farmers in Bergen enjoyed the protection of British soldiers as they brought their goods across the Hudson to New York. These farmers traded with anyone who offered hard money, which Howe had in abundance. Some residents even maintained friendly relations with both sides during this critical period. Philip Van Horne from Somerset, a friend of Livingston's, entertained patriot and British military officers, depending on which were near. Likewise, his eight attractive daughters formed relationships with officers in both armies. These connections allowed men like Van Horne to cement business relations with both sides, as did Abraham Hunt of Trenton, who sold arms and supplies to both Howe and Washington. These relationships remained difficult to detect and even more difficult to snuff out, leaving Livingston and other state officials hoping for more power to insulate the state from loyalist infiltration.[77]

The situational loyalty practiced by New Jerseyans is understandable in view of the physical and economic devastation they had witnessed and in many cases experienced personally. Washington had warned before the invasion that "the Enemy will leave nothing they find," and General Adam Stephen reported to Thomas Jefferson from a camp on the Delaware that the British "like locusts Sweep the Jerseys with the Besom of destruction." Writing from Baltimore in early February, Elizabethtown native Abraham Clark longed "to know the State of our Country and of our Friends"; he believed that the British Army, "the most Savage known among civilized nations, must have Spread desolation through the Country which an age can Scarcely recover." These accounts echoed Livingston's own assessment; reporting to the Assembly, he declared that the British had "marked their progress with devastation and murder and contaminated the British Arms with barbarities unknown to civilized nations." The destruction the British had caused in such a short time became their enduring legacy to New Jerseyans.[78]

The extent of the economic and social dislocation became so important for Livingston to determine that in early February he launched an investigation to understand the impact on the state. The governor inquired about specific attacks on New Jersey troops during the late campaign, especially against Captain Daniel Neil, killed under questionable circumstances at the Battle of Princeton on January 3. Washington substantiated the rumors of brutality inflicted on prisoners of war and civilians in New Jersey. To John Hancock he remarked that it "would be an endless task" to "take depositions concerning the Behaviour of the British and Foreign Troops in Jersey": "their line of march is marked with devastation, and is a thing of such public notoriety, that it demands no further proof." Washington recounted the murder of injured prisoners and believed that these atrocities would invite American retaliation in kind; some believed these acts impelled more members of the state militia to turn out in early 1777. Livingston even ascribed the barbarity to the British practice of employing escaped slaves and claimed that only black troops under patriot colors could inflict the same brutality on the British.[79]

Livingston's investigation identified two primary targets of destruction: economic infrastructure and personal belongings. Especially in East Jersey, where the partisan fighting in early 1777 had been the most intense, residents suffered some of the harshest conditions throughout the war. In August 1777, Ebenezer Hazard, New York's postmaster, traveled from Philadelphia to New York and recorded the devastation he saw along the way. Around Trenton, "all the Fences have been destroyed," and the "Ferry House was burned down." Princeton looked "like the Picture of Desolation. Several Houses have been burned there." Further, the College of New Jersey "is in a very ruinous Situation," its library destroyed and "every room in it looks like a stable." As Hazard continued northward, he again remarked on demolished fences, which, according to Abraham Clark, allowed cattle and other livestock to roam through whatever crops might remain after British and American foraging. Upon reaching Somerset Court House (now Millstone), where "Great Devastation was made," Hazard saw that several churches, houses, and orchards had been destroyed. At Elizabethtown he met a woman whose house had been used to quarter thirty Hessian officers and soldiers, who had plundered everything she owned.[80]

The British and Hessians were responsible for most of the destruction Hazard saw, but many New Jerseyans also suffered from what he described as "the Licentiousness of our own Troops," despite attempts by Livingston and Washington to restrain them. For example, Margaret Morris, a widow from Burlington, recorded in her diary during December and January that locals feared the British and Hessians would set fire to the city, but that the men who searched her house and, in her opinion, acted rudely toward her and her family were patriot militiamen looking for loyalists and Hessians. Likewise, during Washington's encampment at Morristown, residents near Rockaway hid their hogs so that commissioners from the Continental Army could not require their sale and bored and hungry soldiers could not plunder them. Jacob Drake of Succasunna Plains was even bolder, refusing to sell grain to the army and threatening to kill anyone who attempted to take it from him.[81]

Smallpox had a more devastating effect on some New Jerseyans than did warfare. An epidemic had dramatically affected the northern campaign against the British the previous year, and the disease became rampant among the Continental Army during Washington's 1777 Morristown encampment.

At the height of a drive to inoculate the men, more than a thousand soldiers convalesced at converted Morris County churches and houses in the late winter of 1777. Though few of the soldiers died, the disease spread among local residents, most of whom had not received inoculations. Sixty-eight members of the Morristown Presbyterian Church died of smallpox, and, by the end of the year, another two hundred had succumbed to the many other diseases that thrived in the Continental camps and spread to neighboring civilians.[82]

By the early 1780s, the state government allowed residents who experienced economic losses at the hands of either British or Continental forces to file damage claims. The counties bordering New York, especially Bergen, Essex, and Middlesex, had suffered the greatest losses, though numerous claims also came from Somerset and Hunterdon and from areas of Gloucester and Cumberland along the Lower Cohansey River and bordering Pennsylvania. Agricultural goods taken by hungry soldiers accounted for many of these claims. Hogs, for which New Jersey was famous across the Atlantic World, were a particular target, as was wheat, New Jersey's primary agricultural crop. Claims specifically for wheat came from the area running from Bergen County southwest toward Trenton, where soldiers from both sides plundered for the entirety of the war. Many of the claims from East Jersey for the winter of 1777 remarked that Hessian troops and loyalist militias plundered their houses with abandon. For example, Ennis Graham of Middlesex County reported that in December 1776, Hessians and loyalists took his slave Oliver along with much of what he owned, save for a chest containing watches, cash, and jewelry that he had prudently buried. Likewise, Isaac Hull of Bordentown abandoned his house when Hessian soldiers arrived in December 1776 and returned to find damage to his turnips and potatoes and to his fields from wagon wheels amounting to £13 4s.[83]

Livingston himself suffered economically. His daughter Catharine reported on January 12 that she had heard that the British had "wantonly abused" Liberty Hall: "not content with breaking the panes of glass," they had "taken whole sashes out and destroyed them—a small part of the fencing used for fuel and only one tree." Livingston's neighbors successfully concealed portraits of Livingston and John Jay. The Allen family, for example, had "behaved friendly" and "secreted many of our effects," buying them off from the marauding troops with cider so that Livingston could retrieve them. The Allens also secured Livingston's flax harvest in their own barn, while another neighbor, Mrs. Crane, put out the candles left burning around combustible materials in the house's hallway and barn and secured the shutters to protect the vacant house from the elements. In this way, Livingston suffered some of the same depredations experienced by his constituents, though his affluent circumstances certainly set him apart from the economic destruction that ruined some New Jersey families during the war.[84]

In addition to investigating deliberate economic destruction, Congress and Livingston also substantiated numerous accounts of personal attacks against New Jersey's residents, specifically the rape of dozens of women by British and Hessian troops. Multiple congressional delegates recounted these atrocities, including Virginian Thomas Nelson who believed the British "play the very devil with the girls and even old women to satisfy their libidinous appetites. There is scarcely a virgin to be found" anywhere they have marched through, while Samuel Adams believed the Hessians had treated New Jerseyans with "savage Barbarity" and that New Jersey residents had been "most inhumanely used in their persons without regard to sex or age and plundered of all they had without the least compensation." Livingston reported that the enemy had been "ravishing of women" in the state, though it was "more difficult to prove . . . as the person[s] abused . . . are generally reluctant against bringing matters of this kind into public notice." In March 1777, Newark minister Alexander MacWhorter described returning to a town that "looked more like a scene of ruin than a pleasant well cultivated village." Incidents of "murder, robbery, ravishments, and insults" abounded, including the rape of three women by ex-slaves in British employ. Gangs of British soldiers and officers "went about the town at night, entering into houses and openly inquiring for women." Some women came forward and informed on their attackers, including three young women from Hunterdon County. In December 1776, the three refused to follow two British officers to an encampment; several other soldiers proceeded to rape two of them, threatening to kill members of their families if they did not stay quiet. The soldiers then took all three women back to the encampment, where several others repeatedly raped the trio for three days before an officer intervened on their behalf and rescued them. Such reports led Congress at the end of March to confirm the numerous atrocities committed by Hessian and British forces in New Jersey during the winter of 1777.[85]

Instead of dwelling on these destructive events, Livingston, near the end of February, delivered one of his most famous speeches to the legislature, challenging New Jerseyans to look past "the desolation spread through part of this state by an unrelenting enemy" whose "rapacity . . . was boundless, their rapine . . . indiscriminate, and their barbarity unparalleled." Taking up his famously propaganda-laced pen, he argued that the British had been worn down by the enormous effort to send and supply their army across the Atlantic, and that the king was "incapable of concealing his own confusion and distress" at the state of affairs and the growing support from France and Spain for the former colonies. The address, published in the *Pennsylvania Packet*, was noted with approbation by John Adams and John Jay: it identified a "remarkable unanimity" of Americans and "their unshaken resolution to maintain their freedom or perish in the attempt," which encouraged thousands more to stand with the patriot cause. The wanton attacks against New Jersey residents affirmed America's "interest to be detached" from control of the king and Parliament, and, Livingston hoped, would cause New Jerseyans to support the war effort in the spring campaign. In the end, Livingston believed the war would "avenge an injured people" and dispatch their "unfeeling oppressor" with his own "bloody instruments."[86]

*   *   *

Livingston's February call to rouse the legislature and the state's residents made some difference, but by mid-March the lack of support for the militia bill continued to frustrate Livingston. Especially against the backdrop of sustained loyalist activities and significant economic devastation, he grew increasingly concerned about the legislature's failure to take decisive action on almost every major initiative to further the patriot cause. The legislators' indecision reflected the general attitude of average New Jerseyans. The failure in March to pass a stronger militia law that compelled military duty served as a major turning point for Livingston and for the state as a whole: it forced Livingston to see the need for greater executive authority to counter the powerful Whig-infused legislature.[87]

The destruction that Livingston witnessed during the 1776 invasion and the dithering of the legislature in its aftermath convinced him to mold himself yet again to his circumstances and to become that stronger executive. Along with Attorney General William Paterson, Livingston devised options to break out of the constitutional restraints that impaired his ability to do much of anything. Like many former royalists, Livingston still believed the legislature to be problematic in its approach to government. By the end of March 1777, Livingston convinced legislators of the importance of expanding executive authority to deal with both the military crisis and the continued loyalist threat. This solution became the Council of Safety, a group that had previously exerted executive power in 1775 and 1776 when the colony's Provincial Congress was not in session. This smaller independent organization headed by Livingston had wide latitude in dealing with impending crises as they developed. If the invasion had taught New Jerseyans much about the dangers of war and the limitations of their government in responding to it, Livingston hoped to use the next three years to show them a more positive and productive path.[88]

CHAPTER 4

Defending the State,

1777–1778

After patriots reclaimed most of New Jersey in early 1777, they set out to defend it from another British invasion and to root out the growing loyalist threat to their control. The years 1777 and 1778 marked the highest level of military activity in the state, and Livingston became increasingly convinced that the legislature could not defend it against the dual threat of invasion and loyalist disruption. The devastation caused by the invasion, the militia's lackluster performance, and the continuing recruitment and supply problems encouraged the governor to seize additional executive power to fight the state's enemies himself. His flexibility in reshaping his role as a wartime bureaucrat provides a key example of a second-tier founding father working at the local level to prosecute the war effectively. To maintain government operations on the front lines, Livingston relied on the extra powers he had won from the legislature, especially the chairmanships of the state's newly formed Council of Safety and Privy Council. These bodies controlled the state's defense in these two critical years and exercised both executive and judicial functions, allowing Livingston to make policy decisions that enabled the state to begin to turn the tide against the British.

Livingston's push for enhanced executive powers offers an instructive counterexample to prevailing historical thinking about the role militias played during the Revolution. Many historians have argued that the militia formed the infrastructure of the revolutionary government. According to this line of argument, the militia controlled communities during the war and kept vast regions secure from British attack, especially in emergency periods. Further, they interacted with individuals in important ways, using violence and threats of violence to ensure obedience. This type of control and infrastructure was critical on New Jersey's front lines, yet, after two years of war, Livingston consistently felt the militia could not always provide it. He believed that a stronger executive authority, vested in the Council of Safety and the Privy Council, needed to be the infrastructure to interact with individuals and ensure obedience. Only with him in charge of the state's bureaucracy could the war be prosecuted successfully.[1]

Livingston's interactions with New Jerseyans in these two critical years also illuminate the question of loyalty, especially on the local level. New Jersey's contested border abetted the presence and persistence of loyalism; even committed patriots engaged in activities that supported the British, though, as Livingston claimed, such behavior could more often be attributed to economic factors than to ideological beliefs. He consistently argued that the war was one of shared sacrifice and denounced anyone who traded with the British, fought against the patriots, or seemed to do little to aid patriot defenses. However, the physical and economic destruction caused by constant British raiding made the choice of loyalty versus patriotism more complex. Individuals constantly moved across a spectrum of loyalty in ways that Livingston could not accept.[2]

Livingston grew increasingly out of step with the state's population as his own moral and ideological visions of the Revolution contrasted to its realities. These realities, the blurred lines of loyalty, dictated his response as governor. Livingston did everything possible to convince New Jerseyans of the need to support the patriot movement and he punished those who opposed it through confiscation of loyalist-owned property and restricted access to British-held territory. He also drew upon his past propaganda experience to author numerous articles published in the state's newspaper to show New Jerseyans the follies of supporting the king. However, the realities of the wartime economy forced individuals to make pragmatic choices based on their own social and economic positions and to limit their sacrifice to the patriot cause. In a very personal sense, New Jerseyans had to redefine what "loyalty" actually meant. By the end of 1778, Livingston's frustration with men who absented themselves from militia duty, individuals who traded with the British, and legislators who favored their own self-interests illustrates the chasm between Livingston the bureaucrat and the majority of Americans. In his position as a governor prosecuting a still-uncertain war on an ever-changing landscape, he demanded greater self-sacrifice and relied on the consolidation of power within a select group of patriot leaders. In contrast, most New Jerseyans saw Livingston's prosecution of the war as a hindrance to their daily lives and did what they could to ignore his demands on them.[3]

*   *   *

To circumvent the legislature's reluctance to provide adequately for the state's defense, Livingston wanted to create "an executive body, vested with such powers and authorities as may appear requisite for the public safety" in this time of crisis. A twelve-man Council of Safety would exercise, for a period of six months, sweeping judicial and military authority to apprehend "all persons suspected of dangerous designs against the state," specifically in the counties bordering New York, where loyalism ran rampant. In Livingston's view, the constant exchange of information and supplies across enemy lines undermined patriot military success almost as much as the militia's lackluster performance. His former protégé, Alexander Hamilton, agreed. Writing to Livingston from Morristown in April 1777, Hamilton noted that a "spirit of disaffection shows itself with so much boldness and violence in different parts of this state" that Washington hoped that "no delay might be used in making examples of some of the most atrocious offenders." He concluded, "If something be not speedily done to strike a terror into the disaffected, the consequences must be very fatal." Livingston's new council could call out the militia to apprehend suspected loyalists. Equally important, it could try them for treason in place of the many Jersey courts that either had ceased to function or were staffed with disaffected justices and jurors who rendered lenient sentences or acquitted those accused of consorting with the British.[4]

In the midst of wartime, Livingston believed the devolution of power to the legislature, a direct result of the state constitution's Whig origins, had created numerous inefficiencies in the government's response to both invasion and the prosecution of loyalist activities. Attorney General William Paterson agreed, attributing the state's "failure to enforce the law" to the lack of an empowered executive and a functioning court system. Because many local courts and officials had not vigorously administered the laws of the new patriot government, Paterson and Livingston believed that "popular respect for the authority of the government had never really been established." The extralegal county committees of correspondence and the indirect mechanisms of social control they employed could not meet the needs of a state under siege. The proposed council's prosecution of loyalists would augment the local judicial system, demonstrate the government's effectiveness, and reinvigorate confidence in the patriot movement.[5]

The legislature approved the establishment of a Council of Safety modeled after the executive council created by the colony's Provincial Congress to make decisions when the legislature was in recess. Authorized for six months, the Council had its life and authority extended five times until legislators reasserted their power over Livingston by eliminating it in October 1778 as military operations shifted away from New Jersey. The Council could convene anywhere in the state and required only five of its twelve members for a quorum. Livingston routinely gathered this minimum to better control the outcome of its sessions, particularly as he had influenced the legislature to appoint his long-time friend William Peartree Smith and his political allies Caleb Camp, Theophilus Elmer, and Silas Condict. During its roughly eighteen-month existence, the Council and Livingston controlled the issuance of passes to cross enemy lines, mediated elections canceled by British incursions, decided on the disposition of enemy prisoners, expelled families of New Jerseyans who had joined the king's army, and reconstituted courts in counties where none operated. The extent of these activities provided Livingston direct involvement in the prosecution of the war at the local level in ways few other revolutionary leaders ever experienced.[6]

The full extent of loyalist activities in New Jersey remains unknown; estimates of complicity range as high as 37 percent of the state's population, though categorizing someone as a loyalist proved difficult. Situational loyalty became commonplace as the lines between British and American forces shifted regularly from 1776 to 1778. Further, many devout patriots resorted to illegal activities—visiting family behind enemy lines or trading goods to New York—because of economic need or because they did not view them as illegal. Such actions and excuses violated Livingston's sense of morality as he drew increasingly concerned about "those amphibious inmates . . . who seem resolved to the very end of the quarrel to maintain a kind of shameful and most disingenuous neutrality . . . but occasionally and indirectly abetting both, to secure to themselves a favorable reception with the prevailing party." To these "political hypocrites," he believed, "ought by a general test to be dragged from their lurking holes, ferreted out of their duplicity and refuge of lies and be taught" that self-sacrifice to the cause remained critical in distributing the fruits of victory.[7] This almost-daily engagement for eighteen months with individuals who regularly skirted their obligations to the state or traded with the enemy caused Livingston to understand his relationship with the patriot movement through the lens of public virtue and self-sacrifice. He identified those who supported the British in any way as self-interested, morally bankrupt, and deserving of retribution.[8]

This individual engagement against loyalism separated Livingston's revolutionary experience from that of other state leaders. In Connecticut, which did not endure invasion early in the war, patriots dislodged most loyalists in the western part of the state very quickly, with most of them fleeing to New York. The general support in the legislature and from the royal governor, the only royal governor to become a patriot, eased the transition from colony to state and created fewer opponents. The same was true in South Carolina, where low-country planters quickly consolidated power and created a Council of Safety that effectively suppressed loyalists in the upcountry by early 1777. However, the British invasion of Charleston in 1780 destroyed the state's patriot government and unleashed loyalist militias that ravaged the state until the end of the war. Governor John Rutledge then followed Livingston's example: he became the sole representative of the government, traveling throughout the state to organize a resistance movement. Rutledge's strong executive power before the invasion had created an effective organizational structure that enabled independent partisans and militia units to function after the British destroyed the state's command structure. This strong executive framework was exactly what Livingston hoped to create through the Council of Safety in 1777.[9]

Livingston, though, had to set up that structure in the midst of invasion and an active loyalist movement. With "the enemy at both the extremities of the state, a scoundrel pack of Tories in the center, and no inconsiderable numbers of neutrals and mongrels between that and the periphery of the borders," the situation could have "discomforted a man of much greater natural fortitude." Livingston relied on his legal training to take a hard line against loyalists as the leader of the Council of Safety. As he told General Washington, "A Tory is an incorrigible Animal: And nothing but the Extinction of Life, will extinguish his Malevolence against Liberty."[10] Livingston found an ally in William Paterson, who prosecuted many treason cases before the Council after stepping down from it. Paterson agreed that the "only way to deal with the problem of the Tories . . . was to act swiftly and forcefully to make them pay for their transgressions."[11]

Outrage against Jersey loyalists guided most of Livingston's actions even as his own family and friends struggled with abiding loyalist connections. His older brother John remained loyal to the king, as did his partner from his *Independent Reflector* days, William Smith Jr. Smith, who married Livingston's cousin, endured an extended house arrest at Livingston Manor, where other loyalist Livingstons, such as Catherine Livingston Patterson, daughter of William's brother Robert and wife of a loyalist, socialized freely with patriot Livingstons. Likewise, Livingston's sister Sarah, married to Lord Stirling, frequented New York during the occupation to see her daughter Mary and Mary's loyalist husband, John Watts. Despite the loyalism embedded within his own family, Livingston routinely chose to prosecute and punish the disaffected. This determination separated him from average New Jerseyans who struggled against patriot-imposed price controls, confiscation of their goods by the Continental Army, and an inflationary economy. Most saw trading with the British or joining them as logical choices in a difficult situation, while others never agreed that visiting family and friends behind enemy lines or continuing business relations developed before the Revolution represented a criminal offense, much less a serious one.[12]

Even as familial and business relationships stretched the definition of loyalty, most patriot New Jerseyans could agree that anyone who joined the king's army could be classified a traitor. The British invasion increased recruitment of New Jerseyans into loyalist militias and the British-organized Provincial Corps. Cortlandt Skinner, former speaker of the royal Assembly in New Jersey, raised at least 2,450 men for his loyalist New Jersey Volunteers (sometimes called "Skinners") during the war. Even after the British abandoned most of New Jersey, recruitment of disaffected and desperate Jerseymen continued from Staten Island. Livingston and the Council of Safety routinely dispatched the militia to stop this practice, but in many cases the allure of the British proved too strong. In part, recruits were enticed by promises of bounties, but more often they already had intimate relationships with their recruiters. The New Jersey Volunteers often found potential new Skinners in areas where recruiters had familial, business, or personal connections, especially, according to Livingston, in Sussex, which had become an "infernal nest of active Tories." Lieutenant John Troup, for example, was arrested by militiamen in August 1777 on suspicion of recruiting in Sussex and Morris Counties with several other Staten Island loyalists.[13] Under examination by Livingston, Troup testified that he had reentered New Jersey to see his wife and potentially receive a pardon, an explanation that Livingston did not believe. Rather, because Troup held a commission in the Provincial Corps, Livingston recommended that Washington court-martial him; leniency in this case would "have a very unhappy Effect upon . . . future military Exertions" of the local population. Troup's "intimate Knowledge of this part of the Country" made him a "dangerous Man in the Character of a Recruiter." For Livingston, this situation was "really deplorable" because Troup's family members were "all most firmly attached to the Cause of America."[14]

Defending against this type of recruitment occupied a significant amount of the militia's time and pulled the militia away from assisting with the state's defense. For example, during the brief invasion of Essex County in September 1777, militia general Philemon Dickinson reported the apprehension of nearly one hundred men recruited by Jersey loyalist James Moody in Hunterdon and Sussex. Likewise, Livingston complained in April 1778 that John Campbell, the British commander on Staten Island, had routinely sent "a set of dirty Villains who are traitors by the Laws of this State" to recruit at Elizabethtown, where they, "being intimately acquainted" with the inhabitants, had begun "sowing the seeds of disaffection among their old Cronies." Apprehending these loyalist recruiters and recruits while also protecting against British foraging meant that fewer militiamen could reinforce Washington's army. As "hardly a county in the state . . . is not at present exposed to the incursions of the enemy" and the entire state is "nearly encircled by the enemy, to say nothing of our domestic foes," Livingston and the Council understood this type of recruitment would continue unabated without vigilance by the militia as only it could "hinder the Tories from poisoning the minds of the people."[15]

The operations of the loyalist Provincial Corps proved dangerous to the infant state's government by routinely targeting Livingston and other high-ranking officials. In April 1777, twenty-five loyalists used "brutal violence" to capture John Fell, Bergen County's "aged and venerable" Legislative Council member, and confined him in New York. Enraged, Livingston imprisoned as many loyalists as possible to "induce the enemy to release" Fell or at least treat him humanely.[16] Livingston even feared for members of the Council of Safety. Loyalism had become so pervasive by mid-1777 that he thought the Council's militia guard might possibly be "tinctured with Toryism." He therefore requested protection from Washington's Continentals to ensure that members might not "be discouraged from giving their attendance . . . in perpetual danger of being carried off by the Tories." Congress provided Continental troops to protect the Council in late May, urging them to "discharge the trust reposed in them with vigor and strike a terror into the disaffected."[17]

Livingston himself survived an assassination plot and continued harassment from loyalists. He rightly believed that John Troup had planned to kidnap him in early 1778 after Troup escaped Washington's custody, and as Livingston traveled from Morristown back to Liberty Hall in fear of Troup, he learned of another assassination plot hatched by New York loyalists. For his protection, the legislature placed a personal guard of twelve militiamen under his command. Livingston regarded the attempts on him as a badge of honor: he would "certainly despise myself if they did not hate me and suspect myself for a traitor to my country" if he "had their good wishes." Washington echoed Livingston's sentiments, calling the plots "a tax, however severe, which all those must pay who are called to eminent stations of trust."[18]

In the midst of ongoing loyalist recruitment and plots against members of government, the Council of Safety's primary role in identifying and eliminating the state's most dangerous threat to its survival became all the more important. Livingston chaired almost all of the Council's meetings, which rotated across the state throughout 1777 and 1778, with members recording testimony to identify locals who had supported the British. In one of its early meetings in Bordentown in March and April 1777, for example, the Council interviewed dozens of witnesses who exposed their neighbors' loyalist activities. Isaac Potter, a resident of Dover in Monmouth County, testified that Joseph Saltar encouraged him to sign a paper "to put us on the same footing we formerly were under the King" and required that he take General Howe's oath of allegiance. Similarly, Thomas Farr of Upper Freehold saw John Lawrence of Burlington meet with two Hessians and later turn over provisions to them. The Council ordered both men arrested, though they were eventually released; Saltar never stood trial, and Farr was eventually acquitted. Their ultimate release had little bearing on the Council's objective to identify suspected loyalists and jail them. Livingston believed these actions impeded the short-term loyalist threat and, under his supervision, were conducted appropriately.[19]

The Council followed a rapid and routine meeting schedule for almost the entirety of its eighteen-month existence, showing the state's strength in the face of loyalism and Livingston's interest in engaging multiple local issues in support of the war. The Council uncovered the clandestine activities of loyalists and marauders and dispatched the militia to stop them, actions that in the past the legislature would not have been able to undertake. One investigation involved the Woodward family of Monmouth County, affluent Quakers who rallied partisans to support the British during the December 1776 occupation. The Council learned that the Woodwards' pro-loyalist militia had captured former Provisional Congress President Samuel Tucker and confiscated patriot property across Monmouth. The Woodwards had become adept at recruiting their neighbors and enriching themselves by leveraging their long-standing familial and business networks during the power vacuum created by the invasion. They also made efforts to legitimize themselves by claiming authority for their actions through Howe and the British army.[20]

After the liberation of Monmouth in early 1777, most of the Woodwards fled to the largely uninhabited Pine Barrens in the southern part of the county. This region became a contested borderland and haven for clandestine activities for the remainder of the war. The group's ringleaders, Anthony and Jesse Woodward, hid for months in small cabins in the swamps and woods, remaining close to their old homes to gather supplies and information on patriot movements. They were betrayed by another denizen of the Pine Barrens, Thomas Fowler, who was captured during a botched ambush on Lewis Bestedo, a patriot commander who had been searching for the Woodwards.[21]

The Council charged the Woodwards and their allies with treason, riot, and assault, and consigned them to jails in Sussex and Gloucester Counties to await trial in Monmouth, where the courts remained closed until late January 1778. Trying treason cases against men like the Woodwards proved difficult because there were few precedents. Newly appointed New Jersey Chief Justice Robert Morris complained during his first treason prosecutions that "we have a new modeled government, incomplete in parts, young in practice and contingencies unprovided for." Even though the case law on treason was thin, Livingston insisted that the charge be applied to loyalists and used the Council of Safety as the archetype to reestablish nonfunctioning courts and to create new procedures to try treason cases. He mandated that all defendants be tried properly, since those trials would visibly show the reestablishment and operation of the courts, illustrate the strength of New Jersey's new government, and demonstrate Livingston's ability to control government operations in wartime.[22]

Alongside the Council's activities to root out loyalism locally, Livingston and the state legislature enacted a series of laws in 1777 and 1778 to punish recalcitrant loyalists and thereby turn some toward the patriot cause for fear of punishment. The danger of loyalism, which Livingston repeatedly cited when meeting with legislators, forced them to pass stronger laws during the Council of Safety's existence. Livingston's strategy was twofold: provide an incentive to embrace the patriots through a general pardon, or threaten economic ruin by confiscating the property of those who remained disaffected. The matter of confiscation had come up less than a month after the Council first met, when Washington suggested in April 1777 that it allow one of his colonels to take possession of horses, cattle, and grain abandoned by loyalists who withdrew to New York. At this point, the Council had no authority to give such an order, though Livingston believed "it would be highly proper for our Legislature to invest them or some other Body with sufficient Power for that Purpose." This interest in both profiting from abandoned property and punishing the disaffected led Livingston to advocate for what became the June 1777 Act of Free and General Pardon.[23]

In supporting the pardon law, Livingston recognized that many New Jerseyans "have, by the artifices of the enemy or their own criminal hopes of enriching themselves by the spoil of their fellow subjects," been "drawn over to join the British troops," though many had hoped to repent for their transgressions. He believed that these men, "weary of a doleful exile in caves and forests," would happily return "to a participation of the inestimable blessings of liberty enjoyed by the loyal and uncorrupted" residents of New Jersey. In the final law, legislators gave loyalists until August 1, 1777, to return to New Jersey and take an oath of allegiance, a similar timetable and argument used in Connecticut to pardon loyalists who pledged allegiance there. In the meantime, their property would be confiscated; if they failed to return and take the oath, the state would assume ownership of that property. Confiscation was the backbone of the law, according to Livingston, necessary not only to punish those who failed to take the oath but also "to give efficacy to the act." So long as the families of the disaffected benefited from their estates, "they have the less inducement to embrace the proffered clemency." The confiscation system worked in tandem with the Council's mission; the loyalists it identified could be offered the choice of taking the oath. In many cases, fear of lost economic livelihood provided the essential inducement to return to the patriot fold. When the council examined Thomas Welcher of Morris County on August 1, 1777, the deadline for taking the oath, he became "fully convinced of his error in going over to the enemy." He hoped to "defend his country in the future," took the oath of allegiance, and thereby spared himself from prosecution.[24]

After the August 1 deadline, Livingston recommended extending pardons for those who still wished to join the patriots, though this second round came at a higher price—service onboard patriot warships. At this point, he specifically advocated execution for anyone who refused to take the oath after being caught on the way to join the British or crossing British lines without a pass. The addition of the military service requirement also fit Livingston's beliefs on shared sacrifice and the duty of those who had remained recalcitrant to do more to prove their loyalty. Some men, however, still opted to face the possibility of death. James Compton, James Worth, and Benjamin Worth, all of Basking Ridge, confessed that they had voluntarily fled to British Staten Island in May 1777, returning two months later. James Worth gave "no better reason for . . . his conduct, than the gratifying [of] his curiosity."

Compton admitted that he had taken part in the capture of American General Charles Lee, though he claimed he had been forced by the British to accompany them. Each refused a pardon and went to trial.[25]

The confiscation of property remained critical in pushing people to take the oath to the patriots, though in this early phase of the war, many friends, family, and neighbors of loyalists hid large amounts of personal property. They "frequently pretend . . . that they are not possessed of" bonds and promissory notes in order to abscond with them to other states or to keep their existence secret. Wives, especially, were left in limbo after their husbands joined the British Army. Princeton physician Absalom Bainbridge, for instance, withdrew with Howe's army to New York and remained there until 1783. His wife attempted to shepherd their slave Prime and several wagonloads of personal property to her father in Monmouth County. The web of interconnected familial relationships prompted the Council of Safety to order the ejection of all wives and children of loyalists to New York to prevent them from obstructing the confiscation process.[26]

In April 1778, the legislature codified its confiscation efforts and authorized local juries of twenty-four men to hear cases of treason and take over property when the Council of Safety was not in the area. Livingston supported the larger number of jurors, which would limit the ability of a few disaffected from swaying a jury's decision. From 1778 to 1781, more than 1,200 confiscations and sales occurred in New Jersey, yielding approximately £1,388,000 for the state, though depreciation significantly reduced the value of that figure. Estate sales quickly became popular among patriots who blamed the British for their own economic downturn. Patriots in Morris County petitioned the legislature in 1781 to increase the rate of confiscation to punish those who came to the county "in a secret and clandestine manner for the purpose of plundering and taking away the . . . property of the [state's] good inhabitants." Those confiscated goods could be used to compensate law-abiding owners for their losses, a point made by forty-one Monmouth County residents in a 1779 petition. The support for confiscation turned to outrage, however, when residents discovered that some of their commissioners had colluded to sell forfeited estates to themselves, friends, and family at reduced prices. The majority of sales ended in 1781, by which time major military operations had moved elsewhere and patriots had exposed and punished most loyalists.[27]

As the war progressed, Livingston's opinion turned against pardoning loyalists, especially after the 1778 alliance with France lifted his hopes for a victory against Britain. The utilitarian Livingston understood that the state's stronger position meant that he could act more firmly in his treatment of loyalists. In April 1778, Congress requested all states to renew the offer of a general pardon to loyalists, hoping that the news of the French alliance might alter their perception of British success. Even earlier, in December 1777, Chief Justice Robert Morris articulated the need to treat loyalists with leniency and reintegrate them into patriot society. Livingston disagreed, believing that New Jerseyans had "suffered so much from the Tories . . . that the more sanguine Whigs would think it extremely hard to proffer them all the immunities of that happy constitution which they, at the risk of their lives and fortunes, have battled out of the jaws of tyranny." Thus, petitions like that of James Iliff, a loyalist lieutenant captured in late 1777 who hoped to "find refuge under the wings of mercy" instead of confinement, likely would have fallen on deaf ears.[28]

From his local prosecution of the war and his work on the Council of Safety, Livingston knew that the French alliance would deter men from joining the British; therefore, the state should harshly punish those who continued to choose loyalty to the king. Livingston recommended that the legislature reject Congress's request for additional pardons in April 1778. He could never bring himself to provide leniency to those who had joined "the most matchless connoisseurs in the refinements of cruelty, who have exhausted human ingenuity in their engines of torture in introducing arbitrary power and all the horrors of slavery." Those who continued to side with the British would never "make good subjects to a state founded in liberty" and might actually prove harmful by fomenting dissent. Livingston's attitudes provoked roughly three hundred West Jersey loyalists to pledge their loyalty again to General Howe in December 1778. To Livingston, these men were already tainted.[29]

*   *   *

The more insidious type of loyalism that took up much of the Council of Safety's time was the London Trade, the illegal commercial network developed between New Jersey and British New York. In Livingston's view, this practice allowed men and women to reap the benefits of the patriot government while simultaneously trying to kill it by supplying its enemies. Livingston's individual investigations with the council allowed him to see firsthand that this loyalism undermined the new government's chance at victory. Of course, the London Trade had its uses, especially serving as cover for Continental spies operating in New York. Livingston, however, believed that the information they provided could hardly offset the damage caused by the illegal trade. The activities of Essex County resident Baker Hendricks, for example, far exceeded the level needed to maintain his cover. Even more disconcerting was the potential for British spies to gather intelligence to launch foraging raids into New Jersey. In April 1777, for instance, Livingston warned Pennsylvania's president, Thomas Wharton Jr., of the "continual correspondence carried on with the enemy by the way of South Amboy" through "waggoners . . . employed by" Pennsylvania loyalists, who "convey and return . . . intelligence to and from New York and Philadelphia" and undoubtedly from New Jersey as well.[30]

For residents of British New York, the illegal trade represented a boon to their economic well-being, as life under military occupation had soured even the most ardent loyalists. In the absence of effective civilian government, military leaders privileged the supply and operation of the army above all else. Farmers had to surrender two-thirds of their hay, price controls regulated everything from wood to foodstuffs, and regulations on carting fees made even legitimate trade difficult. Long Island and Staten Island could not supply enough food for the swelling population of New York, home to thousands of loyalist refugees, longtime city residents, and British soldiers. The lack of arable land left the city dependent on supply ships from England, an increasingly unreliable source after the French entered the war. Moreover, Parliament's Prohibitory Act restricted trade between New York and England until late 1778; while the colony remained classified as rebellious, New Yorkers looked to the London Trade for survival.[31]

Like their New York counterparts, New Jerseyans flocked to the illegal trade as an economic lifeline. The fear of losing their livelihoods to marauding British forces or through confiscation for Continental troops quartered in New Jersey led many to sell their goods to New York. For example, Trenton and Mercer County magistrates appealed to Washington in early January 1778 when they learned of his decision to winter four regiments of Light Dragoons in Trenton. The city had "suffered so much Injury by the Ravages of the Enemy last Winter . . . that it is yet greatly out of repair." Further, "the neighbouring Country has been so much drained of it's Forage that it is very difficult to get a sufficient Supply" for local stock animals. The requirement to support Continental troops would therefore exacerbate the state's already precarious economic situation and likely encourage "the Enemy to make an Invasion."[32]

If New Jerseyans were likely to lose their livelihoods to British foraging or Continental confiscation, why not sell what they had to whomever could pay hard currency? In his study of the illegal trade in Essex County, historian Gregory Walsh concluded that most convicted smugglers came from society's lowest rungs and saw the London Trade as a way to survive the seismic economic shifts caused by the war. In addition to suffering from the physical destruction caused by both armies, New Jerseyans began by 1777 to suffer from the devaluation of their paper currency, which further encouraged participation in the London Trade. As faith in the Continental dollar plummeted, Jersey merchants either refused to accept the money or charged a premium for its use as opposed to the use of specie. Livingston believed devaluation to be "so atrocious an attempt to stab America in her most vital part and to aid the British troops with weapons for our destruction" that it needed to be stopped. The legislature therefore passed price controls in late 1777 to stabilize the market and the declining currency, fixing prices on foodstuffs, liquor and cider, leather, shoes, salt, iron, and wool, among other commodities. Anyone selling at higher prices would be fined £6 in addition to forfeiting the goods, with additional penalties imposed on those who refused to sell to the army. Legislators identified the hoarding of goods as a particularly pernicious danger: "our poor soldiers who are venturing their lives for the public defense" could not buy enough supplies with their depreciated paper currency to survive. Livingston regarded hoarders as members of the disaffected; they could "easily spare from their own superabundance" but chose not to support the patriot cause.[33]

The price controls and especially the depreciated currency loomed large in the calculations of New Jerseyans who chose to sell their foodstuffs on Staten Island or in occupied Bergen County instead of to the Continental Army. Livingston condemned the "boundless Avarice of some of our Farmers," and he appealed to state residents with the same arguments he had used against granting loyalists pardons. Calling on their "noble ardor" for the "common cause," Livingston hoped that farmers would "disdain in the close of our struggle to sully the honor which New Jersey has deservedly acquired" through its participation in the war. The "infamous traffic" continued, however, and Livingston soon took a harsher tone and promised to punish those who ignored the law.[34]

Few other states took similar actions to control prices, and New Jerseyans petitioned the legislature to repeal the regulations. They argued that residents simply took their goods to other states to sell them at higher prices and that the state would be forced to pay higher prices to purchase supplies for New Jersey's Continental soldiers stationed in states without price controls. Faced with these realities, the legislature approved the suspension of price controls in late June 1778 and voted twice more to suspend them at least until New York, Pennsylvania, and Delaware had passed similar laws.[35]

Even without price controls, the main reason to enter the illegal trade came from the ability to bypass depreciated currency altogether and receive hard-to-find imported manufactured goods or specie. British Captain John Bowater observed that Americans very much enjoyed "our gold and silver better than the Congress paper money," especially by 1778, when inflation and currency depreciation continued to skyrocket. Likewise, tea and cloth from New York merchants became highly sought after in the increasingly barter-based economy that developed as currency depreciation continued. In November 1777, for instance, Livingston reported to Washington that the illegal trade had "grown to so enormous a height that the" British were "plentifully supplied with fresh Provisions, & such a Quantity of British Manufacturers brought back in Exchange as to enable the Persons concerned to set up Shops to retail them."[36]

Although Livingston and other patriot leaders called for greater restrictions on the passage of people and material across enemy lines, the miles of coastline and inlets, not to mention the shifting land boundaries, made it relatively easy for traders to conduct their business undetected. Essex and Monmouth were especially porous. Residents of Monmouth informed the legislature that "large Quantities of Provisions and Forage are daily carted" away and "conveyed to the Enemy." Essex residents complained that, "for Want of Sufficient Guards," a "New mode of Negotiating Between the Publick Enemie and the Disaffected" had evolved: the British received supplies from friendly traders and deposited illicit goods at loyalist homes to be carried into the illegal trade. Connecticut had to deal with some of these same issues; its navy could do little to stop trade across Long Island Sound.[37]

The problem facing state governments was how to distinguish illegal interactions from legitimate ones. Within the familial networks that Livingston himself was part of, visits to family and friends behind enemy lines were viewed as innocuous. Moreover, the business connections that had developed before the war created a web of debt relationships and property ownership that crossed revolutionary boundaries. Many people who fled to New York after the 1776 invasion had been "indebted in large sums" to Jersey patriots and thereby created a chain of financial insecurity linking creditors down the line. Livingston took it upon himself to decide individual claims of legitimate transactions.[38]

Livingston's involvement illustrates the patriot government at work in discriminating between legitimate and less innocent reasons for crossing. In June 1777, the Council of Safety had authorized all legislators, justices of the state supreme court and courts of common pleas, justices of the peace, and field grade officers in the militia to issue permits to cross into New York. Just two months later, the Council realized that this practice was benefiting the illegal trade. Essex County officials, for instance, discovered that Continental officers had delegated authority to their subordinates, who issued passes with little scrutiny. Captain Barnet of the militia, who was "not a little suspected of Disaffection," was likely "guilty of a greater Prostitution of Passports" than any other single individual. To prevent further abuse of passes, Livingston limited their authorization to only George Washington, himself, or a general of the Continental Army or the state militia.[39]

After sixteen months of evaluating requests, Livingston believed that "not above one in twenty" applicants "appeared intitled to that indulgence; and many of them were as venomous Tories as any in the country." Most, in his opinion, hoped to visit New York out of "vain curiosity" or "for the sake of buying tea & trinkets" to resell in New Jersey. Most troubling to Livingston was that rejected applicants simply went to militia or Continental officers who then approved their requests. In denying the request of Mary Martin to journey to Staten Island, he cited his "duty to the public . . . for the sake of adhering to a resolution manifestly beneficial to the state."[40]

Livingston's distrust toward anyone applying for a pass derived from his long-held notion of shared sacrifice in wartime and his determination to stop the illegal trade. Such resolve, developed from his local vantage point, sometimes clashed with attitudes at higher levels of government. In the case of Sarah Yard, for example, Livingston opposed the decision of the Continental Congress to grant her safe passage to Philadelphia from New York. He believed that Yard had been able to deceive the members of Congress because of their inexperience in dealing with individual cases of loyalists and illegal trading. He contended that "not one tenth of" the goods she carried, estimated at close to £20,000, were her "bonafide . . . property . . . but that of Mr. Williams and other Tories."[41]

Livingston carried over this same utilitarian outlook to his dealings with his own relatives. He denied at least two requests from his sister Alida: in 1781 she asked for a pass for her daughter who resided in New York, and in

1782 she wanted to secure funds from her husband to buy books for her son's education in New York. In rejecting her applications, Livingston complained that his family members "have in fact done more to injure my reputation and to furnish my personal enemies with weapons against me than perhaps any twenty families in this state." When they traveled into British lines, "it is presumed by the public to be with my passports." Knowing that Alida's daughter had illegally visited her at Basking Ridge and that other family members had crossed enemy lines, he protested that the family made it "a matter of so little ceremony to insult our laws or to sacrifice my reputation." Livingston likewise denied his cousin Robert's request to bring additional family members into New Jersey; the "precedent would be pernicious" and expose Livingston's administration "to be branded with the reproach of partiality to individuals."[42]

Some of Livingston's reasons for rejecting his family's requests arose from his image of his own self-sacrifice throughout the war. As he wrote to Alida in 1782, "Neither you nor I live as we have been used to live with respect to the ease and affluence in which we were bred." His own "personal estate" had been "so reduced that I can scarcely support my own family even in their present frugal manner of living." Unlike so many who requested passage, Livingston would have rather "with my own hands set fire" to his house "and smile at the conflagration" than "submit to receive one farthing of the debts due" to him behind British lines. Therefore, his self-presentation as a martyr for the patriot cause could be marred if his family benefited from the privileges of his rank. It is not surprising that when Livingston's son Brockholst participated in the London Trade by accompanying a sleigh of fine linen and other cloth owned by a paroled British officer from New York, he hoped to keep the transgression a secret from his father.[43]

Along with stricter limitations on passes, Livingston and the legislature attempted in late 1777 and throughout 1778 to prevent access to British lines by increasing penalties for illegal movement. In August 1777, Livingston used the precedent established in a 1776 state law to propose the death penalty for anyone crossing illegally into New York. Though guilty parties could apply for a pardon if they joined the navy, Livingston endeavored for the remainder of the war to apply the death penalty to deter the practice that he saw as impeding the war every day. The legislature, without the same close interaction with the issue and with a tacit recognition of its constituents' activities, altered the penalty for a first offense to confiscation of goods and a hefty fine or a one-year prison term; a second offense, however, deserved death.[44]

Even with death as a possibility, most New Jerseyans did not see the law as important enough to heed. For enforcement, the Council of Safety and the militia proved to be the state's first line of defense.[45] However, the militia's record in apprehending suspected violators was spotty. Especially in border areas like Bergen and Essex, their numbers failed to stop the constant flow of goods crossing the lines. Frustrated, Livingston declared to Henry Laurens in August 1778 that it would be "utterly impossible" to enforce Congress's resolutions designed to stop the illegal trade "without a greater military force than this state in its present circumstances is able to station" along the New York border. In some areas like New Brunswick, no militia units had been posted, leaving this critical port of entry unpoliced.[46]

Even when the militia captured suspected traders and the Council of Safety's investigation suggested sufficient evidence, local court systems charged with enforcing the law never felt Livingston's intense interest in prosecuting smuggling cases. Few New Jersey smugglers suffered the death penalty, and most of the convicted defendants paid only fines. Livingston offered in an August 1778 proclamation that some "instigated by the most boundless avarice and equally regardless of the blessings of peace and the calamities of war" persisted "in the traitorous practice of enabling the enemy," resulting in the British being able to "continue their savage depredations" on their fellow New Jerseyans. Governor Trumbull of Connecticut likewise argued that because the British could not defeat the Americans on the battlefield, the London Trade was part of a strategy to "catch hold of the avarice, luxury, pride, and vanity" of residents and to seduce them into supporting the British cause. Even these observations failed to end the London Trade. Indeed, in 1780 the legislature eliminated the death penalty for illegal trading to which Livingston responded that "if any crime in the world deserve[d] death . . . it must be that of supplying an enemy in time of war." More suggestive of prevailing attitudes is the treatment of convicted smugglers when they returned to their hometowns; most did not face recrimination, and they continued to conduct commerce and hold positions of trust within their communities. Fellow residents even saw these men as trustworthy enough to sign petitions attesting to their own loyalty to the patriot cause. Livingston's unique position, pressured by the demands of national and local governments, gave him an overview of the intense concerns at both levels, yet he never could win the hearts of those who saw little wrong with trading to support their families.[47]

*   *   *

New Jersey remained the center of military action for much of 1777 and 1778. As Livingston fought against the loyalist threat from within, he also sought greater executive powers to organize a more effective military defense. The militia's lackluster performance during the 1776 invasion and the legislature's failure to pass a stronger militia law led Livingston to rely on the Privy Council, organized under the constitution and consisting of three members of the Legislative Council, to direct the state's military preparedness. While the Council of Safety investigated loyalists, Livingston saw the Privy Council as a de facto executive body; with it, he ensured the delivery of routine government services, reinforced the court system, deployed the militia, and implemented policy in the legislature's absence. It worked in tandem with the courts and the Council of Safety to reinforce the image that New Jersey's government was operational and intent on protecting patriot property and lives. As the chairman of both bodies, Livingston intimately understood the daily operations of the wartime state government and wielded far more executive power than the constitution's framers had intended.[48]

Most legislators saw the utility of the Privy Council and invested it with greater powers, which Livingston was very happy to accept. Legislators granted it authority to direct militia deployments and readiness, even when the legislature was in session, and to appoint militia officials. The Privy Council also worked with the Council of Safety to suppress loyalism after the legislature authorized it in late 1777 to establish special courts to try criminal cases. When the Council of Safety folded in late 1778, legislators empowered the Privy Council to continue policing the illegal trade through the militia. Joined on the Privy Council by staunch ally William Paterson, Livingston exercised authority both to prosecute suspected loyalists and to manage the militia as he deemed appropriate, enabling him to take direct control of the war across the state.[49]

Almost immediately, Livingston and the Privy Council faced the danger of British attacks from New York and parts of Bergen County, New Brunswick, and Perth Amboy, all of which remained occupied in early 1777. For the next eighteen months, the Privy Council directed the militia to secure the state's border from British "irruption[s] into the state" in search of supplies. Foraging raids continued well into 1778 and allowed the British to expand their control of New Jersey, especially in Bergen County. Livingston had to wonder why the British "don't try their hands in Connecticut."[50]

The limited British raiding into Connecticut directly affected the organization of that state's government. The legislature recognized that it needed to support the colony's defense when not in session, yet its Committee of Safety did not have the extrajudicial and legislative powers that New Jersey's Privy Council did. Even as Governor Trumbull carved out more executive power through the Committee of Safety to become the central administrator of his state during the war, his office remained weaker than Livingston's because the war did not engulf Connecticut as much as it did New Jersey.[51]

The effectiveness of the New Jersey militia in preventing routine foraging expeditions proved limited. Some Jersey militiamen continued to serve with Washington, who desperately needed them to fill holes in the Continental Line. More seriously, supply problems led many men to refuse militia duty in early 1777 or limited the usefulness of their units. In April, for example, Livingston confided to Washington that the militia he needed from Middlesex likely would not arrive because most men refused to leave their homes with the British close by in New Brunswick and Perth Amboy. Livingston and the Privy Council recognized that the militia's structure led to its haphazard operation; it relied on friends and neighbors to compel military service, an obligation few wanted to impose on anyone who might have a legitimate excuse for not serving. To Livingston, this failure to enforce militia duty remained the biggest barrier to organizing an effective defense.[52]

In New York, the main body of British forces in North America had survived the winter of early 1777, and General Howe began to think of forcing Washington into a confrontation instead of continuing a prolonged foraging war. In June 1777, he moved additional troops to New Brunswick and pushed toward Philadelphia, attempting to engage Washington in battle somewhere in central New Jersey. Livingston began to mobilize the militia to counter, but Howe instead evacuated all of his troops to New York and opted to attack Philadelphia by sea to minimize casualties.[53]

The move against Philadelphia necessitated that Washington shift his focus toward Pennsylvania, leaving Livingston and the militia as the primary guardians of New Jersey after July 1777. Chief Justice Robert Morris, among others, complained about the response: of the sixty-seven militiamen activated in Bergen County, only twelve appeared for duty. Along with the usual problems of "the season of the year and former services yet unpaid," Morris believed that the "principal cause is that the disaffected among them" have "remained quiet at home and unfined," a situation that "encouraged disaffection and rendered the well affected less zealous" to the cause. The lack of courts operating in Bergen contributed to the failure to fine these men, something that Livingston and the Privy Council worked to remedy.[54]

In the late summer of 1777, Livingston again launched a campaign to revise the state's militia regulations and eliminate the practice of allowing substitutes. He buttressed his utilitarian argument that the military force of New Jersey "ought to be compellable to turn out" with his own ideological stamp. Those who did their duty "were actuated by the spirit of patriotism," he declared, while those who paid fines or supplied substitutes threw "a disproportionate burden on the willing who by that means are extremely harassed" by the breakdown of the system of shared sacrifice. Later in September, the legislature provided additional bounties for those who served in the militia but continued to allow substitutes, again discounting Livingston's recommendations from his local prosecution of the war. Livingston anticipated the lack of legislative response and requested 1,500 Continental troops from John Hancock, arguing that the inadequacy of the state's law would leave East Jersey undefended and "in imminent danger of being lost or at least of suffering the most dreadful depredation" when the British invaded next.[55]

Even the British by this point realized that New Jersey's failures at militia recruitment were caused by inadequate pay, lack of protection for homes and families during absences, and the ease of procuring substitutes. Nevertheless, South Jersey militiamen had been a frequent nuisance and were perceived to be a credible threat to the British invasion of Philadelphia. General Sir Henry Clinton saw the militia's potential and attacked New Jersey from New York in September 1777 to prevent it from supporting Washington after his defeat at Brandywine Creek. Clinton's push into Essex and Bergen lasted less than a week, and the British retreated with more than two thousand head of cattle along with other forage to feed and supply themselves. Livingston informed the Continental Congress that the danger in East Jersey proved too great to answer Washington's calls for assistance at Philadelphia.[56]

The British occupation of Philadelphia created yet another border region in New Jersey, complete with dangers of foraging parties and opportunities for illegal trade. Livingston's pressing concern in the fall of 1777 and spring of 1778 therefore was to organize the reinforcement of critical forts on the Delaware River and to beat back British foraging expeditions throughout Burlington, Salem, and Gloucester Counties. After Washington chose to winter at Valley Forge, Livingston stated to Congress that New Jersey lay "very much exposed"; he hoped the members would not "abandon as a prey to the enemy, a state which has ever been ready to join the troops of the United States and was last winter instrumental in harassing the enemy." Summarizing the state's recent distressing wartime experiences, Livingston managed to secure promises from Washington and Congress to deploy Continental troops to make up for the lack of militiamen ready to defend West Jersey.[57]

The failures of the militia witnessed along the border with New York were repeated along the Pennsylvania border. The militia in the Quaker-dominated western counties routinely refused to appear for religious reasons or because they had been activated so many times before without pay. In December 1777, Gloucester militia colonel Joseph Ellis complained to Livingston that the state owed some men two months' back pay. Moreover, month-long tours of duty proved "so short" that the men "are scarcely entered on duty till they begin to think of returning home."[58] In March 1778, Ellis notified Livingston that none of the Burlington militia had reported for duty and that few from Salem or Cumberland had shown up: "they plead the necessity of guarding their own coast." Gloucester militiamen might have been more willing but now were owed several months' back pay.[59]

While Livingston continued to fight against exemptions and fines, he also advocated for a standing state military force so that New Jersey would not have to rely on the militia. In February 1778, he proposed the creation of two regiments of state troops, which would be better trained and serve for one year rather than the militia's one month. This plan would not only replace the state's "present practice of harassing the husbandman in a state subsisting by agriculture" but also counter the continued problem of militiamen illegally confiscating and impressing goods from residents under pretense of reclaiming the spoils of the London Trade. Joseph Ellis, dealing with the sorry state of the militia in southwest New Jersey, readily agreed that the state needed "some standing force" to prevent enemy incursions, given that "we have little to expect from the militia."[60]

The difficulties of convincing New Jerseyans to serve became even more apparent after the British launched a particularly harsh foraging expedition into Salem County in March 1778. While Livingston and the Privy Council acted quickly to repel the invasion, the militia would not rally, driving Livingston to request Continental troops from Washington. Livingston admitted that "part of our Misfortunes" was caused by "not providing pay for the militia," but it would be "a pity that the Country should be ravaged upon that account." The Salem militiamen who rallied faced detachments commanded by Colonel Charles Mawhood, who threatened to burn the homes of every active militiaman, reducing "their unfortunate wives and children to begging and distress." Further, Mawhood's troops executed militiamen who had surrendered after a skirmish at Quinton's Bridge and bayoneted "in the most cruel manner in cold blood men who were taken by surprise in which they neither could nor did attempt to make any resistance" at Hancock's Bridge. Residents of Salem complained that the "plunder, rapine, and devastation" caused by Mawhood had gone mostly unchecked; the militia had been called so many times that they lacked supplies and were "fast falling into poverty, distress, and into the hands of our enemy." These residents called for the same "body of standing troops" that Livingston had requested to prevent the county from being completely overrun. A standing state force would have prevented some of the devastation caused in Salem, especially as Washington declined to send any troops as they would be insufficient to protect the residents and would spread his already damaged forces even thinner.[61]

Livingston, however, realized that "the State of our Militia" made it impossible "to afford them any effectual relief." Moreover, the legislature declined to support Livingston's plan for a standing military force. Instead, in April 1778, it granted the Privy Council additional powers to call out the militia but retained the one-month term of service, the payment of fines in lieu of service, and the employment of substitutes.[62]

While Livingston and the militia struggled around Philadelphia, British military priorities shifted in early 1778 as French support grew for the American cause after General Horatio Gates's victory over General John Burgoyne at the Battle of Saratoga in October 1777. For the previous year, the French had been reluctant to provide active support to the fledgling United States, though it regarded reconciliation between the colonies and Britain as equally distasteful. At the same time, Britain's prime minister, Lord North, proposed to restore the pre-1763 relationship with the colonies through "a sweeping reconsideration" of their rights. The enticements included the suspension of all legislation enacted by Parliament since the end of the Seven Years' War, a prohibition on keeping a peacetime standing army in the colonies, the direct election of colonial officers, and the possibility of colonial representation in Parliament. Lord North appointed the Earl of Carlisle as the head of a peace commission to negotiate with the Continental Congress. What become known as the Carlisle Commission left for America in April 1778, more than two months after the United States had signed an alliance with France.[63]

News of the Carlisle Commission and the Franco-American alliance forced the Continental Congress and Livingston to decide between continuing the war for independence and accepting reconciliation. Livingston, who had always been skeptical of French support, argued that, "instead of suffering ourselves to be gulled by the finesse of Lord North, it will be a very pleasing reflection to us during the remainder of our lives that we have been instrumental in delivering one of the finest countries upon the globe" from the tyranny of Britain. This resolve must have been difficult for Livingston, given that the loyalist press in New York countered support for the French with the same anti-Catholic tropes Livingston had used during the Seven Years' War. Livingston, though, drew on his experience as a propagandist to argue against the North proposal, writing a number of articles "all calculated to caution America against the insidious arts of enemies." He boasted to Washington that he had "frequently experienced in my political days" the efficacy of "rendering a measure unpopular" by sending letters to newspapers using different names: "the common people collect from it that everybody is against it, and for that reason those who are really for it grow discouraged, from magnifying in their own imagination the strength of their adversaries beyond its true amount." The campaign worked, and Congress quickly rejected the Carlisle Commission and ratified the alliance with France.[64]

The French alliance fundamentally reshaped British military policy and redirected the war away from New Jersey to the American South and the Caribbean. Britain correctly assumed that France would not seek to retake Canada but would focus on the more valuable Caribbean sugar islands, which lay largely undefended. Henry Clinton, the new commander-in-chief in North America, evacuated Philadelphia in June 1778 and deployed five thousand of his men to attack the French on St. Lucia and another three thousand to reinforce Florida. More important, Clinton ceased major land operations in the Middle Colonies and instead supported naval raids on coastal cities while preparing for an assault against the Carolinas and Georgia later that year.[65]

Clinton evacuated the army's supplies and thousands of Philadelphia loyalists by sea, but he chose to march his army across New Jersey back to New York. With Clinton's ultimate destination unclear, Livingston, Washington, and the Privy Council used the militia to oppose Clinton's move into New Jersey while Washington remained in Pennsylvania. This time, local militia leaders successfully rallied their units, leading Livingston to remark to Henry Laurens that the militiamen had turned out "finely," though they could only "skirmish and run" without the support of Washington's larger army. Attesting to their effectiveness, loyalist officer Andrew Bell complained of the militia's constant skirmishing and the destruction of critical bridges. Hunterdon County militia leader Joseph Clark claimed that Clinton's invasion had "roused the militia ... they turned out with such a spirit ... never did the

Jerseys appear more universally unanimous to oppose the enemy." The militia harassment and Clinton's fear of having to cross the Raritan River pushed him southwestward into Monmouth County, where Washington's army fought the British to a standstill in the fiercely contested Battle of Monmouth Courthouse. Clinton retreated to the already occupied Sandy Hook and withdrew to New York, leaving Washington and the militia in control of New Jersey.[66]

For the remainder of 1778, the shift in British military policy limited operations in greater New York to small-scale foraging and skirmishing, yet vividly revealed the woeful shortages of men in Continental service. Washington had hoped to field an army of forty thousand men in 1778, though its real number barely reached thirteen thousand. The lack of recruits for Washington's army had been endemic since early 1777, as recruits increasingly chose not to face the ravages of war and disease despite recruiters using everything from bounties to liquor to encourage enlistments. Common across the country, it was especially the case in New Jersey as by May 1777 Livingston notified the legislature that the legislators needed to act to encourage enlistments to fill the mandated quota that the state was woefully in arrears on. They acted that month by allowing servants or apprentices to enlist in the Continental Line, providing their masters payment for the lost labor and two exemptions from militia service. Of course, Livingston vehemently disagreed with the policy as it again lowered the strength of the militia while it rewarded those who refused to share the burden of military service.[67]

In late 1777, New Jersey's four battalions of the Continental Line remained understaffed as supplies ran low. Looking beyond questions of supplies and pay, Washington identified an even more critical reason for the failure of New Jersey's recruitment efforts: the militia law's sanction of the use of substitutes had drained the pool of eligible men for Continental service, "for what Man will engage to serve during the war, for a Bounty of twenty dollars, when he can get twice as much for serving one month in the militia." Washington proposed that New Jersey adopt a system of conscription, as Virginia had done, to draft men from the militia to fill its Continental quota. Livingston, knowing that the legislature had been adamant about not removing the option to buy substitutes, supported the idea of conscription for its utilitarian value. In February and March, he requested the legislature to begin preparations for such a draft, though he regretted that the "machine of our government moves slower than ever." The legislators "seem terrified at the thought of drafting and some of them were inclined to memorialize for exempting this state," a plea that would have "chagrined me to death." Even the British had launched their own propaganda campaign in Philadelphia newspapers to scare patriots about the draft, claiming that all men currently in uniform or drafted would be required to serve until war's end and that those who refused induction would face death as deserters.[68]

By April 1778, the New Jersey legislature finally passed a conscription law, but one that contained many of the same loopholes found in previous militia laws that Livingston had reviled. The draft system required each militia regiment to be split into eighteen groups, with each class supplying one volunteer to enter Continental service for nine months. The state provided clothing, a blanket, and a forty-dollar bounty (against Washington's wishes). If after ten days no one volunteered, one man in each group would be chosen randomly. He had five days to find a substitute or pay a fine of £300. In effect, the law allowed each group to pool their resources to provide an even larger bounty for a substitute or, because of rampant inflation, to pay the fine easily. Forty percent of the New Jerseyans raised for the New Jersey Line under this system were substitutes; even with these alternates, the state reached only 75 percent of its required strength.[69]

*   *   *

At the same time that Livingston pushed for greater executive power in political and military affairs on the Council of Safety and the Privy Council, he readily understood the power of the press and saw great value in working as a propagandist to argue for the patriot cause in public forums. Livingston convinced the legislature to support a newspaper in late 1777 because he feared the effectiveness of New York's loyalist press in portraying the hopelessness of a war for independence. He penned a series of articles designed to counter false information and to persuade average New Jerseyans to appear for militia duty, to stop participating in the London Trade, and to join the general war effort. Burlington Quaker Isaac Collins, who concurrently served as the legislature's official printer, published the weekly *New-Jersey Gazette* after the legislature subsidized its early operation. The committee that recommended the scheme to the legislature agreed with Livingston and Washington that Collins's paper could counter the enemy's "papers and handbills filled with the grossest falsehoods and misrepresentations, and purposely calculated to abuse and mislead the People." Collins published the *Gazette*'s first edition in December 1777 from Burlington before moving to Trenton in early 1778.[70]

Livingston believed it critical to reach each citizen and therefore made contact with more residents than most other revolutionary politicians through his propaganda writings. From December 1777 to December 1778, Livingston published at least thirty-seven articles under fourteen pseudonyms, discussing one of four topics: minimizing British actions and countering misinformation, illustrating American power and opposing British peace overtures, chiding Americans for not doing their civic duty, and advocating specific policy changes. The first topic, misinformation fed through the loyalist press, had been at the heart of Livingston's initial impulse for the newspaper and appeared in at least ten of his articles, including five written as Hortentius, his most commonly used pseudonym. In December 1777, Hortentius countered reports that the Russians and Prussians had decided to support the British; in fact, he wrote, the interests of Catherine the Great and Prussia lie in severing the American colonies from Great Britain. Anyone who believed that thirty-six thousand Russians would soon arrive in America should be reassured otherwise, Livingston wrote in a second article under a different pseudonym in the same edition. In January 1778, again as Hortentius, he discredited the impartiality of New York's loyalist papers.[71] Livingston also countered many of the king's claims, satirizing his speeches and exposing their false logic. He likewise defended America's protection of freedom of religion—a favorite theme of the anti-Anglican Livingston. More important, he brought reprehensible actions of the British Army into public view, as in April 1778, when he published letters from Salem County militia colonel Elijah Hand to British colonel Mawhood that revealed the execution of surrendering militiamen.[72]

Livingston made his strongest propaganda efforts in articles that promoted the strength of the patriot cause and outlined the folly of accommodation with Great Britain. At least eight of these articles challenged the Carlisle Commission. After the Continental Congress rejected the British peace overtures, the commissioners took the matter of reconciliation directly to the people, using New York newspapers to spread the idea that Congress did not speak for the American populace.[73] Livingston retorted that if Lord North was resorting to peace talks, he obviously had realized that America could beat him; therefore, it was even more important to support the war effort. In a lighter vein, writing as Belinda, Livingston threatened that a wife would "refuse the caresses of her husband" if he supported the "flimsy subterfuge" that in reality was "the dying speech and last groans of Great Britain."[74]

While he exposed the dangers of the Carlisle propaganda campaign, Livingston also launched a literary offensive to check the spread of loyalism and to persuade residents that independence and victory were near. From late 1777 to mid-1778, he wrote several articles that showed, especially after the victory at Saratoga, the strength of the Continental Army and interpreted the British use of propaganda as a recognition that America was too strong to defeat. In January 1778, Hortentius countered loyalist newspaper reports that the patriot leadership had overestimated the willingness of France to enter into an alliance; he even claimed that the victory at Saratoga proved that the colonies did not need France. Livingston had consistently believed an alliance with France to be a remote possibility. In early 1778, he expressed his concerns to Lord Stirling, arguing against "a false dependence upon foreign succours." He retained "little confidence in the Court of Versailles" and therefore worked to promote the nation's readiness for war. Livingston even argued that the British victory at Philadelphia made America stronger because the city had "been the jakes of disaffection to the American cause and the sanctuary of tories and traitors." Howe's occupation would force the area's "timid and the neutral characters" to show their true colors, and when he retreated, he would carry "away all the tory filth with him."[75]

Livingston's third editorial subject allowed him to vent many of his frustrations with the legislature and against individuals who had embraced the London Trade while highlighting the utilitarian vision of the war effort that his work with the Council of Safety had provided him. As Hortentius in late 1777, he challenged the women of Bergen to join in the war's shared sacrifice and renounce the acquisition of luxury goods—in this example, fancy petticoats—through porous British lines. In January 1778, a letter from Cato allowed Livingston to challenge members of the legislature who, he believed, worried more about their own political fortunes than about the good of the entire nation. Livingston delineated the twelve essential characteristics of a good assemblyman, each of which aligned with his own ideas of self-sacrifice, belief in the greater good, and avoidance of selfish motives. In many ways, Livingston believed he upheld these values by rejecting passes for his family members and advocating that all share in militia service.[76]

Finally, Livingston used the press to advocate for specific policy recommendations, most notably the need for a military draft. Under three pseudonyms, Livingston declared that a stronger army meant a quicker victory. Each article remarked on the problems afflicting New Jersey's militia system, specifically the use of substitutes. In April, under the pseudonym De Lisle, Livingston argued that militiamen should sign up for a minimum six months, despite their agricultural and familial duties; an alternative solution was conscription. In February 1778, writing as Persius, he argued for a draft system to alleviate the problems of forcing all men into service. As Adolphus, he agreed with some of his previous stances that civic virtue and shared sacrifice required all men to serve in the militia, yet a draft could be the least oppressive to individual freedoms in ensuring a proper defense.[77]

Though Livingston's influence on New Jerseyans through his writing remains difficult to measure, his articles provoked vehement challenges by the loyalist press, which had already revised its own propaganda campaign in the aftermath of Saratoga. Under the name Integer, New York loyalists Charles Inglis and Ambrose Serle published a series of articles designed to bolster loyalist support by highlighting the economic advantages of staying within the empire, ideas that Livingston countered in his own articles. Likewise, after the announcement of the French alliance, the loyalist press targeted French Catholicism as a direct threat to Americans, in some respects repeating many of Livingston's earlier essays on America's freedom of religion and the separation of state and religion. Other attacks addressed Livingston by name and attempted to discredit his policies and character. For instance, Plain Truth likened the confiscation of loyalist property to highway robbery: Livingston and his "agents are daily plundering" New Jerseyans "for the atrocious crime of adhering to their loyalty and flying from your unsupportable tyranny." A British captain attacked Livingston's character more directly in March 1778: "Thou art that ass which has put on a lion's skin! Thou miserable pettifogging scribbler that can so prostitute the utmost exertion of thy talents in messages and papers signed Adolphus." The captain accused Livingston of using his ill-gotten wealth to "lull the cries of conscience and still the bitter gnawings of remorse." Of course, many old New York political animosities added to the current ones.[78]

Livingston's heightened political and military powers raised concerns among the state legislators who over two years had enabled them. This stronger chief executive had become the opposite of what many fervent Whig supporters had envisioned as their governor and brought forth Livingston's first opponent for reelection, militia general Philemon Dickinson, in 1778. Some legislators claimed to oppose Livingston based on the tenor of his Hortentius writings, though such concerns covered over latent fears of Livingston's growing power within the state. Dickinson received only six votes to Livingston's thirty-one, but the more pressing issue in the fall of 1778 became the retention of the political capital he had acquired over the last two years against those who believed he had reached too far.[79]

John Cooper, a Quaker from Gloucester, and Chief Justice Robert Morris became Livingston's most unwavering opponents on the Legislative Council. In mid-September 1778, they orchestrated a demand by fellow members that Livingston turn over public papers and the proceedings of the Council of Safety to the Legislative Council for examination. In an effort to reassert their power over Livingston, the legislature dissolved the Council of Safety and thereby cut off Livingston's greatest source of authority. In November, Cooper and the Legislative Council attempted to make clear that Livingston had "nothing to do with legislative matters" and that he "ought ever to be under the Government and direction of this house."[80] This attempt to rebalance the state government in favor of the legislature largely failed because Abraham Clark, who had taken Livingston's seat in Congress, proved an unlikely ally and championed the passage of a law to speed confiscation of loyalist estates and beat back some of Cooper's most vehement attacks. Livingston came to respect Clark, who he had despised because he believed Clark had engineered his ousting from the Continental Congress, describing Clark as a legislator who had put his own interests aside for the greater good.[81]

Livingston's power, despite the end of the Council of Safety, survived Cooper's attack. Yet, by the end of 1778, he had become increasingly disillusioned with the daily grind of prosecuting the war. After his second election in 1777, he had remarked to Washington that the burdens of the wartime office had been much greater than he had anticipated because he had expanded his powers and responsibilities. He was further discouraged by the constant need to persuade New Jerseyans of the necessity to share the burden of the war. Above all, the constant movement of the Council of Safety over eighteen months weighed heavy on his personal life. In the summer of 1777, his wife and daughters had moved again with Lord Stirling's family away from the main field of battle, this time to Parsippany and farther away from him. After the Council's dissolution, he hoped that he would "stand some chance of seeing my family at last." Indeed, steady letters from his eldest child, Susannah, telling of familial news and the exploits of his grandchildren caused him stress from being apart from them for so long. New friendships, such as that with congressional president Henry Laurens, provided mild relief. However, Livingston continued to think of his government service as a sacrifice that few of his constituents would ever match.[82]

In many ways, the sacrifice was quite real. Livingston not only dodged assassination attempts but also endured repeated plunderings of Liberty Hall. In November 1777, after Clinton's raid on Elizabethtown earlier that fall, his daughter Kitty found Liberty Hall "in a most ruinous situation"; everything had been carried off by marauding troops, even the "very hinges, locks, and panes of glass." In a larger sense, the real sacrifice Livingston made was the loss of the rural solitude that he at least thought he had wanted by moving to New Jersey. In May 1778, he wrote to Henry Laurens that he had successfully retired to Raritan "for a few days in the most sequestered woods I can find for the purpose of doing something in solitude which I cannot do in the noise and hurry" of the state's executive position. Though he yearned to be in the political spotlight and execute his vision of how to prosecute the war, he continued to be torn between his desire to think and write in solitude and his service as governor.[83]

* * *

Livingston's yearnings for solitude illustrate his perceptions of what he believed had occurred after an especially dangerous and important two years. New Jerseyans had battled consistently with the threats of both invasion and loyalism, and Livingston's role in the center of the war allowed him to examine the multiple vantage points from which the state's residents perceived the revolution. Livingston observed how average New Jerseyans resisted the patriot cause despite his many attempts to encourage full participation through the Council of Safety and his editorial writings. In a larger sense, Livingston's frustrations mirror the difficulties faced by patriots across revolutionary America in maintaining state authority against external and internal enemies. These two years especially highlighted Livingston's experience with the persistence of loyalism and the multiple ways New Jerseyans surreptitiously supported the crown through the London Trade or stayed on their farms and shirked militia duty. Despite Livingston's exertions to destroy loyalism's grip on the state and drive the patriot machine forward, trade with the enemy and the relative lack of support for patriot initiatives continued. The reality on the ground divided Livingston as a military bureaucrat from citizens who largely defended their own economic positions and families above all else.

CHAPTER 5

Fighting the War,

1779–1782

During the last four years of the war, New Jerseyans lived in an increasingly unsound economic environment that was aggravated by the Continental Congress's dependence on ever-larger sums of paper money. This rampant printing of paper destroyed the value of money in circulation and presented already apathetic patriots with yet another reason to withhold support from the revolutionary cause. By 1779, many New Jerseyans believed that an increasingly demanding patriot government could not deliver on its promises of protection and support. Seizures of foodstuffs from Jersey farms accelerated, paid for with more worthless paper. Likewise, as monetary incentives for military service depreciated, fewer and fewer New Jerseyans volunteered for the Continental Line or the state militia. Raids from British New York, as well as an invasion in 1780, encountered weak resistance and spread further devastation.

Livingston responded to this economic crisis as he had to earlier challenges—by securing additional executive authority to try to solve it. Through his Privy Council, Livingston gained control of currency exchange rates and pushed through needed taxation reforms. Yet the economy continued to deteriorate, and the London Trade flourished, the only source of hard currency. This loyalist resurgence angered Livingston, and strategies to suppress it dominated his policy-making efforts in the latter half of the war. In these years, however, Livingston faced a more aggressive band of loyalists. Refugees in New York led by former governor William Franklin stepped up their raids into East Jersey, which further intensified pressure on an already fragile state infrastructure and decreased support for the patriot government because Livingston could not effectively mobilize the militia to stop them.

Though Livingston continued to point to his constituents' lack of revolutionary fervor, he began to admit that the economic and military situation in the state gave New Jerseyans few reasons to support the war. Having been stripped of the executive authority he wielded through the Council of Safety, Livingston repeatedly tried to continue a vigorous prosecution of the war, but his efforts had little effect. Fortunately for Livingston and New Jersey, the theater of war had moved south by the time his powers to enforce the laws and direct the war effort had declined. Although he succeeded at expanding his authority in some areas, the national economic crisis overshadowed what he could do at the state level. The latter half of Livingston's tenure as a wartime bureaucrat became a long and frustrating effort to remain at the center of the political, economic, military, and social action, and to advocate for a stronger and more dedicated response to the war effort than the general population could muster.

* * *

As fighting against the British and loyalists intensified in New Jersey, the state legislature continued to print paper currency to finance the war. With each new issue, that currency's value declined. At the same time, the legislature abandoned price controls enacted earlier to ease inflation. Legislators like Assemblyman Peter Wilson pointed out that such laws were worthless, given that bordering states had not enacted similar ones. Prices therefore increased "with amazing rapidity and where the current will stop is yet in the womb of fate." Yet Wilson also knew the effect "which the depreciation has on the public deliberations of the state": "money is the sinews of war and the substance of almost every law" discussed in New Jersey. Money policy therefore dominated much of Livingston's administrative efforts after 1778.[1]

Congress had compounded New Jersey's dilemma with its own debt. Its plan in 1777 to issue loan certificates to stem the tide of depreciation and remove some currency from circulation had failed. Congress then requested each state to return, through taxes, a quota of paper money based on its population, a momentous shift for New Jersey, where few taxes had been levied before 1778. By March 1778, however, the state taxed land, houses, slaves, animals, and other personal property. But even this effort to remove currency from circulation did little to stop the depreciation of the Continental dollar because Congress needed even more money that year to launch joint operations with France. The nation's debt increased to approximately $140 million by late 1778, and the dollar traded five to one against specie.[2] By the end of 1779, that rate was forty-two to one.

In New Jersey, Continental dollars and loan certificates traded hands along with certificates issued by New Jersey's former royal government and, more devastating, quartermaster supply certificates. While Washington's forces remained in the Mid-Atlantic, certificates issued by Continental Army supply agents to Jersey farmers and merchants became commonplace, especially in East Jersey, which was far more heavily garrisoned than West Jersey.[3] Food became incredibly expensive, and a commodity like salt skyrocketed to thirty-six times its prewar price. In some cases, the British had captured foodstuffs, but most of the great demand came from Continental forces. Few residents wanted to exchange their products for worthless certificates, leading supply officers to confiscate grain and livestock by force. Thomas Carpenter, a supply agent in Salem County, could not buy anything without hard money and repeatedly warned of the lack of forage and other supplies for the military, despite his ability to requisition property. Residents took their animals into the forest to prevent Carpenter from seizing them and ran them to the first butcher who could pay cash—and butchers in Philadelphia always gave hard money for Salem County's cattle. The British understood the rankling bitterness; spies reported that Washington's army had "stripped the people" of their supplies and that his troops traveled from one farmer's house to the next, staying "as long as they have anything to eat then go off," leaving just certificates behind.[4]

The military need was dire. New Jersey congressional delegate William Churchill Houston reported to Livingston in late 1779 that the "army is already at short allowance everywhere, in many places totally destitute."[5] The simultaneous effort to support the French had "created a flood of expense and the means of defraying it are narrowing fast"; each day brought Houston "fresh uneasiness respecting the supply of the general treasury."[6] Even Livingston himself, acknowledging Washington's concerns over the "rapid decline of our currency," knew by 1779 that the economic bottom had fallen out.[7]

The increasingly depressed economic environment decreased the support for the patriot cause that Livingston had tried to cultivate in 1777 and 1778. Depreciation cut incomes and eroded savings, especially for the state's soldiers. William Maxwell, the leader of New Jersey's Continental brigade, chided Livingston and the legislature for having "so shamefully neglected" to supply and pay soldiers. When the men had joined the army, "a continental dollar was worth a Spanish silver dollar"; now it would cost "near twenty continental dollars for what one silver one would have purchased." Maxwell warned that the government should not "say you are not able to pay in full value" because, he claimed, "I know better." These were the same sentiments that Connecticut governor Trumbull made to Washington—no one wanted to serve because of lack of food, pay, and shelter.[8]

Depreciation also crippled creditors owed debts by loyalists. When New Jersey began to sell abandoned loyalist estates, it wiped away millions of dollars of debt by repaying creditors with depreciated money for loans taken out before the war in specie. Those lucky enough to get any money back were better off than the majority, who suffered from "the exorbitant and increasing high prices of the necessities of life." Even Livingston, whose salary increased from £1,000 to £8,000 during 1779, believed legislative attempts to cushion the impact on him "a trifle, considering the depreciation of the money" that had enveloped the state.[9]

Livingston recognized that the "Depreciation of Patriotism has kept full pace with the depreciation of the Currency." An even more "mortifying Consideration" was the "declension of public spirit," which manifested in the London Trade.[10] From the beginning of the war until late 1778, Livingston had attempted in vain to rationalize why so many New Jerseyans were tepid patriots. As the currency crisis reached a tipping point, he admitted that "the money, the money my dear friend, is the grand source of our present calamities." The patriots' "misfortunes are ultimately resolvable into that mighty political evil."[11]

New Jerseyans openly debated solutions to the nation's money dilemma. The Reverend Jacob Green, an author of the state's constitution, became one of the most vocal advocates of change, publishing eight essays in the *New Jersey Journal* on tax policy and depreciation. He too linked "private behavior and public virtue," arguing that "frugality by individuals would allow the larger community to pay off its wartime debts." Unlike congressional leaders who hoped to reform the Continental dollar, Green wanted to replace it with a more stable currency to prevent average New Jerseyans from being victims of unscrupulous speculators.[12]

Like Livingston earlier in the war and Green, other New Jersey politicians attributed the public's reluctance to support the patriot cause to a lack of civic virtue. Bergen's John Fell, for instance, charged that "the people at large complaining of Congress for the depreciation of the money is a false system . . . the real cause is the want of virtue in the people." William Churchill Houston believed that "the people are bewitched." "They seem to have no idea of virtue and patriotism left" as "motives of private gain swallow up every laudable principle." Livingston's years of managing the state had led him toward a more utilitarian answer. He therefore approached this economic emergency just as he had the earlier loyalist emergency, by reasserting the executive authority the legislature had recently taken from him to preside as the prime mediator of New Jersey's war effort.[13]

Livingston's determination to create a stronger tax policy and withdraw as much paper money from circulation as possible required concentrated coordination with the legislature. Through political maneuvering and the alliances he had formed the previous year, Livingston convinced legislators in 1778 and 1779 to approve four tax increases, bringing in revenues of more than £4.5 million. These proposals, though, were not without opposition; more than 70 percent of the negative votes came from West Jersey representatives, whose constituents had suffered far less than their eastern neighbors. This divide became Livingston's battle: how to hold together his legislative coalition while also engaging two disparate sections of a state that experienced the war quite differently.[14]

Livingston, never a fan of paper money, welcomed the new taxes, believing they would finally make strides toward solving the financial emergency. Writing in May 1779 to a New York banker who had taken refuge in New Jersey, Livingston felt obliged to "give our assembly one huzza for having voted a tax of a round million," not one "of dollars" but "fair honest pounds of twenty shillings to the pound."[15] His strong executive support for taxation dovetailed with other actions that he, the Privy Council, and the legislature took to stop inflation. For instance, the legislature followed Livingston's advice and petitioned Congress in September 1779 to set limits on currency emissions and price controls nationally. In response, realizing that the French alliance would not quickly end the war, Congress agreed to set a firm limit on emissions and halt further printings. Moreover, it transferred responsibility for feeding and supplying the army to the states, a plan that Livingston's legislative ally, Abraham Clark, believed problematic nationally yet valuable to New Jerseyans who had suffered from both runaway inflation and property seizures by federal officials.[16]

By the end of 1779, though, Livingston's tax policies had done little to reverse the continued decline of the dollar. Governor Jonathan Trumbull, writing to Livingston in January 1780, observed that price controls, which had failed to curb the inflationary spiral in Connecticut, were only a temporary measure; true relief must come from a national plan put forward by Congress to lay a better foundation for the nation's credit. Abraham Clark agreed, warning that, with all money depreciated to almost nothing, the value of a paper dollar stood in February 1780 at a penny; in his estimation, it would "soon be less than a half penny" without positive action. Bergen's John Fell worried that with so little specie left in New Jersey and so much paper, it was "much easier to find fault then to propose anything new that will" solve the nation's problems.[17]

Livingston could not do much more than wait for Congress finally to admit the true depths of the currency crisis. At last, in March 1780, it devalued the old currency, pegged it at a 40:1 exchange rate with specie, and told the states to collect it in taxes and then destroy it before Congress issued a new paper currency. Samuel Huntington of Connecticut, the sitting president of Congress, told Livingston that this new plan represented "the happiest expedient that could be adopted to extricate" the country "from the embarrassments of a fluctuating medium" and asked him to facilitate New Jersey's quick compliance.[18]

Livingston agreed that the plan made sense and advocated for it strongly in the legislature along with Abraham Clark, recently returned from congressional duties in Philadelphia and elected to the Legislative Council from Essex County. Clark argued forcefully for this new economic strategy and for Livingston and the Privy Council (of which he was a member) to take the lead in its execution. However, the legislature remained divided along regional lines on economic issues. The West Jersey anti-tax faction, led by Gloucester's John Cooper, who believed that Livingston already wielded too much power, rallied his supporters against revaluation, arguing that it would help East Jersey and hurt West Jersey, where fewer quartermaster certificates and more hard money circulated.[19]

Despite West Jersey opposition, Clark and Livingston convinced the legislature to move fast, and by June it had established the new currency as legal tender and created a plan to remove the old money from circulation through taxation. The state would accept all quartermaster certificates as legal tender for the payment of taxes and agreed to sink the requisite debt Congress assigned to it. From Philadelphia, William Churchill Houston applauded the legislature's actions. The former professor of mathematics at the College of New Jersey hoped that "it will be the wisdom" of the nation "to have no more paper"; its continued presence would be "but a mortgage" on America's "future industry."[20]

Livingston's support of the plan cost him some political capital: nine of the thirty-eight legislators (Cooper's faction) voted against his reelection as governor in 1780. His allies, too, worried that devaluing the original currency could cause a crisis of confidence. William Paterson feared devaluation would infuriate creditors because the legislature required that debtors be given a year's grace to repay their debts. On the opposing side, debtors became incensed that they had to pay with the new currency instead of depreciated Continental dollars.[21]

Congress's valuation of the new currency at 40:1 was wildly optimistic. By June 1780, it had declined to 60:1 and continued a downward spiral. New Jerseyans saw the negative effects of the new currency's depreciation almost immediately. As Abraham Clark found, instead of the new bills fixing "the value of the old . . . the value of the new is fixed and varies with the old."[22] New Jerseyans saw the negative effects of the new currency's depreciation. Merchant Manasseh Salter complained to Livingston that he had suffered so much by depreciation that by December 1780 he had lost "upwards of three thousand pounds that" he had accumulated "altogether this fourteen years past with a great deal of industry."[23] Increasing prices encouraged many average New Jerseyans who had not already done so to flock to the London Trade. Reports from East Jersey noted that "every article that may be readily brought from New York cheaper at Elizabethtown," since many sold smuggled goods there, than from places further afield.[24] British intelligence reported that New Jerseyans complained of high taxes, scarce money, and actions by tax collectors to seize monies due—all of which could indicate a shift to embrace the British.[25] These disruptions led Livingston to argue that a stronger executive could react faster to deal with the fluctuating currency and reduce the temptation to enter the London Trade. He convinced the legislature to repeal the 40:1 currency valuation—it stood near 90:1 in some quarters—and allow him and his Privy Council to set the exchange rate as needed. Assemblyman Peter Wilson claimed that these measures answered the people's wishes: "Money, money, the want of money is the universal cry and we have none of it." Even though many legislators had wanted to call in the old money wholesale, Wilson argued that "the people will not accede to such a measure." As a compromise, the legislature affirmed the Privy Council's role in setting the currency exchange rate and agreed that Continental bills of credit could no longer be used as legal tender. These decisions allowed Livingston greater flexibility to make quick adjustments as the currency situation changed.[26]

After securing this greater executive authority, Livingston took his views on the economic crisis directly to the people. In October and November 1780,

he wrote under the name Scipio to identify the root cause of the currency crisis: the United States had entered the war ill prepared and had printed money
with reckless abandon to make up for the "backwardness of the several legislatures to raise money." The faults of the legislatures, however, extended to the
people as well; in his opinion, they "could not deny themselves the pleasure of
possessing whatever they set their hearts upon," thereby triggering a spiral of
price increases and depreciation. "Speculation grew common" as buyers realized that "what they purchased today they could pay for tomorrow with half
the value." In New Jersey, the increasingly common circulation of certificates
issued by military quartermasters had wiped out residents' wealth, leaving
them with "little else to shew for the produce of their labor." By the fall of 1780,
New Jersey had been "drained of supplies, drained of cash, overrun with certificates, and burdened with taxes" in exchange for the service it had provided
in supporting the war effort. Livingston's Privy Council, with new powers over
the currency, would remedy this situation.[27]

In a second Scipio letter, Livingston argued that the people had compounded the faults of the government in the currency crisis. New Jerseyans
must realize that "Congress and the People were the same and that the acts
of the one were the acts of the other." Moral decline, manifested by participation in the London Trade, hoarding goods, charging astronomical prices,
and avoiding taxes, had contributed to the economic crisis. Livingston
wanted to eliminate these dreadful practices to "raise the body politic to
fresh life and vigour," solve the state's economic calamity, and rein in some of
these excesses.[28]

The economic crisis had strong ramifications for Livingston's personal
situation. Even as the legislature increased his gubernatorial salary from
£1,000 to £8,000 in December 1779, the value of his salary continued to decline. In October 1780, legislators added another £300, but the entire amount
of £8,300 was worth less than £150. After the issuance of the new currency,
the legislature set Livingston's salary at £650. By late 1781, he again complained: "that the money is depreciated . . . is not my fault; but should I be
obliged to receive it for what it is not, I should nevertheless bear the punishment." Livingston believed he was not "soliciting for favours" but only asking
for the justice "due to every man."[29]

Like so many other relatively well-off persons, Livingston had to watch his
prewar wealth evaporate. Inflation had eroded the monies he had invested in
individual loans and the sums still owed to him for legal services performed
before his retirement. In 1780, "the extreme depreciation of my personal es-

tate" forced him to apologize to his future son-in-law, John Watkins, for not providing him and daughter Judith any financial support for their impending marriage.[30] His brother Peter Van Brugh Livingston doubted "whether even Congress can" determine the amount owed to their sister Catharine from their father's estate because of depreciation.[31] With Livingston's gubernatorial salary declining, interest payments from loans he had made became a major source of income. This situation aligned him with the creditor position, as he argued that debtors make "no allowance for the depreciation" in their repayments. To Livingston, the debtor had the "opportunity of cheating us" under the present economic situation.[32] Further, after the legislature prohibited the currency from being used as legal tender in 1781 because it had devalued to 175:1, even less money came into Livingston's pockets. Because he did "not receive a single farthing for interest money on all that I have out in bonds," he had "no other resource for supplying the necessities of my own family than my little salary"—which he never received regularly.[33]

Livingston's landholdings likewise had become vulnerable. Almost six thousand acres in central Vermont lay disputed as Congress considered statehood for the region. Livingston fumed that the "depreciation of my personal estate and the robbers of Vermont seizing on the best part of my Estate" would cause "almost the whole family" to be "reduced to straights and difficulties to which we have never been used." Deploring any attempt to settle with the Vermonters, Livingston became increasingly embittered as he saw enemies of the country become wealthy through duplicitous means while he lost his fortune.[34]

Livingston's personal and patriotic reasons to resolve the economic crisis were informed by his attempts as early as 1778 to secure a loan for the United States from Holland. Communicating in the Dutch he had learned growing up in Albany, Livingston carried on an extensive correspondence with Baron Joan Derk van der Capellen, who had adopted the American cause and used its ideals to support the growing republican movement in the United Provinces. Livingston served as an intermediary between Congress and van der Capellen, suggesting that Holland could become a new ally and provide additional loans. Through this communication and through John Jay's diplomatic posting to Spain (where Livingston's son Brockholst was Jay's secretary), Livingston engaged in diplomatic issues far more extensively than other revolutionary governors. Jay even published some of his father-in-law's letters to mobilize Spanish support.[35]

After Holland entered the war against Britain in December 1780,

Livingston heard from members of Congress and from his son that Dutch support for America had waned after the British destruction of St. Eustatius in the Caribbean; they feared losing the Cape of Good Hope next. William Churchill Houston believed that the United Provinces would quickly make peace with England and that Livingston needed to help change Dutch public opinion.[36] Baron van der Capellen advised that the recent invasion of Georgia and South Carolina, the fall of Charleston, and the multiple British victories against American, French, and Dutch forces had made support for America difficult. His own political enemies used his "extreme attachment to the Americans" as a weapon against him. More important, van der Capellen argued that the "dreadful depreciation of American paper currency . . . which can only lead to a national bankruptcy . . . is more than is necessary to totter even an established loan." The nation's lack of financial stability prevented an alliance and a loan. As van der Capellen pointed out, "The Dutch are very good business people, but in general bad narrow-minded politicians." Only if Congress could "interest the underwriters with great profits" by securing a potential debt with gold or the proceeds of exported commodities would a loan be forthcoming.[37]

In the United States, many Americans, like Livingston, understood the increasingly dismal economic situation and saw their savior in Philadelphia businessman Robert Morris. Morris's appointment as superintendent of finance in February 1781 began the dismantling of Congress's committee system and its embrace of individual executive department heads, finance being the most prominent.[38] Morris opposed continued devaluation and repudiation of the old currency, believing the practices symptomatic of Congress's poor fiscal management. Instead, Morris's plan relied on determining the entire cost of the war and apportioning it to each state adjusted for depreciation by when Congress incurred the expense. Further, Morris proposed a congressionally appointed commissioner to adjust quartermaster certificates to reflect the value of the products received by the military.[39] To reinvent the revolutionary monetary system, Morris chartered the private Bank of North America to be Congress's primary bank, to issue private commercial loans, and to circulate its own paper money. This innovation took the power of setting the currency's value out of Congress's hands and allowed the value to float based on market conditions and faith in the bank, thereby folding the interests of private lending and the merchant classes into the success of the nation.[40]

Livingston could only rejoice in the appointment and plans of someone who, like himself, blamed Congress for the years of depreciation and stagnation. He believed that "in these times so chequered with corruption & patriotism, with public depravity & public virtue," the nation would be "rescued from the brink of destruction" by Morris's ascension. The new superintendent will "extricate us out of all the difficulties we labored under for want of cash" for so long. Livingston had personal as well as political and ideological reasons to support Morris. His daughter Kitty often visited Morris's Philadelphia home. Moreover, Morris's political protégé Gouverneur Morris (no relation) had studied with Livingston's legal partner William Smith Jr. before the war and became a frequent visitor to Liberty Hall to admire the charms of Kitty, with whom he had flirted extensively.[41]

Under Livingston's leadership, the state legislature supported the creation of Morris's bank and developed mechanisms to deal with the continued depreciation. In the meantime, legislators received numerous petitions demanding immediate action to stabilize the currency. For example, residents of Salem County and Monmouth County argued in May 1781 for mediation of the fluctuating currency in order to repay debts. As the Salem petitioners observed, if taxes were paid in hard money or the equivalent value in paper money based on depreciation, there would "be no temptation to depreciate" the money, as "evil minded persons" had done in the past, resulting in the ruination of citizens that "defeats the purpose of government, destroys public credit, ruins our army, [and] oppresses the widow and fatherless." These concerns backed up Livingston's and Morris's arguments that the executive should fix currency exchange rates. In April 1781, Livingston's Privy Council had increased the exchange rate to 150:1, and it revised the rate upward again in June to 175:1.[42]

Livingston professed his alignment with Morris in newspaper articles written under his pseudonym Scipio. He blamed depreciation on Congress and rebuked the state legislature for following the 1780 currency plan, though even he had supported it. He applauded legislators for ceding control of exchange rates to the Privy Council, yet he used the newspaper to say what he could not in public: he challenged his own Council for waiting to alter the value until Pennsylvania had acted. Scipio asked, "Is not our money our own? Will they redeem it for us? . . . Will they make good to the people of this state the loss they suffer by receiving it in a depreciated state or holding it in their hands while depreciating?"[43]

State residents had seen Livingston's attempts at fixing the economy but still balked at its depressed state and continued challenges to the repeal of the tender repudiation act of the previous year. Assemblyman Peter Wilson saw

New Jerseyans' despair and believed new congressional policies would subject the state to the harsh realities of life under a restricted monetary supply. Wilson argued that it was "better to see a sum of hard money first in the coffers of the state" raised by taxation where depreciated money or certificates would be refused. Further, because Wilson came from East Jersey, he saw how those in West Jersey had access to greater sums of hard money from selling their goods to Philadelphia, whereas East Jersey residents could only sell their goods to the army for worthless certificates. The hard money that taxes raised could be used to buy supplies for the military and therefore flow into East Jersey pockets. Wilson's assumption that the "western counties live in fullness and plenty" made him believe they would not consent to hard taxes and would instead repay debts in depreciated money—only his plan would stop that.[44]

New Jerseyans reacted to the beginnings of the more centralized currency control system under Livingston and the Privy Council with trepidation. Morris County residents opposed depreciating currency based on issue date, as outlined by Morris, because many of them would have to pay as much as four times more for products they had contracted for in an earlier period. Others invoked their support of the revolutionary cause and argued that in the critical years of 1777 and 1778, as depreciation increased, they had supported the war effort and suffered the most, yet would be repaid the least under Morris's plan. Still others complained that nothing Livingston or Morris did would prevent the "speculator to reap where he has never sown, to sell his country for a few pieces of silver and to roll in ease and affluence" while the nation's soldiers suffered. Of course, men and women of all means speculated in currency, ranging from the likes of Abigail Adams to Livingston's friend William Peartree Smith, who by the early 1780s had heavily invested in loan office certificates.[45]

In the second half of 1782, the plight of the Jersey debtor increased substantially, as creditors began to sue more frequently for outstanding debts to be paid in specie. Both creditors and debtors petitioned for relief just as the state attempted to levy taxes and collect supplies to support the new offensive against the British at Yorktown. Creditors complained that debtors tried to pay off their debts with depreciated paper, and debtors argued that their previous support for the national cause needed to be taken into consideration. Some even petitioned for permission to enter New York City covertly to steal hard money to alleviate the dearth of specie in New Jersey.[46]

Four years of disappointment with the failure of New Jerseyans to change their detrimental habits and support the war convinced Livingston of the necessity to secure greater executive power over the nation's finances. His belief in a strong state executive expanded to encompass a stronger national executive as well. Although New Jersey did not send delegates to the Hartford Convention of November 1780, which discussed the need to compel compliance with requisitions and tax increases, its resolutions aligned with Livingston's experience. He recoiled against the idea of a dictator, but he realized that few states would provide supplies or taxes without compulsion. His own accumulation of executive power in New Jersey confirmed the necessity of centralized executive power at the federal level.[47]

Robert Morris's plan for increasing the power of the national government centered on the creation of a duty, the impost, on imported goods payable directly to Congress, which would give it independence from the states to provide security for foreign loans with a steady revenue source.[48] Robert Livingston, William's second cousin who had studied law with him and was serving as secretary of foreign affairs, took center stage in the impost debate, arguing that a new federal tax structure would increase his ability to negotiate for foreign loans.[49] Livingston agreed with his cousin about the need for a stronger national government and convinced Jersey legislators to support a 5 percent federal impost in June 1781 to help solve the economic crisis. His legislative allies, Abraham Clark among them, presented the plan to constituents as a way to alleviate the burden on New Jersey by equalizing the debt across the nation.[50]

Ultimately, the impost failed after Rhode Island vetoed it, but the debate remains an important source to understand how views on government changed because of depreciation's impact. Livingston and other observers across the country believed that Congress had failed in its duty to regulate the monetary supply, which drove legislators to rebuff congressional requests to make Continental currency legal tender and to resist its attempts to alter the currency. However, Livingston saw promise in Morris's plans to increase national and executive power to change the system in the same ways that he had attempted at the state level. After the failure of the impost, New Jerseyans still struggled with debt, depreciated currency, and animosity toward the system that had done little for them despite Livingston's efforts. The monetary system remained a highly charged political issue throughout the 1780s, pushing Livingston into the center of a monetary debate that led to his eventual service in the Constitutional Convention.[51]

*   *   *

Livingston's strong advocacy for more executive authority in resolving the state's currency crisis was driven in part by an exponential increase in the London Trade. Border cities like Elizabethtown and Woodbridge mimicked what revolutionary leaders in Connecticut had seen—a majority of their residents engaged in some type of illegal trade because of desperation from lack of economic opportunity. Livingston called for the resurrection of the Council of Safety to quell this increased loyalist threat, but his opponents in the legislature, still cautious over his increased executive power, declined to renew the Council's charter. Livingston therefore relied on the Privy Council to expand his control of the militia and limit the trade, again taking a more forceful position within the state's prosecution of the war.[52]

The appeal of the London Trade forced Livingston into action because a significant portion of Jersey foodstuffs went to New York instead of to the Continental Army. The state's central role in military affairs forced the military and the state government in early 1779 to support impressment of foodstuffs and forage as Livingston and Washington reported scarcity of both, especially potent as winter forced the military to rely on New Jersey for most of its subsistence. In January 1779, Livingston warned of the great "possibility that the inhabitants and their livestock will suffer for want" as grain supplies remained limited even as the state instructed quartermasters to leave enough supplies for locals. Livingston identified two reasons for this scarcity: a downturn in supply due to men being called to military service too often, exacerbated by the already high amount of food sent to the military, and food being hoarded and traded into the London Trade. The first issue had some relevance as, during the debates over militia service, those who actually served complained frequently of the burden during harvest season. The more critical issue came from the "great quantities" of food and supplies "carried into the enemies lines" through the London Trade that Livingston had been attempting to stop. By spring 1779, the scarcity of food became endemic and Livingston argued that "our inhabitants instead of cheerfully supplying the army out of their superfluity, hoard it up for a higher market," while the current laws could do little "to wrest it out of their miserly clutches." Washington reiterated the complaint of his officers in New Jersey that "there is too general a disposition, to refuse Forage, prevailing among the Inhabitants"; they "obstinately refus[e] to part with what they can spare unless regularly compelled." In both instances, Livingston and Washington relayed an allied argument that both had used in the past—the commitment of New Jerseyans to the revolutionary cause waned in the face of depreciation.[53]

The supply situation became more dire in late 1779 as Washington faced an even more limited supply of flour and lack of cooperation from residents. Whereas Washington hoped that "a few virtuous individuals in each district" could work to increase the supply of grain coming from farmers, by November Livingston again reported that "without more coercive measures than the legislature seem willing to adopt . . . the farmers will not sell." As in earlier debates over the militia, Livingston believed legislators were at fault for not taking a harder line with residents. The bitter cold winter of 1779–1780 at Morristown did not help as the British, suffering with the same low temperatures and even less food, became more aggressive in luring commerce from New Jersey since British soldiers had resorted to trapping geese and ducks that had frozen on New York's icy waterways for food. Both sides were even more acutely aware of the importance of the London Trade. A raid by Colonel John Simcoe's Queen's Rangers in October 1779 destroyed a massive stockpile of grain in Raritan and discouraged residents continued to refuse to support the military through food or service.[54] Livingston argued that disenchantment was especially strong in West Jersey, where its residents threw "the whole burden of the war upon" East Jersey. By late summer 1780, Washington reported that his troops were "again reduced to an extremity of distress for want of provision" and that coercion could no longer compel support from state residents. Farmers would not "sell any longer for certificates," leading the legislature to complain to the Continental Congress of the glut of certificates in the state and for Livingston personally to guarantee the costs of some goods in order to resupply the army.[55]

Marveling at the ease with which smugglers crossed the front lines in the London Trade, Livingston especially made strong efforts to police the state's borders to prevent the hemorrhaging of foodstuffs. In late 1780, he advised Washington that numerous reports indicated that "the ferry boats at Elizabethtown are most scandalously perverted to the purpose of trade and importing into our lines the most dangerous characters," a practice occurring with great frequency at Perth Amboy as well. Later that month, Livingston urged the militia commander in Elizabethtown to do "something effectual" to stop "that illicit practice of trading with the enemy," lest the region near enemy lines devolve into "a state of anarchy." In June 1781, however, Bergen County residents complained that little prevented intercourse across the Hackensack River and that refugees were hiding in the Ramapo Mountains and raiding patriots.[56]

Livingston became the central bureaucrat in preventing illegal trade by using his authority to restrict movement across enemy lines to only those individuals who possessed a pass from him or from Washington, and he routinely rejected applications. In March 1780, for example, he turned down Abraham Durye's plea to cross into New York to recoup a debt, arguing that Durye had failed to prove that his physical presence would tangibly increase the chance of repayment. Livingston likewise continued his practice of denying passes to most women, believing their appeals to care for ill relatives or to procure money "mere fictions for procuring leave to jaunt it to New York."[57]

Livingston's attempts to quash the illegal trade met with approbation from the state legislature and Congress. The legislature, for example, approved several laws to prevent the illegal trade and to prosecute those who promoted it. Congress recognized that the "infamous practice" would cause "injurious consequences" to all Americans. However, most prosecutions in New Jersey came to naught, as local juries failed to convict their neighbors under the new state laws. Livingston's forceful attempts actually created an even greater problem: condemned smuggled goods were regarded as prizes to be taken and then resold into the London Trade. Militia leaders argued that with "no guards on the lines . . . trade with the enemy goes on very constantly and those who are commissioned to suppress it . . . greatly promote it" by pretending to capture goods from loyalists; then, "by some strange construction of the law they get all such goods condemned to their own benefit" without actually apprehending the supposed loyalist. For example, one prize confiscated by militia officer Baker Hendricks in March 1780 contained fifteen yards of black silk, twelve dozen coat buttons, and fifteen pairs of shoe buckles, among other highly sought-after imported items. They soon reentered the London Trade.[58] In early 1782, Hendricks, now a privateer, seized luxury goods, mainly clothing, from London Traders Alexander Morrison and Samuel Brink. Hendricks brought Morrison and Brink before a local judge to condemn their goods before he sold them back into the London Trade. Opportunists like Hendricks sparked Livingston's ire, but he was only more conspicuous than the many others who operated in the liminal spaces between patriot and loyalist zones of control.[59]

*   *   *

The same reticence for avoiding the London Trade mimicked the continued reluctance of New Jerseyans to serve in the militia, requiring Livingston and the Privy Council to motivate more men to fight. In this, though, Livingston the wartime bureaucrat failed as he had little faith that any militiamen would heed his calls to duty, arguing in early 1779 that the militia would not muster because of their low pay, the value of which was further depreciated by the currency crisis. Washington challenged Livingston on this, imagining that the militia should be "drawn out by the authority of the Government rather than by pecuniary reward" and that if the "former is not sufficient, the latter I apprehend will be found ineffectual." Pay concerns became important for Washington; any increase in militia salary would lure valuable recruits from his army. Along with low pay, militiamen endured the lack of supplies, little to no medical care, and no warm quarters in wintertime. Livingston again blamed the legislature for a failure to require anything of its citizens despite his "utmost exertions." In 1779, even former governor William Franklin, living in New York City, knew from informers that almost no men volunteered for duty in New Jersey's militia, despite a bounty of $1,000. In early 1780, British intelligence reported increased desertions among Pennsylvania and New Jersey militiamen and Continental troops, owing to lack of pay and supplies, hatred of their new French allies, and general disgust at the continued state of war.[60]

Despite Livingston's attempts to compel or to incentivize military service or to do both, the state's failure to fill the ranks continued throughout the war. The governor was thrust into an ever more awkward position, given that his main source of executive authority, the Privy Council, relied heavily on the militia to enforce its decisions. Livingston therefore pushed through legislation that promised courts-martial of those who refused to muster or pay fines, but threats had little effect on recruitment. Livingston believed that low pay and the practice of buying substitutes ensured that it was "not the rich men sons that turns out . . . but it is the needy for the most part and of the poorer classes of mankind who stands in need daily of their wages." Even after the legislature tripled the fine for failure to attend militia duty, wealthy New Jerseyans could buy the services of substitutes for less than the fines. Former Assembly speaker and avowed loyalist Cortlandt Skinner easily paid his fifty-pound militia fine in May 1779.[61]

The lack of support for the militia continued to enrage Livingston. France's entry into the war had siphoned off British troops to the Caribbean and the Carolinas, although New Jersey's frontiers, especially in Monmouth and Bergen Counties, remained contested borderlands. The British even believed that the situation in New Jersey in early 1779 resembled that of Georgia: the absence of hard money and soldiers offered the possibility of an easy

reestablishment of British rule. Livingston himself remained fearful of continued raids, requesting two or three light horsemen for a personal protective
detail. He understood that the "banditti" who continued to infest the state
"are not only a terror to the inhabitants but endanger the communication
necessary" to assist Washington in defending the region.[62]

Livingston had good reason to request personal protection. British
troops had attacked Elizabethtown in February 1779 with the intention of
capturing or assassinating him at Liberty Hall. Finding only his wife and
daughters, they hoped to seize the governor's papers, but the quick-witted
Livingston women instead proffered a pile of old law papers and correspondence from a recently captured British ship. Some reports of the incident
erroneously stated that the British had taken Livingston's daughters captive,
causing legislators like John Fell to wonder about the suitability of Elizabethtown as Livingston's home, so near the front lines. Apparently, the governor agreed that a strong "conspiracy against me" had formed in Essex.
After the summer of 1779 and until the end of the war, he never returned for
significant periods to Liberty Hall. He believed that both he and his wife had
to accept the inevitability that the British would burn their home and that
the couple should "prepare ourselves to bear it with Christian fortitude."
However, he acceded to his wife's plan to stay in Elizabethtown to try to prevent Liberty Hall's destruction.[63]

The 1779 raid was only one episode confirming Livingston's fear of a
British-sponsored assassination plot. A month later, he informed General
Henry Clinton by letter that he had proof that a British officer had offered a
significant sum of money to kidnap or kill him, though Livingston believed it
"highly improbable you should . . . be privy to a design so sanguinary and
disgraceful." He published the letter in the *New-Jersey Gazette*, and it eventually made its way into several New York papers.[64] Clinton's rebuke of Livingston in an open letter to the New York *Royal Gazette*, in which he criticized
Livingston for even intimating that he had been involved, brought a retort
from the governor that the general "entertain[ed] too exalted an opinion of
your own importance in deeming it a condescension in you to answer a letter" on the matter.[65] Three subsequent anonymous correspondents to the
Royal Gazette picked up on this idea of importance and wondered why "the
invisible governor," a man "so intent on masterly productions[,] should be so
little acquainted with the concise elegance of a fine writer" and make ungentlemanly insinuations that Clinton knew anything about the plot.[66]

Livingston put the assassination attempt behind him and joined with other New Jerseyans in mid-1779 in hopeful anticipation of French support of operations against New York. Though the French never came, General Clinton, aware that Washington was readying his men in Morristown for a possible march on the city, strengthened his garrison by evacuating Newport, Rhode Island, and other outlying outposts. By fall 1779, British troops had reinforced Staten Island and conducted multiple raids into New Jersey. The *New-Jersey Gazette* reported in early November that between 1,500 and 2,000 British soldiers looked across the narrow waterway between New Jersey and Staten Island, opposed by a Continental Army that had been weakened by a lack of supplies, a generally unfriendly citizenry, and the transfer of troops to the South. Livingston believed that Clinton's army outnumbered the Continentals by two to one and that only the uncertain actions of the French kept Clinton from destroying New Jersey.[67]

In January 1780, Washington thrust Livingston and New Jersey's state government to the front lines once again when he decided to attack Staten Island. The effort by Lord Stirling to engage the British ultimately failed, and the British responded with attacks against Newark, Elizabethtown, and Woodbridge. Residents from Elizabethtown, tired of "the enemy's having so frequently been over in small parties, plundering and carrying off numbers of the inhabitants" and fearful that their town will "become almost desolate" if something is not "speedily done," petitioned Livingston to secure additional local militiamen. They preferred those men who were "acquainted with the several places the enemy can cross at in this frozen time and can give the alarm before they can make the town," as opposed to the Continentals, who lacked local knowledge. Residents from Essex and Middlesex Counties similarly urged Livingston in early February to ready the militia to oppose a British crossing on the frozen Arthur Kill Strait.[68]

From February to May 1780, raids from Staten Island kept East Jerseyans on constant alert. Livingston, increasingly frustrated by the refusal of militiamen to muster in the midst of the depreciation crisis, recognized the limits of his power. Because the militia could not execute the Privy Council's directives, Livingston reported to the legislature, much of the state had been "perpetually harassed by . . . plundering parties and the inhabitants near the lines cannot without the assistance of their brother citizens . . . defend their possessions against the depredations of the enemy." The state was defended by a small number of Continentals and only the most local of militiamen. It was a "pity indeed" that the residents of East Jersey "should not be more assisted by guards from other counties" and that the most savage attacks by the British had worn out the militia in the border counties while those farther inland ignored his call.[69]

In late spring, the British in New York knew of the lackluster response of the militia and that the enlistments of almost three thousand Continentals would expire in late May; they also knew that much of Washington's army had left for the Carolinas. Furthermore, Livingston had failed to meet the state's recruiting quota for the upcoming campaign. With Washington's men scattered from Connecticut to New Jersey, British intelligence indicated that most Jersey militia would not muster and that many Continentals would soon mutiny. These assumptions formed the basis of a British plan to invade New Jersey in June 1780 through Elizabethtown, take a position in the Short Hills between Springfield and Chatham, and then march on Washington's headquarters at Morristown.[70] Six thousand British and Hessian troops under General Wilhelm von Knyphausen attacked Elizabethtown from Staten Island on the night of June 6, 1780, and quickly occupied the city. Roughly eight hundred Continentals delayed Knyphausen's advance and slowly moved toward nearby Connecticut Farms, where some militiamen had gathered. The delaying tactics near Elizabethtown gave Washington time to mobilize and respond faster than the British had anticipated. With Washington moving toward Springfield and intelligence reporting that detachments of Henry Clinton's army would soon arrive from South Carolina, Knyphausen withdrew to Elizabethtown, having achieved little but the burning of Connecticut Farms.[71]

The British and Hessian retreat worried Livingston because his wife and daughters had been at Liberty Hall when the invasion began. In its immediate aftermath, fearful that "our house and everything in it is doubtless gone," Livingston confided to Susannah that the "thoughts of your situation and that of the poor girls cuts me to the heart." He asked Washington's aide, Tench Tilghman, to identify their whereabouts, if possible. Thankfully, Tilghman reported that the family had survived and that Susannah had prevented Liberty Hall's destruction. However, British intelligence reports indicated animosities toward Livingston because he left his daughters and family alone at Liberty Hall: he was "hated" and "called cruel, miserly, and cowardly" by both patriots and loyalists. More important, the invasion highlighted New Jersey's continued vulnerability and Livingston's inability to defend the state against a sustained threat. Although Livingston and others feared a full-scale invasion, Clinton decided to move his army up the Hudson River, leaving only Knyphausen to push back toward Springfield in mid-June.[72]

The militia, as predicted, failed to materialize in substantial numbers or abandoned their posts with alarming frequency during planting season. Perceiving little resistance, Knyphausen again pushed toward Springfield, yet retreated to Staten Island by the end of June, believing that the troops committed in New Jersey would be needed to defend against the anticipated arrival of the French. Knyphausen's retreat ended the immediate emergency but did nothing to resolve the fundamental issues that had plagued Livingston: the London Trade still flourished, and the militia remained unreliable, no matter what changes Livingston, the Privy Council, or the legislature enacted.[73]

The second half of 1780 played out much like the first. The state could not meet its commitments to the army and could not rally the militia to stop the illegal trading and East Jersey raids. Livingston was "mortified . . . beyond expression" when he learned that only 159 men had joined the Continental Army from New Jersey in the latter half of 1780, far below the required quota. The "propagation of the mischievous doctrine that the enemy had given over all idea of conquest" was resoundingly false, he believed, and the states needed to continue to prepare for the worst, even if some believed that the French would alleviate pressure on New Jersey. Washington reminded Livingston that his army's strength would decline by early 1781 as enlistments ended and therefore implored him to meet the state's quota. Without a professional army, the United States could not hope to negotiate an end to the war. William Churchill Houston suggested to Livingston that "a few hard dollars on the drumhead" would help raise troops; that is, only hard specie, not depreciated paper money or patriotism, could steer New Jerseyans away from the London Trade and toward the patriot cause. Militia commander Jacob Crane agreed, arguing that without an economic motive to support the patriots, New Jerseyans would continue to patronize the London Trade, creating "a state of anarchy and confus[ion] in every place at or near the lines."[74]

The failure of the United States to motivate its soldiers to support the cause resulted in mutinies in Pennsylvania's Continental Line on January 1, 1781, while camped near Morristown. These men had not been paid even in depreciated currency for the previous year and believed they had signed up for only a three-year term instead of the war's duration. Washington asked Livingston to activate the militia to prevent the British from taking advantage of the rebellion. Clinton sent offers of protection and money for any mutineer who defected to New York, though none did, and readied four thousand men to strike into New Jersey should the opportunity arise. Of course, the concerns over terms of service and pay resonated among New Jersey's Continental soldiers. In April and May 1779, officers from the New Jersey Brigade had threatened to abandon their posts if the legislature did not immediately address their pay issues, forcing Lord Stirling to broker a deal that allowed the legislature to pay them without the perception that it had capitulated to their ultimatum.[75]

In late 1780, Livingston's appeals to incentivize militia duty came to fruition as the legislature discussed interventions to compensate for soldiers' depreciated pay. State militia leaders called for payment in specie instead of depreciated paper, whose "nominal sum of pay and substance . . . could by no means answer the idea of pay to the troops." At the same time, Abraham Clark complained of Congress's decision to grant officers half-pay for life when "we are in a perfect state of bankruptcy." It also made no allowances for the depreciation of pay to any soldier currently serving or who had recently left the service. In Clark's view, "Congress appears to be tumbling down fast and will I believe soon retain no more than a name and that I fear not a good one." Especially after the Pennsylvania mutiny, Livingston and New Jersey legislators redoubled their efforts to prevent the same from happening among the state's own disgruntled troops. Less than a week after the Pennsylvania revolt, the legislature authorized a commission to correct soldiers' salary caused by depreciation. This action came too late: two hundred of the New Jersey Line mutinied on January 20.[76]

Washington moved quickly to put down the rebellion. After two days of negotiating with the Jersey mutineers, Colonel Elias Dayton persuaded them to return to duty on a promise that their grievances would be addressed. However, the men continued to disobey orders, forcing Washington to arrest the New Jersey ringleaders and execute two of them. Livingston pointed to the Pennsylvanians as the cause of the "fever of revolt" yet remained "greatly mortified" by the mutiny, apprehensive of the future. Continued currency depreciation, along with the general lack of supplies, would cause the army to suffer over the winter and not bear the conditions with the same "good humor" as in the past. Livingston admitted to himself and Washington that the realities on the ground overrode the patriot fervor he had hoped to inculcate; even the incentives approved by the legislature did little to encourage more men to fight.[77]

The Jersey Line mutiny further damaged the state's ability to defend itself and recruit soldiers. Washington had hoped to use New Jersey as a base in a combined operation with the French to capture New York. Although Clinton had dispatched additional troops to support Cornwallis in the South and thereby relaxed pressure on New Jersey in early 1781, he understood Washington's continued fixation on New York and relished an epic battle against the combined Franco-American force. Clinton therefore kept most of his troops in New York and even recalled some of the troops he had sent south. A French attack on eastern Long Island confirmed his belief that New York remained Washington's primary target. To counter Clinton's growing force, Washington asked Livingston to activate militiamen for three months' duty. Those who did muster in the first half of 1781 more often served on the state's borders, haphazardly interdicting illegal trade rather than supporting Washington. Some Bergen residents, tired of the constant militia musters, argued for the seizure of the real estate of those who refused service. This general lack of support dovetailed with the lack of supplies New Jersey could offer, again highlighting the impact of depreciation and the general downturn in patriot support that Livingston had tried to counter.[78]

The failures of the militia had a direct impact on Livingston's personal safety. In April 1781, Washington intercepted intelligence that four different parties of loyalists and British soldiers had been dispatched from New York to kidnap or assassinate Livingston, Governor George Clinton of New York, Joseph Reed of Pennsylvania, and Washington himself. The wartime bureaucrat Livingston had become a perceived impediment to a British victory. The possibility of another assassination plot did not become especially real until August 1781, when Jersey loyalist James Moody published an article in the *Royal Gazette* offering a reward to anyone who delivered Livingston to New York. No bounty would be paid for his death, though "if his whole person cannot be brought in, half the sum . . . will be paid for his Ears and Nose, which are too well known and too remarkable to be mistaken." Moody's threat frightened Livingston enough to send his daughter Susannah and grandson Peter to Livingston Manor under his brother's care and daughter Kitty back to Philadelphia, believing his "poor girls are so terrified at the frequent incursions of the refugees into Elizabethtown that it is a kind of cruelty to insist on their keeping at home."[79]

The fear of an attack on his person and on Liberty Hall increased in the summer of 1781. The arrival of the French fleet under Admiral François Joseph Paul de Grasse along the East Coast and the strength of New York's garrison persuaded Washington and the Comte de Rochambeau, commander of the French expeditionary force, to attack Lord Cornwallis in Virginia, leaving New Jersey largely undefended. Livingston feared a British attack on New

Jersey or Philadelphia. Only roughly three thousand Continentals and what militia Livingston could muster defended New Jersey. While Washington warned Livingston that the militia must take over defense of the state, petitioners from East Jersey decried the lack of militiamen on the state's borders, and Livingston's friend Elias Boudinot remarked that Philadelphia, and thereby New Jersey, remained largely defenseless. Washington also complained of lackluster support: only three men from New Jersey had joined his army in July 1781. New Jersey was not alone in its neglect of duty: Connecticut could fill no more than a third of its Continental quota. To some degree, the French could be blamed. Originally reviled as former enemies, they brought hard currency that sealed their friendship among cash-poor farmers, who were loathe to abandon that opportunity for military service. By late September, Livingston feared that when the British learned about the Yorktown siege they would "make an excursion to desolate and ravage New Jersey." He warned the head of the state militia that if "Cornwallis experience[s] the fate of Burgoyne . . . Clinton will endeavor to procure some splendor by the blaze of houses and the stealing of forage of which this state . . . is the most likely to feel the effects." These fears were further heightened as British troops massed again on Staten Island in late September.[80]

Although the British did not invade New Jersey, foraging operations continued on the border through the first half of 1782. The victory at Yorktown tempered some resolve in the state. Many believed the war to be near a close, especially after Americans learned of Parliament's vote to end offensive operations in late February 1782 and the downfall of Lord North's government. Livingston, though, remained wary. Writing in the *New-Jersey Gazette* in mid-May under the pseudonym Old Politician, he called upon all New Jerseyans to remain vigilant, even though he knew his Privy Council could do little to mobilize the militia. Two days later, he expressed similar concerns to the legislature, arguing that Britain, despite the acts in Parliament, "is practicing every art to delude us into a belief of their pacific intentions towards us." While irregular fighting continued across the South, he called for the continued recruitment of troops and the readiness of the militia against anyone who engaged in the London Trade. In effect, the changing dynamics of the war politically had little relevance for Livingston; illegal traders and loyalists continued to engage in an increasingly bitter battle against East Jersey patriots, and Livingston had little means to stop them. Fears of his increased power, a lack of resolve by legislators to compel militia service, and the dreadful state of the economy had limited his ability to function as a wartime bureaucrat.[81]

*   *   *

The political limitations placed on Livingston endangered the state in the second half of the war, as attacks by irregular militias of loyalist refugees became common along the New York border. These battles also took on a racial character, especially in Monmouth County, where the notorious Colonel Tye, a former slave from Colts Neck who had escaped to British New York, wreaked havoc in 1779 and 1780. Tye and escaped slaves and white partisans from British-occupied Sandy Hook burned houses, seized supplies, and took patriot militiamen prisoner. Livingston declared martial law after a particularly devastating series of raids in 1780 and sent additional militiamen from West Jersey to defend against Tye. After Tye died in a daring raid to capture a militia officer, his men operated in Monmouth County for the remainder of the war, exacerbating racial tensions in a region that increasingly relied on slavery and deplored the patriots' inability to stop Tye and refugees like him.[82]

Of course, most loyalists along the New York border were white, and they came from every walk of life, including Livingston's own family. In August 1779 Connecticut governor Trumbull informed Livingston that his nephew William Alexander Livingston had been captured attempting to enter New York. Livingston readily agreed that William Alexander "was certainly a British subject at the time of his capture" and hoped the patriots would, "if his name does not stand too much in his way," be able to trade him for an American captive. Loyalism fractured familial lines across the region, and Livingston regretted that his, like "all families, are liable to have degenerate members." He could not forgive men like William Alexander and continued his hard line against loyalism even after others in the state had begun to realize that the war's devastating impact on New Jersey made the motives for some seemingly treasonous activities more ambiguous.[83]

The British took advantage of the discontent caused by the currency crisis and the fear of raids by using media to convince New Jerseyans along the border to stop supporting the patriot cause. In December 1779, an article in the *Royal Gazette* portrayed Livingston as an incompetent buffoon and cited his anti-French leanings as proof that the French alliance would soon sour and that Americans could not count on Paris to save them. Only Britain could protect their rights in the long term. Likewise, a popular song in early 1781 challenged New Jerseyans to "quit it in time and come hither to York . . . if muster fines, taxes imposed beyond reason . . . have washed your means or your patience" under patriot rule.[84]

These propaganda efforts had some success among weary New Jerseyans, but the most concerning danger came from the state's former governor, William Franklin. In an attempt to repair his damaged reputation, he boasted that he could reestablish a royal government in New Jersey and he petitioned British military leaders for a commission to operate against Mid-Atlantic patriots and on the high seas against the French. Generals Clinton and Howe looked at Franklin and his refugee comrades with suspicion, regarding them less as military allies and more as commercial accomplices in operating the critical London Trade. Beginning in 1779, though, Franklin organized the Associated Loyalists with the assistance of New York governor William Tryon, who proposed a plan that would enable Franklin to lead guerrilla attacks against Americans from bases in Rhode Island, Long Island, Staten Island, and Sandy Hook. Clinton scoffed at Tryon's plan, fearful that resources would be taken from his own troops, but in late 1780 London ordered him to supply the Associated Loyalists. Angry and still distrustful of the refugees, Clinton limited their supplies and areas of operation, yet they received the support they needed to begin attacks from Staten Island into Essex County and from Refugeetown on Sandy Hook into Monmouth.[85]

From Monmouth, militia leader Samuel Forman warned Livingston that the southern parts of Monmouth and Burlington Counties had become particularly dangerous. Refugees went there "unmolested and repeatedly joined" the partisans known as Pine Robbers, who operated across the mostly desolate Pine Barrens. This area, especially around Little Egg Harbor, had become the epicenter of the London Trade and attracted hundreds of loyalists, patriots, and neutrals; its few inhabitants and even fewer militiamen created a space for lawless activity to thrive. By late 1781 and early 1782, refugees had fortified Osborn Island, a base they could use to "receive deserters from the American army . . . as well as for the greater convenience of conveying provisions to New York which already go from that neighborhood in immense quantities." The entire region, according to Livingston, had been so long disaffected that most militiamen refused to serve there; those who did were "soon corrupted after being stationed on the lines by the alluring profits of the illicit trade." Patriot inhabitants around Little Egg Harbor petitioned the governor and legislature "to protect them from the ravages and devastation of the refugees," who had treated "them in an inhumane and savage manner." These messages confounded Livingston because other observers were telling him that all inhabitants routinely traded with the refugees. Eventually, Washington called upon Livingston to make illegal trading a capital crime. He readily agreed, but the legislature never took such serious steps against the London Traders.[86]

Livingston could do little to stop the refugee attacks on Monmouth or the lawlessness in the Pine Barrens, leaving local leaders with few reasons to trust the state government. Petitions to legislators in 1779 asking for the redistribution of loyalist property to compensate for damages had failed, and the currency crisis was at its height in 1780, when loyalist refugees increased their attacks. Believing that only direct aggression against loyalists would stop the ongoing violence, Monmouth patriots formed the Association for Retaliation, dedicated to responding "in kind upon the disaffected . . . for all damages, burnings, kidnappings," and appointed Samuel Forman as its leader.[87] Livingston thought the organization dangerous and subversive of state law and gubernatorial power. By late 1780, Forman had been removed from his militia position and he led an increasingly marginalized group. Moderate patriots formed the rival Whig Society of Monmouth County in May 1781, which, like similar groups in other counties, pledged to support changes to the Continental currency, boycott those who refused to accept it, and pursue legal action against the disaffected. The Retaliators, though, continued to support extralegal attacks against any and all loyalists, a practice that escalated violence as the Associated Loyalists began major operations in the county in 1781 and 1782. The situation resembled that in upcountry South Carolina at the same time, where loyalist partisans and criminal elements clashed with patriot militiamen and soldiers in the lawless backcountry. Moderate Monmouth residents could only complain to the legislature.[88]

William Franklin saw the civil war under way in southern New Jersey as an opportunity and enlisted some Pine Robbers into the Associated Loyalists, including Joseph Mulliner, who had received a privateer's commission from the British and ran a gang of ten men who plundered patriot property, traded in contraband goods, privateered, and kidnapped several patriot militiamen. When patriots captured him in the summer of 1781, William Paterson prosecuted him for high treason and won a verdict of death. Mulliner's execution struck a nerve among loyalists because the articles of capitulation at Yorktown treated loyalists as traitors instead of prisoners. The Associated Loyalists petitioned Clinton in New York to threaten retribution for mistreatment of any captured loyalists like Mulliner. Clinton agreed to recognize captured loyalists as prisoners of war in future negotiations but refused any form of retribution, confirming the belief of many Associated Loyalists that London would soon abandon the war.[89]

Yet, even though major military operations ended after Yorktown, the Associated Loyalists conducted daring and destructive raids against the largely undefended New Jersey coastline early in 1782. Forman and his Monmouth Retaliators executed several Associated Loyalists that spring, which incited Franklin and the Associated Loyalists to approve the execution of Monmouth militia captain Joshua Huddy, captured in March after a raid on Toms River. Huddy had been heavily involved with the Retaliators, participating in the execution of loyalist Stephen Edwards. They assigned the task to former New Jerseyan Richard Lippincott, who arranged for Huddy's transfer from New York to Sandy Hook (on the pretense of a prisoner exchange) and his hanging on April 12. They made the intent of their action clear with a sign on Huddy that decried the cruel murders of other loyalists and pledged that vengeance would continue "as long as a refugee is left existing."[90]

Huddy's summary execution placed Livingston and New Jersey at the center of an international incident. George Washington immediately condemned the act and identified a British captain captured at Yorktown, Charles Asgill, to be executed if Clinton did not surrender Lippincott for trial.[91] Such an action would have violated the terms of the surrender at Yorktown and would have reflected badly on the United States. Ultimately, a British court-martial of Lippincott exonerated him, but intercession by the king and queen of France persuaded Congress to release Asgill in November 1782.

In the interlude between Clinton's authorization of Lippincott's court-martial and the trial's beginning, General Sir Guy Carleton assumed command of New York, and Livingston's son Brockholst was captured returning from Spain. Brockholst wrote to his father that, with the Lippincott affair ongoing, "I shall not be set at liberty"; he might even "be thought a proper subject for retaliation" if Washington went through with Asgill's execution. Carleton arranged for Brockholst's parole and had him deliver a letter to his father, demanding that Livingston stop the actions of the Monmouth Retaliators and all forms of retribution, an edict similar to the one Washington delivered after Huddy's execution. Livingston replied to Carleton that he knew of no mistreatment of loyalist or British prisoners; he appreciated Brockholst's release but "never wished to be any farther distinguished from my fellow citizens at large" in any circumstance. In subsequent communications, Livingston argued that the Board of Associated Loyalists had commissioned so many banditti that Carleton should consider investigating them rather than the Americans.[92] Privately, Livingston feared for Brockholst and urged him to take his older brother Billy and immediately leave Elizabethtown for the relative safety of Trenton; because of "the malice of refugees against me," they would be easy targets close to the border. In the end, Livingston's family survived, though the Associated Loyalists did not. New York's British community shunned Franklin for his ungentlemanly behavior in the Huddy affair. He left for England, never to return.[93]

The demise of the Associated Loyalists following the Huddy affair and the news of the downfall of Lord North's government put many Americans at ease, despite Livingston's calls for continued readiness, especially when dealing with loyalists. He believed "a new species of Tories," seeking to leave New York secretly, could increase the activities of loyalists along New Jersey's borders and cause the state to become "a shameful asylum for every self-banished, self-convicted traitor" in the nation. Though Livingston believed that Americans could never let "the rascals return amongst us," he feared that the end of major hostilities would spur even more destruction in the state.[94]

*   *   *

At almost sixty years of age in late 1782, Livingston had felt the impact of war in a multitude of ways. The war had stressed him financially, but, more important, it had strained his family relations and directed him away from some of the pursuits to which he had hoped to dedicate himself in retirement. Throughout the war, Livingston complained that his time was "generally so engrossed by public business" that he could not spend time with his family or pursue his "literary productions."[95] Indeed, despite increasingly bad eyesight, Livingston carried on a significant correspondence with his wife and children, complaining at some moments of their failure to write and at others about his absence from their lives. He truly missed his wife and begged her to visit him in Morristown or Raritan, where he camped near Washington's army. He dreamed of the moment when he could again live with her at Liberty Hall "without the fear of the Tories or the Enemy," when he could "make it [his] constant endeavor to study and promote [her] happiness and to make the remainder of [her] life as agreeable . . . as the tenderest of husbands can."[96]

For his sons, the war represented opportunities for growth. John Jay's appointment to Spain gave Brockholst not only a job but also a means to better himself intellectually and in the public service. Livingston relied on him and Jay to support his post-retirement plans: he asked them to accumulate seeds and report on plants that could be cultivated at Liberty Hall. His attempts to secure a future for Brockholst did not last long. By the summer of

1781, Brockholst's relationship with his sister and brother-in-law had soured to the point that Sarah felt mortified at her brother's "discontent and disgust" as well as his temper and impoliteness. Livingston finally got Brockholst to agree to study law after his return to America, though he hoped eventually to introduce him to Robert Morris, who could tutor him in business, a profession he believed might be more lucrative, especially as his own estate continued to decline in value.[97]

Jay's absence in Spain allowed Livingston to cultivate what became one of his closest familial bonds during the war. The Jays left their son Peter in his grandparents' care, giving Livingston much time to correspond with him. Though they did not live together for any substantial period, William and Peter grew attached to one another. Livingston bought primers for Peter and encouraged him to read. Resurrecting his old pastime as an artist, he drew pictures to accompany his letters to Peter, something he never gave himself license to do in the midst of war. These playful letters let Livingston speak in rhyme and make his grandson guess what his grandfather would soon bring him. He even revealed to Peter his hopes for the future after Yorktown: Washington would quickly drive the British "back again to . . . King George who is a dunce." Even as he publicly warned New Jerseyans of the need to remain vigilant in late 1781 and early 1782, he told Peter the opposite. The British regulars captured at Yorktown, many of whom had marched past Liberty Hall the previous year, "don't look so fierce now that they are prisoners . . . they look like a little dog with his tail between his legs."[98]

The close relationship with Peter tempered some of the loss Livingston felt after his youngest son, John Lawrence, died at sea in 1781 while serving as a midshipman on the *Saratoga*. Livingston had worked hard to gain a commission for his son, even appealing to Robert Morris to arrange for extra seafaring experience for him before his service began. In writing to his cousin Robert Livingston, the secretary of foreign affairs, the governor, in somewhat uncharacteristic fashion, made no apologies for pushing the issue, believing that he had "sacrificed the best part of my fortune to the public . . . while thousands of the most worthless scoundrels on Earth have extorted immense riches from the vitals of their country."[99]

Livingston bitterly blamed King George for the sinking of the *Saratoga* in April 1781. This might then explain some of Livingston's vehement hatred of loyalists and London Traders—he had sacrificed much for the cause and they very little. As no witnesses remained of the ship's fate, however, Livingston held out hope that John Lawrence was alive. Sketchy reports that the *Saratoga* had been captured and had been taken to England encouraged Livingston. He went to work using his contacts in Philadelphia as well as Jay and Brockholst in Spain to confirm the news that John Lawrence might be a prisoner in London. In the end, Sarah reported that "even that ray of hope has been greatly obscured by the unsuccessful enquiries of our friends in Europe."[100]

*   *   *

The end of the war was bittersweet for Livingston. He had lost much of his fortune and his son, and he had lived apart from his family for almost six years. Yet, the conflict had taught him much about how both the government and average Americans would function in this new world. He emerged with a firmer belief in the need for more centralized executive power and a strong understanding of the impact of the economy on the relative strength of the government. Both lessons proved supremely important as the currency crisis continued to rage and as Livingston prepared to attend the Constitutional Convention to address the wrongs that the excesses of legislators had created.

CHAPTER 6

Creating a New Nation,
1783–1789

Almost six years after he had accepted his commission as a general in the militia, Livingston oversaw the demobilization of the army that had been part of life in New Jersey for so long. Although George Washington had hoped to capitalize on the victory at Yorktown and move south toward Charleston, the French evacuated all of their North American forces by October 1782. Washington therefore sat with his army along the Hudson River, waiting for negotiators in Paris to end the conflict. Though fighting continued between the Associated Loyalists and New Jersey's militia, Washington's Continental Army slowly shrank in size from a high of 17,000 men in late 1781 to around 2,500 by summer 1783.[1]

The war's end brought fundamental change to Livingston's daily life; he no longer worried constantly about militia requisitions, calls for additional troops, or London Traders. Still, as he transitioned from wartime bureaucrat to postwar politician, Livingston's experiences in prosecuting the war influenced his actions in the major political battles of the 1780s. State and national finances were of overriding concern, as New Jerseyans battled over paper money and an economic depression that again limited currency's availability. Livingston's personal experience with debt, his hatred of the inflation caused by the Continental dollar, and his long-time opposition to paper money led him to argue forcefully against any remediation of the money supply for the benefit of debtors.

In a scene replicated across the nation, New Jerseyans struggled with debt and a deteriorating economy while understanding that most states never remitted tax revenue to Congress. In 1785, the postwar currency crisis reached a tipping point when Congress called on the states to fill a new tax requisition, a decision that historian Woody Holton argues led to the Constitutional Convention. In New Jersey, legislators refused to allocate the necessary revenue and instead, responding to the concerns of their constituents, approved the creation of a land bank that printed paper money to service the thousands of desperate Jersey debtors. Whereas the requisition in even more heavily indebted New England precipitated Shays' Rebellion and electoral victories by debtors that led to the printing of millions of dollars of worthless paper, New Jersey's internal conflict over the currency remained relatively tame because pro-debtor legislators had already seized control of the state government. Without the executive authority Livingston had acquired during the war, his battle against the excesses of the legislature became a test of political influence, maneuvering, and propaganda. He had excelled in all of these areas before, and his flexible nature served him well again in this postwar gubernatorial role.[2]

An "excess of democracy" arising from the economic crisis of the mid-1780s that created chaos across the nation has been frequently identified as the impetus for the calling of the Constitutional Convention. To Livingston, however, the propensity of legislators to oppose needed but unpopular measures and to pass laws favorable to local over national interests was nothing new. These seemingly never-ending battles taught him the value of a national system that supported efficiency in government and gave greater power to the executive. The ceding of power to the federal government in critical areas such as military affairs, trade, finance, and taxation made sense to him because these very issues had stymied him at the state level. Further, Livingston had supported the royalist argument that King George should regain the prerogatives taken by Parliament from the crown in the years before the Revolution. He was therefore already predisposed to view the legislature with disdain, support stronger executive authority, and join other former royalists in embracing the federalist cause at the Constitutional Convention.[3]

As a delegate to the Convention, Livingston supported federalist proposals that limited the power of the states and the people. He never shied away from lacing his speeches and writings with republican virtue and very much favored the republican ideal of self-sacrifice. However, his condemnations of the working class and debtors in favor of self-sacrifice should be understood as a dialectic Livingston created between an idealized civic virtue and the reality of his own economic and political struggles. He never actually hoped to reorient society in any meaningful way, as his fragile financial condition during and after the war heightened his prewar class anxiety. Further, his wartime experience with legislators who catered to individual interests and his perception that most other Americans had not sacrificed as much as he had assured him that republicanism, while an alluring ideal, needed a stronger executive to persevere. The individual could not be trusted. Livingston's experience therefore reinforces that a stronger royalist trend continued throughout the Revolution and made its way into the Constitution, affecting the relationship among the individual, the state, and the federal government.[4]

                                    *   *   *

With the possibility of peace on the horizon after the patriot victory at the Battle of Yorktown in October 1781, Congress appointed five commissioners, headed by Benjamin Franklin, to negotiate with Great Britain in Paris in the spring of 1782. John Adams, occupied by a treaty with the Dutch, joined later, as did John Jay, who left his less-than-fruitful position in Madrid for Paris. Illness prevented Jay from participating in negotiations from June to September 1782 and also beset Livingston's friend and peace commissioner Henry Laurens. Thomas Jefferson, the fifth commissioner, never ventured to Paris.[5] Though his son-in-law was one of the treaty's primary negotiators, Livingston neither gleaned any insights into the talks nor provided advice. He confessed to Jay that he remained silent because the odds were "at least five to one" that his letters would fall into British hands before they reached Paris. He regretted not having arranged a cypher before Jay's posting to Spain. Instead, he mostly communicated personal information to his daughter Sarah, who only once mentioned the treaty: after negotiators signed the preliminary treaty in late November 1782, Sarah rejoiced that "the dawn of peace seems to approach" and predicted that "brighter days" would be coming soon.[6]

News of the preliminary treaty gave New Jerseyans hope that the war would truly be over soon. The treaty was not final, however, and Livingston's cousin Robert, the secretary of foreign affairs under the Articles of Confederation, asked Livingston in March 1783 to ready New Jersey in case the British rejected it at the last moment. In April, British forces in New York informed Washington of London's orders to cease hostilities, leading Washington to order the remaining Continental forces to stand down. Livingston issued a proclamation on April 14 informing New Jerseyans that peace had been secured. Negotiators signed the final treaty on September 3, and British forces left New York City on November 25, allowing Washington and his remaining eight hundred men to occupy the city. The bloody and destructive conflict that had affected every resident of New Jersey had ended.[7]

The evacuation of British soldiers from New York relieved Livingston of the constant worry of invasion, but it also brought to the fore the bitter question of the fate of the loyalists who had just participated in some of the bloodiest fighting in East Jersey. In these areas, many citizens supported strong anti-loyalist laws to redeem their long suffering and to ensure peace. By late summer 1782, loyalists had realized that Britain no longer opposed American independence. The final treaty's fifth and sixth articles were particularly disheartening to the loyalists because they mandated that Congress only recommend to the states that they restore confiscated loyalist property and stop any future confiscations. Jay, Adams, and Franklin knew that the states would never agree to relinquish seized property, especially in New Jersey and New York, where patriots hungered to confiscate and sell even more to compensate for their losses. In New York, Governor Clinton maneuvered the legislature into passing laws that forgave patriot debts owed to loyalists and allowed lawsuits for damages against those who had used patriot property in New York City during the occupation.[8]

After the terms of the treaty became known, New Jerseyans repeatedly petitioned the legislature to refrain from restoring loyalist property and to prohibit loyalists from returning to the state. Inhabitants of Middletown in war-torn Monmouth County argued that loyalists would become "a pest and disturbers" of the peace, while 125 Middlesex residents "dread[ed] the consequences of such indulgences" as allowing loyalists to return and reclaim their property. The Middlesex petitioners had "fought and bled in the field in support of our cause and had our houses burnt and property taken from us"; having been "reduced almost to want by those very persons," they could not forgive and forget. Describing loyalists as "traitors, robbers, and murderers," Bergen residents warned of danger if the loyalists returned. A Hunterdon petition questioned the possibility of forgiveness, given the "cruel parricides" loyalists had fomented among the Indians and committed themselves. Any loyalists who attempted to return home faced almost certain challenge and retribution. In September 1783, for instance, John Pellet and James Aston of Sussex, former members of the loyalist New Jersey Volunteers, were met by a mob that gave them twenty-one lashes, "tied straw ropes around their necks, cut off their hair," and banished them to New York.[9]

The fate of New Jersey's loyalists became Livingston's first charge as a peacetime politician. He readily agreed with the majority who opposed a quick reconciliation and professed astonishment that any government entity would consider extending an "invitation to all those unnatural rascals who have so long thirsted for our blood and the destruction of our Liberty."[10] Livingston even split with John Jay, writing before the formal signing of the treaty that he and most Jersey patriots opposed reconciliation and doubted that any progress could be made on that point. Jay countered that "a universal indiscriminate condemnation and expulsion" of the loyalists "would partake more of vengeance than of justice" and "would not redound to our honor." Reconciliation needed to begin.[11]

For Livingston, years of defending against relentless incursions and sabotage had limited his ability to forgive, though he did not believe in wholesale retribution, indiscriminate confiscation, or expulsion. As he had championed throughout the war, the rule of law would prevail. He ordered that any suspected loyalist attempting to reenter New Jersey be investigated as a traitor. Likewise, he cautioned militia leaders that, with peace secured, all laws must be respected when it came to loyalists, even using Jay's argument that negative treatment of them would "draw upon us a national reproach for the sake of gratifying a vindictive disposition." However, he likely applauded the legislature's decision in December 1783 to resume sales of confiscated estates. Over the next six years, the state made more than £117,000 and never returned any of the property or proceeds to loyalists, a policy followed in New York as well.[12]

Despite his loathing of loyalists, Livingston and many other New Jerseyans made clear demarcations when it came to friends, family, and business associates who had remained loyal to the king. Livingston's brother John, for instance, lived in occupied New York as the superintendent of derelict property, a position that included some supervision of his family's former sugar refinery, where American prisoners of war were jailed. Even in June 1783, Livingston refused to go to New York to see John (a pass from British commanders was still required), and he recommended that his brother not try to come to New Jersey because "our people still continue so enraged against the loyalists." Even though Livingston believed that John did "not come under that denomination . . . resentment is levelled" without being "always clearly distinguished."[13]

These individual differentiations of loyalty created some space to advocate for the return of loyalists. New Jersey merchant and future senator John Rutherfurd, for example, argued that individuals who had not taken up arms against the United States—specifically, wealthy loyalists—could be lured to New Jersey to increase European trade and rebuild the state's economy. Though never presented as a formal plan, Rutherfurd's ideas appealed to wealthy patriots in New York, Massachusetts, and elsewhere, who saw opportunity in courting their former enemies. They quickly aligned with loyalists like John Livingston on a host of business ventures, seeing opportunities to create stability in the murky postwar economic world instead of inflicting vengeance on those who could help rebuild the nation faster. This same system endured in Massachusetts, as Patriots there welcomed loyalists deemed useful to society with open arms, especially if their transgressions did not involve violence against the American state. Although the political rights of New Jersey loyalists were not restored until 1788, Livingston's peacetime government eventually saw usefulness in forgiving the past.[14]

Forgiveness was the price for strengthening the state's and the nation's economy. John Jay emphatically argued to Livingston that Americans, instead of bickering over the fate of loyalist property, needed to enact wise trade and government regulations to enhance the nation's credit after the signing of the definitive peace treaty. Likewise, George Washington told Livingston that individual concerns should not override a concentrated focus on the nation's economic health; the efforts of each individual and each state were needed to make the nation stronger.[15]

New Jerseyans gradually put aside their disagreements and looked to trade with Europe once again. The reopening of this commerce allowed merchants to import increasingly large quantities of manufactured goods from Britain that began to satisfy the demand only partially served by the London Trade. Imports, however, created a trade imbalance because Americans exported little. High prices had depressed demand for American foodstuffs in Europe, and Parliament's decision in 1783 to close British Caribbean ports to U.S. carriers hurt Jersey farmers, who had few other options to sell their crops. What little hard money remained in New Jersey migrated out of state, and, as the state cycled paper money out of circulation after 1780, merchants and farmers alike began to cry for more cash as New Jerseyans again suffered from a money shortage and a credit collapse—the exact opposite of the inflationary revolutionary financial concerns.[16]

Calls for cash were met with admonitions to curtail the conspicuous consumption that had created this new debt cycle. Livingston believed that American "trade with Britain . . . ever has been and ever will be ruinous to this country." Money drained out of New Jersey to English merchants and, because the state lacked a major port, to New York and Pennsylvania collectors of import duties. Taking to the newspapers under the pen name Caius, Livingston argued that "every friend to America should oppose the introduction of British goods." Just as America is "emerging from a sea of paper money," Britain "is draining us of our current cash." Livingston believed that irresponsible overconsumption had damaged American independence and needed to be restrained in order for the nation to survive. Organizations formed across the nation to lobby for limits on consumption, while Livingston and others worked through intermediaries to develop America's nascent industrial sector, especially in textile manufacturing.[17]

The decline in exports and the resulting lack of cash quickly worsened because of the late eighteenth century's most severe ecological menace: the Hessian fly, or barley midge. The fly, probably brought from Europe in shipments of food to British and Hessian troops in New York in 1777, deposits larvae on wheat stalks that stunt their growth and damage their ability to produce grain. Despite reduced harvests, grain prices slumped from 1782 to 1786. For example, in Mendham Township (Morris County), prices declined 30 percent per bushel for both corn and wheat, a situation repeated across the state that further limited the availability of cash.[18]

The lack of cash became a politically fraught issue for Livingston because New Jerseyans faced increasingly high taxes during and following the agricultural failures and trade imbalance. Complicating the situation, New Jersey had far fewer options to raise revenues than did its neighbors. As Livingston had earlier articulated, both New York and Pennsylvania secured hefty import duties from Jersey consumers and could therefore constrain the taxes levied on their own residents. Other states also had large tracts of western lands to sell. With no significant port, few import duties, and no western territory, New Jersey had to find revenues among the very people who had little money to give to the government as a result of currency contraction.[19]

Per capita taxes increased nationwide several times over their prewar levels from 1784 through 1786 as each state faced the same issues. One group of Jersey petitioners decried these "heavy taxes laid on us" after a war that had begun partly over high taxes. Indeed, many citizens believed their participation in the war merited special dispensation. Essex County petitioners, for example, agreed that taxes must be raised to pay off war debts but argued that they had loaned Congress so much money that they could not deliver the required taxes; the bonds and certificates had "very little prospect as yet of either principal or interest being paid." John Beatty, a New Jersey delegate to the Continental Congress, shared these sentiments. He told Livingston that he would work to have Congress recognize that the state had "borne an unequal share of the public burthen and that proper allowances have not been made for the great devastations committed on our lands, houses, and improvements by the enemy."[20]

Unfortunately for Beatty, Congress needed to receive tax revenue quickly because the world had begun to see cracks in America's ability to repay its debts. The failure of Rhode Island to approve the federal impost and thereby create a dedicated revenue stream for Congress increased congressional reliance on the states. Loans from France, Holland, and other countries had been exhausted and awaited repayment. Writing from Paris, John Jay regretted the reluctance with which "the states in general pay the necessary taxes" because "it injures both their reputation and interest abroad as well as at home." By 1785, even the French ambassador began to complain, arguing that French citizens who held American debt had not been properly paid. John Beatty believed that the failure of states to pay taxes now would later force Congress to "make new and large requisitions of the states."[21]

In December 1783, in response to public outcry against the unfairness of New Jersey's position versus other states, the state legislature authorized the payment of interest due on federal debt instruments held by New Jerseyans directly to them in paper money and deducted that amount from the state's requisition to the federal government. This measure enjoyed some support among bondholders, but it became a ploy to force other states to support the renewed attempt to approve a Continental impost. Livingston, though opposed to the paper-money aspects of the maneuver, agreed that states must pay into the national system and support federal creditors. Under the pen name Scipio, he argued that those who had supported the war in uniform or by lending money should receive quick recompense.[22]

The more disruptive proposal, in Livingston's opinion, came in September 1784, when state legislators required all creditors to accept payment for debts in public securities at their full specie value, a devastating blow to creditors because the value of securities had depreciated significantly. Petitions from across the state argued that legislators had abrogated creditor rights, voided private contracts, and damaged the nation's moral fiber. Livingston, a creditor who had lost much of his fortune because of depreciated money, vigorously agreed with petitions to repeal the law. As Scipio, he argued that the farmers who objected to "paying their proportion of an honest debt" were the same people who had recklessly consumed great amounts of imported manufactured goods. In his view, the solution remained a combination of stopping consumption and withholding "their produce . . . in expectation of a higher market" price, something few poor farmers could attempt with debts mounting and tax collectors searching for them.[23]

The debate over the 1784 law highlighted the differences between East and West Jersey over debt and monetary policy. In general, East Jersey was saddled with more quartermaster certificates and other types of federal debt arising from its position on the war's front lines. Creditors were more likely to be from West Jersey, as they and their fortunes had largely escaped the war's destruction.[24]

Livingston's weak position as governor meant that he could do little to enact policies that conformed to his beliefs. Against his wishes, the 1784 legislative session also passed a tax law that depreciated paper money and removed it from circulation, irrevocably contracting the currency. The governor and the Privy Council had set the exchange rates of all paper-money emissions, but their attempts to ensure that issues held their value failed. Instead, they gradually declined until the legislature fixed their value to specie at 3:1, though even that was generous. In West Jersey, where few of the dollars circulated, residents believed that "paper currency in its present unfixed state is of little use to the public and has detrimental consequences to individuals." East Jersey debtors hoped to redeem the notes at par; but, in this case, several East Jersey legislators defected to join their West Jersey colleagues, acknowledging the farce of redeeming obviously depreciated money at par value. The law not only hurt debtor's hopes but also, in Livingston's mind, damaged the legislature's credibility. The decision to depreciate reinforced the public's opinion that paper money could never be trusted because the legislature could adjust its value at any moment. More critically, this law had the undesired effect of removing one of the last means of paper exchange from the market because holders rushed to redeem their holdings before the legislature changed its mind again. By early 1785, debtors across the state possessed few economic options to survive the contraction of money, crops, and trade.[25]

By September 1785, the Confederation Congress recognized that it was essentially insolvent and issued a new requisition mandating that states pay some of their allotment with hard money, 40 percent of which would pay debt holders. New Jersey's congressional representatives feared the state could not meet its quota. They also worried about the debts held by former army officers, who had threatened to mutiny in the aborted Newburgh Conspiracy of March 1783. These officers had agreed to forgo their lifetime pensions and instead receive commutation certificates valued at five years of full pay, funded by the 1785 requisition. Pensions for officers had been unpopular across the nation. In October 1783, one group of Essex County petitioners argued that, as holders of worthless certificates, they could barely afford to pay their taxes to reduce the mountain of federal debt; even the Continental officers should acknowledge the unreasonableness of paying pensions, given the state of the nation. Officers from the New Jersey Line, however, argued that requisitions to Congress were needed to ensure the stability of the new government and the proper payment of just debts, including their own.[26]

The inclusion of the commutation bonds in the 1785 requisition riled New Jersey's newly elected pro-debtor legislators, who viewed the officers and their large bonuses with suspicion. Joining legislators from New York, Pennsylvania, and almost half of the nation, they refused payment of any interest on bonds issued by Congress after May 1, 1783, including the commutation bonds. Abraham Clark, having returned in 1784 from his three-year appointment to Congress to represent Essex County in the legislature, used this issue to serve as Livingston's foil on monetary issues over the next two years. A strong advocate of paper money and of state over federal power, Clark argued that New Jersey held a unique position in the nation as a holder of significant federal debt; yet the state lacked western land or the ability to raise revenue from imports. Indeed, New Jerseyans had the fourth highest amount of debt per capita, behind only Rhode Island, Pennsylvania, and Massachusetts. Clark saw this obligation as particularly unequal and argued that the requisition might be an attempt not only to support bond speculators but also to limit the potential success of a new federal impost if states paid their share of taxes.[27]

Clark successfully galvanized both pro-debtor and pro-creditor legislators who felt that New Jersey had been treated unfairly by Congress. New Jersey became the first state to reject the 1785 requisition, and legislators also ordered the state's congressional representatives to vote against any measure that would levy an expense on Jersey taxpayers and to refuse to pay Congress anything until it enacted a federal impost. Congress immediately dispatched three congressmen, led by Charles Pinckney of South Carolina, to negotiate with New Jersey legislators. The trio pointed out that the state's actions undermined the security of the Union and eventually convinced legislators to agree to pay; yet the state never made any effort to do so. Connecticut joined New Jersey in opposing the requisition, and New Hampshire flirted with opposition. Heavily indebted states that tried to meet their requisitions became the larger historical story. Attempts to fill the requisition in Rhode Island resulted in the replacement of two-thirds of its assembly with pro–paper-money legislators; in Massachusetts, attempts to impose taxes payable in hard money precipitated Shays' Rebellion. The already pro-debtor legislature in New Jersey used the requisition's rejection as a rallying cry to enact a series of pro-debtor laws over the next two years.[28]

Nationally, men like Clark pursued two related measures to relieve hard-hit taxpayers: a limitation on payments to speculators who had bought debt at depreciated prices and support for the printing of paper money. Clark and other Jersey debtor advocates directed most of their efforts toward forcing the state to issue paper money, given that little currency remained in circulation. Although much of the state remained heavily indebted from the war and the recent economic collapse, taxation, not private debts, took center stage as Clark and his allies had looked at every avenue to reduce the tax burden on Jersey residents. Paper money became yet another option, as it did in every other state that suffered the same poor economic environment. Most paper-money advocates argued that New Jersey had seen several positive experiences with paper before the Revolution, specifically related to the prewar land banks. On the other side, opponents feared the return of the inflationary world from which they had just emerged: inflation would undermine the sanctity of contracts negotiated in hard currency once the paper began to depreciate.[29]

Clark found an easy alliance with voters who signed more than 140 petitions to the legislature asking for paper money in 1785 and 1786. Representing one-quarter of the state's white males, these petitioners gave Clark strong backing to introduce legislation in late 1785 to create a land bank that would issue paper at interest and make it legal tender. To rally support for his plan, Clark adopted Livingston's tactics and published several editorials under the name Willing to Learn. He argued that a land bank would improve the economy without increasing taxes by allowing the state to pay its debts with the interest earned on the bonds and thereby restore the public credit. It would also relieve the indebted by helping them pay their debts, avoid the sale of their property, and reinforce a republican government by tempering some of the wealth inequity that had developed during and after the Revolution. On the creditor side, the plan promised prompt payment of debts instead of delays while lawyers adjudicated cases for years. Further, by linking the paper to land and then retiring a portion of it annually, the currency would retain its value and not depreciate to the extent seen earlier in the decade.[30]

Livingston vehemently opposed Clark's paper-money plan and voiced his concerns both to legislators and to citizens. In January and February 1786, as Primitive Whig, Livingston published six editorials in the *New-Jersey Gazette* to counter Willing to Learn, deploying the same tropes he had used to battle overconsumption in 1783 and 1784. He did not believe Clark's claim that the currency had contracted to the point that money was not available. Instead, the problem was the "lazy, lounging, lubberly fellow sitting nights and days in a tipplinghouse, working perhaps but two days in the week . . . and spending the rest of his time in squandering" his earnings "in riot and debauch and then complaining when the collector calls for his tax, of the hardness of the times, and the want of a circulating medium."[31] For the likes of such men, legislators had performed "the charming and necromatic Hocus Pocus" of passing an act that removed any personal responsibility. Such unconscionable actions would "annihilate all public faith and all private credit," serving not the greater good but only their own reelection. Other observers readily agreed. Former congressman John Beatty, for example, criticized Clark's and the General Assembly's blatant disregard for the security of the Union by refusing to pay the requisition. Instead, Beatty believed that the members of the Privy Council, "the more thinking and prudent part of the state," would kill it.[32]

Livingston's reasons for opposing paper money in 1786 grew out of his vigorous opposition to the London Trade during the Revolution, when his own fortune declined while less patriotic individuals profited. From the war's end through passage of the land bank, Livingston desperately tried to collect debts owed to him but routinely failed or was paid in depreciated paper, leading him to contemplate selling Liberty Hall. His joy at returning to his rural estate in the spring of 1783 for the first time in three years was overshadowed by concern over providing a secure home for his wife in the event of his death. He felt compelled to keep and improve the property, which would "fetch so much the more after our deaths."[33]

Livingston also had larger intellectual concerns about paper money based on his interpretations of morality and republican government. For years he had railed against legislators who had become too beholden to the electorate, challenging their worthiness for leadership. In early 1785, Livingston wrote that all citizens needed to "guard against sinister motives and sacrificing the general welfare to party combinations or personal views."[34] In the midst of this critical period, then, Livingston reiterated the plea of many national leaders for a citizenry that would carry the new nation forward. Throughout the war, Livingston had styled himself in a classical republican mold: "a virile figure" who had "dedicated his life to serving his republic as a warrior, statesmen, and legislator." Despite the elitist tinge, Livingston had served in all three capacities; "service tied to responsibility" had been his "guiding mantra." Financial losses, however, had endangered the economic independence that was a necessary ingredient for a classical republican man, especially because cash rather than land made up much of his estate.[35]

Livingston's beliefs and experiences placed him at the center of an emerging political debate about the traits necessary for a republican citizen and therefore the construction of national identity. Media images used the concept of manliness to depict debtors as the opposite of virtuous citizens; they were slothful, traitorous, degenerate, and ultimately effeminate. In Massachusetts, those who supported Shays' Rebellion were derided for having caused their own destruction by their overconsumption. Livingston readily adapted these tropes to argue that "indulgence in luxurious dress and imported trifles, not high taxes," had brought debtors to their current station. Robert Morris and dozens of other elites declared that debtors lacked "personal discipline and effort" and that a contraction of money, as argued by Paterson, would forge a better citizenry. The characterization of a class of citizens as unable to control themselves made a larger statement about their inability to participate in government and laid the groundwork for their eventual exclusion.[36]

Historians have used Livingston's arguments to buttress the thesis that those who supported the Constitution did so to reinvigorate the virtue of the American people by instilling the values of frugality, industry, and simplicity. Their efforts became emblematic of a larger endeavor to remove special interests from the legislative agenda. Indeed, in early 1787, Livingston wrote to Essex legislator Elijah Clarke that Americans did "not exhibit the virtue that is necessary to support a republican government and without the utmost exertions of the more patriotic part of the community ... I fear that we shall not be able ... to support that independence" that had so dearly cost the nation. He had used similar language with Henry Laurens in 1778 concerning congressional mismanagement and the "degenerate sons of America," whose failures should be redeemed by republican virtue.[37] However, historian Roger Brown could also have used Livingston as evidence for his argument that attacks against luxury were "class-specific responses to popular demands for tax relief and to the popular obstruction and resistance that greeted the governments' tax crackdowns"; elites hoped to stimulate the economy by increasing exports and bringing more specie into the nation.[38]

Livingston's arguments about virtue and republicanism should be read not as a reinforcement of previous historiographic arguments on republicanism but as part of a larger shift in how Americans understood debt and risk. Americans in the colonial period despised debt, viewing it as sinful. Then, the economic crisis of the 1780s accelerated a trend that had begun at the end of the Seven Years' War to view nonpayment as a business instead of a moral failure. Livingston never embraced any part of this gradual reinterpretation and instead continued to denounce debt as a moral failing. Of course, he had enriched himself by suing debtors and struggling merchants in the economic collapse of the 1760s. His revolutionary experiences with debt and his challenges in keeping his family stable during the war reinforced that older colonial mindset: it would be a personal failing if he could not support his family or pay off his own debts. For example, in February 1787 he wrote his family doctor for a summary of his account, because "as of most things in the world I detest the thoughts of dying in debt." He promised to pay within six months, even though he did not "at present abound in cash."[39]

Livingston's former attorney general William Paterson, who reopened his private practice and represented dozens of creditors after the war, returned to the public spotlight to challenge Abraham Clark's plans alongside his former political ally. Publishing an essay "On Legal Order," Paterson agreed with Livingston that paper would always depreciate as it had during the Revolution, and he distrusted legislators who acted primarily for their own benefit. In addition, Paterson asserted that no scarcity of money existed, given that legislators continually voted themselves pay increases, laborers earned more than they had during the war, and "people of all ranks purchase from foreign manufacturers and are emulous to excel in dress, in living, and in all fashionable and expensive amusements." A group of Cumberland County residents agreed with Livingston and Paterson on the availability of currency, and they published an extensive memorial to that effect in response to Livingston's editorials. The Cumberland petitioners believed that the economy would cure itself and that paper money would stymie the acquisition of specie. Moreover, they worried that paper money would further sink the economy by destroying the state's credit and encouraging people to buy more European luxuries. In fact, Paterson had recommended a "decrease of money," which would "introduce a spirit of industry and frugality [and] restrain luxury, extravagance, and thoughtless profusion." Encouraging debtors to spend more and tempting them into "knavish acts" would endanger the stability of law, something that Paterson and Livingston had desperately tried to protect during the Revolution.[40]

Other responses to Primitive Whig's essays portrayed Livingston and Paterson as out of touch. One writer found little common sense in Livingston's belief that debtors hoped for paper money so that they could pay back less than they borrowed. Rather, the payment of taxes, not personal debt, was driving debtors to paper money. Moreover, depreciation was not preordained; the land bank plan held no relation to the turbulent revolutionary inflation but instead provided a secure means for men to repay their debts with a strong and legal currency. Clark buttressed this view with the publication of a pamphlet, *The True Policy*, that outlined the need for paper money and the reasoning by which the hard-money advocates sought to disparage those who needed the government to work to relieve the burdens of taxation.[41]

The bill to create the land bank passed the General Assembly in March 1786, but the Legislative Council voted it down 8 to 5, with most of the opposition coming from West Jersey. As president of the Council, Livingston had a vote but routinely declined to exercise it except in cases of a tie. In this case, he broke a tie to move the bill to a final reading but abstained from voting on the final version, likely knowing that he had mobilized enough West Jersey votes against it. Outraged citizens dragged Livingston's effigy through the streets of Elizabethtown.[42]

Clark believed that the political mobilization of disenchanted debtors would cause the Council to change its mind. Over the next two months, mounting pressure from the electorate convinced many legislators to alter their stance and support the land bank—including Livingston himself. If, as he declared in a letter to an assemblyman, the state would comply with the 1785 congressional requisition, "emit such a sum of paper currency as would not prove inconsistent with that compliance," and ensure that it be redeemed with "a reasonable prospect of its maintaining its credit and not enable every knave to defraud his neighbor," then he would support its passage. He even claimed that the paper would "relieve many honest people in distress . . . without injury to the commonwealth." Of course, Livingston had always believed the exact opposite; but, as a realistic politician, he recognized that his would have been one of the sole remaining voices against it.[43]

New Jersey therefore joined Pennsylvania, New York, the Carolinas, and Rhode Island in setting up land banks that emitted paper money during the critical Confederation period. The state established loan offices in each county that allowed borrowers to mortgage their land for loans at 6 percent interest for twelve years, the proceeds of which would circulate as legal tender. When the offices began operation in November 1786, applications quickly overwhelmed the available supply of money. (Ironically, anti-paper legislators Joseph Ellis and Franklin Davenport arrived promptly at the Gloucester loan office with their applications ready for processing.) Initially, the paper held its value because of its relation to the land and to the limits placed on the amount of both individual loans and the total emission, restraints that prevented the type of unbridled printing practiced by Congress before 1780.[44]

These limitations likely encouraged Livingston to concede that Clark had outmaneuvered him and that failure to compromise would end his political career. Livingston continued to believe in his obligation to serve in New Jersey to push for his vision for the nation. Even though he had expressed his "ardent passion" to leave public life as recently as November 1783, he nevertheless, in that same month, considered that the state would be better served by "an old hand . . . than a new one" and assented to serve once again as governor. He used a similar argument in March 1785, in the midst of the battle over the land bank, when he declined Congress's offer of appointment as minister to Holland, where his language skills and wartime contacts would have been useful. Livingston at first cited his age (sixty-two) but also expressed his deep desire to honor the long-standing faith New Jerseyans had placed in him. Despite the "many disagreeable truths" he had "told them respecting their conduct as to public faith and integrity," he believed his long tenure as governor made him a more effective leader than others. Of course, as New Jersey Congressman Charles Stewart knew, there were "persons in the state who would wish you abroad to make room for a new governor." In the 1786 election, Abraham Clark received eight votes for governor from those who had hoped to see Livingston at The Hague instead of in Trenton.[45]

Clark's popularity was based on his support for the land bank and a variety of other measures that Livingston begrudgingly accepted as his influence declined. The most important of these was the "bull law," which allowed debtors to pay creditors in goods instead of cash, thereby circumventing auctions of goods at less than half their value. After the passage of the land bank bill and Clark's election to Congress in 1786, the new legislature repealed the bull law, an action that coincided with the eventual depreciation of the loan office currency, something Clark claimed would not happen. The currency declined between 10 and 15 percent from its par value, a significant amount, though far less than the 80 percent drop in Rhode Island's currency. Still, in a blow to those who relied on trade with New York, merchants there refused to accept New Jersey money. Livingston complained years later to John Jay of the "rotten part" played by New Jersey's legislature "with our paper currency." Combined with New York's own fluctuations, depreciation made it "prejudicial to an honest man to purchase any commodity which is daily fluctuating in value."[46]

Paper money became a rallying point that forced Livingston and national elites to reassess their understanding of debt, Congress's role, and the actions of the legislatures in their respective states. In New Jersey, future senator John Rutherfurd believed "Jersey is outrageous" for refusing congressional requisitions. After the legislature passed the land bank and bull law, Rutherfurd published *Notes on the State of New Jersey* (August 1786), in which he lambasted the legislature for sinking the state's credit and supporting "fraudulent measure[s]" that defrauded creditors and "destroyed all credit and confidence both in and without the state."[47] Rutherfurd was in good company. Many observers across the nation feared the "excess of democracy" that had pressured legislators to acquiesce to the demands of debtors at the expense of the federal government. Thomas Paine warned that the proceedings of the Pennsylvania legislature "are marked with such vehemence of party spirit and rancorous prejudice" that no country could survive under "such manifest misconduct."[48] In New Jersey, where nearly all white men could vote, the encroachment of the lower classes into the political arena had been more pervasive and therefore increasingly worrisome for Livingston and other Jersey elites. For those in less egalitarian states, such as James Madison, the realization of a need for change came relatively late. Madison adopted a radical reform agenda only after he returned to Virginia from Congress in 1783 and struggled with his own legislature and others who refused to fund and support national unity. Under certain circumstances, Madison believed in a nationalist agenda and argued emphatically about the larger problem of a lack of civic virtue, just as Livingston had. However, Madison realized that the impasse on important national issues came from a lack of congressional power to execute decisions, not a lack of virtue. Trade and taxation issues dominated Madison's thinking and undergirded his agenda at the Constitutional Convention. An underfunded government could not negotiate on a world stage, battle pirates in the Mediterranean, or force Britain to comply with the Paris Treaty. Likewise, Madison and Jefferson both saw westward movement as critical for the nation's future. A strong federal government could effectively battle Spain for control of the Mississippi and ensure the nation's growth. The root of the problem lay in the state governments, in which individual interests prohibited solutions like the federal impost and forced men like Madison to turn to a renegotiation of the federal compact.[49]

Like Madison, Livingston believed that the "perpetual variations of the manner of paying or rather not paying our public creditors have been so multiplied by our different legislatures." Because New Jerseyans seemed to be interested only in the "science of getting money" printed through the legislature, Livingston understood the problems that Congress faced in trying to buttress the nation's independence.[50] However, Livingston's long tenure in state government gave him a perspective different from Madison's. The solution was not necessarily to dilute the power of the common people in a new federal government by expanding electoral districts to eliminate "incompetent legislators" who had passed "too many laws" that had damaged the nation's integrity. Rather, Livingston's road to becoming a Federalist more closely followed his interest in building an efficient government instead of reinforcing a republican citizenry. As the nation's longest-serving revolutionary governor, Livingston had long contended with legislative self-interest and understood how to govern effectively with an uncooperative legislature. Governmental bodies like the Privy Council and the Council of Safety allowed him to bypass the legislature and use his position within state government to his advantage. His stronger executive authority made the government more efficient. Thus, instead of seeing the debates over finances in the critical period as the reason for radical constitutional reforms, historians must look beyond the money, as Livingston did. Concerns with the legislature, the failures of Congress, and New Jersey's own uniquely vulnerable position during the Revolution influenced Livingston's acceptance of the federalism that Madison would eventually bring to the Constitutional Convention.[51]

Livingston was already predisposed to promote Madison's brand of federalism; his original support of the royalist position in 1775 arose from his perception of the dangers represented by Parliament's meddling in American affairs and its usurpation of the king's prerogatives. Like Alexander Hamilton and James Wilson, Livingston believed a new constitution could restore proper government by eliminating legislative tyranny and creating a strong executive office. His wartime experiences had only reinforced these beliefs; a true republican citizenry might be too difficult to create. New Jersey became one of four states to support Hamilton's plan of creating a life term for the presidency and insulating the executive as a strong check against legislative excesses. The powerful presidential system Livingston supported in the new government created real power for the American executive branch, something British kings never achieved.[52]

Roger Brown's interpretation of the desire for government efficiency and the revived spirit of royalism aligns with Madison's determination to free Congress from its reliance on individual states—exactly the ends Livingston tried to achieve by carving out power for himself throughout the war as the individual legislator could not be trusted. Thus, Livingston's path toward federalism was not a campaign to protect creditor rights or utilize republicanism to create a stronger citizenry but one to create a stronger national state that could defend American interests against European actors without interference from legislative excesses. As Massachusetts governor James Bowdoin advocated to Livingston in July 1785, Congress needed to be "vested with more efficient powers" concerning "commerce and our national credit." This stronger federal state would control national finances and commerce, and it would exercise stronger authority over the military, all powers that Livingston had enlarged for himself during the war. Livingston argued this point to legislators in August 1788: in the aftermath of the Revolution, the nation had "been in eminent danger of losing the great and important blessings to be expected from Independence" because of the absence of "an efficient national government." The Constitution provided hope for "reestablishment of public faith and private credit, of being respected abroad and revered at home." In a rebuke to their previous behavior, he warned that legislators needed to encourage and promote the nation's growth by abstaining "most religiously and inflexibly" from enacting laws that "aim at the relief of the distresses of some individuals at the expense and to the view of others."[53]

* * *

The opportunity to create a more efficient national government came when Virginia called for a national discussion on congressional trade power. Legislators jumped at the chance to reorient trade policies that hurt New Jersey and sent a delegation headed by Abraham Clark to the Annapolis meeting in September 1786. With only five states in attendance, the convention dissolved, but it called for wider discussions to reform the Articles of Confederation. Clark readily agreed, as did Livingston, but for different reasons. Both saw the need for an independent Congress, but Livingston wanted that Congress to limit the power of the states whereas Clark hoped an empowered Congress could reduce taxation on the states.[54]

In late 1786, after word of Shays' Rebellion reached New Jersey, Livingston wrote to William Churchill Houston that he had "strange forebodings of calamitous times." He had recently settled into the more relaxed pace of the peacetime governorship, which allowed him "to return to my library and rural solitude," pleasures he enjoyed "with infinitely greater satisfaction than any posts or titles which it is in the power of men to confer upon me." Yet he accepted the need to call a national convention to reframe not just trade policies but also the larger government system to ensure a stable country able to collect taxes, pay its debts, and act independently of the unstable legislatures. Livingston, however, was not New Jersey's first choice to attend the Constitutional Convention. In November, legislators had approved the appointments of David Brearley, William Churchill Houston, William Paterson, and John Neilson. Ultimately, Neilson declined his appointment, leading the legislature to appoint Livingston and Abraham Clark a week before the Convention began. Clark believed his recent election to Congress was incompatible with serving at Philadelphia and declined, leaving Livingston, Paterson, Houston, and Brearley to represent New Jersey. Livingston had a strong relationship with Houston, who had served in the Continental Congress and later joined the governor on the Council of Safety in 1778. Livingston had also worked closely with Brearley, chief justice of the New Jersey Supreme Court, and of course he counted Paterson as his closest political ally.[55]

Although the Constitutional Convention began on May 25, Livingston decided to stay in Trenton until the legislative session ended and did not arrive in Philadelphia until June 5. Jonathan Dayton came two weeks after Livingston to replace the ailing Houston. In this national assembly, Livingston served with no members of his extended familial networks. Eleven members from other states were known to him from his service in the First and Second Continental Congresses from 1774 to 1776, including Robert Morris, with whose family his daughter Kitty had lived. Yet, even though the New Jersey governor was unknown personally to many delegates, James Madison commented to Livingston's first biographer that "there was a predisposition in all to manifest the respect due to the celebrity of his name."[56]

As during his previous service in Philadelphia, Livingston's speaking abilities did not match his wit with the pen. Neither James Madison nor the Convention's official secretary recorded any speech delivered by Livingston on the floor during his eleven weeks there. Madison reminisced that he himself had only a passing acquaintance with Livingston, though Livingston's fame as the author of the *Independent Reflector* preceded him, as did his service as a trustee of the College of New Jersey while Madison studied there. Georgia delegate William Pierce recorded that Livingston, though "a Man of the first rate talents," was "no Orator, and seems little acquainted with the guiles of policy," even though his "writings teem with satyr and a neatness of style." In Pierce's opinion, Livingston appeared "rather to indulge a sportiveness of wit, than a strength of thinking." The sketch sent to France's minister of foreign affairs was kinder, citing Livingston's education, patriotism, and preference to support "the public good" over "bad laws."[57]

Livingston's silence remains curious because New Jersey's delegation challenged Madison's Virginia Plan and began one of the most significant debates in the Convention over the issue of representation. David Brearley, Jonathan Dayton, and especially William Paterson took the lead in advocating for equal representation in any potential national legislature. Paterson, though, was no advocate of states' rights; he feared that larger and more economically sound states would dominate the new government, prevent small states from receiving equal shares of impost revenue and western lands, and thereby increase the tax burden already shouldered by New Jerseyans. Paterson and a coalition of delegates from small states rejected Madison's plan for a bicameral legislature with proportional representation and instead supported a unicameral legislature with a single vote for each state. Though Livingston sat with Paterson on June 15, when he announced the New Jersey plan, no evidence points to Livingston's participation in its formulation. His interest in the efficiency of the federal government would have to be balanced with New Jersey's interests and the potential for ratification; he would have likely supported Paterson because he believed New Jersey needed protection from the larger states and a share of federal lands and revenue. According to one historian, the plan's defeat four days later did not end debates on Paterson's ideas but actually began them. Believing that "much remains to be done and the work is full of labor and difficulty," Paterson remained in Philadelphia over the Convention's Independence Day recess to consider a compromise plan while Livingston returned to Liberty Hall. Weighing the fact that New Jersey, Delaware, Maryland, and Connecticut might not approve proportional representation or ratify it in a final document, Madison moved to adopt equal representation in the Senate in the Great Compromise. Livingston's absence from Philadelphia from July 3 to 21 left him out of the decision making on both the representation issue and the three-fifths compromise that awarded representatives in the House of Representatives based on a proportion of each state's enslaved population.[58]

When Livingston returned to Philadelphia in late July, he seemed more intent on spending time with his daughter Kitty and her husband, Matthew Ridley, whom she had married in April. Livingston was absent again from July 27 to August 6 while visiting Ridley's country home in Maryland. After his return on August 6, Livingston devoted himself more productively to the Convention's business. Madison recalled that Livingston had been "placed on important committees, where it may be presumed he had an agency and a due influence." Livingston chaired two committees that proposed major compromises on the payment of state debts, the status of the militia, and the continuation of the Atlantic slave trade.[59]

One of those committees resolved two of the major efficiency problems—state debts and militia service—that Livingston had struggled with in New Jersey. The committee recommended that the federal government should assume all debts incurred by the states for the prosecution of the Revolution, a proposal that the Convention unanimously endorsed. Livingston's friend Gouverneur Morris and other federalists readily supported this idea because it centered power on the federal system and allowed for the systematic improvement of the nation's credit by enabling the new government to service all outstanding loans. This issue had been a constant vexation for Livingston because New Jersey's legislators had always bent to the short-term interests of their constituents and had never made hard choices about payment of debts. Livingston then echoed the arguments of Madison and Hamilton who had seen the inefficiencies of government during the war. Hamilton especially, serving on Washington's general staff, understood the chaos created in the military when the states refused to fund the army. Livingston too believed strongly in the need for the national government to secure its own source of revenue and voted to give the federal government power to set import and export tariffs, to bar the states from enacting the same, and, most important, to prohibit the states from issuing paper money. After the Constitution went into effect, the federal government financed all its debt payments on tariff revenue, effectively reducing the debt burden on individual Americans and thereby allowing many states to lower their effective tax rates to prewar levels. The steady payment of the debt at its par value created a median of exchange, backed by taxes, which resisted depreciation.[60]

The committee's second task, to provide Congress with the power to make laws to organize and regulate the militia, likewise addressed frustrations Livingston had experienced during the war when he could not convince legislators to equip or deploy the state's militia. Particularly in the wake of Shays' Rebellion, many feared the new government would use the military to overpower the states, while others, especially Madison, saw an effective militia as a national tool in the service of everyone. Livingston argued that federal standards would negate the supply, training, and recruitment issues seen in wartime New Jersey. Therefore, in supporting a regulated militia, Livingston adhered to the federalist idea of interdependency between military and financial issues: the federal government could not efficiently support itself without being able to enforce the laws. Despite apprehensions by some delegates, the Convention overwhelmingly approved Livingston's plan for congressional regulation of the militia; however, in a bow to concerns over the power of the federal government, it reserved the appointment of officers and issues of training to the states under regulations approved by Congress.[61]

Livingston's more memorable August committee developed a compromise on slavery, the issue that had created fissures in the Convention over the past month. In what some historians have called the "dirty compromise," Livingston's committee agreed to extend the life of the Atlantic slave trade in exchange for commerce and trade concessions that benefited New Englanders and, by default, New Jerseyans. Maryland's Luther Martin began this debate by proposing to limit the slave trade through the imposition of a tax on imported slaves, citing fears that the already approved three-fifths compromise would increase the number of slaves and thereby the chances of slave revolt. New Englanders vigorously opposed Martin's plan, even though their states had already prohibited the slave trade. They profited from shipping southern products to the Caribbean and Europe and therefore found common cause with their compatriots in the Deep South, who made it known that any restriction on the slave trade would precipitate South Carolina's exit from the Union. Of course, Madison and his fellow Virginians had prohibited the trade before the Revolution to shore up falling tobacco prices and reduce the possibility of slave rebellion. Moreover, after the war, Virginians had a surplus of slaves and hoped to sell them in the newly acquired western territories instead of continuing importation.[62]

South Carolina, though, needed northern help to defeat export taxes that threatened the steady trade of its rice into the Atlantic World. New Englanders, whose ships carried slave products, readily agreed to support the Deep South on eliminating export duties, as did Livingston, but they needed something in exchange. They had opposed the Virginia plan's required two-thirds congressional vote to pass tariff and navigation laws, fearing that their commercial interests might be restricted. Therefore, Livingston's committee brought forward a four-pronged compromise that aligned New England and the Deep South: export taxes would be prohibited, the slave trade would continue unfettered by the federal government until at least 1800 (later amended to 1808), slave imports could be taxed, and a congressional majority could set future tariff laws.[63]

Livingston's appointment to this committee put him in a difficult posi-

No state shall, without the consent of Congress, ✗ imposts or duties on imports or exports, and with such consent, but to the use of the treasury of the United States, ✗ keep troops nor ships of war in time of peace, nor enter into any agreement or compact with another state, nor with any foreign power, nor engage in any war, unless it shall be actually invaded by enemies, or the danger of invasion be so imminent, as not to admit of delay until the Congress can be consulted.

II.

Sect. 1. The executive power shall be vested in a president of the United States of America. He shall hold his office during the term of four years, and, together with the vice-president, chosen for the same term, be elected in the following manner ~

Each state shall appoint, in such manner as the legislature thereof may direct, a number of electors, equal to the whole number of senators and representatives to which the state may be entitled in Congress: but no senator or representative shall be appointed an elector, nor any person holding an office of trust or profit under the United States.

The electors shall meet in their respective states, and vote by ballot for two persons, of whom one at least shall not be an inhabitant of the same state with themselves. And they shall make a list of all the persons voted for, and of the number of votes for each, which list they shall sign and certify, and transmit sealed to the seat of the general government, directed to the president of the senate. The president of the senate shall in the presence of the senate and house of representatives open all the certificates, and the votes shall then be counted. The person having the greatest number of votes shall be the president, if such number be a majority of the whole number of electors appointed; and if there be more than one who have such majority, and have an equal number of votes, then the house of representatives shall immediately chuse by ballot one of them for president; and if no person have a majority, then from the five highest on the list the said house shall in like manner chuse the president. But in chusing the president, the votes shall be taken by states, and not by persons, the representation from each state having one vote. A quorum for this purpose shall consist of a member or members from two-thirds of the states, and a majority of all the states shall be necessary to a choice. In every case, after the choice of the president by the representatives, the person having the greatest number of votes of the electors shall be the vice-president. But if there should remain two or more who have equal votes, the senate shall chuse from them by ballot the vice-president.

The Congress may determine the time of chusing the electors, and the day on which they shall give their votes, but the election shall be on the same day throughout the United States.

No person except a natural born citizen, or a citizen of the United States, at the time of the adoption of this constitution, shall be eligible to the office of president; neither shall any person be eligible to that office who shall not have attained to the age of thirty-five years, and been fourteen years a resident within the United States.

In case of the removal of the president from office, or of his death, resignation, or inability to discharge the powers and duties of the said office, the same shall devolve on the vice-president, and the Congress may by law provide for the case of removal, death, resignation or inability, both of the president and vice-president, declaring what officer shall then act as president, and such officer shall act accordingly, until the disability be removed, or the period for electing another president arrive, or a President be elected.

The president shall, at stated times, receive a fixed compensation for his services, which shall neither be encreased nor diminished during the period for which he shall have been elected.

Before he enter on the execution of his office, he shall take the following oath or affirmation: "I ———, do solemnly swear (or affirm) that I will faithfully execute the office of president of the United States, and will to the best of my judgment and power, preserve, protect and defend the constitution of the United States."

Sect. 2. The president shall be commander in chief of the army and navy of the United States, and of the militia of the several states. He may require the opinion, in writing, of the principal officer in each of the executive departments, upon any subject relating to the duties of their respective offices, when called into the actual service of the United States, and he shall have power to grant reprieves and pardons for offences against the United States, except in cases of impeachment.

He shall have power, by and with the advice and consent of the senate, to make treaties, provided two-thirds of the senators present concur; and he shall nominate, and by and with the advice and consent of the senate, shall appoint ambassadors, other public ministers and consuls, judges of the supreme court, and all other officers of the United States, whose appointments are not herein otherwise provided for, which shall be established by law. And the president shall have power to fill up all vacancies that may happen during the recess of the senate, by granting commissions which shall expire at the end of their next session.

Sect. 3. He shall from time to time give to the Congress information of the state of the union, and recommend to their consideration such measures as he shall judge necessary and expedient; he may, on extraordinary occasions, convene both houses, or either of them, and in case of disagreement between them, with respect to the time of adjournment, he may adjourn them to such time as he shall think proper; he shall receive ambassadors and other public ministers; he shall take care that the laws be faithfully executed, and shall commission all the officers of the United States.

Sect. 4. The president, vice-president and all civil officers of the United States, shall be removed from office on impeachment for, and conviction of treason, bribery, or other high crimes and misdemeanors.

III.

Sect. 1. The judicial power of the United States, both in law and equity, shall be vested in one supreme court, and in such inferior courts as the Congress may from time to time ordain and establish. The judges, both of the supreme and inferior courts, shall hold their offices during good behaviour, and shall, at stated times, receive for their services, a compensation, which shall not be diminished during their continuance in office.

Sect. 2. The judicial power shall extend to all cases, both in law and equity, arising under this constitution, the laws of the United States, and treaties made, or which shall be made, under
their

William Livingston's copy of a draft from the 1787 Constitutional Convention's Committee of Style, page 3 of 4. Image #74650. Courtesy of the New-York Historical Society.

tion. His fellow Jersey delegates had opposed the three-fifths compromise that diluted northern power at the national level, and a continuation of the slave trade could mean further growth of southern power. However, as a slaveholder who had made his fortune as a lawyer to the shipping industry, Livingston brought a unique perspective that in the end benefited New Jersey. The state's other delegates joined the Upper South and border North in voting against extending the slave trade, which was already outlawed in New Jersey. The more important prize to Livingston was the simple majority vote in Congress for commercial regulations that protected New Jerseyans from high taxes in New York and Philadelphia.[64]

Livingston's service on this important committee had special significance in the light of his involvement in the abolition movement. Discussions of abolition had begun in the late 1600s among Quakers in Pennsylvania and West Jersey, though serious debate on the issue did not come until the 1760s. On the eve of the Revolution, the Philadelphia Yearly Meeting of the Society of Friends banned its members from holding slaves and campaigned to convince non-Quakers to support abolition as well. The war with Britain gave Quakers a rhetorical opportunity to compare the plight of the enslaved American colonists with that of enslaved Africans. Prominent Jersey Quaker Samuel Allinson used this argument in 1778 when he began a long-term dialogue with Livingston that eventually convinced the governor of the comparison's validity. Livingston became Allinson's ally, agreeing that slavery "is utterly inconsistent both with the principles of Christianity and humanity"; he found it "particularly odious and disgraceful" among Americans who had "idolized liberty." He asked the legislature to consider measures to end slavery, but the military situation in New Jersey provided an excuse to defer action, especially as any move toward abolition would have angered already disgruntled constituents.[65]

Pennsylvania's passage of a gradual abolition law in 1780 spurred a wider discourse in New Jersey's newspapers on the merits of slave freedom. Quaker abolitionist and legislator John Cooper argued forcefully for freedom, while Presbyterian minister Jacob Green challenged patriots to adhere to the rhetoric that they espoused. In response, opponents warned that abolition would invite slave rebellion and an apocalyptic end for Jersey whites. Green countered that slaveholders were more threatening to Americans than slaves and reiterated that Americans needed to uphold the values stated in the Declaration. Green, however, realized the futility of battling against slavery in the midst of a destructive war.[66]

At war's end, Connecticut, New Hampshire, and Rhode Island passed gradual abolition laws, and Livingston redoubled his efforts to attack slavery. In 1785, John Jay, Alexander Hamilton, and other elites formed the New York Manumission Society, and Livingston applied for membership the following year, calling slavery "an indelible blot" upon humanity. He also aligned himself with Quaker abolitionists who had reinvigorated the Pennsylvania Abolition Society to spearhead a proposal to end the slave trade and enact gradual abolition. Ultimately, the plan failed because of continued economic instability and opposition from slave-rich East Jersey. Livingston also identified a "fatal error": the sale of confiscated loyalist-owned slaves at the end of the war. Livingston argued that these sales for the state's benefit gave "greater sanction to legitimate the practice" and that legislators could not allow the state to profit from slavery and simultaneously mandate that their constituents abandon the institution to their own economic detriment.[67]

Victory for Livingston finally came in 1786, when the legislature banned the slave trade and approved a series of reforms, ranging from fewer manumission restrictions to better slave treatment. These achievements were won by abandoning gradual abolition. Whatever his own personal hopes, Livingston's "experience in business and especially in political affairs" had taught him that when the demand to obtain everything runs "the risk of obtaining nothing, it is then prudence not to insist upon it but to get what we can and which obtained paves the way for procuring the rest."[68] He reminded Quaker James Pemberton, "Rome was not built in a day" and slavery needs "more than a day to abolish."[69]

This 1786 legislative battle to end the slave trade illustrates Livingston's practice as a peacetime politician. His acceptance of one victory on a path toward a greater one in the future may have influenced his work at the Constitutional Convention. The slave trade, the most reviled part of the institution, was easier to outlaw because Americans had imported few slaves since the beginning of the Revolution and saw slim gain in restarting the trade. Likewise, expanding the availability of manumission did little harm to slaveholders yet gave West Jersey Quakers the ability to begin dismantling the institution. In the end, Livingston might have thought that the constitutional compromise for a future end of the slave trade in exchange for immediate and important economic concessions for New Jersey to be equitable, even though he opposed slavery.[70]

On a personal level, Livingston's work on the committee might have accelerated his efforts against the institution in his own household. As late as

1785, while fighting for abolition in New Jersey, he had inquired about buying two slaves to work at Liberty Hall. Instead of purchasing them, he acquired the indenture of a German servant, Nicholas Henry Wickessen, who, after stealing food from Livingston for three months, made his escape in late April 1786, just at the beginning of planting season. Even though Livingston complained to John Jay about the difficulty of finding qualified laborers, he freed his two slaves, an adult woman named Bell and her male child, Lambert, a month after he returned from the Constitutional Convention. However, even though he had promised both publicly and privately to work to abolish slavery—and held up the manumission of his own slaves as evidence—in early 1790 he agreed to take on several of his daughter Kitty's slaves after the death of her husband. He never offered an explanation.[71]

*   *   *

After more than three months of debate, Livingston and the rest of the New Jersey delegation signed the Constitution and reported to the legislature that they had reached an equitable agreement with the other states. Personally, the governor felt his long absence from home "will be worth it" for the future, even if his personal affairs had been neglected because some of his fellow delegates were "more pleased with their own speeches than they can prevail upon anybody else."[72] From late September until late November, New Jersey-ans, along with the rest of the nation, debated the Constitution among themselves and in print. A letter from Salem County reprinted in the *Pennsylvania Herald* remarked that "nothing is talked of here either in public or private but the New Constitution." Livingston's friend Elias Boudinot judged the final document, considering "the difficulty of reconciling thirteen jarring interests," to be better than he expected.[73]

The print debate highlighted several of Livingston's concerns—the excesses of the legislature, paper money, and national taxes—and predicted that the Constitution would be a boon for New Jersey. For example, Cassius declared in the *New-Jersey Journal* that the Constitution prevented "the encroachments of puerile legislatures" and created a foundation to build national happiness. Marcus agreed and suggested that the document's only opponents would be "those who enjoy state consequence which would be lost in the assemblies of the states"; their "narrow vision . . . cannot extend . . . to continental concerns."[74] A Salem County correspondent took up the matter of state-issued paper money, arguing that the Constitution would "guard against that great instrument of fraud."[75] Finally, commentators wrote extensively about the ways in which the founding document regulated commerce to New Jersey's advantage and allowed for equitable profit sharing from western lands among all the states.[76]

The preservation of equal representation in at least one branch of Congress, the intent of Paterson's original New Jersey plan, delighted most New Jerseyans. The most extensive pamphlet published on the question, by A Farmer of New-Jersey, argued that the new federal government would protect minority interests and ensure that both the Union and New Jersey could thrive. Just as Georgia could benefit from protection against Indian attacks, the additional revenue from national duties alone would lower taxes in New Jersey and eliminate the major complaints of the mid-1780s.[77]

Anti-federalist agitation remained limited in New Jersey. Livingston received word that Virginians had mobilized against ratification, but he thought the opposition was more about that state losing "domination over the smaller states" and thereby reducing "the Dominion Strut to a level with the humble and natural gait of her Sister States." New Jersey had little to gain from staying in a confederation without the Constitution. Some critics, like Abraham Clark, opposed parts of the new government, citing presidential power, the cost of paying the new representatives, and the limits imposed on state legislators. But even Clark realized that the benefits outweighed the potential costs and stayed silent on the question of ratification. Seeing little opposition, Livingston said nothing on the issue in personal correspondence or in public essays. Even though he had maintained a strong relationship with John Jay, there is no evidence that he collaborated or even communicated with Jay regarding the Federalist Papers published in his native New York.[78]

The *Pennsylvania Gazette* reported in mid-October that its correspondents traveling through New Jersey had encountered only one opponent of the Constitution—and that person was actually a Pennsylvanian. Petitions to the legislature unanimously supported adoption, and, in late November 1787, New Jerseyans elected thirty-nine delegates to discuss the new government. None had been involved in the earlier paper-money debate, and few had been active at all in state politics after the Revolution; only one member of the General Assembly and one member of the Legislative Council had been elected. Livingston played no part in their deliberations, returning to Liberty Hall for the entire month of December. The delegates began their debates on December 11, 1787, in a Trenton tavern and emerged on December 18 with a unanimous vote to ratify, making New Jersey the third state to do so. The state also offered a ten-square-mile piece of land on the Delaware for a new national capital. Reports in the *Pennsylvania Packet* claimed that "the yeomanry of New Jersey love liberty"; because "every field in that state had been dyed with the blood of its militia" in the Revolution, a unanimous vote by its convention surely meant that the Constitution was a just and an equitable arrangement for the new nation.[79]

*　*　*

The winter of 1787–1788 marked a change for Livingston. In February 1788, he remarked that "Mrs. Livingston & I have never spent so solitary a winter" as this past one at Liberty Hall with little company and little travel. Though he believed both of them were "reconciled to solitude beyond most people," he uncharacteristically claimed that "too much of it is irksome." Despite his frequent expressions of desire for rural solitude when in Philadelphia or Trenton, political action remained more alluring. He did carve out time to restart his writing career, working on several new pieces as well as revisiting several speeches he wrote during the Revolution, many of which Mathew Carey included in his magazine, *The American Museum*.[80]

Politics called Livingston from his winter of solitude on two important issues: the still-nagging problem of paper money and the impending 1789 congressional election. By 1788, more conservative forces from West Jersey had taken control of the legislature and confronted a rising tide of inflation from the paper issued two years earlier by the state's land banks. Though inflation never increased to levels seen in New England, Jersey residents worried that the inflated currency would affect the state's economy and wanted the legislature to limit the damage. At this session, Livingston spoke to legislators about the Constitution's power to limit future economic disruption. He challenged them to take actions that accorded with the Constitution and to reject laws that supported individual interests. The West Jersey legislators did just that by blocking the continued issuance of paper money and acting to call in and cancel outstanding bills. The legislature even took some loans out of circulation and by 1789 had reduced the amount of bills and revenue money by a third. These measures started the slow process of reducing paper in circulation and over the next ten years totally removed it. Livingston himself began to loan his own money again, something he had not done since before the Revolution; he likely felt he had a fair chance of receiving payment in hard money or nondepreciated paper.[81]

The disputed congressional election of 1789 was the larger issue Livingston mediated after ratification of the Constitution. New Jersey had been apportioned four representatives in the first Congress and elected them on a statewide ticket. The more conservative West Jersey forces, who later became Federalists that controlled the legislature, rallied around four candidates, including Livingston's long-time friend Elias Boudinot, known as the Junto ticket. Abraham Clark and Jonathan Dayton quickly rose as the two major candidates opposing the Junto with significant support from East Jersey. The Junto soon realized that it would likely gain little support from East Jersey, where Clark remained popular. Likewise, Dayton and Clark knew that West Jersey voters would not support them because Clark had been the driving force behind paper money, rabidly opposed in the West, and because Dayton had speculated in certificates, aligning him with East Jersey debtor interests. Therefore, both sides realized that they needed to secure every possible vote from their respective regions to win.[82]

The election quickly became a dirty affair with the Junto ticket lambasting Abraham Clark for supposedly opposing the Constitution to New Jersey's detriment as well as supporting the land bank in order to allow him to pay his own debts in depreciated paper. Despite these slanderous attacks, Clark's continuing popularity and Dayton's service in the Constitutional Convention proved tough to defeat. Dayton ally Joseph Bloomfield reported that as of late February 1789, Clark and Dayton led the other candidates with 35 and 29 percent of the vote, respectively, not even counting their home county of Essex. Junto supporters countered by supplying preprinted ballots for their people, a stark difference from the voice voting used in East Jersey. Moreover, polls in the West stayed open far longer than in the East. With the Junto ticket still trailing, Livingston, as the head of the Privy Council and the ultimate authority on declaring the election winners, declined to name anyone at the Council's meeting on March 3, 1789, the date appointed to do so. Livingston postponed action until the March 18 meeting, providing more time for ballots to come in from the West after polls had closed in much of the East. At the March 18 meeting, without the results from Essex County reported, Livingston declared the election of the four Junto candidates.[83]

Understandably, many Dayton and Clark supporters denounced Livingston over the election irregularities. Matthias Ogden, a member of the Privy Council from Essex County and Dayton's son-in-law, demanded that Livingston turn over specific details about vote totals and the dates they had been reported. Livingston refused, declaring such a request improper and any impropriety false. Despite Livingston's claims, vote totals in many counties reached 80 to 90 percent of the eligible population, a much higher turnout than in any previous election and therefore suspect. Dayton believed the situation created such resentment in the East that "the present temper and spirit of the people" could increase "into a flame not easily to be extinguished" and "resolve itself into a violent contention and dispute between Eastern and Western New Jersey." Dayton and Clark supporters ultimately applied to Congress, which held the final authority in seating members. After four months of deliberation, the House accepted the four Junto members—a victory for Livingston in his last major decision as governor and the last time he exerted his executive influence through the Privy Council.[84]

*   *   *

Thirteen years as governor had put Livingston in the unique position of dealing with almost every issue to come before New Jersey in its revolutionary moment. This experience had a profound impact on his understanding of the Constitutional Convention and his support of federalism. New Jersey, unlike several other states, needed the Constitution, and Livingston needed it too. Broken by the inflationary wartime currency and further beaten by the postwar economic crisis, Livingston saw his personal battles intersect with the larger legislative ones over the future of the state's currency and economy. His long governorship on the front lines of some of the war's fiercest military, economic, and social battles provided a vantage point distinct from that of most other revolutionary leaders. His consistent condemnation of legislators who neglected the common good and his predisposition for a stronger independent chief executive motivated him to see the need for a stronger federal system to protect New Jersey's interests and to ensure the progress of its citizens along what he believed was the better path forward in independence.

Epilogue

After the controversy concerning the first congressional election, Livingston returned to a simple life at Liberty Hall. He remained entrenched in his library, continuing to tutor himself in French and writing for various publications. He also pursued his love of gardening. Though he had created a model farm at Liberty Hall early on, his return to Elizabethtown after the Revolution brought a much greater engagement with horticulture. He asked everyone possible for seed samples for his garden, especially the harder-to-find plants from Europe. John Jay, for example, returned from his stint in Spain and France with cuttings from various fruit trees and shrubs and with many flower seeds, though Livingston's daughter Sarah cautioned him that European fruits "bear no comparison to those" grown previously at Liberty Hall. Livingston even acquired vegetable seeds from the gardens of Louis XVI, hoping that America's "republican soil" would not subvert "the products of a monarchical climate." Only fishing with Jay and with his grandson Peter took Livingston away from his library and garden.[1]

Politically, Livingston became increasingly marginal in his last two years in office. The legislature reelected him governor in November 1788 and 1789, but after November 1788, he remained at Liberty Hall for all but nine weeks, until his death in July 1790. Aside from a brief flirtation with a possible nomination as vice president, Livingston settled into a state of semi-retirement, believing that he had fulfilled his obligations to the state and to the nation.[2]

Worry over his family replaced concerns over loyalists and monetary policy, as the life choices of his two sons Brockholst and William Jr. (Billy) routinely dissatisfied him. Brockholst, in particular, caused Livingston ongoing frustration. In 1783, Brockholst had finally agreed to read for the bar, succumbing to his father's wishes after his release from British imprisonment following the Huddy affair. He built his new career as a private lawyer in New York but clashed with his father again in 1784 over his choice of a wife, his first of three. This act was particularly devastating to Livingston because he "had placed the greatest hopes of my future happiness in the evening of my life" in Brockholst, only to have his son marry a woman "altogether unworthy of that alliance," a "landlady's daughter." Perhaps remembering his own father's disapproval of his marriage to a woman of lower social standing, William decided to reconcile with Brockholst but only on the condition of not interacting with the new wife. Eventually, Brockholst regained Livingston's respect, becoming a politician in New York in his own right. Livingston likely would have been proud of Brockholst as he eventually became a justice on the New York Supreme Court in 1802. From that position, Thomas Jefferson appointed Brockholst an associate justice of the U.S. Supreme Court, a position he held from 1807 until his death in 1823.[3]

Billy, Livingston's oldest son, never fully redeemed himself in his father's eyes. He remained financially dependent on Livingston, who provided him various government commissions. In his father's twilight years, Billy's gambling and drinking debts became excessive to the point that he engaged in illegal actions in his last office as surrogate of the chancery court. Forced by his father to resign in 1789, Billy fathered an illegitimate daughter, the last straw for Livingston. He disowned Billy and gave him an ultimatum: behave properly for one year or be permanently disowned. For Livingston's last year of life, Billy somehow managed to reform himself, and his father restored his share of the estate less than three weeks before he died. After Livingston's death, though, Billy occupied the family farm in Parsippany and refused to leave. Only a lawsuit filed by Brockholst evicted him in 1792. From there, he served for approximately three years in debtors' prison in Newark before leaving for Long Island, where he managed to acquire a commission as a surrogate. He began to gather Livingston's writings for publication, possibly because he thought he could make money on them, though he never saw the project through.[4]

Livingston's youngest son, John Lawrence, caused him the most stress in his final year at Liberty Hall. Livingston continued to hope that his son had survived the destruction of the *Saratoga* in 1781 and eagerly received a visit in January 1790 from a sailor who claimed to have been captured by Algerian pirates in 1785 and to have been imprisoned for three years until the Spanish liberated him. While in Algiers, he met an American who recounted that pirates had captured him during the American Revolution and that his name was John Livingston. He described his father William, brothers William and Brockholst, and four sisters, all living in New Jersey. Livingston quickly asked John Jay to use his contacts as secretary of foreign affairs to determine the validity of the claim. Jay replied that he believed the sailor had spun a web of lies, hoping for a reward. Piece by piece, Jay discredited the story but still made inquiries in North Africa. Livingston eventually agreed with Jay, yet remained depressed by the bad memories the episode had awoken.[5]

The affair concerning John Lawrence highlighted a larger problem: Livingston felt incredibly alone. He wrote to Jay that he was "so solitary here," with "little inclination to seek society beyond" Liberty Hall, that he hoped to reproach his relations in New York into visiting him in his old age. Of course, the "gaiety and splendor" of the city "affords but little leisure to think of the obscure retirement of any old fellow in New Jersey." Over the previous six months, Livingston had grown lonelier and therefore more susceptible to trickery because his wife, Susannah, had died in July 1789. His distress at her passing and increasing loneliness exacerbated his already deteriorating health. His oldest daughter, Susannah, who had not married, cared for him, as did her sister Kitty, who had returned home after her husband's death in 1789.[6]

In early spring 1790, Brockholst learned that his father's declining health had confined him to Liberty Hall for much of the year. His sister Judith reported that he had "almost lost his memory, asking the same questions, and telling the same stories several times in the space of a day." Brockholst acted quickly to contradict those stories to maintain his father's reputation, but word spread after Livingston's visit to Perth Amboy in May to meet with the Legislative Council. Political allies and friends sent their well wishes to Susannah and hoped to be informed of the governor's condition and the date of his funeral at the earliest moment so that they could plan on attending. The day before Livingston's death, Susannah knew her father would not live much longer. She notified her siblings, but Brockholst could not return from Albany soon enough to see his father one last time. William Livingston died at the age of sixty-six on July 25, 1790, just over one year after his beloved Susannah.[7]

Livingston's will, after he restored Billy, was quite ordinary, dividing his estate equally among his seven living children. He made sure, though, that shares provided to daughters Mary and Judith were controlled by Brockholst and John Jay, respectively, because he did not trust their husbands. Brockholst also received several sentimental items above his share, including books, maps, and a silver hilted sword. Susannah was left a silver coffee pot in recognition of her care during Livingston's illness. His favorite grandson, Peter Jay, was presented with a gold watch to remember him by.[8]

Few remembrances of Livingston focused on his engagement with monetary policy, loyalist prosecutions, or military affairs. Instead, the death notice published in the *New-Jersey Journal* lauded his imagination, his literary accomplishments, his strong moral fiber, and his "political principles altogether republican." Likewise, his epitaph barely mentions his time as governor, citing instead his republicanism and his sacrifice for the good of the nation. This emphasis on sacrifice became important for William Paterson, Livingston's staunch political ally throughout the Revolution, who succeeded him as governor. Paterson wrote a poem as a eulogy to Livingston, describing him as a "man of humanity and courage, of genius and learning . . . who, in devotion to public service, emerged 'second in fame to Washington alone.'" Sacrifice became central to the memory of Livingston: few could review his personal papers without seeing that ideal surface in a multiplicity of ways.[9]

Throughout his life, however, Livingston waged a constant internal battle between the political operative and the solitary writer. Often these personas aligned well, as when his prolific political writings influenced Americans of all classes before and during the Revolution. At the same time, the Livingston who loved to polemicize also loved to draw, paint, and write poetry, pursuits more appropriate for a country gentleman than a politician. At his core, that was the real Livingston. The politician whose life and experiences helped to organize a government on the war's front lines was the real Livingston, too, but more forced at times by circumstance. In the end, his flexible personality in constantly changing roles made him a mostly perfect leader for the times in which he served. But to be remembered as a literary master more than as a politician is likely what Livingston himself would have wanted.

ABBREVIATIONS

Adams Papers

The Adams Papers
*Series I: Diaries: Diary and Autobiography of John
Adams*, ed. Lyman Butterfield et al., 4 vols.
(Cambridge, MA: Harvard University Press, 1961).
Series II: Adams Family Correspondence, ed. Lyman
Butterfield et al. (Cambridge, MA: Harvard
University Press, 1963–).
*Series III: General Correspondence and Other Papers of
the Adams Statesmen*, ed. Robert J. Taylor et al.
(Cambridge, MA: Harvard University Press, 1977–).

AM Papers

New Jersey Department of State, Secretary of State's
Office, AM [Autograph Manuscript] Papers, 1693–
1905, New Jersey State Archives, Trenton
(collection SSTSE052).

BAH MS Collection

New Jersey State Library, Bureau of Archives and
History, Manuscript Collection, 1680s–1970s, New
Jersey State Archives, Trenton (collection
SEDSL006).

Clinton Papers

Henry Clinton Papers, 1736–1850, 304 vols.,
Manuscripts Division, William L. Clements
Library, University of Michigan, Ann Arbor.

DHRC

*The Documentary History of the Ratification of the
Constitution*, vol. 3, *Ratification of the Constitution
by the States: Delaware, New Jersey, Georgia,
Connecticut*, ed. Merrill Jensen (Madison: State
Historical Society of Wisconsin, 1978).

Founders Online

National Archives, *Founders Online*, https://
founders.archives.gov/.

GW

George Washington

HSP	Historical Society of Princeton, New Jersey
JCC	*Journals of the Continental Congress, 1774–1789*, ed. Worthington C. Ford et al., 34 vols. (Washington, DC: GPO, 1904–1937).
Jefferson Papers	*The Papers of Thomas Jefferson*, ed. Julian P. Boyd et al. (Princeton, NJ: Princeton University Press, 1950–).
LDC	*Letters of Delegates to Congress, 1774–1789*, ed. Paul H. Smith et al., 26 vols. (Washington, DC: Library of Congress, 1976–2000).
Madison Papers	*The Papers of James Madison, Congressional Series*, ed. William T. Hutchinson et al., 17 vols. (Chicago: University of Chicago Press; Charlottesville: University Press of Virginia, 1962–1991).
MHS	Massachusetts Historical Society, Boston
Minutes	*Minutes of the Provincial Congress and the Council of Safety of the State of New Jersey [1775–1776]* (Trenton, NJ: Naar, Day & Naar, 1879).
NJA	*New Jersey Archives: Documents Relating to the Colonial, Revolutionary, and Post-Revolutionary History of the State of New Jersey*, 42 vols. (Newark: New Jersey Historical Society, 1880–1949).
NJHS	New Jersey Historical Society, Newark
NJSA	New Jersey State Archives, Trenton
PWL	*The Papers of William Livingston*, ed. Carl E. Prince et al., 5 vols. (Trenton: New Jersey Historical Commission; New Brunswick, NJ: Rutgers University Press, 1979–1988).
RUSCUA	Special Collections and University Archives, Rutgers University Libraries, Rutgers University, New Brunswick, NJ
Washington Papers	*The Papers of George Washington Revolutionary War Series*, ed. Philander D. Chase et al. (Charlottesville: University Press of Virginia, 1985–).
WL	William Livingston
WLP	*William Livingston Papers*, microfilm edition, 25 reels (Ann Arbor, MI: University Microfilms, 1986)

NOTES

Introduction

1. William Livingston (hereafter WL) to John Henry Livingston, September 29, 1778, *PWL*, 2:450–51.

2. David Bernstein, "New Jersey in the American Revolution: The Establishment of a Government Amid Civil and Military Disorder, 1770–1781" (PhD diss., Rutgers University, 1970), examines some of these issues relating to the establishment of governmental authority amid revolutionary crisis. However, Bernstein plays down the interactions between the legislature and the executive, even though he credits Livingston's leadership as the only reason the state survived, which is a bit of an overstatement. He provides a rudimentary analysis of some of the key issues relating to loyalty, but he does not delve deeply into the limits of patriot government in the second half of the war (his project ends in 1781) or examine how the Revolution set New Jersey toward ratification of the Constitution.

3. The last biography published was Theodore Sedgwick, *A Memoir of the Life of William Livingston* . . . (New York: J & J. Harper, 1833). Sedgwick was married to Susan Anne Ridley Sedgwick, Livingston's granddaughter, who lived with Livingston briefly after her mother, Catharine, moved home after her husband died. Livingston has also been the subject of two other works. In 1993, Garland published a largely unrevised 1954 dissertation by Milton Klein, *The American Whig*, which focuses almost exclusively on Livingston before 1773. I rely heavily on Klein's work in my first chapter. In addition, Cynthia Kierner, *Traders and Gentlefolk: The Livingstons of New York, 1675–1790* (Ithaca, NY: Cornell University Press, 1992), surveys multiple generations of Livingstons. In addition, several unpublished dissertations and theses also examine Livingston and his family, which I utilize throughout as well.

4. There has been significant scholarship on the Livingstons in New York and the family's role in building the colony as a political and an economic powerhouse. For example, see Kierner, *Traders and Gentlefolk*; Patricia Joan Gordon, "The Livingstons of New York, 1675–1860: Kinship and Class" (PhD diss., Columbia University, 1959); Mary Lou Lustig, *Privilege and Prerogative: New York's Provincial Elite, 1710–1776* (Madison, NJ: Fairleigh Dickinson University Press, 1995); Lawrence Leder, *Robert Livingston, 1654–1728, and the Politics of Colonial New York* (Chapel Hill: University of North Carolina Press, 1961); Alan Tully, *Forming American Politics: Ideals, Interests, and Institutions in Colonial New York and Pennsylvania* (Baltimore: Johns Hopkins University Press, 1994); Simon Middleton, *From Privileges to Rights: Work and Politics in Colonial New York City* (Philadelphia: University of Pennsylvania Press, 2006); Ned Landsman, *Crossroads of Empire: The Middle Colonies in British North America* (Baltimore: Johns Hopkins University Press, 2010); Dorothy Dillon, *The New York Triumvirate: A Study of the Legal and Political Careers of William Livingston, John Morin Scott, William Smith, Jr.* (New York: Columbia University Press,

1949); Cathy Matson, *Merchants and Empire: Trading in Colonial New York* (Baltimore: Johns Hopkins University Press, 1998); Barnet Schecter, *The Battle for New York: The City at the Heart of the American Revolution* (New York: Walker, 2002).

5. Livingston was related to a multitude of revolutionary leaders, including Robert R. Livingston (cousin; Continental Congress delegate, first U.S. Secretary of Foreign Affairs); John Jay (son-in-law; president of the Continental Congress, ambassador to Spain); Philip Livingston (brother; Continental Congress delegate); Walter Livingston (nephew; Continental Congress delegate, commissioner of the U.S. Treasury); James Duane (nephew-in-law; Continental Congress delegate, mayor of New York City); William Alexander, Lord Stirling (brother-in-law; Continental Army general); and William Duer (nephew-in-law; Continental Congress delegate). He also had personal or business connections with dozens of other holders of federal and state offices.

6. Leonard Lundin, *Cockpit of the Revolution: The War for Independence in New Jersey* (Princeton, NJ: Princeton University Press, 1940); Mark Edward Lender, "The 'Cockpit' Reconsidered: Revolutionary New Jersey as a Military Theater," in *New Jersey in the American Revolution*, ed. Barbara J. Mitnick (New Brunswick, NJ: Rutgers University Press, 2005), 45–46; James J. Gigantino II, "Introduction" in *The American Revolution in New Jersey: Where the Battlefront Meets the Home Front*, ed. James J. Gigantino II (New Brunswick, NJ: Rutgers University Press, 2014), 1–8.

7. Eric Nelson, *Royalist Revolution: Monarchy and the American Founding* (Cambridge, MA: Harvard University Press, 2014), 6–7, 31–37, 149.

8. Social historians have been interested in the movement toward revolution by the lower sort for some time. The following works have strongly influenced this movement as well as my thinking about the role of the individual in this process: Gary Nash, *The Unknown American Revolution: The Unruly Birth of Democracy and the Struggle to Create America* (New York: Viking, 2005); Gary Nash, *The Urban Crucible: Social Change, Political Consciousness, and the Origins of the American Revolution* (Cambridge, MA: Harvard University Press, 1979); Woody Holton, *Forced Founders: Indians, Debtors, Slaves, and the Making of the American Revolution in Virginia* (Chapel Hill: University of North Carolina Press, 1999); T. H. Breen, *American Insurgents, American Patriots: The Revolution of the People* (New York: Hill and Wang, 2010); Ronald Hoffman, *A Spirit of Dissension: Economics, Politics, and the Revolution in Maryland* (Baltimore: Johns Hopkins University Press, 1973); Richard Ryerson, *The Revolution Is Now Begun: The Radical Committees of Philadelphia, 1765–1776* (Philadelphia: University of Pennsylvania Press, 1978); Edward Countryman, *A People in Revolution: The American Revolution and Political Society in New York, 1760–1790* (Baltimore: Johns Hopkins University Press, 1981); Dirk Hoerder, *Crowd Action in Revolutionary Massachusetts, 1765–1780* (New York: Academic Press, 1977); Jack Greene, *Pursuits of Happiness: The Social Development of Early Modern British Colonies and the Formation of American Culture* (Chapel Hill: University of North Carolina Press, 1988).

9. John Shy, *A People Numerous and Armed: Reflections on the Military Struggle for American Independence* (Ann Arbor: University of Michigan Press, 1990), 177, 217–19. The republican synthesis controlled much of revolutionary historiography and influenced the thinking of historians for a generation, especially those who looked at men like Livingston. It is easy to understand how historians saw Livingston through this republican lens, since these themes are constant in his writings. Yet, even though he discussed republican values that influenced his outlook on the war, they are not controlling. For the republican synthesis, see Robert Shalhope, "Toward a Republican Synthesis: The Emergence of an Understanding of Republicanism in

American Historiography," *William and Mary Quarterly* 29.1 (January 1972): 69–72; Daniel Rodgers, "Republicanism: The Career of a Concept," *Journal of American History* 79.1 (June 1992): 34–37; Robert Shalhope, "Republicanism, Liberalism, and Democracy: Political Culture in the Early Republic," *Proceedings of the American Antiquarian Society* 102, pt. 1 (April 1992): 37–57; Jack N. Rakove, "Gordon Wood, the 'Republican Synthesis,' and the Path Not Taken," *William and Mary Quarterly* 44.3 (July 1987): 619–20.

10. Judith Van Buskirk, *Generous Enemies: Patriots and Loyalists in Revolutionary New York* (Philadelphia: University of Pennsylvania Press, 2002).

11. Historical understanding of loyalism has increased significantly in the past two decades. Studies have expanded the definition of loyalty to include African Americans, Native Americans, and situational loyalty as seen in New Jersey and New York. See Maya Jasanoff, *Liberty's Exiles: American Loyalists in the Revolutionary World* (New York: Knopf, 2011); Ruma Chopra, *Unnatural Rebellion: Loyalists in New York City During the Revolution* (Charlottesville: University of Virginia Press, 2011); Jim Piecuch, *Three Peoples, One King: Loyalists, Indians, and Slaves in the Revolutionary South, 1775–1782* (Columbia: University of South Carolina Press, 2008); Cassandra Pybus, *Epic Journeys of Freedom: Runaway Slaves of the American Revolution and Their Global Quest for Liberty* (Boston: Beacon Press, 2006); Robert Calhoon, Timothy Barnes, and George Rawlyke, eds., *Loyalists and Community in North America* (Westport, CT: Greenwood Press, 1994); Joseph Tiedemann, Eugene Fingerhut, and Robert Venables, eds., *The Other Loyalists: Ordinary People, Royalism, and the Revolution in the Middle Colonies, 1763–1787* (Albany: State University of New York Press, 2009); and Gregory Walsh, "Most Boundless Avarice," in Gigantino, ed., *American Revolution in New Jersey.* Foundational works on loyalism that stress ideology or other factors that do not apply to all loyalists include William Nelson, *The American Tory* (Oxford: Clarendon Press, 1961); Wallace Brown, *The King's Friends: The Composition and Motives of American Loyalist Claimants* (Providence, RI: Brown University Press, 1965); Bernard Bailyn, *The Ordeal of Thomas Hutchinson* (Cambridge, MA: Harvard University Press, 1974); Robert Calhoon, *The Loyalists in Revolutionary America, 1760–1781* (New York: Harcourt Brace Jovanovich, 1973); John Ferling, *The Loyalist Mind: Joseph Galloway and the American Revolution* (University Park: Pennsylvania State University Press, 1977).

12. Woody Holton, *Unruly Americans and the Origins of the Constitution* (New York: Hill and Wang, 2007).

13. The creation and meaning of the Constitution has inspired a vibrant historiography. Many recent works have diverged from Gordon Wood's *The Creation of the American Republic, 1776–1787* (Chapel Hill: University of North Carolina Press, 1969) and investigated the relationships between economics and power in the critical postwar period. The following are influential in understanding Livingston's role in the Constitution: Holton, *Unruly Americans*; Lance Banning, *The Sacred Fire of Liberty: James Madison and the Founding of the Federal Republic* (Ithaca, NY: Cornell University Press, 1995); Jack N. Rakove, *James Madison and the Creation of the American Republic* (Glenview, IL: Scott, Foresman/Little, Brown, 1990); Roger Brown, *Redeeming the Republic: Federalists, Taxation, and the Origins of the Constitution* (Baltimore: Johns Hopkins University Press, 1993); Richard Beeman, Stephen Botein, and Edward Carter, eds., *Beyond Confederation: Origins of the Constitution and American National Identity* (Chapel Hill: University of North Carolina Press, 1987); Bruce Mann, *Republic of Debtors: Bankruptcy in the Age of American Independence* (Cambridge, MA: Harvard University Press, 2002); Jack N. Rakove, *Original Meanings: Politics and Ideas in the Making of the Constitution* (New York: Knopf, 1996); Jack N. Rakove, *The Beginnings of National Politics: An Interpretive History of the*

Continental Congress (Baltimore: Johns Hopkins University Press, 1979); Max Edling, *Revolution in Favor of Government: Origins of the U.S. Constitution and the Making of the American State* (New York: Oxford University Press, 2003). Brown, *Redeeming the Republic*, emphasizes the idea of efficiency in government as opposed to the Madisonian interpretations concerning the removal of power from the lower sort advanced by Holton, *Unruly Americans*. For Livingston, though, the two goals intertwined to stop legislative excess.

14. Annette Gordon-Reed, "Writing Early American Lives as Biography," *William and Mary Quarterly* 71.4 (October 2014): 492, 498–99, 503–4, 507–8. Biography as a mode of historical exploration has played a central role since the early nineteenth century when Parson Weems's *Life of George Washington* unleashed "biographical mania" and has remained, as Gordon-Reed argued recently, one of the best ways to effectively engage American history.

Chapter 1

1. Milton Klein, *The American Whig: William Livingston of New York* (New York: Garland, 1993), 4–6; Patricia Joan Gordon, "The Livingstons of New York, 1675–1860: Kinship and Class" (PhD diss., Columbia University, 1959), 1–4; Mary Lou Lustig, *Privilege and Prerogative: New York's Provincial Elite, 1710–1776* (Madison, NJ: Fairleigh Dickinson University Press, 1995), 27; Cynthia Kierner, *Traders and Gentlefolk: The Livingstons of New York, 1675–1790* (Ithaca, NY: Cornell University Press, 1992), 10–19.

2. Gordon, "Livingstons of New York," 5–13, 15–16, 24–29; Lustig, *Privilege and Prerogative*, 27; Theodore Sedgwick, *A Memoir of the Life of William Livingston . . .* (New York: J. & J. Harper, 1833), 24, 38–39; Lawrence Leder, *Robert Livingston, 1654–1728, and the Politics of Colonial New York* (Chapel Hill: University of North Carolina Press, 1961), esp. 211–26; Kierner, *Traders and Gentlefolk*, 20, 22, 24, 39–43.

3. Gordon, "Livingstons of New York," 37–40, 45–46, 54–55, 62, 84; Klein, *American Whig*, 14–15; Sedgwick, *Memoir of William Livingston*, 43; Lustig, *Privilege and Prerogative*, 60–62; Kierner, *Traders and Gentlefolk*, 50–54.

4. Klein, *American Whig*, 31–38; Sedgwick, *Memoir of William Livingston*, 45–46; Gordon, "Livingstons of New York," 76, 84, 91–99, 116; Walter Peterson, "William Livingston: A Study of a Political Center Before, During, and After the Revolution" (master's thesis, University of Iowa, 1948), 1–4; Gloria Bulotti, "William Livingston: American Patriot and Publicist" (master's thesis, Stanford University, 1947), 3–4; Kierner, *Traders and Gentlefolk*, 54, 64–66, 70–71.

5. Sedgwick, *Memoir of William Livingston*, 47; Harold Thatcher, "Social Philosophy of William Livingston" (PhD diss., University of Chicago, 1938), 3; Klein, *American Whig*, 31, 39–48; WL to Noah Welles, May 27, 1742, as cited in Klein, *American Whig*, 48; Bulotti, "William Livingston," 5–8.

6. Gordon, "Livingstons of New York," 119, 128–29; Ned Landsman, *Crossroads of Empire: The Middle Colonies in British North America* (Baltimore: Johns Hopkins University Press, 2010), 186–87; Thatcher, "Social Philosophy of William Livingston," 4, 7–10; Klein, *American Whig*, 57–60, 61–66 (quote on 64); Sedgwick, *Memoir of William Livingston*, 57–58; Bulotti, "William Livingston," 11–15; Kierner, *Traders and Gentlefolk*, 69, 88.

7. WL to Susannah French, November 17, 1744, December 29, 1744, January 1, 1744/45, WL Letterbook, William Livingston Family Collection, microfilm reel 5, MHS.

8. Ibid., August 11 and 14, 1744.

9. Ibid., December 4, 1744; Klein, *American Whig*, 93–100; Sedgwick, *Memoir of William Livingston*, 59; Gordon, "Livingstons of New York," 131–32.

10. Klein, *American Whig*, 66–68, 88–92; Kierner, *Traders and Gentlefolk*, 143. For quote, see Charles Levermore, "The Whigs of Colonial New York," *American Historical Review* 1.2 (January 1896): 241, as cited in Peterson, "William Livingston," 15.

11. Thatcher, "Social Philosophy of William Livingston," 11–12; Klein, *American Whig*, 66–71; Gordon, "Livingstons of New York," 129; Bulotti, "William Livingston," 10–15; Kierner, *Traders and Gentlefolk*, 145.

12. Klein, *American Whig*, 71–79.

13. Ibid., 101–3; Gordon, "Livingstons of New York," 131–32; Peterson, "William Livingston," 8; Bulotti, "William Livingston," 16–17.

14. Klein, *American Whig*, 107–9; Kierner, *Traders and Gentlefolk*, 74, 88.

15. Klein, *American Whig*, 143, 152–53; Sedgwick, *Memoir of William Livingston*, 63–66; Gordon, "Livingstons of New York," 170; Peterson, "William Livingston," 9–10; Bulotti, "William Livingston," 18–19; Thatcher, "Social Philosophy of William Livingston," 14.

16. Klein, *American Whig*, 128–31, 169–71; Simon Middleton, *From Privileges to Rights: Work and Politics in Colonial New York City* (Philadelphia: University of Pennsylvania Press, 2006), 212–13.

17. Alan Tully, *Forming American Politics: Ideals, Interests, and Institutions in Colonial New York and Pennsylvania* (Baltimore: Johns Hopkins University Press, 1994), 126–35; Lustig, *Privilege and Prerogative*, 64–66, 72–73; Kierner, *Traders and Gentlefolk*, 171–72.

18. Middleton, *From Privileges to Rights*, 213–15 (quote on 215); Lustig, *Privilege and Prerogative*, 73; Klein, *American Whig*, 183–85, 325.

19. Peterson, "William Livingston," 15, 18; Klein, *American Whig*, 182, 188–89, 269–71; Lustig, *Privilege and Prerogative*, 80–83; Milton Klein, "Church, State, and Education: Testing the Issue in Colonial New York," *New York History* 45 (1964): 296–97; Thomas Curry, *First Freedoms: Church and State in America to the Passage of the First Amendment* (New York: Oxford University Press, 1986), 121; Landsman, *Crossroads of Empire*, 138–39, 151; Gordon, "Livingstons of New York," 171–73; Kierner, *Traders and Gentlefolk*, 147.

20. Lustig, *Privilege and Prerogative*, 83–88; Klein, *American Whig*, 275–83; Tully, *Forming American Politics*, 136–38; Klein, "Church, State, and Education," 296–99; Don Gerlach and George DeMille, "Samuel Johnson and the Founding of King's College, 1751–1755," *Historical Magazine of the Protestant Episcopal Church* 44.3 (September 1975): 336–40; Curry, *First Freedoms*, 121–24; Patricia U. Bonomi, *A Factious People: Politics and Society in Colonial New York* (Ithaca, NY: Cornell University Press, 1971), 177; Peterson, "William Livingston," 19–20; Gordon, "Livingstons of New York," 174–75; quotes from the *Independent Reflector*, March 22, 1753, in the *Independent Reflector, or, Weekly Essays on Sundry Important Subjects, More Particularly Adapted to the Province of New York*, ed. Milton Klein (Cambridge, MA: Harvard University Press, 1963), 173–74, also see March 29, 1753, page 182; WL to Aaron Burr, May 29, 1754, WL Letterbook, William Livingston Family Collection, microfilm reel 5, MHS; Kierner, *Traders and Gentlefolk*, 176. For other treatments of King's College, also see Bulotti, "William Livingston," 115–52; Dorothy Dillon, *New York Triumvirate: A Study of the Legal and Political Careers of William Livingston, John Morin Scott, William Smith, Jr* (New York: Columbia University Press, 1949), 31–35; and Thatcher, "Social Philosophy of William Livingston," 18–60.

21. WL to Chauncey Whittoliog, August 22, 1754, WL Letterbook, William Livingston Family Collection, microfilm reel 5, MHS.

22. Klein, *American Whig*, 305–7, 316–28, 338–39; Tully, *Forming American Politics*, 139–40; Klein, "Church, State, and Education," 301; Bonomi, *A Factious People*, 177; Peterson, "William

Livingston," 21; WL to Noah Welles, October 18, 1754, WL Letterbook, William Livingston Family Collection, microfilm reel 5, MHS; Bulotti, "William Livingston," 53–59. Also see Thatcher, "Social Philosophy of William Livingston," 61–69.

23. Klein, *American Whig*, 236; Frank Lambert, *The Founding Fathers and the Place of Religion in America* (Princeton, NJ: Princeton University Press, 2003), 189; John Mulder, "William Livingston: Propagandist Against Episcopacy," *Journal of Presbyterian History* 54.1 (Spring 1976): 83–88; Sedgwick, *Memoir of William Livingston*, 86–87; Bulotti, "William Livingston," 85–87.

24. Klein, *American Whig*, 223–35 (quote on 233); Curry, *First Freedoms*, 23; Klein, "Church, State, and Education," 295. For deism, see Thatcher, "Social Philosophy of William Livingston," 289–90.

25. Tully, *Forming American Politics*, 136–38; Landsman, *Crossroads of Empire*, 139–40, 161, 201 (quotes on 140); David Hoeveler, *Creating the American Mind: Intellect and Politics in the Colonial Colleges* (Lanham, MD: Rowman and Littlefield, 2002), 134–35; Lustig, *Privilege and Prerogative*, 82; Peterson, "William Livingston," 21–23; Lambert, *Founding Fathers and Religion*, 188; Ned Landsman, *From Colonials to Provincials: American Thought and Culture, 1680-1760* (New York: Twayne, 1997), 153–55, 159–60; Bulotti, "William Livingston," 61–62; Bernard Bailyn, *Ideological Origins of the American Revolution* (Cambridge, MA: Harvard University Press, 1967), 35–37, 53, 250; Kierner, *Traders and Gentlefolk*, 161.

26. Lambert, *Founding Fathers and Religion*, 181, 185–95; Landsman, *From Colonials to Provincials*, 150, 160–61.

27. *Independent Reflector*, August 9, 1753, in Klein, *Independent Reflector*, 313–15.

28. Ibid., August 16, 1753, 319–27 (quotes on 324); Thatcher, "Social Philosophy of William Livingston," 254–55, 260–63; Landsman, *From Colonials to Provincials*, 161–63.

29. Klein, *American Whig*, 358–68; Landsman, *Crossroads of Empire*, 197–201; Lustig, *Privilege and Prerogative*, 89; quotes from WL to David Thompson, October 28, 1754, in WL Letterbook, William Livingston Family Collection, microfilm reel 5, MHS; quotes from *Watch-Tower* in *New York Mercury*, January 13, 1755, as cited in Klein, *American Whig*, 367; Peter Silver, *Our Savage Neighbors: How Indian War Transformed Early America* (New York: Norton, 2008), 1–8; Lustig, *Privilege and Prerogative*, 89–91; Thatcher, "Social Philosophy of William Livingston," 70–71.

30. Landsman, *Crossroads of Empire*, 197–98; Klein, *American Whig*, 360–68; Lustig, *Privilege and Prerogative*, 89–91; Thatcher, "Social Philosophy of William Livingston," 70–71; WL to David Thompson, October 28, 1754, WL Letterbook, William Livingston Family Collection, microfilm reel 5, MHS (for quote).

31. Klein, *American Whig*, 370–77; Lustig, *Privilege and Prerogative*, 93–100; Kierner, *Traders and Gentlefolk*, 74.

32. Milton Klein, "William Livingston's *A Review of Military Operations in North America*," in *The Colonial Legacy, Volume II: Some Eighteenth-Century Commentators*, ed. Lawrence Leder (New York: Harper & Row, 1971), 124–33; Peterson, "William Livingston," 26; Lustig, *Privilege and Prerogative*, 94–100.

33. Klein, *American Whig*, 378–86; Kathy Matson, *Merchants and Empire: Trading in Colonial New York* (Baltimore: Johns Hopkins University Press, 1998), 274; Lustig, *Privilege and Prerogative*, 103–5; Bulotti, "William Livingston," 179–80; Thatcher, "Social Philosophy of William Livingston," 72–80.

34. Klein, *American Whig*, 382–86; Matson, *Merchants and Empire*, 267–70, 274, 281–283.

35. Tully, *Forming American Politics*, 168–69; Klein, *American Whig*, 412–15; Lustig, *Privilege*

and Prerogative, 115–16; Dillon, *New York Triumvirate*, 66–81; Peterson, "William Livingston," 31; Thatcher, "Social Philosophy of William Livingston," 82–87; Kierner, *Traders and Gentlefolk*, 178–80.

36. Lustig, *Privilege and Prerogative*, 115–17; Klein, *American Whig*, 421–22; Tully, *Forming American Politics*, 168–69; Middleton, *From Privileges to Rights*, 223; Bulotti, "William Livingston," 62; Thatcher, "Social Philosophy of William Livingston," 81–87; Kierner, *Traders and Gentlefolk*, 181–82.

37. Klein, *American Whig*, 421–24, 429–32, 439–41; Lustig, *Privilege and Prerogative*, 121–23; Tully, *Forming American Politics*, 169; Thatcher, "Social Philosophy of William Livingston," 90–92.

38. Barnet Schecter, *The Battle for New York: The City at the Heart of the American Revolution* (New York: Walker & Co., 2002), 13–15; Klein, *American Whig*, 430, 432–34, 438–42; Tully, *Forming American Politics*, 170 (for quote); Lustig, *Privilege and Prerogative*, 129–31; Dillon, *New York Triumvirate*, 83, 87, 91, 94; Thatcher, "Social Philosophy of William Livingston," 92–96; Gordon, "Livingstons of New York," 176; Kierner, *Traders and Gentlefolk*, 185–87.

39. Ruma Chopra, *Unnatural Rebellion: Loyalists in New York City During the Revolution* (Charlottesville: University of Virginia Press, 2011), 11; Klein, *American Whig*, 442–46; Schecter, *Battle for New York*, 21–22; Tully, *Forming American Politics*, 171; Dillon, *New York Triumvirate*, 95–96.

40. Lustig, *Privilege and Prerogative*, 134–35; Bonomi, *A Factious People*, 234; Klein, *American Whig*, 443–47; Dillon, *New York Triumvirate*, 96–97; Schecter, *Battle for New York*, 23 (first two quotes); Sedgwick, *Memoir of William Livingston*, 126 (last quote); Bulotti, "William Livingston," 189.

41. Gordon, "Livingstons of New York," 134, 170–71; Sung Bok Kim, *Landlord and Tenant in Colonial New York: Manorial Society, 1664–1775* (Chapel Hill: University of North Carolina Press, 1978), 347, 367, 381–88, 397–401; Lustig, *Privilege and Prerogative*, 74, 139; Bonomi, *A Factious People*, 219–22, 225; Klein, *American Whig*, 132–36, 449; Kierner, *Traders and Gentlefolk*, 110–15.

42. Tully, *Forming American Politics*, 171; Bonomi, *A Factious People*, 223; Mulder, "William Livingston," 96; Klein, *American Whig*, 132; Gordon, "Livingstons of New York," 170; Lustig, *Privilege and Prerogative*, 140; Kierner, *Traders and Gentlefolk*, 116–24, 144, 154–55 (first quote on 124); Bulotti, "William Livingston," 40 (second quote).

43. Bonomi, *A Factious People*, 254–62; Lustig, *Privilege and Prerogative*, 148–55; Schecter, *Battle for New York*, 27–35; Klein, *American Whig*, 517–22, 527–31; Dillon, *New York Triumvirate*, 106–23; Tully, *Forming American Politics*, 177–81, 250–52; Kierner, *Traders and Gentlefolk*, 191–94.

44. Carl E. Prince, *William Livingston, New Jersey's First Governor* (Trenton: New Jersey Historical Commission, 1975), 6; Klein, *American Whig*, 522–25, 543.

45. Klein, *American Whig*, 534–36; Milton Klein, "The Rise of the New York Bar," in *Essays in the History of Early American Law*, ed. David Flaherty (Chapel Hill: University of North Carolina Press, 1969), 402, 414–15; *New-York Gazette, and Weekly Mercury*, April 6 and 13, 1772; William Willcocks to WL, March 24, 1773, *WLP*, reel 1; Deborah Rosen, "Courts and Commerce in Colonial New York" *American Journal of Legal History* 36.2 (April 1992): 142, 149–50.

46. Thatcher, "Social Philosophy of William Livingston," 14–15; Klein, *American Whig*, 66–68, 534; Prince, *William Livingston*, 6; Rob Wilson, "William Livingston's Philosophic Solitude and the Ideology of the Natural Sublime," *Early American Literature* 24.3 (1989): 218–22; Bulotti, "William Livingston," 64–68.

47. Paul David Nelson, *William Alexander, Lord Stirling* (Tuscaloosa: University of Alabama Press, 1987), 12; George Adams Boyd, *Elias Boudinot, Patriot and Statesman, 1740–1821* (Princeton, NJ: Princeton University Press, 1952), 20–21; Klein, *American Whig*, 535; Sedgwick, *Memoir of William Livingston*, 157; Ron Chernow, *Alexander Hamilton* (New York: Penguin Press, 2004), 42–46; James Thomas Flexner, *The Young Hamilton: A Biography* (Boston: Little, Brown, 1978), 55–56; Willard Randall, *Alexander Hamilton: A Life* (New York: Harper Collins, 2003), 50–56; Bulotti, "William Livingston," 26–27; Thatcher, "Social Philosophy of William Livingston," 135–36.

48. Klein, *American Whig*, 544–47; Liberty Hall Floor Plans, Misc. Collections NJSA; WL to Paparel Bloodgood, December 9, 1772, *WLP*, reel 1.

49. Whitehead Hicks to WL, unknown date, 1772, *WLP*, reel 1.

50. Klein, *American Whig*, 546–47; *John Jay, The Making of a Revolutionary: Unpublished Papers, 1745–1780*, ed. Richard Morris et al. (New York: Harper & Row, 1975), 71–72, 123–24, 138–39.

51. Klein, *American Whig*, 545–46; Walter Rutherfurd to WL, July 14, 1773, *WLP*, reel 1.

52. Larry R. Gerlach, *Prologue to Independence: New Jersey in the Coming of the American Revolution* (New Brunswick, NJ: Rutgers University Press, 1976), 178–85; Sheila Skemp, *William Franklin: Son of a Patriot, Servant of a King* (New York: Oxford University Press, 1990), 123–24; Chief Justice Smyth to Earl of Hillsborough, October 5, 1772, *NJA*, 10:379–80; David Bernstein, "New Jersey in the American Revolution: The Establishment of a Government Amid Civil and Military Disorder, 1770–1781" (PhD diss., Rutgers University, 1970), 44–45.

53. Skemp, *William Franklin*, 126–29; Stephen Skinner memorials to the legislature, December 6 and 17, 1773, BAH MS Collection, box 5-1, nos. 61 and 62; *Votes and Proceedings of the General Assembly of the Colony of New-Jersey [1773–1774]* (Burlington, NJ: Isaac Collins, 1774), 5–6, 85–112; Bernstein, "New Jersey in the American Revolution," 45–47.

54. Klein, *American Whig*, 546; Sedgwick, *Memoir of William Livingston*, 161–65; Larry R. Gerlach, "Politics and Prerogatives: The Aftermath of the Robbery of the East Jersey Treasury in 1768," *New Jersey History* 90.3 (August 1972): 155.

55. Gerlach, "Politics and Prerogatives," 155; Prince, *William Livingston*, 7–8; WL legal opinion, June 1, 1773, and WL to unknown person, March 7, 1774, *WLP*, reel 1; Bailyn, *Ideological Origins of the American Revolution*, 11, 14.

56. Inhabitants of Hunterdon County to William Franklin, Council, and General Assembly, February 14, 1774, BAH MS Collection, box 5-1, no. 63.

57. Gerlach, "Politics and Prerogatives," 154–56; Gerlach, *Prologue to Independence*, 183; Skemp, *William Franklin*, 129; *Votes and Proceedings [1773–1774]*, 164–67.

58. *Votes and Proceedings [1773–1774]*, 176–77; Gerlach, *Prologue to Independence*, 184; Skemp, *William Franklin*, 129–30; Bernstein, "New Jersey in the American Revolution," 47–49.

59. Peter O. Wacker and Paul G. E. Clemens, *Land Use in Early New Jersey: A Historical Geography* (Newark: New Jersey Historical Society, 1995), 35, 44, 141–47; James J. Gigantino II, *The Ragged Road to Abolition: Slavery and Abolition in New Jersey, 1775–1865* (Philadelphia: University of Pennsylvania Press, 2015), 2, 11–16; John Pomfret, *The Province of East New Jersey, 1609–1702* (Princeton, NJ: Princeton University Press, 1962), 3–17, 82–101, 182–98, 336–64; Paul Clemens, *The Uses of Abundance: A History of New Jersey's Economy* (Trenton: New Jersey Historical Society, 1992), 13–15; Gerlach, *Prologue to Independence*, 9, 16; Joseph Tiedemann, "Interconnected Communities: The Middle Colonies on the Eve of the American Revolution," *Pennsylvania History* 76.1 (January 2009): 2–9, 19–20; Joseph Tiedemann, "A Tumultuous

People: The Rage for Liberty and the Ambiance of Violence in the Middle Colonies in the Years Preceding the American Revolution," *Pennsylvania History* 77.4 (Autumn 2010): 388.

60. Bernstein, "New Jersey in the American Revolution," 30; Michael Batinski, *The New Jersey Assembly, 1738–1775: The Making of a Legislative Community* (Lanham, MD: University Press of America, 1987), 186–87; David J. Fowler, "'These Were Troublesome Times Indeed': Social and Economic Conditions in Revolutionary New Jersey," in *New Jersey in the American Revolution*, ed. Barbara J. Mitnick (New Brunswick, NJ: Rutgers University Press, 2005), 20; Thomas Purvis, *Proprietors, Patronage, and Paper Money: Legislative Politics in New Jersey, 1703–1776*, 171; Gerlach, *Prologue to Independence*, 42–44.

61. Purvis, *Proprietors, Patronage, and Paper Money*, 144–49, 152–54, 168–71; Gerlach, *Prologue to Independence*, 42–44.

62. Gerlach, *Prologue to Independence*, 46; Klein, *American Whig*, 515–16, 520–22.

63. Skemp, *William Franklin*, xi–xiii, 71, 78–79, 86.

64. William Franklin to Earl of Hillsborough, August 24, 1768, *NJA*, 10:48–50; Gerlach, *Prologue to Independence*, 45–46.

65. Skemp, *William Franklin*, 86–87; Bernstein, "New Jersey in the American Revolution," 31, 34; Hillsborough to Franklin, November 15, 1768, *NJA*, 10:60–62; Gerlach, *Prologue to Independence*, 46–47.

66. Skemp, *William Franklin*, 87, 112–15; Bernstein, "New Jersey in the American Revolution," 35, 36, 41; Gerlach, *Prologue to Independence*, 71–78; Batinski, *New Jersey Assembly*, 189.

67. Brendan McConville, *These Daring Disturbers of the Public Peace: The Struggle for Property and Power in Early New Jersey* (Philadelphia: University of Pennsylvania Press, 1999), 1–27, 223–28 (quote on 223); T. H. Breen, *Marketplace of Revolution: How Consumer Politics Shaped American Independence* (New York: Oxford University Press, 2004), 72–101; Kierner, *Traders and Gentlefolk*, 134–38.

68. McConville, *Daring Disturbers*, 12–19; Clemens, *The Uses of Abundance: A History of New Jersey's Economy* (Trenton, NJ: New Jersey Historical Commission, 1992), 13–15; Pomfret, *The Province of West New Jersey*, 49–64; Pomfret, *The Province of East New Jersey*, 82–101, 182–98; Hodges, *Root and Branch*, 36–39, 44–45; Gigantino, *Ragged Road to Abolition*, 13–14; Bernstein, "New Jersey in the American Revolution," 10–11.

69. McConville, *Daring Disturbers*, 230–34.

70. *Votes and Proceedings of the General Assembly of the Province of New-Jersey [March 1770]* (Woodbridge, NJ: James Parker, 1770), 5–6.

71. McConville, *Daring Disturbers*, 235–37; Gerlach, *Prologue to Independence*, 47, 185–90; Dennis Ryan, "Six Towns: Continuity and Change in Revolutionary New Jersey, 1770–1792" (PhD diss., New York University, 1974), 110–12, 114; Leonard Lundin, *Cockpit of Revolution: The War for Independence in New Jersey* (Princeton, NJ: Princeton University Press, 1940), 55–58, 60–64; Bernstein, "New Jersey in the American Revolution," 10–11, 31–32; Batinski, *New Jersey Assembly*, 186; WL to Robert Rosebrugh, June 7 and August 13, 1772, receipt, July 4, 1772, WL to William Colwell, August 13, 1772, WL to Peter Van Brugh Livingston, August 13, 1772, and January 27, 1773, WL to Walter Rutherfurd, August 23, 1772, David Clarkson to WL, December 26, 1772, *WLP*, reel 1.

72. McConville, *Daring Disturbers*, 239–46; Ryan, "Six Towns," 112, 115; Lundin, *Cockpit of Revolution*, 63–64; Bernstein, "New Jersey in the American Revolution," 32; Gerlach, *Prologue to Independence*, 190–91. For previous interpretations of New Jersey's decision to join the revolutionary cause, see Gerlach, *Prologue to Independence*, xv, 52; Fowler, "These Were Troublesome

Times Indeed," 20; and John O'Connor, *William Paterson: Lawyer and Statesman, 1745–1806* (New Brunswick, NJ: Rutgers University Press, 1979), 64–65.

73. Edward Countryman, *The American Revolution* (New York: Hill and Wang, 2003), 74–104; Pauline Maier, *From Resistance to Revolution: Colonial Radicals and the Development of American Opposition to Britain, 1765–1776* (New York: Knopf, 1972), xviii–xxi.

74. Petition from the inhabitants of Evesham to Colonial Assembly, no date, BAH MS Collection, box 1-19, no. 12.

75. Bernstein, "New Jersey in the American Revolution," 56–57; Gerlach, *Prologue to Independence*, 50–51; William Franklin to Earl of Dartmouth, June 13, 1774, *NJA*, 10:461–63.

76. *Votes and Proceedings [March 1770]*, 7–9.

77. Bernstein, "New Jersey in the American Revolution," 32–33; O'Connor, *William Paterson*, 48–52, 58; John O'Connor, "William Paterson: The Conservative as Revolutionary," in *New Jersey in the American Revolution*, vol. 3, ed. William Wright (Trenton: New Jersey Historical Commission, 1976), 40, 44.

78. Klein, *American Whig*, 423, 527, 550.

Chapter 2

1. Eric Nelson, *Royalist Revolution: Monarchy and the American Founding* (Cambridge, MA: Harvard University Press, 2014), 7.

2. Ibid., 4–7 (quote on 6).

3. Ibid., 4–7, 30–37, 63, 148–49.

4. Milton Klein, *American Whig: William Livingston of New York* (New York: Garland, 1993), 535; David Bernstein, "New Jersey in the American Revolution: The Establishment of a Government Amid Civil and Military Disorder, 1770–1781" (PhD diss., Rutgers University, 1970), 67–68; William Franklin to the Earl of Dartmouth, May 31, 1774, *NJA*, 10:457–59.

5. Circular Letter of the Boston Committee of Correspondence, May 13, 1774 (http://avalon.law.yale.edu/18th_century/circ_let_boston_1774.asp; accessed January 22, 2015); Committee of Correspondence of the New Jersey Assembly to the Boston Committee of Correspondence, May 31, 1774, and James Kinsey to Elias Boudinot, June 14 and July 2, 1774, in *New Jersey in the American Revolution, 1763–1783: A Documentary History*, ed. Larry R. Gerlach (Trenton: New Jersey Historical Commission, 1975), 67–68, 73–75; Larry R. Gerlach, *Prologue to Independence: New Jersey in the Coming of the American Revolution* (New Brunswick, NJ: Rutgers University Press, 1976), 206–7; Bernstein, "New Jersey in the American Revolution," 74–75.

6. Essex County Resolves on the Boston Port Act, June 11, 1774, in Gerlach, *New Jersey in the American Revolution*, 70–72; Gerlach, *Prologue to Independence*, 207; Theodore Sedgwick, *A Memoir of the Life of William Livingston . . .* (New York: J. & J. Harper, 1833), 168; Essex County Resolutions, June 11, 1774, *PWL*, 1:16–19; Bernstein, "New Jersey in the American Revolution," 69–70; John Pomfret, *Colonial New Jersey: A History* (New York: Scribner, 1973), 247–48; Harold Thatcher, "Social Philosophy of William Livingston" (PhD diss., University of Chicago, 1938), 137.

7. *Independent Reflector*, December 7, 1752, as cited in Klein, *American Whig*, 431, also see 431–34.

8. Brendan McConville, *These Daring Disturbers of the Public Peace: The Struggle for Property and Power in Early New Jersey* (Philadelphia: University of Pennsylvania Press, 1999), 239–46; Gerlach, *Prologue to Independence*, 208–9; Committee of the People of Essex County to the Inhabitants of Monmouth County, June 13, 1774, *NJA*, 10:459–61, also see 464–65 for William Franklin's response to the Essex County Resolves.

9. For resolutions of Bergen, Morris, Hunterdon, Middlesex, Sussex, and Monmouth, see *Minutes*, 9–25; Resolves of the New Brunswick Convention, July 23, 1774, in Gerlach, *New Jersey in the American Revolution*, 76–78; resolutions of a meeting of county committees at New Brunswick, July 21, 1774, in *Pennsylvania Journal*, July 27, 1774, *NJA*, 29:430–32; Bernstein, "New Jersey in the American Revolution," 73–76; Gerlach, *Prologue to Independence*, 212–13; Pomfret, *Colonial New Jersey*, 248–49; Nelson, *Royalist Revolution*, 32.

10. Bernstein, "New Jersey in the American Revolution," 75–80.

11. BN on the Continental Congress, *New-York Journal, or General Advertiser*, August 4, 1774, and John Witherspoon, "Thoughts on American Liberty," [August 1774], in Gerlach, *New Jersey in the American Revolution*, 78–81, 85–87; John Adams Diary, August 27, 1774, *Adams Papers, Series I*, 2:111–13; John Fea, *The Way of Improvement Leads Home: Philip Vickers Fithian and the Rural Enlightenment in Early America* (Philadelphia: University of Pennsylvania Press, 2008), 69, 137–42; Jeffry H. Morrison, *John Witherspoon and the Founding of the American Republic* (Notre Dame, IN: University of Notre Dame Press, 2005), 45–69, 72–73; Gerlach, *Prologue to Independence*, 220–23.

12. John Adams Diary, September 1, 1774, *Adams Papers, Series I*, 2:118–19.

13. Klein, *American Whig*, 551–53; *John Jay, The Making of a Revolutionary: Unpublished Papers, 1745–1780*, ed. Richard Morris et al. (New York: Harper & Row, 1975), 135; John Adams Diary, August 22, 1774, *Adams Papers, Series I*, 2:105–8; John Adams to Thomas Jefferson, November 12, 1813, *Founders Online* (http://founders.archives.gov/documents/Adams/99-02-02-6195; accessed January 27, 2015). For Adams on Anglicanism, see Sui Juris to the *Boston Gazette*, May 23, 1768, *Adams Papers, Series III*: 1:211–14.

14. John Adams's Notes of Debates, September 8, 1774, *LDC*, 1:46–49; Robert Middlekauff, *The Glorious Cause: The American Revolution, 1763–1789* (New York: Oxford University Press, 2005), 235, 243–44; Klein, *American Whig*, 48, 229, 264, 438, 553; Governor Franklin to Earl of Dartmouth, September 6, 1774, *NJA*, 10:473–78; Richard Beeman, *Our Lives, Our Fortunes, and Our Sacred Honor: The Forging of American Independence* (New York: Basic Books, 2013), 163–65; Nelson, *Royalist Revolution*, 32–33.

15. *JCC*, 1:62, 75, 81–90; John Jay to John Adams, January 31, 1818, *Founders Online* (http://founders.archives.gov/documents/Adams/99-02-02-6846; accessed January 23, 2015); Committees of Correspondence and Commerce, November 1775–January 1776, *Adams Papers, Series I*, 3:339–41; John Adams to John Jay, January 9, 1818, *Founders Online* (http://founders.archives.gov/documents/Adams/99-02-02-6835; accessed January 27, 2015). For Jefferson on Jay's authorship, see Thomas Jefferson, Autobiography, January 6, 1821, *Founders Online* (http://founders.archives.gov/documents/Jefferson/98-01-02-1756; accessed January 27, 2015); Klein, *American Whig*, 553; Middlekauff, *Glorious Cause*, 243–44; Jack N. Rakove, *The Beginnings of National Politics: An Interpretive History of the Continental Congress* (Baltimore: Johns Hopkins University Press, 1979), 53–54; James Henderson, *Party Politics in the Continental Congress* (New York: McGraw-Hill, 1974), 37; Jerrilyn Marston, *King and Congress: The Transfer of Political Legitimacy, 1774–1779* (Princeton, NJ: Princeton University Press, 1987), 93–96; Neil York, "The First Continental Congress and the Problem of American Rights" *Pennsylvania Magazine of History and Biography* 122.4 (October 1998): 359–61; Beeman, *Our Lives*, 163–65; Thatcher, "Social Philosophy of William Livingston," 138; Nelson, *Royalist Revolution*, 32–33, 37, 63.

16. Middlekauff, *Glorious Cause*, 243–45; Klein, *American Whig*, 554; Merrill Jensen, *Founding of a Nation: A History of the American Revolution, 1763–1776* (New York: Oxford University Press, 1968), 493, 498–99; Rakove, *Beginnings of National Politics*, 54–55, 60–61; Henderson,

Party Politics in the Continental Congress, 39; Marston, *King and Congress*, 92–93; Jane Calvert, *Quaker Constitutionalism and the Political Thought of John Dickinson* (New York: Cambridge University Press, 2009), 232; Beeman, *Our Lives*, 125–30, 131.

17. John Adams to *Boston Patriot*, October 31, 1810, *Founders Online* (http://founders.archives .gov/documents/Adams/99-02-02-5573; accessed January 27, 2015).

18. WL to Henry Laurens, February 5, 1778, *PWL*, 2:207–13. Also see Rakove, *Beginnings of National Politics*, 101–2, and York, "First Continental Congress," 362.

19. Essex County Committee of Correspondence to the Freeholders of Essex County, November 28, 1774, *Minutes*, 34–35; Klein, *American Whig*, 553–54; Sedgwick, *Memoir of William Livingston*, 176–77; Rakove, *Beginnings of National Politics*, 60–61.

20. Essex County Assembly, Newark Committee, and Elizabethtown Resolutions, *Minutes*, 36–41 (for other county resolutions, see 42–55).

21. Gerlach, *Prologue to Independence*, 233–36; Gary Nash, *The Unknown American Revolution: The Unruly Birth of Democracy and the Struggle to Create America* (New York: Viking, 2005), 178–79; Woody Holton, *Forced Founders: Indians, Debtors, Slaves, and the Making of the American Revolution in Virginia* (Chapel Hill: University of North Carolina Press, 1999), 46–65; T. H. Breen, *American Insurgents, American Patriots: The Revolution of the People* (New York: Hill and Wang, 2010), 167–69, 198–99 (quote on 168).

22. A Freeholder to the Essex County Committee, *Rivington's New-York Gazetteer*, January 5, 1775, in Gerlach, *New Jersey in the American Revolution*, 102–4.

23. Z on the Continental Congress, *Rivington's New-York Gazetteer*, November 19, 1774, in Gerlach, *New Jersey in the American Revolution*, 91–94.

24. Gerlach, *Prologue to Independence*, 233–36; William Franklin to Lord Dartmouth, December 6, 1774, *NJA*, 10:503–4; Nash, *Unknown American Revolution*, 178–79.

25. Fea, *Way of Improvement*, 142–53 (quote on 142); Gerlach, *Prologue to Independence*, 198–202; Cumberland County Committee Proceedings on the Greenwich Tea Party, December 22–23, 1774, in Gerlach, *New Jersey in the American Revolution*, 100–101; Breen, *American Insurgents, American Patriots*, 3–9.

26. Circular Letter from Earl of Dartmouth to William Franklin, January 4, 1775, and Franklin to Dartmouth, April 3, 1775, *NJA*, 10:534, 570–71; Bernstein, "New Jersey in the American Revolution," 90–92; William Franklin to the General Assembly, January 13, 1775, in Gerlach, *New Jersey in the American Revolution*, 109–11; Nottingham petition to the legislature, BAH MS Collection, box 5-1, no. 70; Sheila Skemp, *William Franklin: Son of a Patriot, Servant of a King* (New York: Oxford University Press, 1990), 160; Gerlach, *Prologue to Independence*, 243–45; Pomfret, *Colonial New Jersey*, 250.

27. William Franklin to Earl of Dartmouth, February 1, 1775, and Franklin letter abstract, March 12, 1775, *NJA*, 10:537–38, 575–76; William Livingston et al. to the General Assembly, January 11, 1775, *PWL*, 1:23–24; *Votes and Proceedings of the General Assembly of the Colony of New-Jersey [January 11–February 13, 1775]* (Burlington, NJ: Isaac Collins, 1775), 15–17. Also see Bernstein, "New Jersey in the American Revolution," 92–93; Gerlach, *Prologue to Independence*, 243–46; Pomfret, *Colonial New Jersey*, 250–51; Sedgwick, *Memoir of William Livingston*, 179.

28. Bernstein, "New Jersey in the American Revolution," 93–95; Gerlach, *Prologue to Independence*, 246–48, 252–53; Skemp, *William Franklin*, 162; New Jersey Assembly Petition of Grievances to George III, February 13, 1775, in Gerlach, *New Jersey in the American Revolution*, 117–20; William Franklin letter abstract, March 12, 1775, *NJA*, 10:575–77; Jensen, *Founding of a Nation*, 532; Henderson, *Party Politics in the Continental Congress*, 48; Marston, *King and*

Congress, 209–10; Barnet Schecter, *The Battle for New York: The City at the Heart of the American Revolution* (New York: Walker & Co., 2002), 50–51.

29. John Adams Diary, August 22, 1774, *Adams Papers, Series I*, 2:105–8 [for Philip Livingston quotes]; Marston, *King and Congress*, 182–88 (second quote on 186); Jensen, *Founding of a Nation*, 484; Cynthia Kierner, *Traders and Gentlefolk: The Livingstons of New York, 1675–1790* (Ithaca, NY: Cornell University Press, 1992), 206.

30. *New-York Journal, or General Advertiser*, April 20, 1775, and Elias Boudinot to the Morris County Committee, April 30, 1775, in Gerlach, *New Jersey in the American Revolution*, 125–27, 132–34. Also see Gerlach, *Prologue to Independence*, 258.

31. Gerlach, *Prologue to Independence*, 256–64; Bernstein, "New Jersey in the American Revolution," 107; William Franklin to Council and Assembly, May 16, 1775, BAH MS Collection, box 5-1, no. 71.

32. New Jersey General Assembly, "Address to His Majesty," May 19, 1775, BAH MS Collection, box 1-14, no. 18b.

33. Gerlach, *Prologue to Independence*, 263–66; Bernstein, "New Jersey in the American Revolution," 109–14; Skemp, *William Franklin*, 167–70.

34. Petition of several inhabitants of Bridgewater Township to the Legislative Council and General Assembly, March 3, 1776, Petitions, Resolutions, Transactions, Accounts, and Misc. Papers, 1700–1845, no. 7, NJSA.

35. *Minutes*, 169–83 (quote on 173); Gerlach, *Prologue to Independence*, 267–70; Bernstein, "New Jersey in the American Revolution," 109–10, 117–18; Pomfret, *Colonial New Jersey*, 253–54; Skemp, *William Franklin*, 184; William Franklin to Earl of Dartmouth, June 5, 1775, *NJA*, 10:601–6 (quote on 604).

36. Gerlach, *Prologue to Independence*, 271; *JCC*, 2:85, 212, 238; Elias Boudinot to the Morris County Committee, April 30, 1775, in Gerlach, *New Jersey in the American Revolution*, 132–34.

37. *JCC*, 2:105, 128–30; *Jefferson Papers*, 1:187–92 (quote on 189); Julian Boyd, "The Disputed Authorship of the Declaration on the Causes and Necessity of Taking Up Arms, 1775," *Pennsylvania Magazine of History and Biography* 74.1 (January 1950): 51–73; Jensen, *Founding of a Nation*, 617; Rakove, *Beginnings of National Politics*, 28; Milton Flower, *John Dickinson, Conservative Revolutionary* (Charlottesville: University Press of Virginia, 1983), 133; Calvert, *Quaker Constitutionalism*, 234; Beeman, *Our Lives*, 248–51; Nelson, *Royalist Revolution*, 31–37.

38. *JCC*, 2:128–57.

39. John Adams to William Tudor, July 6, 1775, *Adams Papers, Series III*, 3:59–60.

40. William Bradford to James Madison, July 10, 1775, and Madison to Bradford, July 28, 1775, *Madison Papers, Congressional Series*, 1:154–57, 159–62.

41. John Jay to Gouverneur Morris, August 1775, John Jay to Sarah Livingston, September 18 and 29, 1775, in *John Jay Unpublished Papers*, 161–62, 166–68.

42. Earl of Dartmouth to William Franklin, July 5, 1775, Franklin to Dartmouth, August 2, 1775, and copy of letter from Daniel Coxe to Cortlandt Skinner, July 4, 1775, *NJA*, 10:645–47, 652–53, 654–55.

43. Gerlach, *Prologue to Independence*, 275–79; Bernstein, "New Jersey in the American Revolution," 120–21; Pomfret, *Colonial New Jersey*, 255; Skemp, *William Franklin*, 184; Minutes of the Sussex County Committee, August 10–11, 1775, in Gerlach, *New Jersey in the American Revolution*, 158–59.

44. WL and James Kinsey to Samuel Tucker, October 9, 1775, and WL to Lord Stirling, December 9, 1775, *PWL*, 1:25–26, 29; *Minutes*, 212–13, 215–16, 236–37, 246; Milton Klein, "William

Livingston's *A Review of Military Operations in North America*," in *The Colonial Legacy, Volume II: Some Eighteenth-Century Commentators*, ed. Lawrence Leder (New York: Harper & Row, 1971), 119–23, 129–33 (quote on 119); Klein, *American Whig*, 359–79.

45. Philip Vickers Fithian Journal, November 13, 1775, in Gerlach, *New Jersey in the American Revolution*, 163; Fea, *Way of Improvement*, 172, 180–81.

46. Petition from Burlington County freeholders to General Assembly, November 25, 1775, AM Papers, box 12, no. 1699 AM; Skemp, *William Franklin*, 186.

47. William Franklin to the Council and Assembly, November 16, 1775, BAH MS Collection, box 5-1, no. 79; Skemp, *William Franklin*, 186–88; Pomfret, *Colonial New Jersey*, 256–57; Gerlach, *Prologue to Independence*, 291–98.

48. Notes on John Dickinson Speech Before the House of Assembly, *NJA*, 10:689–90.

49. *Votes and Proceedings of the General Assembly of the Colony of New-Jersey [November 15–December 6, 1775]* (Burlington, NJ: Isaac Collins, 1775), 19–20; Skemp, *William Franklin*, 188–90; *JCC*, 3:404; Gerlach, *Prologue to Independence*, 296–99; Pomfret, *Colonial New Jersey*, 257; Cortlandt Skinner to William Skinner, December 1775, in Gerlach, *New Jersey in the American Revolution*, 165–66; Bernstein, "New Jersey in the American Revolution," 138, 204–5; Marston, *King and Congress*, 213–15; Beeman, *Our Lives*, 287–88.

50. Lord Stirling to WL, December 12, 1775, WL to Lord Stirling, December 19, 1775, WL to unknown, December 22, 1775, *PWL*, 1:30–33; WL to Samuel Tucker, December 27, 1775, BAH MS Collection, box 2-1.

51. Klein, *American Whig*, 555–56; Diary of Richard Smith, December 22, 1775, *LDC*, 2:512–13; David Jacobson, *John Dickinson and the Revolution in Pennsylvania, 1764–1776* (Berkeley: University of California Press, 1965), 90–92; John Dickinson's Notes for a Speech in Congress, May 23–25, 1775, *LDC*, 1:371–83; Kierner, *Traders and Gentlefolk*, 208.

52. *LDC*, 2:xviii–xix; WL to unknown, December 22, 1775, *PWL*, 1:32–33; *Minutes*, 289, 307; John DeHart to General Assembly, November 13, 1775, in Gerlach, *New Jersey in the American Revolution*, 161–63; Klein, *American Whig*, 555.

53. William Franklin to Lord Dartmouth, January 5, 1776, *NJA*, 10:676–77; Bernstein, "New Jersey in the American Revolution," 138.

54. Bernstein, "New Jersey in the American Revolution," 138–42; Dennis Ryan, "Six Towns: Continuity and Change in Revolutionary New Jersey, 1770–1792" (PhD diss., New York University, 1974), 119; Gerlach, *Prologue to Independence*, 320.

55. Paul David Nelson, *William Alexander, Lord Stirling* (Tuscaloosa: University of Alabama Press, 1987), 68–71; Bernstein, "New Jersey in the American Revolution," 139; *JCC*, 4:17–18; Plain Dealer, January 2, 1776, in Gerlach, *New Jersey in the American Revolution*, 174–75; Fea, *Way of Improvement*, 152–55.

56. Richard Smith Diary, January 10, 1776, *LDC*, 3:80; *JCC*, 4:16–18 (quote on 17); Committee Report (in WL's hand), January 23, 1776, *PWL*, 1:33–35; Nelson, *William Alexander, Lord Stirling*, 68.

57. *JCC*, 4:42, 54, 77; Richard Smith Diary, January 9 and 15, 1776, *LDC*, 3:71–72, 80; Nelson, *William Alexander, Lord Stirling*, 68–70; Skemp, *William Franklin*, 193–97; George Adams Boyd, *Elias Boudinot, Patriot and Statesman, 1740–1821* (Princeton, NJ: Princeton University Press, 1952), 27–28.

58. Lord Stirling to WL, February 9, 1776, *PWL*, 1:38–39; *Minutes*, 361–62; *New-York Gazette, and the Weekly Mercury*, February 19, 1776.

59. WL to John Hancock, February 3, 1776, *PWL*, 1:37–38.

60. Richard Smith Diary, January 3 and 5, 1776, *LDC*, 3:27–28, 38–39; New York Provincial Congress to Continental Congress, December 21, 1775, *American Archives, Fourth Series . . . March 7, 1774 to the Declaration of Independence . . .*, 6 vols. (Washington, DC, 1837–1846), 4:434; *New-York Journal, or General Advertiser*, December 28, 1775, in Gerlach, *New Jersey in the American Revolution*, 171; WL to Samuel Tucker, December 27, 1775, BAH MS Collection, box 2-1; Gerlach, *Prologue to Independence*, 304; Pomfret, *Colonial New Jersey*, 258.

61. Richard Smith Diary, February 20, 1776, WL to Philip Schuyler, March 9, 1776, and Francis Lewis to WL, March 20, 1776, *LDC*, 3:291–92, 362, 417; John Adams to Benjamin Rush, February 21, 1813, *Founders Online* (http://founders.archives.gov/documents/Adams/99-02-02 -5961; accessed January 31, 2015); WL et al. to Baltimore Committee of Observation, February 27, 1776, *PWL*, 1:40–41; Middlekauff, *Glorious Cause*, 322; Henderson, *Party Politics in the Continental Congress*, 58–60; Beeman, *Our Lives*, 267–69.

62. Milton Klein, "Failure of a Mission: The Drummond Peace Proposal of 1775," *Huntington Library Quarterly* 35.4 (August 1972): 347–52; Beeman, *Our Lives*, 301–3.

63. Klein, "Failure of a Mission," 352–57; James Duane to Robert Livingston, January 5, 1776, and James Duane to Cornelius Duane, December 9, 1775, *LDC*, 3:33–34, 464–65.

64. Klein, "Failure of a Mission," 357–58; Lord Drummond's Notes, January 3–9, 1776, *LDC*, 3:21–27 (quotes on 23); *Historical Memoirs of William Smith, 1778–1783*, ed. W. H. W. Sabine (New York: New York Times, 1971), 18–19.

65. Klein, "Failure of a Mission," 358.

66. Ibid., 359–67; Lord Drummond's Minutes, January 6, 1776, Joseph Hewes to Samuel Johnston, January 6, 1776, John Dickinson's Proposed Resolutions on a Petition to the King, January 9–24, 1776, Lord Drummond's Minutes, January 14, 1776, and John Jay's Essay on Congress and Independence, January 1776, *LDC*, 3:39–40, 42–43, 63–64, 91–92, 175–78; GW to John Hancock, February 14, 1776, *Washington Papers, Revolutionary War Series*, 3:306–8.

67. Klein, "Failure of a Mission," 366–69; John Jay to Robert Livingston, January 6, 1776, and Richard Smith Diary, March 5, 1776, *LDC*, 3:47, 335–36; Klein, *American Whig*, 555–56; Middlekauff, *Glorious Cause*, 315–16; Jensen, *Founding of a Nation*, 650; Rakove, *Beginnings of National Politics*, 90; Marston, *King and Congress*, 215–16.

68. *Minutes*, 367; GW to Lord Stirling, March 19, 1776, *Washington Papers, Revolutionary War Series*, 3:497–98; Unknown to Stirling, March 16, 1776 (for quotes), and Stirling to Samuel Tucker, March 23, 1776, William Alexander Papers, Manuscripts and Archives Division, New York Public Library; Gerlach, *Prologue to Independence*, 305; Richard Smith Diary, March 28, 1776, *LDC*, 3:458; Lord Stirling to WL, March 24, 1776, William Heath to WL and WL to William Heath, April 1, 1776, *PWL*, 1:44–45, 46–47; Nelson, *William Alexander, Lord Stirling*, 72–79; GW General Orders, New York, April 15, 1776, *Washington Papers, Revolutionary War Series*, 4:65–66; Middlekauff, *Glorious Cause*, 311; Schecter, *Battle for New York*, 67–72, 82–85.

69. Skemp, *William Franklin*, 202; Bernstein, "New Jersey in the American Revolution," 153–54; John Witherspoon, "On the Controversy About Independence," in Gerlach, *New Jersey in the American Revolution*, 198–200; Fea, *Way of Improvement*, 137, 142; Gideon Mailer, "Anglo-Scottish Union and John Witherspoon's American Revolution," *William and Mary Quarterly* 67.4 (October 2010): 733–35.

70. Elias Boudinot versus John Witherspoon on Independence, in Gerlach, *New Jersey in the American Revolution*, 195–96; Ruth Bogin, *Abraham Clark and the Quest for Equality in the Revolutionary Era, 1774–1794* (Rutherford, NJ: Fairleigh Dickinson University Press, 1982), 19–20; Mailer, "Anglo-Scottish Union," 737.

71. Robert Livingston to Edward Rutledge, October 10, 1776, and Landon Carter to GW, May 9, 1776, as cited in Henderson, *Party Politics in the Continental Congress*, 76, for Rutledge, see 77; Nash, *Unknown American Revolution*, 201–3; John O'Connor, *William Paterson: Lawyer and Statesman, 1745–1806* (New Brunswick, NJ: Rutgers University Press, 1979), 78.

72. Ryan, "Six Towns," 146; Bernstein, "New Jersey in the American Revolution," 131–32, 157; Petition of inhabitants of Salem County asking for the right to vote, no date, BAH MS Collection, box OV 1–48, no. 156 (for quotes); Gerlach, *Prologue to Independence*, 288–89, 318; Rakove, *Beginnings of National Politics*, 82; Nash, *Unknown American Revolution*, 187, 201–3.

73. O'Connor, *William Paterson*, 79–80; Pomfret, *Colonial New Jersey*, 260; Jonathan Dickinson Sergeant to John Adams, April 11, 1776, *LDC*, 3:507–8; Michal Rozbicki, *Culture and Liberty in the Age of the American Revolution* (Charlottesville: University of Virginia Press, 2011), 102–3.

74. Breen, *American Insurgents, American Patriots*, 3–9; Nash, *Unknown American Revolution*, 178–88; Nelson, *Royalist Revolution*, 148.

75. Klein, *American Whig*, 557; John Hancock to Philip Schuyler, May 24, 1776, *LDC*, 4:66–67; Holton, *Forced Founders*, 44–65; Nelson, *Royalist Revolution*, 148–49.

76. Beeman, *Our Lives*, 344–45; *LDC*, 3:xix; *JCC*, 4:362, 419; Committee Report (in WL's hand), June 7, 1776, *PWL*, 1:53–54; New Jersey Supreme Court Case Files, 1704–1844, #20456*, NJSA; Thatcher, "Social Philosophy of William Livingston," 142–43.

77. Skemp, *William Franklin*, 203; Bernstein, "New Jersey in the American Revolution," 159, 167; Gerlach, *Prologue to Independence*, 331–33; *Minutes*, 454–57; William Franklin to His Majesty's Council and to the House of Representatives of the Province of New Jersey, June 17, 1776, BAH MS Collection, box 1-1, no. 57a.

78. Jonathan Dickinson Sergeant to Samuel Adams, June 24, 1776, as reproduced as footnote in Abraham Clark to Elias Dayton, July 4, 1776, *LDC*, 4:378–79n. 1.

79. *Minutes*, 450, 452, 472, 473; *LDC*, 3:xix, 4:xvii; Klein, *American Whig*, 557–58; Bernstein, "New Jersey in the American Revolution," 168; WL to Samuel Tucker, July 26 and August 9, 1776, *PWL*, 1:107–8, 114 (quote on 114); Gloria Bulotti, "William Livingston: American Patriot and Publicist" (master's thesis, Stanford University, 1947), 190–91; Thatcher, "Social Philosophy of William Livingston," 144–45.

80. John Adams Diary, June 28 and July 1, 1776, *Adams Papers, Series I*, 3:395–98; John Adams to Thomas Jefferson, September 18, 1823, *Founders Online* (http://founders.archives.gov /documents/Jefferson/98-01-02-3760; accessed January 31, 2015); Sedgwick, *Memoir of William Livingston*, 187–90; Klein, *American Whig*, 558.

81. WL to Henry Laurens, February 5, 1778, *PWL*, 2:207–13; Rakove, *Beginnings of National Politics*, 101–3; Sedgwick, *Memoir of William Livingston*, 185; Klein, *American Whig*, 557.

82. John Dickinson's Notes for a Speech in Congress, July 1, 1776, *LDC*, 4:351–57; Jensen, *Founding of a Nation*, 699–700; Rakove, *Beginnings of National Politics*, 94; Jacobson, *John Dickinson and the Revolution in Pennsylvania*, 113–14; Flower, *John Dickinson*, 162–64; Calvert, *Quaker Constitutionalism*, 241.

83. Marston, *King and Congress*, 219–22; John Adams to Patrick Henry, June 3, 1776, John Adams to William Cushing, June 9, 1776, Richard Henry Lee to Landon Carter, June 2, 1776, and Edward Rutledge to John Jay, June 8, 1776, *LDC*, 4:122–23, 174–75, 177–78. Middlekauff, *Glorious Cause*, 321, 323; Jensen, *Founding of a Nation*, 688, 690; Rakove, *Beginnings of National Politics*, 93–94, 98–99; James Haw, *John & Edward Rutledge of South Carolina* (Athens: University of Georgia Press, 1997), 91–93.

84. Jensen, *Founding of a Nation*, 690–91; *Papers of Thomas Jefferson*, 1:299–313; WL to Henry Laurens, February 5, 1778, *PWL*, 2:207–13 (for quotes). Also see Sedgwick, *Memoir of William Livingston*, 185; Klein, *American Whig*, 557; and Bulotti, "William Livingston," 195 (last quote).

85. WL to Henry Laurens, February 5, 1778, *PWL*, 2:207–13; Calvert, *Quaker Constitutionalism*, 241–44 (second quote on 243).

86. Rakove, *Beginnings of National Politics*, 103–7; Kierner, *Traders and Gentlefolk*, 202, 208, 221–24.

Chapter 3

1. David Bernstein, "New Jersey in the American Revolution: The Establishment of a Government Amid Civil and Military Disorder, 1770–1781" (PhD diss., Rutgers University, 1970), 307–8; Mark Kwasny, *Washington's Partisan War, 1775–1783* (Kent, OH: Kent State University Press, 1996), 56.

2. John Shy, *A People Numerous and Armed: Reflections on the Military Struggle for American Independence* (New York: Oxford University Press, 1976), 127, 219, 237–38.

3. Eric Nelson, *Royalist Revolution: Monarchy and the American Founding* (Cambridge, MA: Harvard University Press, 2014), 4–7.

4. Robert Middlekauff, *The Glorious Cause: The American Revolution, 1763–1789* (New York: Oxford University Press, 2005), 333, 338; David Hackett Fischer, *Washington's Crossing* (New York: Oxford University Press, 2004), 77–78; Arthur Lefkowitz, *The Long Retreat: The Calamitous American Defense of New Jersey, 1776* (New Brunswick, NJ: Rutgers University Press, 1999), 1–2, 6–7.

5. Fischer, *Washington's Crossing*, 77–82; Kwasny, *Washington's Partisan War*, 56, 65–66; Middlekauff, *Glorious Cause*, 333–35; GW to John Hancock, September 8, 1776, *Washington Papers, Revolutionary War Series*, 6:248–54; *Minutes*, 548–51.

6. GW to WL, June 28, 1776, *PWL*, 1:56–57 (for quote); Jonathan Trumbull to GW, June 22, 1776, *Washington Papers, Revolutionary War Series*, 5:76–77; George Adams Boyd, *Elias Boudinot, Patriot and Statesman, 1740–1821* (Princeton, NJ: Princeton University Press, 1952), 29; Bernstein, "New Jersey in the American Revolution," 307–8; Kwasny, *Washington's Partisan War*, 56.

7. GW to WL, June 29, 1776, *WLP*, reel 1; WL to GW, June 28, 1776, *PWL*, 1:57.

8. General Orders, July 2, 1776, *Washington Papers, Revolutionary War Series*, 5:179–82; Kwasny, *Washington's Partisan War*, 56.

9. WL to Hugh Mercer, July 3, 1776, *PWL*, 1:62–63; Barnet Schecter, *The Battle for New York: The City at the Heart of the American Revolution* (New York: Walker & Co., 2002), 100–101.

10. Elizabethtown Committee of Safety to GW, July 3, 1776, and Newark Committee of Correspondence to GW, July 4, 1776, *Washington Papers, Revolutionary War Series*, 5:189–90, 207–8; WL to Joseph Reed, July 3, 1776, *PWL*, 1:60–61; Woodbridge Committee of Correspondence to WL, July 4, 1776, *WLP*, reel 1.

11. Abraham Clark to Elias Dayton, July 4, 1776, Abraham Clark to Samuel Tucker, July 9, 1776, and Abraham Clark to Elias Dayton, July 14, 1776, *LDC*, 4:378, 418, 451–52; Larry R. Gerlach, *Prologue to Independence: New Jersey in the Coming of the American Revolution* (New Brunswick, NJ: Rutgers University Press, 1976), 350–52; John Adams to Abigail Adams, August 12, 1776, *LDC*, 4:660; *Minutes*, 494; Leonard Lundin, *Cockpit of the Revolution: The War for Independence in New Jersey* (Princeton, NJ: Princeton University Press, 1940), 115; Boyd, *Elias Boudinot*, 30. Also see Lewis Ogden to WL, July 3, 1776, *WLP*, reel 1.

12. WL to Samuel Tucker, July 3, 1776, and WL to GW, July 4, 1776, *PWL*, 1:61–62, 64–65; Jonathan Deare to WL, July 4, 1776, *PWL*, 1:64 (for quote); GW to WL, July 5, 1776, and WL to GW, July 5, 1776, *PWL*, 1:65–67, 69–70; GW to Hugh Mercer, July 4, 1776, *Washington Papers, Revolutionary War Series*, 5:206–7; WL to GW, July 7, 1776, *PWL*, 1:79–80; *Minutes*, 487, 516–17.

13. Kwasny, *Washington's Partisan War*, 57; GW to Hugh Mercer, July 4, 1776, *Washington Papers, Revolutionary War Series*, 5:206–7; WL to GW, July 4, 1776, *PWL*, 1:64–65 (for quotes); GW to WL, July 5, 6, and 8, 1776, *PWL*, 1:65–67, 75–76, 80–81.

14. WL to Samuel Tucker, July 6, 1776, *PWL*, 1:72–74.

15. Samuel Tucker to WL, July 9, 1776, and WL to William Hooper (second quote), August 29, 1776, *PWL*, 1:86–87, 128–29.

16. WL to Samuel Tucker, July 6, 1776, *PWL*, 1:72–73; Schecter, *Battle for New York*, 103.

17. *Minutes*, 488; Bernstein, "New Jersey in the American Revolution," 168–74; Scott Rohrer, *Jacob Green's Revolution: Radical Religion and Reform in a Revolutionary Age* (University Park: Pennsylvania State University Press, 2014), 153–60.

18. Rohrer, *Jacob Green's Revolution*, 153–60; Irwin Gertzog, "The Author of the New Jersey Constitution of 1776," *New Jersey History* 110.3–4 (Fall/Winter 1992): 1–7; Charles Erdman, "The New Jersey Constitution of 1776" (PhD diss., Princeton University, 1929), 26–40; Maxine Lurie, "New Jersey: Radical or Conservative in the Crisis Summer of 1776?" in *New Jersey in the American Revolution*, ed. Barbara J. Mitnick (New Brunswick, NJ: Rutgers University Press, 2005), 36–38; Gary Nash, *The Unknown American Revolution: The Unruly Birth of Democracy and the Struggle to Create America* (New York: Viking, 2005), 273–79; Harold Thatcher, "Social Philosophy of William Livingston" (PhD diss., University of Chicago, 1938), 249–52; Bernstein, "New Jersey in the American Revolution," 168–74, 209, 231; Michael Levine, "Transformation of a Radical Whig Under Republican Government: William Livingston, Governor of New Jersey, 1776–1790" (PhD diss., Rutgers University, 1975), 58–62; Maxine Lurie, "Envisioning a Republic: New Jersey's 1776 Constitution and Oath of Office," *New Jersey History* 119.3 (Fall/Winter 2001): 3–7.

19. *Dunlap's Pennsylvania Packet; or, the General Advertiser*, July 15, 1776, in *New Jersey in the American Revolution, 1763–1783: A Documentary History*, ed. Larry R. Gerlach (Trenton: New Jersey Historical Commission, 1975), 219–20; Gerlach, *Prologue to Independence*, 348; *Minutes*, 511, 546–47; Joseph Barton to Henry Wisner, July 9, 1776, in Gerlach, *New Jersey in the American Revolution*, 221; John Fea, *The Way of Improvement Leads Home: Philip Vickers Fithian and the Rural Enlightenment in Early America* (Philadelphia: University of Pennsylvania Press, 2008), 194–95; Schecter, *Battle for New York*, 107–9.

20. John Adams to Jonathan Dickinson Sergeant, July 21, 1776, *Adams Papers, Series III*, 4:397–98.

21. Ibid.; Jonathan Dickinson Sergeant to John Adams, July 19, 1776, *Adams Papers, Series III*, 4:393–94; *Minutes*, 561–63.

22. Schecter, *Battle for New York*, 95; Lundin, *Cockpit of the Revolution*, 107; John Adams to John Sullivan, June 23, 1776, *Adams Papers, Series III*, 4:330–31; William Ellery to Benjamin Ellery, July 10, 1776, *LDC*, 4:430; Gerlach, *Prologue to Independence*, 356.

23. GW to Essex County Committee of Safety, June 21, 1776, and William Burnet to GW, June 25, 1776, *Washington Papers, Revolutionary War Series*, 5:63–64, 98–99; John Duyckinck to WL, July 6, 1776, and Hugh Mercer to WL, July 9, 1776, *PWL*, 1:74, 88; GW to WL and WL to GW, July 6, 1775, *PWL*, 1:74–76; Lundin, *Cockpit of the Revolution*, 119.

24. WL to Samuel Tucker, July 29, 1776, *PWL*, 1:110–11; *Minutes*, 486, 492, 524, 539; WL to John Dickinson, August 1, 1776, *PWL*, 1:112. Also see Lord Stirling to WL, July 15, 1776, *WLP*, reel 2.

25. Nathaniel Woodhull to GW, July 26, 1776, *Washington Papers, Revolutionary War Series*, 5:478–79n. 1; *Minutes*, 476–77, 489, 491–92; Gerlach, *Prologue to Independence*, 353; Lundin, *Cockpit of the Revolution*, 116–17; GW to Samuel Tucker, August 7, 1776, *Washington Papers, Revolutionary War Series*, 5:616–18. Also see GW to WL, July 8, 1776, and WL to Samuel Tucker, July 26, 1776, *PWL*, 1:80–81, 107–8; Certain Inhabitants of New York City to GW, July 9–14, 1776, *Washington Papers, Revolutionary War Series*, 5:252; David J. Fowler, "Egregious Villains, Wood Rangers, and London Traders: The Pine Robber Phenomenon in New Jersey During the Revolutionary War" (PhD diss., Rutgers University, 1987), 43–46.

26. Jonathan Elmer, Address to the Residents of Cumberland County, August 7, 1776, in Gerlach, *New Jersey in the American Revolution*, 225–27; John Witherspoon's Speech in Congress, July 30, 1776, *LDC*, 4:584–85; Jeffry Hays Morrison, "John Witherspoon and 'The Public Interest of Religion,'" *Journal of Church and State* 41.3 (January 1999): 563–66. For an overview of loyalists in this period, see Robert M. Calhoon, *The Loyalists in Revolutionary America, 1760–1781* (New York: Harcourt Brace Jovanovich, 1973), 360–67.

27. WL to Samuel Tucker, July 13–15, 1776, *PWL*, 1:97–98. Also see WL to Samuel Tucker, July 6, 1776, *PWL*, 1:72–74.

28. WL to Thomas Johnson, July 10, 1776, *WLP*, reel 2. Also see GW to John Hancock, July 4–5, 1776, *Washington Papers, Revolutionary War Series*, 5:199–203, and WL to Joseph Reed, July 11, 1776, *WLP*, reel 2.

29. WL to Samuel Tucker, July 6, 1776, *PWL*, 1:73 (first quote); *Minutes*, 481, 518; Joseph Reed to WL, July 6, 1776, and WL to Joseph Reed, July 7, 1776, *PWL*, 1:77–78.

30. WL to Samuel Tucker, July 13–15, 1776, *PWL*, 1:97–98 (first quote).

31. Thomas Cadmus, David Cundit, Philip Van Cortland, and Mathias Ward to WL, July 2, 1776, *WLP*, reel 1 (first quote); John Duyckinck to WL, July 7, 1776, *PWL*, 1:78–79 (second quote); Jacob Drake Jr. to WL, July 12, 1776, *PWL*, 1:95 (third quote).

32. WL to Jacob Drake Jr., July 12, 1776, *PWL*, 1:96 (for quotes); WL to Hugh Mercer, July 15, 1776, and WL to Samuel Tucker, July 16, 1776, *PWL*, 1:99–101; Howard H. Peckham, ed., *Memoirs of the Life of John Adlum in the Revolutionary War* (Chicago: Caxton Club, 1968), 17. Also see Kwasny, *Washington's Partisan War*, 57–59; Lundin, *Cockpit of the Revolution*, 123; Abraham Clark to Elias Dayton, August 6, 1776, *LDC*, 4:626; and Levine, "Transformation of a Radical Whig," 73–75.

33. Middlekauff, *Glorious Cause*, 338; Lefkowitz, *Long Retreat*, 14–17; *Minutes*, 521; Richard Stockton to Thomas Jefferson, July 19, 1776, *LDC*, 4:491; John Hancock to the New Jersey Convention, July 22, 1776, *LDC*, 4:517; GW to John Hancock, July 27, 1776, *Washington Papers, Revolutionary War Series*, 5:180–81; GW to WL, August 8, 1776, *PWL*, 1:112–13; Hugh Mercer to GW, July 30, 1776, and GW to Samuel Tucker, August 7, 1776, *Washington Papers, Revolutionary War Series*, 5:522–23, 616–18; GW to WL, August 8, 1776, WL to GW, August 12, 1776, WL Order, August 13, 1776, *PWL*, 1:112–13, 115–18; *Minutes*, 540, 568–69; WL to Philemon Dickinson, *PWL*, 1:118.

34. Jonathan Dickinson Sergeant to John Adams, August 13, 1776, *Adams Papers, Series III*, 4:453–55; John Adams to Jonathan Dickinson Sergeant, August 17, 1776, *LDC*, 5:11–12; James J. Gigantino II, *The Ragged Road to Abolition: Slavery and Freedom in New Jersey* (Philadelphia: University of Pennsylvania Press, 2015), 54–55.

35. GW to New York Convention, August 17, 1776, *Washington Papers, Revolutionary War Series*, 6:54–55; Judith L. Van Buskirk, *Generous Enemies: Patriots and Loyalists in Revolutionary New York* (Philadelphia: University of Pennsylvania Press, 2002), 20; Schecter, *Battle for New York*, 120–21; Fischer, *Washington's Crossing*, 86–87.

36. Schecter, *Battle for New York*, 112–16, 123–29; Middlekauff, *Glorious Cause*, 340–41; Fischer, *Washington's Crossing*, 89–91; Kwasny, *Washington's Partisan War*, 66; WL to GW, August 21, 1776, *PWL*, 1:120–21; Lefkowitz, *Long Retreat*, 9.

37. Middlekauff, *Glorious Cause*, 343–46; Fischer, *Washington's Crossing*, 91–101; Hugh Mercer to WL, August 27, 1776, and WL to William Hooper, August 29, 1776, *PWL*, 1:127, 128–29 (for quote). Also see GW to John Hancock, August 31, 1776, *Washington Papers, Revolutionary War Series*, 6:177–79, for the retreat to New York; Fea, *Way of Improvement*, 198–203; and Andrew Hunter Jr. Diary, in Gerlach, *New Jersey in the American Revolution*, 329–32, for specific details on the Battle of Long Island.

38. Gerlach, *Prologue to Independence*, 357; Bernstein, "New Jersey in the American Revolution," 245–46; Levine, "Transformation of a Radical Whig," 53–55; Richard McCormick, "The First Election of Governor William Livingston," *Proceedings of the New Jersey Historical Society* 92 (April 1974): 92–99; Joint Meeting Minutes, *PWL*, 1:132; John Pomfret, *Colonial New Jersey: A History*, (New York: Charles Scribner's Sons, 1973), 264; Boyd, *Elias Boudinot*, 30.

39. John Adams to William Tudor, June 24, 1776, and Jonathan Dickinson Sergeant to John Adams, September 14, 1776, *Adams Papers, Series III*, 4:335–36, 5:24–25; William Hooper to WL, September 11, 1776, *LDC*, 5:132–33.

40. WL to Henry Brockholst Livingston, September 2, 1776, *PWL*, 1:136; WL to Hugh Mercer, September 1, 1776, *PWL*, 1:133–34.

41. Jacob Ford Jr. to WL, September 3, 1776, *PWL*, 1:134–35; Michael S. Adelberg, "'I am as Innocent as an Unborn Child': The Loyalism of Edward and George Taylor," *New Jersey History* 123.1 (Spring/Summer 2005): 12–17, 22–26.

42. Address to the Legislature, September 13, 1776, *PWL*, 1:143–45; John Adams to Abigail Adams, September 22, 1776, *Adams Papers, Series II*, 2:131–33.

43. Address to the Legislature, September 13, 1776, *PWL*, 1:143–45; Bernstein, "New Jersey in the American Revolution," 309; GW to John Augustine Washington, September 22, 1776, *Washington Papers, Revolutionary War Series*, 6:371–74; Kwasny, *Washington's Partisan War*, 75–77, 79; Schecter, *Battle for New York*, 177–93; Middlekauff, *Glorious Cause*, 347–49; Lefkowitz, *Long Retreat*, 11–12.

44. Matthias Williamson to WL, September 15 and 21, 1776, *PWL*, 1:146–47, 149–50; WL to New Jersey Delegates to the Continental Congress, September 19, 1776, *PWL*, 1:148–49; Shy, *People Numerous and Armed*, 127–28.

45. WL to Assembly, September 24 and 26, October 5 and 8, 1776, *PWL*, 1:150–51, 153, 158, 164; John Hart to WL, October 5, 1776, and WL to Hugh Gaine, October 17, 1776, *PWL*, 1:160, 167.

46. Clement Biddle to WL, September 3, 1776, and William Maxwell to WL, October 18, 1776, *WLP*, reel 3; William Paterson to WL, October 21, 1776, as cited in *PWL*, 1:168; WL to Philip Schuyler, *PWL*, 1:168.

47. John Cushing, comp, *First Laws of the State of New Jersey* (Wilmington, DE: M. Glazier, 1981), 1–2; Kwasny, *Washington's Partisan War*, 77–82; Schecter, *Battle for New York*, 224–43; Middlekauff, *Glorious Cause*, 350–51.

48. November 9, 1776, *JCC*, 6:939; John Hancock to WL, November 12, 1776, *PWL*, 1:176; Lord Stirling to WL, November 18, 1776, and WL to Lord Stirling, November 20, 1776, *PWL*, 1:180–81; WL to GW, November 9, 1776, *PWL*, 1:174–75; WL to the Assembly, November 21, 1776, *PWL*, 1:183; Van Buskirk, *Generous Enemies*, 63–68; *Minutes*, 84.

49. GW to John Hancock, November 6, 1776, *Washington Papers, Revolutionary War Series*, 7:96–100 (first quote); GW to Nathanael Greene, November 7, 1776, *Washington Papers*,

Revolutionary War Series, 7:107–9 (second quote); GW to WL, November 7, 1776, *Washington Papers, Revolutionary War Series*, 7:110–12 (third quote); Kwasny, *Washington's Partisan War*, 82–83; Adrian Leiby, *The Revolutionary War in the Hackensack Valley: The Jersey Dutch and the Neutral Ground* (New Brunswick, NJ: Rutgers University Press, 1962), 54–55; Lefkowitz, *Long Retreat*, 20–23.

50. WL to GW, November 9, 1776, *PWL*, 1:174–76; Kwasny, *Washington's Partisan War*, 82–84; Schecter, *Battle for New York*, 244, 248–49; Lefkowitz, *Long Retreat*, 25–32.

51. WL to the New Jersey Militia Colonels, November 17–24, 1776, *PWL*, 1:177–79 (see 179 n. 4 for *New-York Gazette* article); Isaac Smith to WL, November 20, 1776, *PWL*, 1:182; Middlekauff, *Glorious Cause*, 351–54.

52. Schecter, *Battle for New York*, 209–10, 255; Kwasny, *Washington's Partisan War*, 84–87; Leiby, *Revolutionary War in the Hackensack Valley*, 65–67; Lefkowitz, *Long Retreat*, 35–53; Lord Stirling to WL, November 21, 1776 (two letters), *WLP*, reel 3; GW to WL, November 21, 1776, *Washington Papers, Revolutionary War Series*, 7:195–96; Matthias Williamson to WL, November 21, 1776, *WLP*, reel 3. For a complete overview of the invasion, see Fischer, *Washington's Crossing*, 126–35; Lundin, *Cockpit of the Revolution*, 137–59; Middlekauff, *Glorious Cause*, 354–57; and Lefkowitz, *Long Retreat*, 54–126.

53. Susannah French Livingston to WL, February 7, 1777, *PWL*, 1:218; WL to Philemon Dickinson, November 24, 1776, WL to Matthias Williamson, November 25, 1776, WL to the Assembly, November 25, 1776, WL to GW, November 27, 1776, *PWL*, 1:187–89 (see p. 188n. 2 for militia bounty); Cushing, *First Laws of New Jersey*, 6.

54. GW to WL, November 30, 1776, *PWL*, 1:191; GW to WL, December 1, 1776, *WLP*, reel 3 (first quote); Kwasny, *Washington's Partisan War*, 85; Matthias Williamson to GW, December 8, 1776, *Washington Papers, Revolutionary War Series*, 7:280–82 (second quote); William Hooper to Joseph Hewes, November 30, 1776, and Samuel Adams to James Warren, December 4, 1776, *LDC*, 5:557–58, 567–68 (last quote). For WL's response to militia failures, see WL to Philemon Dickinson, January 14, 1777, *PWL*, 1:197–98.

55. GW to John Hancock, December 5, GW to Jonathan Trumbull Sr., December 12, and GW to Samuel Washington, December 18, 1776, *Washington Papers, Revolutionary War Series*, 7:262–64, 321–22, 369–72; Kwasny, *Washington's Partisan War*, 89.

56. Schecter, *Battle for New York*, 260–63; Kwasny, *Washington's Partisan War*, 90–93; Fischer, *Washington's Crossing*, 138–41; Lefkowitz, *Long Retreat*, 66–67.

57. Alexander McDougall to GW, December 22 and 30, 1776, *Washington Papers, Revolutionary War Series*, 7:410–11, 485–88. See Editor's Introduction, *PWL*, 1:195, for information on WL's disappearance.

58. Fischer, *Washington's Crossing*, 160–65; Kwasny, *Washington's Partisan War*, 90–91, 97–98; Leiby, *Revolutionary War in the Hackensack Valley*, 82–83; John Bray to Andrew Bray, December 17, 1776, in Gerlach, *New Jersey in the American Revolution*, 364–65; GW to Colonel David Forman, November 24, 1776, *Washington Papers, Revolutionary War Series*, 7:203; Adam Stephen to WL, November 22, 1776, *PWL*, 1:186; Mark Edward Lender, "The Cockpit Reconsidered: Revolutionary New Jersey as a Military Theater," in Mitnick, *New Jersey in the American Revolution*, 48.

59. Kwasny, *Washington's Partisan War*, 90–91, 97–98; Leiby, *Revolutionary War in the Hackensack Valley*, 77–80, 82–83, 89; Lundin, *Cockpit of the Revolution*, 160–65; Fischer, *Washington's Crossing*, 160–65; Calhoon, *Loyalists in Revolutionary America*, 360–61; Peter Parker to Henry Clinton, December 20, 1776, Clinton Papers, vol. 19.

60. WL to John Hancock, December 7, 1776, *PWL*, 1:192; WL to Philemon Dickinson, January 14, 1777, *PWL*, 1:197; December 1776–March 1777 essay on Livingston, *PWL*, 1:194–95.

61. Lord Stirling to WL, December 28, 1776, *WLP*, reel 3. For war powers, see WL to John Hancock, February 3, 1777, *PWL*, 1:208; Kwasny, *Washington's Partisan War*, 101; Fischer, *Washington's Crossing*, 144–45; and Thatcher, "Social Philosophy of William Livingston," 249. For accounts of the Trenton and Princeton campaigns, see Kwasny, *Washington's Partisan War*, 99–105; Fischer, *Washington's Crossing*, 204–62, 308–45; Lundin, *Cockpit of the Revolution*, 194–215; Middlekauff, *Glorious Cause*, 359–62; and Lender, "Cockpit Reconsidered," 49–50.

62. Schecter, *Battle for New York*, 268; Kwasny, *Washington's Partisan War*, 105–6; GW, Proclamation to the Friends of America in the State of New Jersey, December 31, 1776, GW to John Hancock, January 1, 1777, *Washington Papers, Revolutionary War Series*, 7:497–98, 503–5; William Whipple to John Langdon, January 15, 1777, and John Adams to Abigail Adams, February 17, 1777, *LDC*, 6:110–11, 305; Fowler, "Egregious Villains," 48–49; Michael S. Adelberg, "'A Combination to Trample All Law Underfoot': The Association for Retaliation and the American Revolution in Monmouth County, New Jersey," *New Jersey History* 115 (February 1997): 5.

63. WL to Philemon Dickinson, January 14, 1777, WL Order, January 20, 1777, *PWL*, 1:197–98, 201; GW to WL, January 24, 1777, *Washington Papers, Revolutionary War Series*, 8:147–48; Shy, *People Numerous and Armed*, 225.

64. WL to Assembly, January 24 and 31, February 3 and 5, 1777, *PWL*, 1:202–3, 206, 209–10, 214–15 (quotes on 209–10); GW, Circular Letter to Eleven States, January 31–February 1, 1777, *Washington Papers, Revolutionary War Series*, 8:196–97; Mark Edward Lender, "The Conscripted Line: The Draft in Revolutionary New Jersey," *New Jersey History* 103 (1985): 24–26. Also see Assembly to WL, February 5, 1777, *PWL*, 1:213; and Theodore Thayer, *Colonial and Revolutionary Morris County* (Morristown, NJ: Morris County Heritage Commission, 1975), 175.

65. James Haw, *John & Edward Rutledge of South Carolina* (Athens: University of Georgia Press, 1997), 83–84, 101–2, 120; Gregory Massey, *John Laurens and the American Revolution* (Columbia: University of South Carolina Press, 2000), 132–34; John Gordon, *South Carolina and the American Revolution: A Battlefield History* (Columbia: University of South Carolina Press, 2003), 49.

66. Richard Hixson, *Isaac Collins, A Quaker Printer in 18th Century America* (New Brunswick, NJ: Rutgers University Press, 1968), 64–65; David Morris Roth, *Connecticut's War Governor, Jonathan Trumbull* (Guilford, CT: Pequot Press, 1974), 52–53, 61–66; Richard Buel, *Dear Liberty: Connecticut's Mobilization for the Revolutionary War* (Middletown, CT: Wesleyan University Press, 1980), 82–83, 95–96.

67. WL to GW, February 15, 1777, *PWL*, 1:225 (first quote); "The Impartial Chronicle," *PWL*, 1:226–39; Hixson, *Isaac Collins*, 64–66.

68. WL to GW, February 10, 1777, *PWL*, 1:219 (first quote); Simon Schama, *Rough Crossings: Britain, the Slaves, and the American Revolution* (New York: Ecco, 2006), 113 (second quote); Fischer, *Washington's Crossing*, 346–51; Leiby, *Revolutionary War in the Hackensack Valley*, 103–6, 116–17; Kwasny, *Washington's Partisan War*, 106; David J. Fowler, "These Were Troublesome Times Indeed: Social and Economic Conditions in Revolutionary New Jersey," in Mitnick, *New Jersey in the American Revolution*, 24–25; Middlekauff, *Glorious Cause*, 363; Lender, "Cockpit Reconsidered," 52–53; Jeffrey A. Denman, "Fighting for Forage," *Military Historical Quarterly* 26.3 (Spring 2014): 53.

69. Fischer, *Washington's Crossing*, 346–61 (Harcourt quote on 358); Denman, "Fighting for Forage," 54 (Waldeck quote); Lundin, *Cockpit of the Revolution*, 223–26; Kwasny, *Washington's*

Partisan War, 113–17; Jared Lobdell, "Six Generals Gather Forage: The Engagement at Quibbletown, 1777," *New Jersey History* 102.1–2 (February 1984): 36–46; Elias Boudinot to WL, June 20, 177, *WLP*, reel 5.

70. Israel Putnam to WL, February 18, 1777, *PWL*, 1:241 (first quote); Oliver Spencer to WL, February 24, 1777, *PWL*, 1:252; WL to Philemon Dickinson, March 1, 1777, *PWL*, 1:260 (second quote); WL to John Jay, March 3, 1777, *PWL*, 1:264–65 (third quote).

71. Loftus Cliffe to John Cliffe, March 5, 1777, Loftus Cliffe Papers, Manuscripts Division, William L. Clements Library, University of Michigan, Ann Arbor; WL to Assembly, March 7, 1777, *PWL*, 1:268–69 (first and fourth quotes); WL to GW, March 3, 1777, *PWL*, 1:266 (second quote); WL to John Hancock, March 4, 1777, *PWL*, 1:267 (third quote); Bernstein, "New Jersey in the American Revolution," 197–99, 313; Buel, *Dear Liberty*, 95–96.

72. For passage of the militia bill, see *PWL*, 1:269n. 2; *Votes and Proceedings of the General Assembly of the State of New-Jersey [August 1776]* (Burlington, NJ: Isaac Collins, 1777), 94–95; Philemon Dickinson to GW, February 19, 1777, *Washington Papers, Revolutionary War Series*, 8:368–69; John Hancock to WL, February 25, 1777, Nathanael Greene to WL, March 8, 1777 (for quote), and GW to WL, March 9, 1777, *WLP*, reel 4; Kwasny, *Washington's Partisan War*, 131–32.

73. Leiby, *Revolutionary War in the Hackensack River Valley*, 106–7; Lundin, *Cockpit of the Revolution*, 217–20; Fischer, *Washington's Crossing*, 349–50; WL to Assembly, February 3, 1777, and WL Proclamation, February 5, 1777, *PWL*, 1:209, 214–15; Lender, "Cockpit Reconsidered," 50–51.

74. WL to George Clinton, January 15, 1777, *PWL*, 1:198–99. Also see George Clinton to WL, January 12, 1777, *PWL*, 1:196.

75. WL, Proclamation, February 5, 1777, *PWL*, 1:214; Cushing, *First Laws of New Jersey*, 4–5; Bergen County Oath of Allegiance, January 28, 1777, in Gerlach, *New Jersey in the American Revolution*, 365–66; Ruth Bogin, *Abraham Clark and the Quest for Equality in the Revolutionary Era, 1774–1794* (Rutherford, NJ: Fairleigh Dickinson University Press, 1982), 24–26; Thayer, *Colonial and Revolutionary Morris County*, 175.

76. WL to GW, March 3, 1777, *PWL*, 1:266–67 (first quote); Supreme Court of New Jersey Case Files, 1704–1844, no. 34552, NJSA; Samuel Forman to WL and Legislature, February 21, 1777, *WLP*, reel 4 (second quote); GW to William Maxwell, February 12, 1777, *Washington Papers, Revolutionary War Series*, 8:319–20 (third quote).

77. Leiby, *Revolutionary War in the Hackensack River Valley*, 108–9; Fischer, *Washington's Crossing*, 166–68, 170–71.

78. GW to Nathanael Greene, November 7, 1776, *Washington Papers, Revolutionary War Series*, 7:107–9 (first quote); Adam Stephen to Thomas Jefferson, December 20, 1776, *Jefferson Papers*, 1:659–60 (second quote); Abraham Clark to James Caldwell, February 4, 1777, *LDC*, 6:209–11 (third quote); WL to Assembly, January 24, 1777, *PWL*, 1:202 (fourth quote); Gigantino, *Ragged Road to Abolition*, 36–37.

79. WL to GW, February 6, 1777, GW to WL, February 14, 1777, *PWL*, 1:217–18, 224; GW to John Hancock, February 5, 1777, *Washington Papers, Revolutionary War Series*, 8:249–53; WL to GW, February 22, 1777, *PWL*, 1:251; Gigantino, *Ragged Road to Abolition*, 36–37.

80. Ebenezer Hazard Diary, August 1777, in Gerlach, *New Jersey in the American Revolution*, 298–300; Abraham Clark to John Hart, February 8, 1777, *LDC*, 6:240–41. Also see Fischer, *Washington's Crossing*, 173–77; John Stevens to U.S. Congress, April 3, 1778, BAH MS Collection, box 5-2, no. 137; and Mark A. Noll, "Princeton in the Revolutionary Era, 1757–1815," *Journal of Presbyterian History* 85.2 (Fall/Winter 2007): 93.

81. Ebenezer Hazard Diary, August 6, 1777, and Margaret Morris Journal, December 1776, in Gerlach, *New Jersey in the American Revolution*, 283–84, 299; WL to Owen Biddle, February 22, 1777, Thomas Wharton to WL, March 1, 1777, *PWL*, 1:247–48, 262–64; Lundin, *Cockpit of the Revolution*, 173–75, 245–46; Thayer, *Colonial and Revolutionary Morris County*, 173–74.

82. Thayer, *Colonial and Revolutionary Morris County*, 169–71; GW to Horatio Gates, February 5–6, 1777, and GW to William Shippen Jr., February 6, 1777, *Washington Papers, Revolutionary War Series*, 8:248–49, 264; Elizabeth Fenn, *Pox Americana: The Great Smallpox Epidemic of 1775–1782* (New York: Hill and Wang, 2001).

83. Peter O. Wacker and Paul G. E. Clemens, *Land Use in Early New Jersey: A Historical Geography* (Newark: New Jersey Historical Society, 1995), 141–44, 185–86; Dennis Ryan, "Six Towns: Continuity and Change in Revolutionary New Jersey, 1770–1792" (PhD diss., New York University, 1974), 129–34, 283; Damage Claim of Ennis Graham, Middlesex County Inventories of Damages by the British and Americans in New Jersey, pages 1–2, and Burlington County Inventories of Damages by the British and Americans in New Jersey, page 168, NJSA.

84. Catharine Livingston to WL, January 12, 1777, *WLP*, reel 3.

85. Thomas Nelson to Thomas Jefferson, January 2, 1777, *Jefferson Papers*, 2:3–4; Samuel Adams to John Adams, January 9, 1777, *Adams Papers, Series III*, 5:68–71; WL to Caesar Rodney, February 24, 1777, *PWL*, 1:251, 252n. 1; Alexander MacWhorter in *Pennsylvania Evening Post*, April 26, 1777, in Gerlach, *New Jersey in the American Revolution*, 296; James J. Gigantino II, "The Trouble with Quakers: Creating Racial Tensions in East and West Jersey," in *Quakers and Their Allies in the Abolitionist Cause, 1754–1808*, ed. Maurice Jackson and Susan Kozel (London: Pickering and Chatto, 2015), 121. Also see Fischer, *Washington's Crossing*, 178; Lundin, *Cockpit of the Revolution*, 177; Gigantino, *Ragged Road to Abolition*, 36–37; and Holger Hoock, *Scars of Independence: America's Violent Birth* (New York: Crown, 2017), 160–65, 172–77.

86. WL to the Legislature, February 25, 1777, *PWL*, 1:254–60, 260n. 4; John Adams to James Warren, March 6, 1777, *Adams Papers, Series III*, 5:100–101; Walter Peterson, "William Livingston: A Study of a Political Center Before, During, and After the Revolution" (master's thesis, University of Iowa, 1948), 72.

87. Bernstein, "New Jersey in the American Revolution," 309–14.

88. Ibid.; John O'Connor, *William Paterson, Lawyer and Statesman, 1745–1806* (New Brunswick, NJ: Rutgers University Press, 1979), 90–91; Editor's Note, *PWL*, 1:272; Nelson, *Royalist Revolution*, 149.

Chapter 4

1. John Shy, *A People Numerous and Armed: Reflections on the Military Struggle for American Independence* (New York: Oxford University Press, 1976), 177, 217–19.

2. Robert M. Calhoon, *The Loyalists in Revolutionary America, 1760–1781* (New York: Harcourt Brace Jovanovich, 1973), 360–69; Gary Nash, *The Unknown American Revolution: The Unruly Birth of Democracy and the Struggle to Create America* (New York: Viking, 2005), xvi.

3. Judith L. Van Buskirk, *Generous Enemies: Patriots and Loyalists in Revolutionary New York* (Philadelphia: University of Pennsylvania Press, 2002), 2–5.

4. WL to Assembly, March 11, 1777, *PWL*, 1:273–75; Michael Levine, "Transformation of a Radical Whig Under Republican Government: William Livingston, Governor of New Jersey, 1776–1790" (PhD diss., Rutgers University, 1975), 65–67, 80; Alexander Hamilton to WL, April 29, 1777, *The Papers of Alexander Hamilton*, ed. Harold C. Syrett et al., 27 vols. (New York: Columbia University Press, 1961–1979), 1:242–44.

5. John O'Connor, *William Paterson, Lawyer and Statesman, 1745–1806* (New Brunswick, NJ: Rutgers University Press, 1979), 90–95 (quotes on 92 and 93); Leonard Lundin, *Cockpit of the Revolution: The War for Independence in New Jersey* (Princeton, NJ: Princeton University Press, 1940), 269.

6. Calhoon, *Loyalists in Revolutionary America*, 402–4; David Bernstein, "New Jersey in the American Revolution: The Establishment of a Government Amid Civil and Military Disorder, 1770–1781" (PhD diss., Rutgers University, 1970), 280–88, 294; Act for investing the governor and a council . . . with certain powers, March 15, 1777, *Acts of the General Assembly of the State of New-Jersey [1776–1777]* (Burlington, NJ: Isaac Collins, 1777), 40–42; Levine, "Transformation of a Radical Whig," 80–84, 86; Carl E. Prince, *William Livingston, New Jersey's First Governor* (Trenton: New Jersey Historical Commission, 1975), 17–18; Theodore Sedgwick, *A Memoir of the Life of William Livingston . . .* (New York: J. & J. Harper, 1833), 231; Lundin, *Cockpit of the Revolution*, 270; O'Connor, *William Paterson*, 96; WL to Assembly, November 6, 1777, *PWL*, 2:103; Theodore Thayer, *Colonial and Revolutionary Morris County* (Morristown, NJ: Morris County Heritage Commission, 1975), 190–96.

7. WL to Assembly, May 29, 1778, *PWL*, 2:346.

8. David Fowler, "Loyalty Is Now Bleeding in New Jersey: Motivations and Mentalities of the Disaffected," in *The Other Loyalists: Ordinary People, Royalism, and the Revolution in the Middle Colonies, 1763–1787*, ed. Joseph S. Tiedemann, Eugene R. Fingerhut, and Robert W. Venables (Albany: State University of New York Press, 2009), 49; Van Buskirk, *Generous Enemies*, 61; Levine, "Transformation of a Radical Whig," 73–76; Dennis Ryan, "Six Towns: Continuity and Change in Revolutionary New Jersey, 1770–1792" (PhD diss., New York University, 1974), 182–83; Walter Peterson, "William Livingston: A Study of a Political Center Before, During, and After the Revolution" (master's thesis, University of Iowa, 1948), 69.

9. David Morris Roth and Freeman Meyer, *From Revolution to Constitution: Connecticut, 1763–1818* (Guilford, CT: Pequot Press, 1975), 23; David Morris Roth, *Connecticut's War Governor, Jonathan Trumbull* (Guilford, CT: Pequot Press, 1974), 40–41; John Gordon, *South Carolina and the American Revolution: A Battlefield History* (Columbia: University of South Carolina Press, 2003), 104; Jim Piecuch, *Three Peoples, One King: Loyalists, Indians, and Slaves in the Revolutionary South, 1775–1782* (Columbia: University of South Carolina Press, 2008), 17, 44, 50–56, 91–96, 177–85, 190–99; Walter Edgar, *Partisans and Redcoats: The Southern Conflict That Turned the Tide of the American Revolution* (New York: Morrow, 2001), 30–33, 67–68; John Pancake, *This Destructive War: The British Campaign in the Carolinas, 1780–1782* (Tuscaloosa: University of Alabama Press, 2003), 53, 123–39; Holger Hoock, *Scars of Independence: America's Violent Birth* (New York: Crown, 2017), 303–35.

10. WL to Henry Laurens, June 8, 1778, *PWL*, 2:362 (first quote); WL to GW, October 5, 1777, *PWL*, 2:86 (second quote).

11. O'Connor, *William Paterson*, 98.

12. Van Buskirk, *Generous Enemies*, 45–55, 61; Peterson, "William Livingston," 80; Ruma Chopra, *Unnatural Rebellion: Loyalists in New York City During the Revolution* (Charlottesville: University of Virginia Press, 2011), 39.

13. WL to John Sullivan, August 16, 1777, *WLP*, reel 5.

14. Paul Smith, "New Jersey Loyalists and the British 'Provincial' Corps," *New Jersey History* 87.2 (1969): 72–73, 76; Calhoon, *Loyalists in Revolutionary America*, 362–63; WL to GW, August 15–16, 1777, *PWL*, 2:32–35, 36–37n. 4 (for quotes); WL to GW, September 3, 1777, *PWL*, 2:59–61.

15. Philemon Dickinson to WL, September 14, 1777, WL to John Hancock, September 17, 1777, and WL to Assembly, September 19, 1777, *PWL*, 2:70–71, 74–76; WL to John Hancock, October 4, 1777, *PWL*, 2:84–85 (for quotes); WL to GW, April 15, 1778, *PWL*, 2:291 (for dirty villains quote); Gregory F. Walsh, "'Most Boundless Avarice': Illegal Trade in Revolutionary Essex," in *The American Revolution in New Jersey: Where the Battlefront Meets the Home Front*, ed. James J. Gigantino II (New Brunswick, NJ: Rutgers University Press, 2015), 40; GW to WL, April 1, 1777, *PWL*, 1:290 (for poisoning mind quote).

16. WL to GW, April 30, 1777, *PWL*, 1:317; WL to Assembly, May 9, 1777, *PWL*, 1:326–27 (for quotes).

17. WL to John Witherspoon, May 7, 1777, *PWL*, 1:322–24; May 8, 1777, *JCC*, 7:335.

18. WL to GW, January 13, 1778, WL to GW, January 26, 1778, WL to Henry Laurens, February 5, 1778, and WL to Levinus Clarkson, April 10, 1778, *PWL*, 2:176–77, 193, 211, 287–88; GW to WL, February 2, 1778, *Washington Papers, Revolutionary War Series*, 13:441–42 (for quote); WL to John Fell, December 14, 1778, *PWL*, 2:506. Also see Henry Laurens to WL, July 17, 1778, *WLP*, reel 7; and Sedgwick, *Memoir of William Livingston*, 242.

19. Deposition of Thomas Farr, April 5, 1777, and Deposition of Isaac Potter, April 7, 1777, *PWL*, 1:294, 299; *Minutes of the Council of Safety of the State of New Jersey* (Jersey City: J. H. Lyon, 1872), 15–16. For other examples of depositions, see *WLP*, reel 4, and *PWL*, 1:287–330.

20. For an example of using the militia, see WL to William Winds, July 3, 1777, *PWL*, 2:8. For the Woodwards, see David J. Fowler, "Egregious Villains, Wood Rangers, and London Traders: The Pine Robber Phenomenon in New Jersey During the Revolutionary War" (PhD diss., Rutgers University, 1987), 49, 54, 58–60, 64–78, 107–8.

21. Fowler, "Egregious Villains," 50–51, 78–87; Deposition of Lewis Bestedo, April 15, 1777, *PWL*, 1:306–7.

22. Fowler, "Egregious Villains," 93; WL to Assembly, May 7, 1777, and Robert Morris to WL, June 14, 1777, *PWL*, 1:321, 352–53; Robert Morris to WL, November 12, 1777, *PWL*, 2:111–12; Ruth Bogin, *Abraham Clark and the Quest for Equality in the Revolutionary Era, 1774–1794* (Rutherford, NJ: Fairleigh Dickinson University Press, 1982), 29–30.

23. GW to WL, April 1, 1777, and WL to GW, April 4, 1777, *PWL*, 1:289–91, 292–93; Levine, "Transformation of a Radical Whig," 23.

24. WL to Assembly, May 28, 1777, *PWL*, 1:341–42 (first quotes); *Minutes of the Council of Safety*, 110 (last quote); WL to Assembly, June 7, 1777, *PWL*, 1:347; Act of free and general pardon, June 5, 1777, *Acts of the General Assembly [1776–1777]*, 71–74; Michael Riccards, "Patriots and Plunderers: Confiscation of Loyalist Lands in New Jersey, 1776–1786," *New Jersey History* 86.1 (February 1968): 15–16; WL to GW, July 8, 1777, *PWL*, 2:11; Roth and Meyer, *From Revolution to Constitution*, 25.

25. WL Proclamation, August 14–17, 1777, *PWL*, 2:28–30; *Minutes of the Council of Safety*, 126–27.

26. WL to Assembly, September 3, 1777, and February 16, 1778, *PWL*, 2:55, 223–24; Riccards, "Patriots and Plunderers," 18; Bainbridge Petition, Loyalist Claims Commission, British Public Records Office, AO 12/14/139-144, AO 12/101/255-56, and AO13/108/31-46; James J. Gigantino II, *The Ragged Road to Abolition: Slavery and Freedom in New Jersey* (Philadelphia: University of Pennsylvania Press, 2015), 31–32; Van Buskirk, *Generous Enemies*, 3; Joseph Hedden Jr. to WL, June 21, 1777, and Order in Council of Safety, June 24, 1777, *PWL*, 1:358; Joseph Hedden to WL, July 9, 1777, *WLP*, reel 5.

27. Wallace Brown, *The King's Friends: The Composition and Motives of the American Loyalist*

Claimants (Providence, RI: Brown University Press, 1965), 115; Riccards, "Patriots and Plunderers," 16–26; Act for . . . forfeiting the personal estates of certain fugitives and offenders," April 18, 1778, *Acts of the General Assembly of the State of New-Jersey [1777–1778]* (Burlington, NJ: Isaac Collins, 1778), 73–82; Inhabitants of Morris County to the Legislative Council and General Assembly, May 28, 1781, and Inhabitants of Monmouth County to the Governor, Legislative Council, and General Assembly, May 25, 1779, BAH MS Collection, box 4-1a, nos. 76, 110; Gigantino, *Ragged Road to Abolition*, 58–59.

28. Henry Laurens to WL, April 27, 1778, *PWL*, 2:312; April 23, 1778, *JCC*, 10:381–82; Robert Morris to Gouverneur Morris, December 11, 1777, in *New Jersey in the American Revolution, 1763–1783: A Documentary History*, ed. Larry R. Gerlach (Trenton: New Jersey Historical Commission, 1975), 254–56; WL to Henry Laurens, May 7, 1778, *PWL*, 2:329 (first quote); Petition of James Iliff to WL and Legislative Council, [October 1777], BAH MS Collection, box 1-1, no. 74.

29. WL to Assembly, May 29, 1778, *PWL*, 2:343–44, 347–49, 351; Levine, "Transformation of a Radical Whig," 23–24; Petition of the Underwritten Gentleman and Landholders and Inhabitants of the Province of West Jersey to General Howe, December 1778, Clinton Papers, vol. 49.

30. WL to Elias Dayton, July 22, 1777, WL to GW, January 26, 1778, *PWL*, 2:24–25, 193–95; Walsh, "Most Boundless Avarice" 32–33; Van Buskirk, *Generous Enemies*, 119; WL to Thomas Wharton Jr., April 5, 1777 (two letters), *PWL*, 1:296–98 (for quotes).

31. Walsh, "Most Boundless Avarice," 37–39; Van Buskirk, *Generous Enemies*, 29, 107–14; Chopra, *Unnatural Rebellion*, 64–77, 126; Bernstein, "American Revolution in New Jersey," 274.

32. Walsh, "Most Boundless Avarice," 38; Van Buskirk, *Generous Enemies*, 35–36; Trenton and Mercer County Magistrates to GW, January 2, 1778, *Washington Papers, Revolutionary War Series*, 13:122–24.

33. Bernstein, "New Jersey in the American Revolution," 294, 378–80; WL to Assembly, November 7, 1777, *PWL*, 2:105–6; WL to GW, December 1, 1777, *PWL*, 2:129–30, esp. n. 7; Act for regulating and limiting the prices of sundry articles, December 11, 1777, *Acts of the General Assembly [1777–1778]*, 16–20; Peterson, "William Livingston," 76; WL to Assembly, September 21, 1777, *PWL*, 2:77–78; Cortlandt Skinner to Henry Clinton, June 7, 1781, Clinton Papers, vol. 158.

34. William Burnet to WL and Council of Safety, February 25, 1778, *WLP*, reel 6; WL to GW, January 12, 1778, *PWL*, 2:175; WL to GW, November 11, 1777, *PWL*, 2:110; WL to Inhabitants of New Jersey, February 25, 1778, *PWL*, 2:238; Proclamation, March 9, 1778, *PWL*, 2:248–49. The British occupation of Philadelphia turned that city into another popular trading spot for illegal traders; see February 21, 1778, *Minutes of the Governor's Privy Council, 1777–1789*, ed. David A. Bernstein (Trenton: New Jersey State Library, 1974), 61–62.

35. Petition to the General Assembly requesting that price limits be suspended, January 16, 1778, BAH MS Collection, box 1-14, no. 35; Act to suspend . . . An Act for regulating and limiting the price, June 22, 1778, and October 7, 1778, *Acts of the General Assembly [1777–1778]*, 89, 101; Act to further suspend the operation of . . . An Act for regulating and limiting the price, December 3, 1778, *Acts of the General Assembly of the State of New-Jersey [1778–1779]* (Burlington, NJ: Isaac Collins, 1779), 8.

36. Walsh, "Most Boundless Avarice," 34–37, 43–45 (Bowater quote at 44); WL to GW, November 22, 1777, *PWL*, 2:120.

37. Walsh, "Most Boundless Avarice," 34–35; March 2, 1778, *Votes and Proceedings of the General Assembly of the State of New-Jersey [1777–1778]* (Trenton, NJ: Isaac Collins, 1779), 72–73 (Monmouth petition); Residents of Essex County to the General Assembly on Trade with the

Enemy, undated, in Gerlach, *New Jersey in the American Revolution*, 399–401; Richard Buel, *Dear Liberty: Connecticut's Mobilization for the Revolutionary War* (Middletown, CT: Wesleyan University Press, 1980), 257–59; Roth, *Connecticut's War Governor*, 71.

38. Walsh, "Most Boundless Avarice," 40–41; Inhabitants of the state to Council of New Jersey, May 24, 1778, BAH MS Collection, box 4-1a, no. 63; Testimony of Abel Thomas and James Thomas, May 26, 1778, *PWL*, 2:342.

39. Order in Council of Safety, June 9, 1777, *PWL*, 2:347–48; Essex County Grand Jury to WL, August 13, 1777, *PWL*, 2:27; WL to GW, August 15–16, 1777, *PWL*, 2:36; Walsh, "Most Boundless Avarice," 40–41; Proclamation, August 14–17, 1777, *PWL*, 2:28–30.

40. WL to GW, December 21, 1778, *PWL*, 2:518–19; WL to Mary Martin, February 16, 1778, *PWL*, 2:232–33; Van Buskirk, *Generous Enemies*, 65–67; Walsh, "Most Boundless Avarice," 41–43. Even Livingston was occasionally fooled; see WL to Henry Laurens, November 29, 1778, *PWL*, 2:486, for a case in which he issued a pass to a loyalist.

41. Walsh, "Most Boundless Avarice," 35–37, 40–41; WL to Joseph Reed, October 22, 1778, *PWL*, 2:471–72; Van Buskirk, *Generous Enemies*, 61; Levine, "Transformation of a Radical Whig," 73–76.

42. WL to Alida Hoffman, October 29, 1782, *PWL*, 4:484–85; WL to Robert Livingston, April 22, 1782, *PWL*, 4:394–95.

43. WL to Alida Hoffman, October 29, 1782, *PWL*, 4:484–85; Van Buskirk, *Generous Enemies*, 126; Sedgwick, *Memoir of William Livingston*, 236–39; WL to Henry Brockholst Livingston, January 4, 1778, *PWL*, 2:158–59. Other Livingston allies also illegally imported goods. See Prince, *William Livingston*, 18, for a discussion of Elias Boudinot.

44. Proclamation, August 14–17, 1777, *PWL*, 2:28–30; Van Buskirk, *Generous Enemies*, 58–59; Peterson, "William Livingston," 79; Proclamation, July 28, 1778, *PWL*, 2:405; Act to prevent the subjects of this state from going into, or coming out of, the enemy's lines, October 8, 1778, *Acts of the General Assembly [1777–1778]*, 104–6; Act to explain and amend . . . An Act to prevent, December 11, 1778, *Acts of the General Assembly [1778–1779]*, 41–42.

45. *Minutes of the Council of Safety*, 204, 249–50.

46. WL to Henry Laurens, August 22, 1778, *PWL*, 2:423 (for quote); WL to Lord Stirling, October 12, 1778, *PWL*, 2:462; GW to WL and Joseph Reed, December 17, 1778, *WLP*, reel 8.

47. Proclamation, August 22, 1778, *PWL*, 2:421–22 (first quote); WL to GW, January 26, 1782, *PWL*, 4:373 (second quote); Walsh, "Most Boundless Avarice," 39–40, 42–48; Buel, *Dear Liberty*, 266 (Trumbull quote).

48. Bernstein, "New Jersey in the American Revolution," 328–32; Introduction, *Privy Council Minutes*, 7–11.

49. Bernstein, "New Jersey in the American Revolution," 328–32; Introduction, *Privy Council Minutes*, 12–16.

50. GW to WL, April 1 and 5, 1777, *PWL*, 1:290, 298; WL to GW, April 4, 1777, *PWL*, 1:292–93; WL to Assembly, October 3, 1777, *PWL*, 2:83; WL to Assembly, December 5, 1777, *PWL*, 2:132–33 (first quote); WL to Silvanus Seely, December 9, 1777, *PWL*, 2:133; WL to Joseph Ellis, January 8, 1778, *PWL*, 2:170; WL to Henry Laurens, September 24, 1778, *PWL*, 2:447; WL to Henry Laurens, September 24 and 28, 1778, *PWL*, 2:447, 448–49 (third quote); WL to John Henry Livingston, *PWL*, 2:450–51; WL to Lord Stirling, October 5, 1778, *PWL*, 2:455–56 (last quote); Mark Kwasny, *Washington's Partisan War, 1775–1783* (Kent, OH: Kent State University Press, 1996), 191.

51. Roth, *Connecticut's War Governor*, 61–66.

52. WL to Assembly, March 15, 1777, *PWL*, 1:279–80; GW to WL, April 1, 1777, *PWL*, 1:289–90; Petition of Eight Persons in Newark to WL, April 24, 1777, *WLP*, reel 4; WL to GW, April 4, 1777, *PWL*, 1:292–93; Nathaniel Heard to WL, April 1, 1777, *WLP*, reel 4; Levine, "Transformation of a Radical Whig," 90.

53. Robert Middlekauff, *The Glorious Cause: The American Revolution, 1763–1789* (New York: Oxford University Press, 2005), 365–69, 384; Lundin, *Cockpit of the Revolution*, 308–12, 320–29; Kwasny, *Washington's Partisan War*, 141–51; John Ferling, *Almost a Miracle: The American Victory in the War of Independence* (New York: Oxford University Press, 2007), 209–10, 242–43; Paul David Nelson, *William Alexander, Lord Stirling* (Tuscaloosa: University of Alabama Press, 1987), 106–7; Mark Edward Lender, "The Cockpit Reconsidered: Revolutionary New Jersey as a Military Theater," in *New Jersey in the American Revolution*, ed. Barbara J. Mitnick (New Brunswick, NJ: Rutgers University Press, 2005), 53.

54. Kwasny, *Washington's Partisan War*, 151–53, 162; Nelson, *William Alexander*, 105; Robert Morris to WL, July 5, 1777, *PWL*, 2:12–14.

55. WL to Assembly, September 3, 1777, *PWL*, 2:53; WL to John Hancock, September 7, 1777, *PWL*, 2:65; Peter Dubois to Henry Clinton, January 24, 1778, Clinton Papers, vol. 30; Act to explain and amend . . . An Act for better regulating the militia, September 23, 1777, *Acts of the General Assembly [1776–1777]*, 98–101; Bernstein, "New Jersey in the American Revolution," 317–18.

56. Henry Clinton to John Burgoyne, September 11, 1777, Clinton Papers, vol. 22; Kwasny, *Washington's Partisan War*, 164–66; Leiby, *Revolutionary War in the Hackensack Valley*, 134–39; Philemon Dickinson to WL, September 3, 6, and 17, 1777, *WLP*, reel 5; Philemon Dickinson to WL, September 14, 1777, *PWL*, 2:70–71, esp. n. 1, WL to Philemon Dickinson, September 14, 1777, *PWL*, 2:72, esp. n. 2; John Hancock to WL, September 12, 1777, *PWL*, 2:67; WL to John Hancock, September 14, 1777, *PWL*, 2:74; Henry Clinton to William Hotham, September 3, 1777, Clinton Papers, vol. 23; Henry Clinton to Edward Harvey, September 19, 1777, Clinton Papers, vol. 24; Shy, *People Numerous and Armed*, 237.

57. Ferling, *Almost a Miracle*, 253; WL to John Hancock, September 13, 1777, *PWL*, 2:68; WL to GW, October 10, 1777, *PWL*, 2:90; GW to WL, October 1, 1777, *PWL*, 2:82. For protection of Delaware forts, see GW to WL, October 22, 1777, *PWL*, 2:94, and WL to Philemon Dickinson, October 26, 1777, *PWL*, 2:95. For foraging and protection of West Jersey in winter, see Christopher Greene to WL, November 23, 1777, *PWL*, 2:121; WL to Militia of Hunterdon, Burlington, Gloucester, Salem, and Cumberland Counties, November 23, 1777, *PWL*, 2:123; WL to Henry Laurens, December 22, 1777, *PWL*, 2:140 (for quote); GW to WL, December 31, 1777, *PWL*, 2:157; and WL to Henry Laurens, January 9, 1778, *PWL*, 2:171.

58. Joseph Ellis to WL, December 6, 1777, *WLP*, reel 6.

59. Ibid., March 23, 1778, *PWL*, 2:270.

60. WL to Assembly, February 16, 1778, *PWL*, 2:223–25 (first and second quotes at 223 and 224); Bernstein, "New Jersey in the American Revolution," 318, 321–22; Robert Lawrence to Legislature, October 1777, in Gerlach, *New Jersey in the American Revolution*, 252–53; Joseph Ellis to WL, March 23, 1778, *PWL*, 2:270.

61. WL to GW, March 18, 1778, *PWL*, 2:263; WL to Israel Shreve, March 23, 1778, *PWL*, 2:269; *Privy Council Minutes*, March 21, April 1, April 2, and April 8, 1778, 71–74; WL to GW, March 23, 1778, *PWL*, 2:271 (first quote); Elijah Hand to Charles Mawhood, March 22, 1778, Revolutionary Era Collection, NJHS (second quote); Petition of Civil and Military Officers to WL, March 28, 1778, *WLP*, reel 7 (final quotes); Lundin, *Cockpit of the Revolution*, 388; Report on Ravages of War in Southwest New Jersey, in Gerlach, *New Jersey in the American Revolution*, 302–5.

62. WL to Nathaniel Scudder, April 9, 1778, *PWL*, 2:284–85; WL to GW, April 9, 1778, *PWL*, 2:285–86 (for quote); GW to WL, April 14, 1778, *WLP*, reel 7; Kwasny, *Washington's Partisan War*, 193; A Supplementary Act to An Act . . . for the better regulating the militia, December 12, 1777, *Acts of the General Assembly [1777–1778]*, 24.

63. Ferling, *Almost a Miracle*, 260–68 (quote on 264); Chopra, *Unnatural Rebellion*, 94–95.

64. WL to Henry Laurens, April 27, 1778, *PWL*, 2:310 (first quote); Henry Laurens to WL, April 27, 1778, *PWL*, 2:311–12, esp. n. 1; WL to Henry Laurens, June 20, 1778, *PWL*, 2:370; WL to GW, April 27, 1778, *PWL*, 2:313 (second quote); GW to WL, April 22, 1778, *Washington Papers, Revolutionary War Series*, 14:586–87; Henry Laurens to WL, June 10, 1778, *WLP*, reel 7; Henry Laurens to WL, June 17, 1778, *PWL*, 2:366–67; Chopra, *Unnatural Rebellion*, 92–93; Peterson, "William Livingston," 72; Ferling, *Almost a Miracle*, 271–73.

65. Chopra, *Unnatural Rebellion*, 94–97; Kwasny, *Washington's Partisan War*, 199; Ferling, *Almost a Miracle*, 268; Middlekauff, *Glorious Cause*, 407–10.

66. GW to WL, June 1, 1778, *Washington Papers, Revolutionary War Series*, 15:292; WL to Philemon Dickinson, June 16, 1778, *PWL*, 2:365–66, esp. n. 5; *Privy Council Minutes*, June 16, 1778, 81; WL to Henry Laurens, June 20, 1778, *PWL*, 2:370 (first quotes); Andrew Bell Diary, esp. June 23 and 24, 1778, Andrew Bell Papers, box 1, folder 1, NJHS; Joseph Clark Diary, June 1778, Joseph Clark, Revolutionary War Officer Papers, June 1778, NJHS (second quote); WL to GW, June 22, 1778, *PWL*, 2:372. For full treatment of the Battle of Monmouth, see Kwasny, *Washington's Partisan War*, 199–221; Ferling, *Almost a Miracle*, 293–308; Lundin, *Cockpit of the Revolution*, 394–400; Middlekauff, *Glorious Cause*, 426–34; Lender, "Cockpit Reconsidered," 56–58; Nelson, *William Alexander*, 125–30; Account of Battle of Monmouth, July 1, 1778, *PWL*, 2:375–79; George Washington's Account of the Battle of Monmouth, in Gerlach, *New Jersey in the American Revolution*, 306.

67. Kwasny, *Washington's Partisan War*, 226–29; Nelson, *William Alexander*, 134–36; Ferling, *Almost a Miracle*, 195–97, 300; WL to Assembly, May 9 and June 4, 1777, *PWL*, 1:324–25, 346; Act for completing the four battalions . . . in the Continental service, May 28, 1777, *Acts of the General Assembly [1776–1777]*, 51–53; Moses Hagen to Thomas McKean, September 29, 1778, Thomas McKean Papers, HSP.

68. Ferling, *Almost a Miracle*, 195–97; WL to Assembly, November 5, 1777, *PWL*, 2:100–101; GW to WL, November 1, 1777, *PWL*, 2:97 (first quote); WL to GW, November 5, 1777, *PWL*, 2:102; Mark Edward Lender, "The Conscripted Line: The Draft in Revolutionary New Jersey," *New Jersey History* 103 (1985): 25–27, 30–31; WL to Assembly, February 16 and March 16, 1778, *PWL*, 2:219, 254; WL to Nathaniel Scudder, March 20, 1778, *PWL*, 2:265 (second quote); WL to GW, April 15 and 17, 1778, *PWL*, 2:291 (third quote), 293, esp. n. 1.

69. Lender, "Conscripted Line," 30–35; Act for the speedy and effectual recruiting of the four New-Jersey regiments . . . , April 3, 1778, *Acts of the General Assembly [1777–1778]*, 64–71; WL to Assembly, May 29, 1778, *PWL*, 2:344.

70. Richard Hixson, *Isaac Collins, A Quaker Printer in 18th Century America* (New Brunswick, NJ: Rutgers University Press, 1968), 55–57, 67–69, 75 (quote on 68); WL to Assembly, October 11, 1777, *PWL*, 2:91; *Votes and Proceedings*, November 5, 1777, 8–9; Richard Hixson, "Faithful Guardian of Press Freedom," *Proceedings of the New Jersey Historical Society* 81.3 (1963): 155; Bernstein, "New Jersey in the American Revolution," 234–35; Levine, "Transformation of a Radical Whig," 184–86; Peterson, "William Livingston," 69–70.

71. WL to Isaac Collins, November 25, 1777, *PWL*, 2:125; Hortentius, December 24, 1777, and January 7, 1778, *PWL*, 2:141–43, 168–69; Correspondent, December 24, 1777, *PWL*, 2:527; Hixson,

Isaac Collins, 88–89, 93. For an overview of Livingston and his writings, see Levine, "Transformation of a Radical Whig," 185–89.

72. For challenges against the king, see Hortentius, January 21 and February 11, 1778, *PWL*, 2:191–92, 214–17. For religious freedom, see Cato, February 4 and 18, 1778, *PWL*, 2:203–5, 234–38. For Mawhood, see WL to Isaac Collins, April 15, 1778, *PWL*, 2:534–35.

73. WL to Henry Laurens, July 22, 1779, *PWL*, 2:396–97. For Carlisle Commission writings, see Carlisle Commission to Lord Germain, November 15, 1778, Clinton Papers, vol. 46.

74. America's True Friend, May 6, 1778, *PWL*, 2:319–22; Belinda, May 6, 1778, *PWL*, 2:322. For other examples of anti-Carlisle writings, see A Correspondent, April 23, 1778, *PWL*, 2:308–9; H.I., April 29, 1778, *PWL*, 2:316; Hortentius, May 6, September 9, and October 21, 1778, *PWL*, 2:323–26, 428–33, 464–65; and Trismegistus, May 20, 1778, *PWL*, 2:337–38. For WL discussing his efforts against the peace plan, see WL to Henry Laurens, April 27, 1778, and WL to GW, April 27, 1778, *PWL*, 2:310, 313. Also see Bernstein, "New Jersey in the American Revolution," 235–38.

75. Proclamation, October 21, 1778, *PWL*, 2:466–67; De Lisle, December 31, 1777, and January 7, 1778, *PWL*, 2:150–55, 165–67; Hortentius, January 28, 1778, *PWL*, 2:201–2; WL to Lord Stirling, February 17, 1778, *PWL*, 2:233. Also see WL to Henry Laurens, February 5, 1778, *PWL*, 2:209, for the same sentiment about France. For Philadelphia, see De Lisle, January 14, 1778, *PWL*, 2:180–85. For other examples under this trope, see Hortentius, December 8, 1777, and April 1, 1778, *PWL*, 2:137–39, 277–80; Adolphus, February 25, 1778, *PWL*, 2:239–41; De Lisle, March 25, 1778, *PWL*, 2:273–76; Camillus, April 29, 1778, *PWL*, 2:316–19.

76. Hortentius, December 31, 1777, *PWL*, 2:156; Cato, January 7, 1778, *PWL*, 2:162–65.

77. Adolphus, January 8, 1778, *PWL*, 2:188–91; De Lisle, April 23, 1778, *PWL*, 2:300–305; Persius, February 18, 1778, *PWL*, 2:530–31; Lender, "Conscripted Line," 27–28.

78. Chopra, *Unnatural Rebellion*, 84–85, 92–95; Plain Truth, September 9, 1778, *PWL*, 2:426–28; A British Captain, March 17, 1778, *PWL*, 2:255–57. For other examples, see A Member of the Sentimental Society, *PWL*, 2:435–36; Charon and Pluto, December 5, 1778, *PWL*, 2:496–98; and Hixson, *Isaac Collins*, 93.

79. Bernstein, "New Jersey in the American Revolution," 248–49; WL to Theophilus Elmer, December 9, 1778, *PWL*, 2:500–501, esp. n. 3; Lundin, *Cockpit of the Revolution*, 281–82.

80. WL to Theophilus Elmer, December 9, 1778, *PWL*, 2:501n. 4 (for quotes).

81. WL to Nathaniel Scudder, December 14, 1778, *PWL*, 2:507. Also see WL to Nathaniel Scudder, November 24 and December 9, 1778, *PWL*, 2:484, 502–3; WL to Theophilus Elmer, December 9, 1778, *PWL*, 2:500; Bogin, *Abraham Clark*, 48–49; Bernstein, "New Jersey in the American Revolution," 219–22.

82. Susannah Livingston to WL, May 30, 1777, *PWL*, 1:345; Nelson, *William Alexander*, 134; WL to Henry Laurens, October 9, 1778, *PWL*, 2:458 (first and third quotes); WL to John Henry Livingston, September 29, 1778, *PWL*, 2:450–51 (second quote); WL to GW, November 11, 1777, *PWL*, 2:110; Susannah Livingston to WL, November 12 and 29, 1777, *WLP*, reel 6; WL to Susannah Livingston, April 6, 1778, *PWL*, 2:281–82; Prince, *William Livingston*, 15–16. For friendship with Laurens, see Henry Laurens to WL, January 27, 1778, *PWL*, 2:196, and WL to Henry Laurens, February 5 and November 9, 1778, *PWL*, 2:207, 475.

83. Susannah Livingston to WL, November 29, 1777, *WLP*, reel 6 (first quote); WL to Henry Laurens, May 13, 1778, *PWL*, 2:332 (second quote); Henry Brockholst Livingston to WL, July 12, 1777, *PWL*, 2:20.

Chapter 5

1. E. James Ferguson, *Power of the Purse: A History of American Public Finance, 1776–1790* (Chapel Hill: University of North Carolina Press, 1961), 26–33; Edward Fuhlbruegge, "New Jersey Finances During the American Revolution: Address Before the Historical Forum at the New Jersey Historical Society, April 20, 1937," *Proceedings of the New Jersey Historical Society* 55 (July 1937): 15; David Bernstein, "New Jersey in the American Revolution: The Establishment of a Government Amid Civil and Military Disorder, 1770–1781" (PhD diss., Rutgers University, 1970), 371, 378–80; Peter Wilson to Dirck Romeyn, February 26, 1780, Peter Wilson Papers, NJHS (for quote).

2. Ferguson, *Power of the Purse*, 35–40; Bernstein, "New Jersey in the American Revolution," 381–84; Clarence Ver Steeg, *Robert Morris: Revolutionary Financier* (New York: Octagon Books, 1972), 42–44; John Ferling, *Almost a Miracle: The American Victory in the War of Independence* (New York: Oxford University Press, 2007), 349–50.

3. Ferling, *Almost a Miracle*, 349–51; Bernstein, "New Jersey in the American Revolution," 371–73.

4. Ferling, *Almost a Miracle*, 399; Intelligence Report of David Babcock and Thomas Ward, November 29, 1779, Clinton Papers, vol. 77. See also David Coxe to Henry Clinton, December 10, 1779, Clinton Papers, vol. 79, for the impact of the lack of supplies and depreciation. For Carpenter, see Colonel A. Dunham to Thomas Carpenter, May 17 and July 31, 1780, and Thomas Carpenter to Colonel Dunham, May 6, July 12, August 20, and September 1, 1780, Carpenter Family Papers, HSP.

5. William Churchill Houston to WL, December 20, 1779, *WLP*, reel 10.

6. Ibid., November 12, 1779, *WLP*, reel 10.

7. GW Circular to the States, May 22, 1779, *Washington Papers, Revolutionary War Series*, 20: 568–70. Also see WL to GW, May 27, 1779, *PWL*, 3:99.

8. William Maxwell to WL and Legislature, April 25 and 26, 1779, *WLP*, reel 9; David Morris Roth, *Connecticut's War Governor, Jonathan Trumbull* (Guilford, CT: Pequot Press, 1974), 53.

9. Petition of John Dennis to WL, December 6, 1779, Petitions, Resolutions, Transactions, Accounts, and Misc. Papers, 1700–1845, no. 12, NJSA; Petitions of the inhabitants of Morris County . . . concerning inflation and the depreciation of bills of credit, March 9, 1779, AM Papers, box 6, no. 1055 AM; WL to Susannah French Livingston, June 17, 1779, *PWL*, 3:115 (for quote); *Acts of the General Assembly of the State of New-Jersey [1777–1778]* (Burlington, NJ: Isaac Collins, 1778), 65; *Acts of the General Assembly of the State of New-Jersey [1778–1779]* (Trenton, NJ: Isaac Collins, 1779), 31.

10. WL to GW, October 8, 1779, *PWL*, 3:178.

11. WL to Nathaniel Scudder, November 8, 1779, *PWL*, 3:197–99; Michael Levine, "Transformation of a Radical Whig Under Republican Government: William Livingston, Governor of New Jersey, 1776–1790" (PhD diss., Rutgers University, 1975), 120.

12. Scott Rohrer, *Jacob Green's Revolution: Radical Religion and Reform in a Revolutionary Age* (University Park: Pennsylvania State University Press, 2014), 198–209, esp. 204–5.

13. John Fell to Robert Morris, June 13, 1779, and William Churchill Houston to Robert Morris, October 2, 1779, Robert Morris Papers, RUSCUA; Levine, "Transformation of a Radical Whig," 120, 135–36.

14. Petitions of the inhabitants of Morris County; Bernstein, "New Jersey in the American Revolution," 385–91; Fuhlbruegge, "New Jersey Finances," 12.

15. WL to Anthony Bleecker, May 1, 1779, *PWL*, 3:77–78.

16. Petition of inhabitants of Burlington County concerning measures to appreciate the currency, August 23, 1779, BAH MS Collection, box 1-1, no. 92; Bernstein, "New Jersey in the American Revolution," 388, 445–47; Ruth Bogin, *Abraham Clark and the Quest for Equality in the Revolutionary Era, 1774–1794* (Rutherford, NJ: Fairleigh Dickinson University Press, 1982), 72–73; Jack N. Rakove, *The Beginnings of National Politics: An Interpretive History of the Continental Congress* (New York: Knopf, 1979), 275–76; Ferguson, *Power of the Purse*, 46.

17. Bernstein, "New Jersey in the American Revolution," 391, 445–47; Jonathan Trumbull to WL, January 27, 1780, *PWL*, 3:291–92; Abraham Clark to Caleb Camp, February 17, 1780, BAH MS Collection, box 5-2, no. 180; John Fell to Robert Morris, March 5, 1780, Robert Morris Papers, RUSCUA.

18. WL to Baron van der Capellen, March 15, 1780, *PWL*, 3:331; Samuel Huntington to WL, March 20, 1780, *WLP*, reel 11; Bernstein, "New Jersey and the American Revolution," 391–92; Ferling, *Almost a Miracle*, 399–400; Ferguson, *Power of the Purse*, 51. Also see WL to John Jay, March 17, 1780, *PWL*, 3:341–42; and Samuel Huntington to WL, September 3, 1780, *WLP*, reel 13.

19. WL to William Churchill Houston, May 24, 1780, *PWL*, 3:392–93; Bernstein, "New Jersey in the American Revolution," 217–23, 391–93.

20. William Churchill Houston to WL, October 2, 1780, *WLP*, reel 13; Bernstein, "New Jersey in the American Revolution," 391–93; WL to Joshua Wallace, November 9, 1779, *PWL*, 3:204.

21. Bernstein, "New Jersey in the American Revolution," 391–93; John O'Connor, *William Paterson, Lawyer and Statesman, 1745–1806* (New Brunswick, NJ: Rutgers University Press, 1979), 122–23; An Act for establishing a fund for sinking and redeeming the proportion of the bills of credit . . . , June 9, 1780, *Acts of the General Assembly of the State of New-Jersey [1779–1780]* (Trenton, NJ: Isaac Collins, 1780), 92; Act to empower the collectors to receive certain certificates in payment of taxes, June 13, 1780, *Acts of the General Assembly of the State of New-Jersey [1779–1780]* (Trenton, NJ: Isaac Collins, 1780), 102; WL to William Churchill Houston, May 24, 1780, *PWL*, 3:392–93n. 3.

22. Abraham Clark to Josiah Hornblower, October 31, 1780, BAH MS Collection, box 5-2, no. 230.

23. Manasseh Salter to WL, December 1, 1780, *WLP*, Reel 13.

24. Peter Wilson to Dirck Romeyn, November 18, 1780, Peter Wilson Collection, NJHS.

25. Hugh Haggerty Intelligence Report, January 2, 1781, Clinton Papers, vol. 138.

26. Bernstein, "New Jersey in the American Revolution," 393–96; Samuel Huntington to WL, November 9, 1780, *PWL*, 4:86–87; Ferling, *Almost a Miracle*, 470; Representation of the New Jersey Legislature to the Continental Congress, November 20, 1780, *PWL*, 4:92–93 (see n. 3 on the repeal of the 40:1 standard); Act for ascertaining the value of the Continental currency in the payment of debt, January 5, 1781, *Acts of the Fifth General Assembly of the State of New-Jersey [1780–1781]* (Trenton, NJ: Isaac Collins, 1781), 30; Peter Wilson to Dirck Romeyn, November 22, 1780, Peter Wilson Collection, NJHS.

27. Scipio, *New-Jersey Gazette*, October 25, 1780, *PWL*, 4:76–80.

28. Ibid., November 1, 1780, *PWL*, 4:82–86 (quote on 86); Levine, "Transformation of a Radical Whig," 140–45, 165–66.

29. A supplementary act . . . for the support of the government of the state, June 8, 1779, *Acts of the General Assembly [1778–1779]*, 65; Act to provide for the payment of the several officers of the government of the state, December 23, 1779, and Act to amend . . . An Act to provide for the payment, October 6, 1780, *Acts of the General Assembly [1779–1780]*, 31, 136; WL to Josiah

Hornblower, November 1, 1780, *PWL*, 4:81; Act for striking the sum of thirty thousand pounds in bills of credit, January 9, 1781, *Acts of the Fifth General Assembly*, 55; WL to John Mehelm, November 21, 1781, *PWL*, 4:334–35 (for quote); Theodore Sedgwick, *A Memoir of the Life of William Livingston* . . . . (New York: J. & J. Harper, 1833), 355; Levine, "Transformation of a Radical Whig," 163–64. Also see WL to Lord Stirling, December 8, 1781, *PWL*, 4:343; and WL to Assembly, June 18, 1782, *PWL*, 4:430.

30. WL to John Watkins, March 13, 1780, *PWL*, 3:329.

31. Peter Van Brugh Livingston to WL, May 5, 1781, *PWL*, 4:191.

32. WL to Catharine Livingston, April 21, 1781, *PWL*, 4:182–83.

33. WL to Judith Watkins, August 22, 1782, *PWL*, 4:460; Levine, "Transformation of a Radical Whig," 160–71; Bernstein, "New Jersey in the American Revolution," 394.

34. WL to Catharine Lawrence, April 21, 1781, *PWL*, 4:182 (for quote). Also see WL to John Witherspoon, May 10, 1781, and John Witherspoon to WL, May 15, 1781, *PWL*, 4:192, 196; Levine, "Transformation of a Radical Whig," 162–63; Bernstein, "New Jersey in the American Revolution," 240; Sedgwick, *Memoir of William Livingston*, 362.

35. Baron van der Capellen to WL, July 16, 1779, *PWL*, 3:131–41; Essay, "The European Powers and the American Revolution," *PWL*, 3:147; John de Neufville and Son to WL, July 31, 1779, *PWL*, 3:155; WL to John Henry Livingston, November 24, 1779, *PWL*, 3:231–32; WL to Henry Remsen, November 24, 1779, *PWL*, 3:232; WL to William Churchill Houston, December 6, 1779, *PWL*, 3:249; WL to Samuel Huntington, December 6, 1779, *PWL*, 3:252; WL to GW, November 27, 1779, *PWL*, 3:234–36; Henry Brockholst Livingston to WL, February 23, 1780, *PWL*, 3:305; WL to Baron van der Capellen, March 15, 1780, *PWL*, 3:331; WL to John Jay, March 17, 1780, *PWL*, 3:341–42; Henry Brockholst Livingston to WL, July 12, 1780, *PWL*, 4:6–8; Henry Brockholst Livingston to WL, April 29, 1781, *PWL*, 4:187; Gloria Bulotti, "William Livingston: American Patriot and Publicist" (master's thesis, Stanford University, 1947), 210.

36. William Churchill Houston to WL, March 22, 1781, *PWL*, 4:160; Henry Brockholst Livingston to WL, April 1, 1781, *PWL*, 4:166–68.

37. Baron van der Capellen to WL, May 25, 1781, *PWL*, 4:199–205 (for quotes); Baron van der Capellen to WL, May 25, 1781, *PWL*, 4:251 (final quote). John Adams secured a loan in 1782 after the victory at Yorktown and through a realignment of Dutch politics. See Henry Brockholst Livingston to WL, December 3, 1781, *PWL*, 4:341–42; and Jacob Gerhard Diriks to WL, April 29, 1782, *PWL*, 4:400–401n. 1.

38. Charles Rappleye, *Robert Morris: Financier of the American Revolution* (New York: Simon & Schuster, 2010), 215–16, 226–27.

39. Ibid., 212; Ver Steeg, *Robert Morris*, 90–93; William C. Houston to Thomas McKean, March 31, 1781, Thomas McKean Papers, HSP.

40. Rappleye, *Robert Morris*, 236–39; Ver Steeg, *Robert Morris*, 93, 117.

41. WL to Robert Morris, February 23, 1781, *PWL*, 4:151 (first quote); WL to Sarah Jay, August 21, 1781, *PWL*, 4:256–57 (second quote); Robert Morris to WL, June 11, 1781, *PWL*, 4:220; Rappleye, *Robert Morris*, 203; William Trent to WL, June 3, 1781, *WLP*, reel 15.

42. Act to promote and support the National Bank, May 30, 1782, *Acts of the Sixth General Assembly of the State of New-Jersey [1781–1782]* (Trenton, NJ: Isaac Collins, 1782), 67; Petition of [inhabitants of Pittsgrove Township, Salem County] . . . urging that state taxes be paid in hard money, May 11, 1781 (for quote), and Petition of inhabitants of Monmouth County . . . concerning trade and taxation, May 12, 1781, BAH MS Collection, box 1-14, nos. 64, 65; WL to John Stevens Sr., April 20, 1781, *PWL*, 4:181; WL, Proclamation, April 28 and June 2, 1781, *PWL*, 4:186,

212; Act to repeal part of sundry acts making the bills of credit issued on the faith of this state a legal tender, June 13, 1781, and Act to declare the value of the Continental currency, through the several periods of its depreciation, and to provide for the more equitable payment of debts, June 22, 1781, *Acts of the Fifth General Assembly*, 83, 102.

43. Scipio, *New-Jersey Gazette*, April 25, 1781, *PWL*, 4:185–86 (for quote); WL to John Stevens Sr., April 20, 1781, *PWL*, 4:181; Peter Wilson to Dirck Romeyn and Mr. Zabriskie, May 19 and 20, 1781, Peter Wilson Collection, NJHS.

44. Act to amend an act entitled an Act to declare the value of the Continental currency . . . , December 25, 1781, *Acts of the Sixth General Assembly*, 29; Peter Wilson to Dirck Romeyn, June 12, 1781, Peter Wilson Collection, NJHS (for quotes); Stephen Reed Grossbart, "The Revolutionary Transition: Politics, Religion, and Economy in Eastern Connecticut, 1765–1800" (PhD diss., University of Michigan, 1989), 135.

45. Petitions of "Freemen" of Morris County . . . concerning depreciation of Continental currency, May 23, 1782, Petition of freeholders and inhabitants of Morris and Sussex Counties . . . for payment of debts in Continental currency, November 16, 1782, and Petition of inhabitants of Hunterdon County . . . concerning speculation in state notes, December 17, 1782 (for quote), BAH MS Collection, box 1-15, nos. 5, 24, 30; Daniel Jones, "From War to Peace: The Revolutionary War Letters of William Peartree Smith, 1780–1783," *New Jersey History* 104 (1986): 50; Elias Boudinot to William Peartree Smith, 1781, Boudinot Family Papers, RUSCUA.

46. Bogin, *Abraham Clark and the Quest for Equality*, 107; Petition of inhabitants of Sussex County . . . concerning independence of Continental money, September 19, 1782, BAH MS Collection, box 1-1, no. 103; Abraham Clark to John Mehelm, September 26, 1782, BAH MS Collection, box 5-2, no. 269; Petition Concerning the use of state money for paying taxes, December 12, 1782, Petitions, Resolutions, Transactions, Accounts, and Misc. Papers, 1700–1845, no. 27, NJSA; Petition of Charles Barclay . . . concerning the depreciation of currency, Middlesex County, November 16, 1782, AM Papers, box 12, no. 1635 AM; John Covenhoven, David Forman, Thomas Henderson to WL, July 20, 1782, *PWL*, 4:440.

47. William Bradford to Thomas Jefferson, November 22, 1780, *Jefferson Papers*, 4:138–41; John Witherspoon to WL, December 16, 1780, and WL to John Witherspoon, December 28, 1780, *PWL*, 4:110–12, 113–14; WL to John Mathews, February 2, 1781, *PWL*, 4:136–37 (quote).

48. John Mathews to WL, January 29, 1781, *PWL*, 4:131–33; Rakove, *Beginnings of National Politics*, 282–84; Levine, "Transformation of a Radical Whig," 147; Ferguson, *Power of the Purse*, 111–17.

49. Rappleye, *Robert Morris*, 279–82, 284–86, 291–93; Ferguson, *Power of the Purse*, 119–21; Rakove, *Beginnings of National Politics*, 282–84.

50. Act to enable the Congress of the United States to levy duties of five percentum, June 2, 1781, *Acts of the Fifth General Assembly*, 75; Bogin, *Abraham Clark and the Quest for Equality*, 75, 84–85.

51. Levine, "Transformation of a Radical Whig," 147; Ferguson, *Power of the Purse*, 116–17; Ver Stegg, *Robert Morris*, 131; Rappleye, *Robert Morris*, 329; Harold Thatcher, "Social Philosophy of William Livingston" (PhD diss., University of Chicago, 1938), 302; Walter Peterson, "William Livingston: A Study of a Political Center Before, During, and After the Revolution" (master's thesis, University of Iowa, 1948), 75.

52. Adrian Leiby, *The Revolutionary War in the Hackensack Valley: The Jersey Dutch and the Neutral Ground* (New Brunswick, NJ: Rutgers University Press, 1962), 111; Bernstein, "New Jersey in the American Revolution," 363–65; Grossbart, "Revolutionary Transition," 203.

53. Clement Biddle to WL, January 17, 1779, *WLP*, reel 9 (first quote); WL to GW, January 15, 1779, *PWL*, 3:22 (second quote); Proclamation, January 14, 1779, *PWL*, 3:20–21; WL to Jeremiah Powell, February 7, 1779, *PWL*, 3:31–32; WL to G. Morris and William Whipple, January 30, 1779, *PWL*, 3:26–27 (third quote); Blair to Furman, March 26, 1779, Department of Defense record #4734, NJSA; WL to GW, April 12, 1779, *PWL*: 3:54–55 (fourth quote); GW to WL, April 12, 1779, *Washington Papers, Revolutionary War Series*, 20:43–45 (fifth quote); WL to Henry Laurens, April 23, 1779, *PWL*, 3:67.

54. GW to WL, September 7, 1779, *Washington Papers, Revolutionary War Series*, 22: 375 (first quote); WL to Nathaniel Scudder, November 8, 1779, *PWL*, 3:197–99 (second quote); WL to GW, December 19, 1779, *PWL*, 3:271–72; Ferling, *Almost a Miracle*, 412–13; Leiby, *Revolutionary War in the Hackensack Valley*, 233; Levine "Transformation of a Radical Whig," 138–39; WL to John Simcoe, November 9, 1779, *PWL*, 3:203; Essay, "Imprisoned Men and Inflated Dollars," *PWL*, 3:207, 212–14; Kwasny, *Washington's Partisan War, 1775-1783* (Kent, OH: Kent State University Press, 1998), 233, 251; Bernstein, "New Jersey in the American Revolution," 354.

55. Joseph Lewis to Thomas Anderson, July 11, 1780, Anderson Family Papers, NJHS; WL to GW, August 4, 1780, *PWL*, 4:26 (first quote); GW to WL, August 27, 1780, *WLP*, reel 12 (second quote); John Goetschius to WL, November 20, 1780, *WLP*, reel 13 (fourth quote); WL to Joseph Reed, September 8, 1781, *PWL*, 4:288; Memorial of the New Jersey Legislature to the Continental Congress, November 9/14, 1781, *WLP*, reel 16; Bernstein, "New Jersey in the American Revolution," 356, 433; Rakove, *Beginnings of National Politics*, 277–80.

56. Petition of Inhabitants of Bergen County, June 26, 1781, *PWL*, 4:233–34 (first quote); WL to GW, December 20, 1780, *WLP*, reel 13 (second quote); Robert Hude to WL, November 20, 1780, *PWL*, 4:100; Jacob Crane to WL, December 23, 1780, *WLP*, reel 13; David Brearly to WL, May 13, 1782, *PWL*, 4:409–10; WL to GW, May 13, 1782, *PWL*, 4:411–12; GW to WL, May 10, 1782, *Founders Online* (http://founders.archives.gov/documents/Washington/99-01-02-08387; accessed July 27, 2017). Also see Barrent Hartwick to WL, June 13, 1782, *WLP*, reel 17; and WL Proclamation, May 13, 1782, *PWL*, 4:406.

57. WL to Abraham Durye, March 3, 1780, *PWL*, 3:313; WL to John Cochran, March 9, 1780, *PWL*, 3:320–21 (first quote); WL to George Clinton, August 31, 1781, *PWL*, 4:262 (second quote); WL to Jacobus Van Zandt, April 25, 1779, *PWL*, 3:75–76; WL to Timothy Johns, April 15, 1782, *PWL*, 4:393.

58. Josiah Hornblower to WL, January 16, 1782, *WLP*, reel 16.

59. Act more effectually to prevent . . . trading with the enemy or going within their lines, December 22, 1780, *Acts of the Fifth General Assembly*, 11; Act to amend . . . Act more effectually to prevent . . . , June 28, 1781, *Acts of the Fifth General Assembly.*, 115; Act for preventing an illicit trade and intercourse between the subjects of this state and the enemy, June 24, 1782, *Acts of the Sixth General Assembly*, 95; John Hanson to WL, June 24, 1782, *WLP*, reel 17; Petition of inhabitants of Essex County protesting acts of disaffection by dangerous men, November 21, 1781, BAH MS Collection, box 5-2, no. 251; John Isaac Ryker v. Ralph Post, and Samuel Craig v. John Piatt, Supreme Court Case Files, nos. 32784 and 8110, NJSA. Also see WL to John Mead, February 5, 1779, *PWL*, 3:29; WL to Silvanus Seely, November 26, 1779, *PWL*, 3:233; WL to Joseph Reed, December 5, 1780, *PWL*, 4:103; and WL to Assembly, June 7, 1782, *PWL*, 4:423.

60. WL to Assembly, April 24, 1779, *PWL*, 3:69–70; WL to GW, May 1, 1779, *PWL*, 3:79–80; GW to WL, May 4, 1779, *WLP*, reel 9 (first quote); John Taylor to WL, September 25, 1779, *WLP*, reel 10; WL to GW, May 8, 1779, *PWL*, 3:84–85 (second quote); John Neilson to WL, May 15, 1779, *PWL*, 3:89–90; WL to Baron von Steuben, May 22, 1779, *PWL*, 3:95; WL to Samuel

Huntington, June 11, 1780, *PWL*, 3:432, esp. n. 2; Isaac Gillam to WL, July 23, 1781, *WLP*, reel 13; William Franklin to John André, June 11, 1779, Clinton Papers, vol. 60; Intelligence report of John Cunningham, February 26, 1780, Clinton Papers, vol. 87.

61. WL to GW, October 7, 1779, *PWL*, 3:172; WL to Assembly, March 13, 1780, *PWL*, 3:325–26; WL to GW, August 6, 1781, *PWL*, 4:249; Joseph Scudder to WL, March 30, 1781, *WLP*, reel 14 (for quote); Kwasny, *Washington's Partisan War*, 236; Cortlandt Skinner to Henry Clinton, May 11, 1779, Clinton Papers, vol. 58.

62. Kwasny, *Washington's Partisan War*, 234; WL to Assembly, June 5, 1779, *PWL*, 3:105–6; WL to Jonathan Deare, March 1, 1779, *WLP*, reel 9 (for quote); Cortlandt Skinner to Henry Clinton, April 11, 1779, Clinton Papers, vol. 56.

63. Sidney Berry to Colonel Furman, February 26, 1779, Department of Defense, Adjutant General's Office, Revolutionary War Numbered MSS, box 39, Record #4524, NJSA; John Fell to WL, March 25, 1779, *PWL*, 3:47–48; WL to Susannah French Livingston, June 17, 1779, *PWL*, 3:115 (first quote); WL to William Livingston Jr., June 24, 1779, *PWL*, 3:123–24; WL to Susannah French Livingston, June 17, 1779, *PWL*, 2:115 (second quote); WL to Catharine Livingston, November 16, 1779, *PWL*, 3:221; WL to Susannah French Livingston, March 9, 1780, *PWL*, 3:322–23; Essay, "WL Domestic Life," *PWL*, 3:174–77; Sedgwick, *Memoir of William Livingston*, 322–23; Bulotti, "William Livingston," 207; George Adams Boyd, *Elias Boudinot, Patriot and Statesman, 1740–1821* (Princeton, NJ: Princeton University Press, 1952), 78.

64. WL to Sir Henry Clinton, March 29, 1779, *PWL*, 3:49–50.

65. Sir Henry Clinton to WL, April 10, 1779, *PWL*, 3:54; WL to Sir Henry Clinton, April 15, 1779, *PWL*, 3:56 (for quote).

66. Pluto, April 17, 1779, *PWL*, 3:59; Detector, May 8, 1779, *PWL*, 3:86–87; Humphry Clinker, April 24, 1779, *PWL*, 3:71–72; Bulotti, "William Livingston," 208.

67. Kwasny, *Washington's Partisan War*, 248–52; George Clinton to WL, October 4, 1779, *WLP*, reel 10; John Taylor to WL, September 26, 1779, *WLP*, reel 10; WL to Susannah French Livingston, October 15, 1779, *PWL*, 3:180–81; WL to John Sullivan, November 2, 1779, *PWL*, 3:193, esp. n. 2; WL to GW, December 21, 1779, *PWL*, 3:277.

68. Petition of the inhabitants of Elizabethtown, February 1, 1780, *WLP*, reel 11 (for quotes); Petition of the inhabitants of Essex and Middlesex Counties, February 2, 1780, *WLP*, reel 11; Kwasny, *Washington's Partisan War*, 257–58; Levine, "Transformation of a Radical Whig," 56–57.

69. WL to Assembly, March 13, 1780, *PWL*, 3:325–26 (first quote); WL to Baron van der Capellen, March 15, 1780, *PWL*, 3:331 (second quote); WL to Peter Ward, April 19, 1780, *PWL*, 3:363–64 (third quote); WL to Aaron Hankinson, May 29, 1780, *PWL*, 3:399–400. Also see Peter Ward to WL, April 18, 1780, *PWL*, 3:355; WL to Samuel Huntington, May 16, 1780, *PWL*, 3:379; and Kwasny, *Washington's Partisan War*, 259.

70. WL to GW, February 26, 1780, *PWL*, 3:309; Kwasny, *Washington's Partisan War*, 260–61.

71. Nathaniel Heard to WL, June 10, 1780, *PWL*, 3:425; Kwasny, *Washington's Partisan War*, 260–62.

72. WL to Susannah French Livingston, June 9, 1780, *PWL*, 3:424; WL to Tench Tilghman, June 9, 1780, *PWL*, 3:424; Tench Tilghman to WL, June 14, 1780, *PWL*, 3:434; WL to Samuel Huntington, June 20, 1780, *PWL*, 3:436; Kwasny, *Washington's Partisan War*, 263–64; William Maxwell to WL, June 14, 1780, *WLP*, reel 12; Sedgwick, *Memoir of William Livingston*, 349–54; Intelligence report of John Cunningham, February 26, 1780, Clinton Papers, vol. 87.

73. WL to Samuel Huntington, June 11, 1780, *PWL*, 3:432–33; Baron von Steuben to WL, June 20, 1780, *PWL*, 3:437; WL to Baron von Steuben, June 21, 1780, *PWL*, 3:438; Kwasny, *Washington's Partisan War*, 264–68; Bernstein, "New Jersey in the American Revolution," 347–49.

74. Robert Morris to WL, July 29, 1780, *PWL*, 4:22–23; John Mathews to WL, August 18, 1780, *PWL*, 4:45; WL to GW, August 21, 1780, *PWL*, 4:48–49 (first quote); WL to GW, October 23, 1780, *PWL*, 4:75 (second quote); GW to WL, October 18, 1780, *PWL*, 4:72; William Churchill Houston to WL, September 30, 1780, *WLP*, reel 13 (third quote); Jacob Crane to WL, December 23, 1780, *WLP*, reel 13 (fourth quote).

75. Bernstein, "New Jersey in the American Revolution," 357; Ferling, *Almost a Miracle*, 466; Kwasny, *Washington's Partisan War*, 281–82; Petition of officers of the 1st New Jersey Regiment, May 6, 1779, BAH MS Collection, box 5-2, no. 159; Memorial of the Officers of the New Jersey Brigade to the Legislature, April 17, 1779, in *New Jersey in the American Revolution, 1763–1783: A Documentary History*, ed. Larry R. Gerlach (Trenton: New Jersey Historical Commission, 1975), 344–45; Brigadier General William Maxwell to GW, May 6, 1779, and GW to Maxwell, May 7, 1779, BAH MS Collection, box 5-2, nos. 158 and 160; Paul David Nelson, *William Alexander, Lord Stirling* (Tuscaloosa: University of Alabama Press, 1987), 141–42; James Burnside to WL, January 11, 1781, *PWL*, 4:122; Intelligence report of William Curlis, Philip Burden, and Thomas Kants, January 15, 1781, Clinton Papers, vol. 141; Lord George Germain to Henry Clinton, March 7, 1781, Clinton Papers, vol. 148.

76. Petition of New Jersey Militia Officers to WL and Legislature, December 16, 1780, *WLP*, reel 13 (first quote); Abraham Clark to WL, October 22, 1780, *WLP*, reel 13 (second quote); Act for making compensation to the troops . . . for depreciation of their pay, January 6, 1781, *Acts of the Fifth General Assembly*, 32; WL to GW, January 28, 1781, *PWL*, 4:130n. 2; Essay, "Men and Money," *PWL*, 4:96–99; GW to WL, January 23, 1781, *PWL*, 4:128.

77. GW to WL, January 23 and 27, 1781, *PWL*, 4:128–29; WL to GW, January 28 and February 4, 1781, *PWL*, 4:130, 139; Ferling, *Almost a Miracle*, 469; Kwasny, *Washington's Partisan War*, 281–84; Francis Barber to Jonathan Dayton, February 28, 1781, in Gerlach, *New Jersey in the American Revolution*, 350–51.

78. WL to John Jay, January 14, 1781, *PWL*, 4:123; Kwasny, *Washington's Partisan War*, 271–79, 292–301; GW to WL, June 15, 1781, *Founders Online* (http://founders.archives.gov/documents /Washington/99-01-02-06069; accessed July 27, 2017); Ferling, *Almost a Miracle*, 505, 510, 515, 523–24; Bergen County Citizens Petition, May 21, 1781, Department of Defense, Adjutant General's Office, Revolutionary War Numbered MSS, box109, Record #10949, NJSA.

79. For the assassination plot, see Robert Hoops to WL, April 2, 1781, *PWL*, 4:173; GW to WL, April 8, 1781, *PWL*, 4:176; WL to Joseph Reed, April 11, 1781, *PWL*, 4:178; WL to GW, April 14, 1781, *PWL*, 4:180; James Moody to WL, August 25, 1781, *PWL*, 4:258–59 (for quote); WL to Henry Brockholst Livingston, October 24, 1781, *PWL*, 4:319; Essay, "Livingston Family and the War," *PWL*, 4:172; Essay, "WL Domestic Life," *PWL*, 3:174–77; WL to Susannah Livingston, October 25 and December 17, 1781, *PWL*, 4:320, 351; and WL to Robert Livingston, December 17, 1781, *PWL*, 4:350. For more on Moody, see James Moody, *Narrative of the Exertions and Sufferings of Lieut. James Moody . . .*, ed. Charles I. Bushnell (New York: privately printed, 1865).

80. Kwasny, *Washington's Partisan War*, 302–5; Ferling, *Almost a Miracle*, 523–25; GW to WL, August 21, 1781, *PWL*, 4:254–55; Petition of inhabitants of Newark, September 23, 1781, *WLP*, reel 15; Elias Boudinot to WL, September 29, 1781, *PWL*, 4:306; WL to Assembly, September 20, 1781, *PWL*, 4:300 (first quote); WL to William Heath, September 15, 1781, *PWL*, 4:293 (second quote); William Heath to WL, September 28, 1781, *WLP*, reel 15; GW to WL, August 2,

1781, *PWL*, 4:247; Robert A. Selig, "Rochambeau in New Jersey: The Good French Ally," in *The American Revolution in New Jersey: Where the Battlefront Meets the Home Front*, ed. James J. Gigantino II (New Brunswick, NJ: Rutgers University Press, 2015), 97–98; Robert Middlekauff, *The Glorious Cause: The American Revolution, 1763–1789* (New York: Oxford University Press, 2005), 560–64; Thomas McKean to GW, September 11 and 21, 1781, Thomas McKean Papers, HSP. For British debate about preparation for the Yorktown campaign, see Cortlandt Skinner to Henry Clinton, July 22 and 24, 1781 (vol. 166), Andrew Gautier to Henry Clinton, August 22, 1781 (vol. 171), William Sproule intelligence report, August 23, 1781 (vol. 171), Intelligence report, August 27, 1781 (vol. 172), and Cortlandt Skinner to Henry Clinton, September 22, 1781 (vol. 175), Clinton Papers; Richard Buel, *Dear Liberty: Connecticut's Mobilization for the Revolutionary War* (Middletown, CT: Wesleyan University Press, 1980), 176–77.

81. Old Politician, May 15, 1782, *PWL*, 4:413–14; WL to Assembly, May 17, 1782, *PWL*, 4:414–15; Ferling, *Almost a Miracle*, 546–47.

82. Simon Schama, *Rough Crossings: Britain, the Slaves and the American Revolution* (New York: Ecco, 2006), 114–15; Douglas Egerton, *Death or Liberty: African Americans and Revolutionary America* (New York: Oxford University Press, 2009), 65–67; WL to Asher Holmes, March 21, 1780, *PWL*, 3:343–44; Graham Hodges, *Slavery and Freedom in the Rural North: African Americans in Monmouth County, New Jersey 1665–1865* (Madison, WI: Madison House, 1997), 102–6; James J. Gigantino II, *The Ragged Road to Abolition: Slavery and Freedom in New Jersey* (Philadelphia: University of Pennsylvania Press, 2015), 51–52; Holger Hoock, *Scars of Independence: America's Violent Birth* (New York: Crown, 2017), 341–42.

83. WL to Jonathan Trumbull, August 23, 1779, *PWL*, 3:163.

84. Copy of a letter from a gentleman in New Jersey to his friend in this city, December 1, 1779, *PWL*, 3:241–45; Loyalist verse, January 1781, Samuel Smith Papers, RUSCUA.

85. Ruma Chopra, *Unnatural Rebellion: Loyalists in New York City during the Revolution* (Charlottesville, VA: University of Virginia Press, 2013), 118, 122, 127, 167–73; Harry Ward, *Between the Lines: Banditti of the American Revolution* (Westport, CT: Praeger, 2002), 52–58; WL to New Jersey Militia Colonels, March 18 and 20, 1780, *PWL*, 3:339–41; Samuel Forman to WL, August 6, 1780, *PWL*, 4:28; William Franklin to John André, November 10, 1779, Clinton Papers, vol. 74; Hoock, *Scars of Independence*, 339–44.

86. Samuel Forman to WL, November 7, 1781, *PWL*, 4:326 (first quote); Andrew Brown to WL, December 29, 1781, *PWL*, 4:356; WL to GW, January 1, 1782, *PWL*, 4:357 (second quote); Petition of the inhabitants of Little Egg Harbor, November 12, 1781, *PWL*, 4:328; Captain Andrew Brown to WL, January 10, 1782, *WLP*, reel 16; GW to WL, January 12, 1782, *PWL*, 4:361; WL to GW, January 26, 1782, *PWL*, 4:372–73 (third quote); David Fowler, "Egregious Villains, Wood Rangers, and London Traders: The Pine Robber Phenomenon in New Jersey During the Revolutionary War" (PhD diss., Rutgers University, 1987), 204–10. Also see Abiel Akin to WL, January 10, 1782, *WLP*, reel 16.

87. Nathaniel Scudder to Joseph Scudder, July 12, 1780, Revolutionary Era Collection, NJHS; Hoock, *Scars of Independence*, 342.

88. WL v. John Beatty, Supreme Court Case Files, no. 23143, NJSA; Monmouth County petition on conditions in the county, May 12, 1781, Department of Defense, Adjutant General's Office, Revolutionary War Numbered MSS, box 109, Record #11037, NJSA; Ward, *Between the Lines*, 60; Michael S. Adelberg, "A Combination to Trample All Law Underfoot: The Association for Retaliation and the American Revolution in Monmouth County, New Jersey," *New Jersey History* 115 (February 1997): 6–8, 10–16, 18; Bernstein, "New Jersey in the American Revolution," 366–69.

89. Fowler, "Egregious Villains," 214–24; Ward, *Between the Lines*, 111–13; Richard Koke, "War, Profit, and Privateers Along the New Jersey Coast: Letters of 1782 Relating to an Obscure Waterfront of the American Revolution," *New York Historical Society Quarterly* 41.3 (July 1957): 284–86; Chopra, *Unnatural Rebellion*, 194–95, Sheila Skemp, *William Franklin: Son of a Patriot, Servant of a King* (New York: Oxford University Press, 1990), 253–55; Henry Clinton to unknown, January 1782, Clinton Papers, vol. 191; Hoock, *Scars of Independence*, 343.

90. Skemp, *William Franklin*, 256–59 (quote on 257); Samuel Forman to WL, March 25, 1782, *PWL*, 4:388; Ward, *Between the Lines*, 64–65; Essay, "The Prince and the Patriot, William Henry and Joshua Huddy," *PWL*, 4:362–63; Hoock, *Scars of Independence*, 339–48.

91. Skemp, *William Franklin*, 259–61; GW to WL, May 6, 1782, *PWL*, 4:104; "The Prince and the Patriot" *PWL*, 4:363–64; GW to Elias Dayton, June 22, 1782, Elias Dayton Papers, NJHS; Andrew Elliot reports, June 15, August 9, and October 30, 1782, Clinton Papers, vols. 194, 195.

92. Henry Brockholst Livingston to WL, May 3, 1782, *PWL*, 4:403 (first quote); Guy Carleton to WL, May 7, 1782, *PWL*, 4:405; WL to Guy Carleton, May 13, 1782, *PWL*, 4:407 (second quote); Skemp, *William Franklin*, 261; Essay, "The Prince and the Patriot," *PWL*, 4:364; Guy Carleton to WL, June 12, 1782, *PWL*, 4:426–28; WL to Guy Carleton, June 25, 1782, *PWL*, 4:436–37. WL made the same argument to GW as Carleton concerning lack of evidence of prisoner abuse; see WL to GW, May 14, 1782, *PWL*, 4:412.

93. WL to Henry Brockholst Livingston, June 7, 1782, *PWL*, 4:422; Skemp, *William Franklin*, 261–65; Essay, "The Prince and the Patriot," *PWL*, 4:364.

94. WL to Elias Boudinot, January 19, 1782, *PWL*, 4:368 (first quote); WL to Assembly, June 3, 1782, *PWL*, 4:420–21 (second quote); WL to Henry Brockholst Livingston, December 17, 1781, *PWL*, 4:348–49 (third quote); Adelberg, "A Combination to Trample All Law Underfoot," 22–26.

95. WL to Hugh Brackenridge, January 13, 1779, *PWL*, 3:18–19.

96. WL to Susannah French Livingston, June 17, 1779, November 15 and 29, 1779, and March 9, 1780 (for quote), *PWL*, 3:115, 219, 237, 322–23; WL to Catharine Livingston, December 14, 1779, *PWL*, 3:265–66; WL to Catharine Livingston, February 23, 1781, and March 9, 1782, *PWL*, 4:150, 384; WL to Caesar Rodney, April 24, 1781, *PWL*, 4:184.

97. Sarah Jay to WL, June 24, 1781, *PWL*, 4:225–27 (for quote); WL to Catharine Livingston, March 16, 1782, *PWL*, 4: 85. For gardening, see WL to John Jay, March 17, 1780, *PWL*, 3:341–42; John Jay to WL, November 22, 1780, *PWL*, 4:100–101; and Essay, "Livingston Family and the War," *PWL*, 4:171.

98. WL to Sarah Jay, January 14, 1781, *PWL*, 4:124; Peter Augustus Jay to WL, January 30, March 13, and November 25 (for quote), 1781, and WL to Peter Augustus Jay, January 26, 1782, *PWL*, 4:134, 158, 336–37, 372.

99. WL to Robert Morris, April 10, 1780, *PWL*, 3:350–51; Robert Morris to WL, April 17, 1780, *PWL*, 3:353; WL to Francis Lewis, April 19, 1780, *PWL*, 3:353; WL to John Lawrence Livingston, April 19, 1780, *PWL*, 3:358–59; WL to Robert Livingston, April 19, 1780, *PWL*, 3:361–62 (for quote).

100. Catharine Livingston to WL, June 8, 1781, *PWL*, 4:217–18; WL to Sarah Jay, August 21, 1781, *PWL*, 4:256; WL to Henry Brockholst Livingston, September 17, 1781, *PWL*, 4:298–99; WL to Henry Brockholst Livingston, October 24, 1781, *PWL*, 4:319; WL to William Semple, November 2, 1781, *PWL*, 4:324; Sarah Jay to WL, January 31, 1782, *PWL*, 4:377–78 (for quote); Essay, "Livingston Family and the War," *PWL*, 4:170–71; Sedgwick, *Memoir of William Livingston*, 345–48.

Chapter 6

1. John Ferling, *Almost a Miracle: The American Victory in the War of Independence* (New York: Oxford University Press, 2007), 546–49, 554–56.

2. Woody Holton, *Unruly Americans and the Origins of the Constitution* (New York: Hill and Wang, 2007), 48, 58–60, 66, 72.

3. Proceedings of the Convention, June 18, 1787, *Records of the Federal Convention of 1787*, ed. Max Farrand, 4 vols. (New Haven, CT: Yale University Press, 1911–1937), 1:301 (for excess quote by Alexander Hamilton); Roger H. Brown, *Redeeming the Republic: Federalists, Taxation, and the Origins of the Constitution* (Baltimore: Johns Hopkins University Press, 1993), 3–7; Andrew Shankman, *Original Intents: Hamilton, Jefferson, Madison, and the American Founding* (New York: Oxford University Press, 2017), 9; Eric Nelson, *The Royalist Revolution: Monarchy and the American Founding* (Cambridge, MA: Harvard University Press, 2014), 149, 161–62, 185–96, 217–18.

4. Robert Shalhope, "Toward a Republican Synthesis: The Emergence of an Understanding of Republicanism in American Historiography," *William and Mary Quarterly* 29.1 (January 1972): 69–72; Daniel T. Rodgers, "Republicanism: The Career of a Concept," *Journal of American History* 79.1 (June 1992): 34–37; Gordon Wood, "Classical Republicanism and the American Revolution," *Chicago-Kent Law Review* 66.1 (April 1990): 13–16, 22–29.

5. Ferling, *Almost a Miracle*, 549–50; Sarah Jay to WL, October 14, 1782, *PWL*, 4:476–77.

6. WL to John Jay, January 8, 1783, *PWL*, 4:507–8 (first quote); Sarah Jay to WL, December 14, 1782, *PWL*, 4:499–500 (second quote).

7. WL to Elias Boudinot, March 24, 1783, *WLP*, reel 19; Robert Livingston to WL, March 18, 1783, *PWL*, 4:514; WL, Proclamation, April 14, 1783, *PWL*, 4:516; Ferling, *Almost a Miracle*, 557–58; Mark V. Kwasny, *Washington's Partisan War, 1775–1783* (Kent, OH: Kent State University Press, 1996), 324–26.

8. Ruma Chopra, *Unnatural Rebellion: Loyalists in New York City During the Revolution* (Charlottesville: University of Virginia Press, 2011), 198, 206, 210; Joseph Tiedemann, "Patriots, Loyalists, and Conflict Resolution in New York, 1783–1787," in *Loyalists and Community in North America*, ed. Robert Calhoon, Timothy Barnes, and George Rawlyk (Westport, CT: Greenwood Press, 1994), 78–82.

9. Petition of inhabitants of Middletown Township against the return of loyalists or restoration of their property, May 10, 1783, BAH MS Collection, box 4-1b, no. 132; Petition of inhabitants of Middlesex County against an act of grace for loyalists and to exempt them from citizenship, May 15, 1783, BAH MS Collection, no. 136; Petition of inhabitants of Bergen County against treaty articles holding states liable to recompense loyalists, May 3, 1783, BAH MS Collection, box 5-2, no. 280; Petition of inhabitants of Hunterdon County against an act of grace for loyalists, 1782, BAH MS Collection, box 4-1b, no. 129; Chopra, *Unnatural Rebellion*, 211 (for Pellet and Aston quote); Holger Hoock, *Scars of Independence: America's Violent Birth* (New York: Crown, 2017), 370–72.

10. WL to Samuel Hayes, September 1, 1782, *PWL*, 4:462.

11. WL to John Jay, May 21, 1783, *PWL*, 5:17–18; John Jay to WL, July 19, 1783, *WLP*, reel 19.

12. WL to David Forman, January 17, 1784, *PWL*, 5:77 (quote); Henry Brockholst Livingston to WL, March 30, 1784, *PWL*, 5:108–9; Mary Murrin, *To Save This State from Ruin: New Jersey and the Creation of the United States Constitution, 1776–1789* (Newark: New Jersey Historical Society, 1987), 36–37; Richard McCormick, *Experiment in Independence: New Jersey in the*

Critical Period, 1781–1789 (New Brunswick, NJ: Rutgers University Press, 1950), 27, 33–35; Chopra, *Unnatural Rebellion*, 211.

13. WL to John Livingston, June 30, 1783, *PWL*, 5:30; Judith L. Van Buskirk, *Generous Enemies: Patriots and Loyalists in Revolutionary New York* (Philadelphia: University of Pennsylvania Press, 2002), 171–72; Hoock, *Scars of Independence*, 389–90.

14. Murrin, *To Save This State from Ruin*, 37–38; McCormick, *Experiment in Independence*, 29; Van Buskirk, *Generous Enemies*, 185–89; Biographical essay on John Livingston, *PWL*, 5:541–42; David Maas, "The Massachusetts Loyalists and the Problem of Amnesty, 1775–1790," in Calhoon, Barnes, and Rawlyk, *Loyalists and Community in North America*, 68–70; Hoock, *Scars of Independence*, 386–89.

15. John Jay to WL, May 21, 1783, *PWL*, 5:16; GW to WL, June 8, 1783, *PWL*, 5:23.

16. Holton, *Unruly Americans*, 28, 47; John Kaminski, *Paper Politics: The Northern State Loan Offices During the Confederation, 1783–1790* (New York: Garland Publishing, 1989), 10–13, 16–18; McCormick, *Experiment in Independence*, 107; Brown, *Redeeming the Republic*, 39.

17. WL to Assembly, May 19, 1783, *PWL*, 5:14–15; WL to Monsieur de Marbois, September 24, 1783, *PWL*, 5:46–47 (first quote); Caius editorial, August 21, 1782, *PWL*, 4:455 (second quote); Edmund Clegg to WL, April 21, 1784, *WLP*, reel 20; Holton, *Unruly Americans*, 48–52; William Finkelstein, "An Examination of Three Attempts to Promote Manufacturing in Early America" (Honors thesis, University of Arkansas, 2016); John Beatty to WL, April 13, 1785, *PWL*, 5:184–87.

18. Philip Pauly, "Fighting the Hessian Fly: American and British Responses to Insect Invasion, 1776–1789," *Environmental History* 7 (2002): 485–88, 500; Peter O. Wacker and Paul G. E Clemens, *Land Use in Early New Jersey: A Historical Geography* (Newark: New Jersey Historical Society, 1995), 147–49; Kaminski, *Paper Politics*, 8.

19. Robert Becker, *Revolution, Reform, and the Politics of American Taxation, 1763–1783* (Baton Rouge: Louisiana State University Press, 1980), 173; Mary Murrin, "New Jersey and the Two Constitutions," in *The Constitution and the States: The Role of the Original Thirteen in the Framing and Adoption of the Federal Constitution*, ed. Patrick T. Conley and John P. Kaminski (Madison, WI: Madison House, 1988), 57; Kaminski, *Paper Politics*, 8; Brown, *Redeeming the Republic*, 36; Ruth Bogin, *Abraham Clark and the Quest for Equality in the Revolutionary Era, 1774–1794* (Rutherford, NJ: Fairleigh Dickinson University Press, 1982), 93; McCormick, *Experiment in Independence*, 111–12, 115–16.

20. Petition of inhabitants of Hunterdon County concerning tax oppression, December 12, 1783, AM Papers, box 18, no. 3007 AM (first quote); Holton, *Unruly Americans*, 29–30; Brown, *Redeeming the Republic*, 33–34; Petition of inhabitants of Essex County for relief, November 3, 1783, BAH MS Collection, box 1-15, no. 47 (second quote); John Beatty to WL, February 10, 1784, *PWL*, 5:81 (third quote).

21. Holton, *Unruly Americans*, 29–30; John Jay to WL, May 21, 1783, *WLP*, reel 19; Charles Thomson to S. Hardy, July 28, 1784, and Charles Thomson to Read, July 23, 1784, Charles Thomson Papers, HSP; Robert Morris to WL, July 11, 1783, *PWL*, 5:31–32; John Jay to WL, July 19, 1783, *WLP*, reel 19 (first quote); John Beatty to WL, April 13, 1785, *PWL*, 5:184–87; John Beatty to WL, February 25, 1783, *PWL*, 5:87–89 (second quote).

22. Petition of freeholders and inhabitants of Salem County for redemption of state money, May 31, 1783, and Petition of the subscribers and inhabitants of Essex County for relief, November 3, 1783, BAH MS Collection, box 1-15, nos. 42 and 47; Act for raising a revenue ... for the purpose of paying the interest and principal of debts due from the United States, December 20, 1783, *Acts of the Eighth General Assembly of the State of New-Jersey* (Trenton, NJ: Isaac Collins,

1784), 44; James Mott to WL, November 17, 1784, *PWL*, 5:165–67; Bogin, *Abraham Clark and the Quest for Equality*, 123–25; Scipio editorial, May 24, 1784, *PWL*, 5:131–34.

23. Act for the relief of persons holding publick securities, September 2, 1784, *Acts of the Eighth General Assembly*, 118. For petitions on repealing the law, see Petition of freeholders and inhabitants of Essex and Middlesex Counties, [1784], Petition of sundry persons, October 12, 1784, Petition of the grand jury of Burlington County, November 3, 1784, Petition of freeholders and inhabitants of Hunterdon County, November 4, 1784, and Petition of the grand jury of Hunterdon County, November 11, 1784, BAH MS Collection, box 1-15, nos. 55, 66, 68, 69, 71; and Scipio editorial, May 24, 1784, *PWL*, 5:131–34 (quote at 133).

24. Murrin, "New Jersey and the Two Constitutions," 59; Carl Prince, *New Jersey's Jeffersonian Republicans: The Genesis of an Early Party Machine, 1789–1817* (Chapel Hill: University of North Carolina Press, 1967), 6; Jackson Turner Main, *Political Parties Before the Constitution* (Chapel Hill: University of North Carolina Press, 1973), 156–57, 162–65; Murrin, *To Save This State from Ruin*, 39–44; McCormick, *Experiment in Independence*, 100–101, 147–55; Bogin, *Abraham Clark and the Quest for Equality*, 87–88.

25. Bogin, *Abraham Clark and the Quest for Equality*, 91–93; Petition of subscribers, freeholders, and other electors of Hunterdon County . . . concerning the redemption of state money, 1783, BAH MS Collection, box 1-15, no. 32 (for quote); McCormick, *Experiment in Independence*, 162–70, 179–80; Theodore Sedgwick, *A Memoir of the Life of William Livingston . . .* (New York: J. & J. Harper, 1833), 394.

26. John Beatty to WL, April 13, 1785, *PWL*, 5:184–87; Petition of inhabitants of Essex County . . . against an act to pay officers five years of pay, October 22, 1783, BAH MS Collection, box 4-1b, no. 139; Petition of Officers of Jersey Line to Legislative Council and General Assembly, May 23, 1783, Department of Defense, Adjutant General's Office, Revolutionary War Numbered MSS, box 90, Record #9957, NJSA; Holton, *Unruly Americans*, 66–69.

27. Holton, *Unruly Americans*, 63, 67–69, 70–71; James Mott to WL, November 17, 1784, *WLP*, reel 20; Bogin, *Abraham Clark and the Quest for Equality*, 124–27; McCormick, *Experiment in Independence*, 174–75, 208; Murrin, "New Jersey and the Two Constitutions," 66–67; Woody Holton, "'From the Labours of Others': War Bonds Controversy and the Origins of the Constitution in New England," *William and Mary Quarterly* 61.2 (April 2004): 315.

28. Holton, *Unruly Americans*, 71–77; Murrin, *To Save This State from Ruin*, 62–63, 65–66; Murrin, "New Jersey and the Two Constitutions," 66; McCormick, *Experiment in Independence*, 234–43; Bogin, *Abraham Clark and the Quest for Equality*, 127–31.

29. Holton, *Unruly Americans*, 55–61; Murrin, "New Jersey and the Two Constitutions," 59–61; Murrin, *To Save This State from Ruin*, 44–45; Kaminski, *Paper Politics*, 18–23; Brown, *Redeeming the Republic*, 151.

30. Bogin, *Abraham Clark and the Quest for Equality*, 93–99; Kaminski, *Paper Politics*, 110–11.

31. Primitive Whig, *New-Jersey Gazette*, January 9, 1786, *PWL*, 5:215–19.

32. Ibid., January 16, 1786, *PWL*, 5:220–21. Also see Harold Thatcher, "The Social and Economic Ideas of New Jersey's First Governor," *Proceedings of the New Jersey Historical Society* 60.4 (1942): 44; Maxine N. Lurie, "New Jersey Intellectuals and the United States Constitution," *Journal of the Rutgers University Libraries* 49.2 (1987): 69–70; Walter Peterson, "William Livingston: A Study of a Political Center Before, During, and After the Revolution" (master's thesis, University of Iowa, 1948), 93–94; and John Beatty to Josiah Hornblower, March 6, 1786, Hornblower Family Collection, NJHS (for last quote). For other Primitive Whig letters, see *PWL*, 5:223–28, 235–41.

33. WL to William Hooper, November 10, 1783, *PWL*, 5:52–53; John Jay to WL, May 21, 1783, *PWL*, 5:16; WL to Susannah French Livingston, no date [1783], *PWL*, 4:504–5 (for quote); WL to Isaac Plume, May 2/3, 1783, *PWL*, 5:11; WL to John Jay, March 21, 1785, *PWL*, 5:181–82;Phillip Phillip Livingston to WL, May 19, 1785, *PWL*, 5:192; Michael Levine, "Transformation of a Radical Whig Under Republican Government: William Livingston, Governor of New Jersey, 1776–1790" (PhD diss., Rutgers University, 1975), 235–37, 242–44.

34. WL to Charles Stewart, March 15, 1785, *PWL*, 5:175–77.

35. Carroll Smith-Rosenberg, *This Violent Empire: The Birth of an American National Identity* (Chapel Hill: University of North Carolina Press, 2010), 60–66 (quotes on 60 and 61); Lurie, "New Jersey Intellectuals and the United States Constitution," 70; Levine, "Transformation of a Radical Whig," 233, 239–40; Cynthia Kierner, *Traders and Gentlefolk: The Livingstons of New York, 1675–1790* (Ithaca, NY: Cornell University Press, 1992), 166.

36. Smith-Rosenberg, *This Violent Empire*, 88–91, 98–109, 116–17, 128–31 (first quote on 107); Brown, *Redeeming the Republic*, 48–49 (second quote on 49).

37. WL to Elijah Clarke, February 17, 1787, *PWL*, 5:277; WL to Henry Laurens, January 8, 1778, *PWL*, 2:170–71.

38. Brown, *Redeeming the Republic*, 157; Gordon S. Wood, *Creation of the American Republic 1776–1787* (Chapel Hill: University of North Carolina Press, 1998), 404–18; Shalhope, "Toward a Republican Synthesis," 69–72; Robert E. Shalhope, "Republicanism, Liberalism, and Democracy: Political Culture in the Early Republic," *Proceedings of the American Antiquarian Society* 102, pt. 1 (April 1992): 99–152.

39. WL to William Burnet Sr., February 23, 1787, *PWL*, 5:277–78; Brown, *Redeeming the Republic*, 156–61, 167; Bruce H. Mann, *Republic of Debtors: Bankruptcy in the Age of American Independence* (Cambridge, MA: Harvard University Press, 2002), 4–5, 35–59, 120–21, 172–80; Kaminski, *Paper Politics*, 40–42; Wood, *Creation of the American Republic*, 404–18; Shalhope, "Toward a Republican Synthesis," 69–72; Jack N. Rakove, "Gordon Wood, the 'Republican Synthesis,' and the Path Not Taken," *William and Mary Quarterly* 44.3 (July 1987): 619–20; Rodgers, "Republicanism," 34–37.

40. "On Legal Order," William Paterson Papers, RUSCUA; Lurie, "New Jersey Intellectuals and the United States Constitution," 71–75; Murrin, "New Jersey and the Two Constitutions," 60–61; Murrin, *To Save This State from Ruin*, 45–49; Cumberland response to Primitive Whig, *New-Jersey Gazette*, February 6, 1786, *PWL*, 5:232–35; John O'Connor, *William Paterson, Lawyer and Statesman, 1745–1806* (New Brunswick, NJ: Rutgers University Press, 1979), 123–26, 134.

41. *New-Jersey Gazette*, February 6, 1786, *PWL*, 5:229–32; Bogin, *Abraham Clark and the Quest for Equality*, 99.

42. Sedgwick, *Memoir of William Livingston*, 397; Kaminski, *Paper Politics*, 114–15; Peterson, "William Livingston," 95–97; Bogin, *Abraham Clark and the Quest for Equality*, 103–6.

43. Bogin, *Abraham Clark and the Quest for Equality*, 103–6; WL to Benjamin Van Cleve, May 5, 1786, *PWL*, 5:248–49; Sedgwick, *Memoir of William Livingston*, 397; Kaminski, *Paper Politics*, 114–15; Peterson, "William Livingston," 95–97.

44. McCormick, *Experiment in Independence*, 200–203; Brown, *Redeeming the Republic*, 151; Kaminski, *Paper Politics*, 116–19; Bogin, *Abraham Clark and the Quest for Equality*, 106.

45. WL to William Hooper, November 10, 1783, *PWL*, 5:52–53 (first quote); John Jay to WL, March 21, 1785, *PWL*, 5:179–80; WL to Charles Stewart, March 21, 1785, *PWL*, 5:180–81 (second quote); WL to John Jay, March 21, 1785, *PWL*, 5:181–82; Charles Stewart to WL, March 25, 1785, *PWL*, 5:183–84 (third quote); Charles Thomson to WL, June 23, 1785, *PWL*, 5:197; WL to Charles

Thomson, June 25, 1785, *PWL*, 5:197–98; Robert Pemberton to Elias Boudinot, June 24, 1785, Boudinot Family Papers, RUSCUA; Sedgwick, *Memoir of William Livingston*, 389; Peterson, "William Livingston," 93.

46. Brown, *Redeeming the Republic*, 151; WL to John Jay, March 23, 1790, *PWL*, 5:427–28 (for quotes); Kaminski, *Paper Politics*, 119–21; Bogin, *Abraham Clark and the Quest for Equality*, 110–13; McCormick, *Experiment in Independence*, 205; O'Connor, *William Paterson*, 121.

47. John Rutherfurd to General Robertson, April 29, 1787, Walter Eastburn Collection, NJHS (first quote); *Notes on the State of New Jersey* (Trenton, 1786), in *Proceedings of the New Jersey Historical Society* 2.1–2 (1867–1872), 83.

48. Thomas McKean to John Adams, April 30, 1787, Thomas McKean Papers, HSP; Thomas Paine to Daniel Clymer, September 1786, George Clymer Papers, HSP.

49. Lance Banning, *The Sacred Fire of Liberty: James Madison and the Founding of the Federal Republic* (Ithaca, NY: Cornell University Press, 1995), 14–30, 42, 44–45, 71–73, 117, 125–29; Holton, *Unruly Americans*, 4–8, 28; Jack N. Rakove, *James Madison and the Creation of the American Republic* (Glenview, IL: Scott Foresman, 1990), 44–46; Brown, *Redeeming the Republic*, 3–4, 25, 156–61; Gordon S. Wood, "Interests and Disinterestedness in the Making of the Constitution," in *Beyond Confederation: Origins of the Constitution and American National Identity*, ed. Richard Beeman, Stephen Botein, and Edward C. Carter II (Chapel Hill: University of North Carolina Press, 1987), 73–76; Wood, *Creation of the American Republic*, 404–7, 417–18; Levine, "Transformation of a Radical Whig," 245–48, 254–56; Mann, *Republic of Debtors*, 4–5, 35–59, 120–21, 172–80; Kaminski, *Paper Politics*, 40–42; Shankman, *Original Intents*, 14–15, 36–37, 41–43.

50. WL to Baron von Steuben, September 25, 1786, *PWL*, 5:259–60 (first quote); WL to Chauncey Whittelsey, February 2, 1787, *PWL*, 5:268–70. Also see Becker, *Revolution, Reform, and the Politics of American Taxation*, 154.

51. Rakove, *Madison and the Creation of the American Republic*, 37, 44–51 (quote on 47); Brown, *Redeeming the Republic*, 3–7; Jack N. Rakove, *The Beginnings of National Politics: An Interpretive History of the Continental Congress* (New York: Knopf, 1979), 368–73; Wood, "Interests and Disinterestedness," 82–86, 92; Lance Banning, "The Republican Interpretation: Retrospect and Prospect," *Proceedings of the American Antiquarian Society* 102, pt. 1 (April 1992): 153–79; Shalhope, "Republicanism, Liberalism, and Democracy," 55–59.

52. Nelson, *Royalist Revolution*, 149, 161–62, 169, 185–96, 217, 218, 232.

53. Brown, *Redeeming the Republic*, 3–7; Rakove, *Madison and the Creation of the American Republic*, 37; Max M. Edling, *A Revolution in Favor of Government: Origins of the U.S. Constitution and the Making of the American State* (New York: Oxford University Press, 2003), 3–8, 73–76, 93–97, 163–66, 172–73; Jack N. Rakove, *Original Meanings: Politics and Ideas in the Making of the Constitution* (New York: Knopf, 1996), 44, 50, 54; James Bowdoin to WL, July 1, 1785, *WLP*, reel 21; WL to Assembly, August 29, 1788, *PWL*, 5:354–55 (for quotes).

54. Murrin, *To Save This State from Ruin*, 66; McCormick, *Experiment in Independence*, 253–55; Brown, *Redeeming the Republic*, 29–30; Rakove, *Beginnings of National Politics*, 374–75; Bogin, *Abraham Clark and the Quest for Equality*, 131–32.

55. WL to William Churchill Houston, December 22, 1786, *WLP*, reel 21 (first quotes); WL to John Tabor Kempe, March 3, 1787, *PWL*, 5:281 (second quotes); Appointment to Constitutional Convention, November 23, 1786, *PWL*, 5:263–64; Appointment of WL and Abraham Clark to Federal Convention, May 18, 1787, *PWL*, 5:289–90; Bogin, *Abraham Clark and the Quest for Equality*, 133–34; Brown, *Redeeming the Republic*, 142, 149.

56. WL to David Brearley, May 19, 1787, *PWL*, 5:290–91; James Madison, *Notes of Debates in*

the Federal Convention of 1787 (New York: Norton, 1987), 163; James Madison to Theodore Sedgwick, February 12, 1831, *Founders Online*, (http://founders.archives.gov/documents/Madison/99-02-02-2282; accessed July 27, 2017); McCormick, *Experiment in Independence*, 258; WL to John Jay, September 11, 1787, *PWL*, 5:300–301n. 4, George Washington, George Read, John Dickinson, John Rutledge, John Langdon, Roger Sherman, Benjamin Franklin, Thomas Mifflin, Gouverneur Morris, George Clymer, and James Wilson all served in the First or Second Continental Congress with Livingston.

57. James Madison to Theodore Sedgwick, February 12, 1831, *Founders Online*, (http://founders.archives.gov/documents/Madison/99-02-02-2282; accessed July 27, 2017); William Pierce, Character sketches of delegates to the Federal Convention, in Farrand, *Records of the Federal Convention of 1787*, 3:90; Liste des membres et officiers du Congres, in Farrand, *Records of the Federal Convention of 1787*, 3:235.

58. Rakove, *Original Meanings*, 37–38, 61–65; Murrin, *To Save This State from Ruin*, 71–74; O'Connor, *William Paterson*, 135–60; Brown, *Redeeming the Republic*, 192–94; William Paterson to Euphemia Paterson, July 2, 1787, William Paterson Papers, RUSCUA (for quote). On western land, see Elias Boudinot to WL, June 8, 1783, *PWL*, 5:22; Remonstrance of New Jersey Legislature to Continental Congress, June 14, 1783, *PWL*, 5:23; and McCormick, *Experiment in Independence*, 220–23. For Paterson and slavery, see Paul Finkelman, "Slavery and the Constitutional Convention," in Beeman, Botein, and Carter, *Beyond Confederation*, 201–2, 212–13.

59. Jonathan Dayton to WL, July 13, 1787, *PWL*, 5:293–94; Matthew Ridley to WL, July 15, 1787, *PWL*, 5:294–95; WL to John Jay, July 19, 1787, *PWL*, 5:295; James Madison to Theodore Sedgwick, February 12, 1831, Madison Papers (for quote); Journal, August 17 and 22, 1787, in Farrand, *Records of the Federal Convention of 1787*, 2:322, 366.

60. Holton, *Unruly Americans*, 266–68; Report to the Convention, August 21, 1787, *PWL*, 5:297–98; Robert McGuire, *To Form a More Perfect Union: A New Economic Interpretation of the United States Constitution* (New York: Oxford University Press, 2003), 65, 86–89; Peterson, "William Livingston," 100–101; Shankman, *Original Intents*, 12–14, 27.

61. Report to the Convention, August 21, 1787, *PWL*, 5:297–98; Farrand, *Records of the Federal Convention of 1787*, 2:380–95; Saul Cornell, *A Well-Regulated Militia: The Founding Fathers and the Origins of Gun Control in America* (New York: Oxford University Press, 2006), 39–44; Edling, *Revolution in Favor of Government*, 7–8, 73–76.

62. Finkelman, "Slavery and the Constitutional Convention," 213–14; David Waldstreicher, *Slavery's Constitution: From Revolution to Ratification* (New York: Hill and Wang, 2010), 94–97; Christopher Collier, *All Politics Is Local: Family, Friends, and Provincial Interests in the Creation of the Constitution* (Hanover, NH: University Press of New England, 2003), 64–66; Rakove, *Original Meanings*, 87–88; Woody Holton, *Forced Founders: Indians, Debtors, Slaves, and the Making of the American Revolution in Virginia* (Chapel Hill: University of North Carolina Press, 1999), 51–73.

63. Finkelman, "Slavery and the Constitutional Convention," 214, 217–20; Waldstreicher, *Slavery's Constitution*, 95–101; Collier, *All Politics Is Local*, 67–71; Rakove, *Original Meanings*, 88–89; Report of Committee of Eleven, August 24, 1787, *PWL*, 5:98; Peterson, "William Livingston," 101; McGuire, *To Form a More Perfect Union*, 86–89; Farrand, *Records of the Federal Convention of 1787*, 2:355, 366, 396, 400.

64. Peterson, "William Livingston," 101; McGuire, *To Form a More Perfect Union*, 86–89; Farrand, *Records of the Federal Convention of 1787*, 2:355, 366, 396, 400; James J. Gigantino II, *The Ragged Road to Abolition: Slavery and Freedom in New Jersey* (Philadelphia: University of Pennsylvania Press, 2015), 72–73.

65. Samuel Allinson to WL, July 13, 1778, and WL to Samuel Allinson, July 25, 1778, Allinson Family Papers, RUSCUA (for quotes); Gigantino, *Ragged Road to Abolition*, 25–26, 34–39; Scott Rohrer, *Jacob Green's Revolution: Radical Religion and Reform in a Revolutionary Age* (University Park: Pennsylvania State University Press, 2014), 213–14. For other conversations with Allinson, see Samuel Allinson to WL and WL to Samuel Allinson, May 27, 1780, and June 2, 1780, *PWL*, 3:396–97, 407–9; WL to Samuel Allinson, December 22, 1781, *WLP*, reel 16.

66. *New-Jersey Journal*, May 3 and 10, 1780, November 29, 1780, December 27, 1780, and January 10, 17, 24, and 31, 1781; Gigantino, *Ragged Road to Abolition*, 26–29; Rohrer, *Jacob Green's Revolution*, 210–18.

67. WL to New York Manumission Society, June 26, 1786, *PWL*, 5:255 (first quote); WL to James Pemberton, December 21, 1788, *PWL*, 5:365–68 (second quote); Gigantino, *Ragged Road to Abolition*, 65–67; Shane White, *Somewhat More Independent: The End of Slavery in New York City, 1770–1810* (Athens: University of Georgia Press, 1991), 27–28, 82, 86.

68. WL to James Pemberton, October 20, 1788, *PWL*, 5:357–58.

69. Ibid., December 21, 1788, *PWL*, 5:365–68; Gigantino, *Ragged Road to Abolition*, 72–74.

70. Gigantino, *Ragged Road to Abolition*, 72–74.

71. Timothy Brush to WL, March 5, 1785, *PWL*, 5:174–75; WL to Susannah French Livingston, February 19, 1786, *PWL*, 5:242; WL to John Jay, May 1, 1786, *PWL*, 5:247–48; Bill of manumission for his slaves, October 1787, *PWL*, 5:302; Catharine Livingston Ridley to WL, January 20 and February 2, 1790, *PWL*, 5:413–14, 419–20.

72. WL to Legislative Council, October 25, 1787, *PWL*, 5:303–4; WL to John Jay, September 4 and 11, 1787, *PWL*, 5:299–300, 300–301 (for quotes).

73. *Pennsylvania Herald*, October 27, 1787, *DHRC*, 3:140–41 (first quote); Elias Boudinot to William Bradford Jr., September 28, 1787, *DHRC*, 3:134 (second quote).

74. *New-Jersey Journal*, October 31 and November 14, 1787, *DHRC*, 3:141–42, 152–53.

75. *Pennsylvania Herald*, October 27, 1787, *DHRC*, 3:140–41.

76. *Trenton Mercury*, November 6, 1787, *DHRC*, 3:146–51; Lambert Cadwalader to George Mitchell, October 8, 1787, *DHRC*, 3:137–38; Bernard Bailyn, ed, *The Debate on the Constitution: Federalist and Antifederalist Speeches, Articles, and Letters During the Struggle Over Ratification* (New York: Viking, 1993), 1:160, 283.

77. Lambert Cadwalader to George Mitchell, October 8, 1787, *DHRC*, 3:137–38; *Pennsylvania Gazette*, October 10, 1787, *DHRC*, 3:140; A Farmer of New-Jersey [John Stevens], *Observations on Government: Including Some Animadversions on Mr. Adams's Defence of the Constitutions of Government of the United States of America and on Mr. De Lolme's Constitution of England* (New York: printed by W. Ross, 1787), 14, 39, 52–53; Bogin, *Abraham Clark and the Quest for Equality*, 135–36; Collier, *All Politics Is Local*, 4, 10; McCormick, *Experiment in Independence*, 261–63, 272–75. For pro-Constitution petitions from Gloucester, Burlington, Salem, and Middlesex, see *DHRC*, 3:136–37.

78. WL to Ephraim Harris, December 3, 1787, *PWL*, 5:316–17 (for quotes); Murrin, *To Save This State from Ruin*, 75–76; Bogin, *Abraham Clark and the Quest for Equality*, 135–37.

79. Election of Convention Delegates, *DHRC*, 3:173; New Jersey Ratification Convention Notes, *DHRC*, 3:177, 188; *Pennsylvania Packet*, December 21, 1787, *DHRC*, 3:192; Murrin, *To Save This State from Ruin*, 76–80; McCormick, *Experiment in Independence*, 266–67.

80. WL to John Jay, February 14, 1788, *PWL*, 5:329–30. For *American Museum*, see WL to Mathew Carey, June 26, 1788, August 4, 1788, and August 19, 1788, *PWL*, 5:335–36, 340, 351–53; and Mathew Carey to WL, July 30, 1788, *PWL*, 5:339.

81. McCormick, *Experiment in Independence*, 280–86; Petition of the inhabitants of Burlington County concerning depreciation of currency, August 19, 1788, BAH MS Collection, box 1-16, no. 1; WL to Assembly, August 29, 1788, *PWL*, 5:354–55; Rudolph J. Pasler and Margaret C. Pasler, *The New Jersey Federalists* (Rutherford, NJ: Fairleigh Dickinson University Press, 1974), 26; Levine, "Transformation of a Radical Whig," 257.

82. Richard Cox to Jonathan Dayton, May 19, 1789, Jonathan Dayton Family Papers, Manuscripts Division, William L. Clements Library, University of Michigan, Ann Arbor; McCormick, *Experiment in Independence*, 290–91, 294.

83. Bogin, *Abraham Clark and the Quest for Equality*, 138–40; Joseph Bloomfield to Jonathan Dayton, February 29, 1789, Jonathan Dayton Papers, folder 60, NJHS; McCormick, *Experiment in Independence*, 291–99; WL Proclamation, March 19, 1789, *PWL*, 5:381–82; Pasler and Pasler, *New Jersey Federalists*, 26–29.

84. Murrin, *To Save This State from Ruin*, 82–85; Prince, *New Jersey's Jeffersonian Republicans*, 7–8; WL to Matthias Ogden, June 8, 1789, *PWL*, 5:385–86; Elias Boudinot to WL, September 2, 1789, *PWL*, 5:391; Jonathan Dayton to Majors Ross and Cox, March 15, 1789, Jonathan Dayton Family Papers (for quotes); Matthias Ogden to Jonathan Dayton, June 6, 1789, Jonathan Dayton Family Papers; McCormick, *Experiment in Independence*, 90, 297–302.

Epilogue

1. Milton M. Klein, *The American Whig: William Livingston of New York* (New York: Garland, 1993), 563; WL to John Jay, January 8, 1783, *PWL*, 4:507; Sarah Jay to WL, July 18, 1783, *PWL*, 5:33 (first quote); WL to Monsieur de Marbois, September 24, 1783, *PWL*, 5:46–47 (second quote).

2. Klein, *American Whig*, 562–65; Theodore Sedgwick, *A Memoir of the Life of William Livingston . . .* (New York: J. & J. Harper, 1833), 432.

3. Klein, *American Whig*, 562; WL to Peter Yates, August 19, 1782, *PWL*, 4:453; WL to Henry Brockholst, August 20, 1782, *PWL*, 4:454; WL to John Jay, January 5 and February 13, 1785, *PWL*, 5:171–72, 173 (for quotes).

4. William Livingston Jr. biographical entry, *PWL*, 5:556–58; Henry Brockholst Livingston to Susannah Livingston, July 15, 1791, *PWL*, 5:446; William Livingston Jr. to William Paterson, May 29, 1801, *PWL*, 5:447–48; Last Will and Testament of William Livingston, *PWL*, 5:442–45; Klein, *American Whig*, 562.

5. WL to John Jay, January 18 and 28, 1790, *PWL*, 5:410–12, 418–19; John Jay to WL, January 25, 1790, *PWL*, 5:416–17.

6. WL to John Jay, January 28, 1790, *PWL*, 5:419 (for quote); Klein, *American Whig*, 565; Sedgwick, *Memoir of William Livingston*, 433–34.

7. Sedgwick, *Memoir of William Livingston*, 435–37; Henry Brockholst Livingston to Susannah Livingston, March 24, 1790, *PWL*, 5:428–29; John Beatty to Susannah Livingston, July 19, 1790, *PWL*, 5:436–37; Susannah Livingston to Catharine Ridley, July 24, 1790, *PWL*, 5:437–38; Henry Brockholst Livingston to Susannah Livingston, August 2, 1790, *PWL*, 5:441.

8. William Livingston Last Will and Testament, *PWL*, 5:442–45.

9. Death Notice, July 28, 1790, *PWL*, 5:439–40 (first quote); WL Epitaph, Statesmen Collection, NJHS; William Paterson to WL Jr., December 21, 1790, William Paterson Papers, NJHS; John O'Connor, *William Paterson: Lawyer and Statesman* (New Burnswick, N.J: Rutgers University Press, 1979), 183–84 (for second quote).

INDEX

ACKNOWLEDGMENTS

When I first met William Livingston almost ten years ago, I never thought I would write a whole book about him or ever feel that I knew so well someone who died almost two hundred years before I was born. Like most authors who examine a single human subject in this way, I find that Livingston has gotten in my head. If I met him, I am not sure I would like him, but I definitely understand him and even see a bit of myself in him. Without Livingston, this book obviously would not be possible and therefore I owe him the greatest gratitude.

Beyond Livingston himself, the work of Carl Prince and the other editors and staff who collected, edited, and published the *Papers of William Livingston* sped this project to completion. Though deciphering Livingston's notoriously bad handwriting on microfilm in the unpublished papers was not the most exciting part of my academic career, doing it from the comfort of my own library instead of traveling to dozens of others certainly made up for that. Special thanks to the staff members of Arkansas's interlibrary loan office, especially to Robin Roggio, for all their work in bringing Livingston to Arkansas. When I did travel for this project, the archivists and staff at the institutions I visited never failed to lend a helping hand and offer a kind word. Thank you to the archivists and staff at the New Jersey State Archives (especially Bette Epstein), the New Jersey Historical Society (especially James Amemasor), Rutgers University, the Historical Society of Pennsylvania, the New-York Historical Society, and the William Clements Library at the University of Michigan.

I could not have completed this book without support from those organizations that during my academic career have believed in me the most. Financial assistance from the University of Arkansas History Department and the J. William Fulbright College of Arts and Sciences as well as a research grant from the New Jersey Historical Commission, a division of the Department of State, provided the funds necessary for research. I thank the people of both

New Jersey and Arkansas for this support. Likewise, I thank Misti Harper, Sarah Riva, Nate Conley, and Amanda McGee for research assistance, helping me slog through newspapers, microfilm, and numerous French sources.

Beyond money, though, the people who have been with me over the last few years made this project possible. A special thanks to Bob Lockhart for believing in me for now two books with him and for the kind critical comments that helped bring the final version of this book to life. The two anonymous reviewers for Penn Press gave me pointed feedback to refine my arguments, and Gretchen Oberfranc worked her magic with editing for clarity and style. I also thank Lucia McMahon and Randall Woods who heard me drone on about Livingston far too often. I would be remiss if I did not thank Calvin White Jr. for his support. We often appear to be the odd couple walking across campus together, but, for some reason, it just works. I have been proud to call him a friend these past several years.

The debt to my family continues to go beyond what I can describe. My sister, Diane, and brother-in-law, Joseph, are models of what a good family can be like. I often look with wonder as my sister mobilizes my four nephews for all their varied and exciting activities when I am dog-tired after a day with Livingston. I continue not to understand how she can be such a good mother and sister without being exhausted every day. Though the time I spend with them can be exhausting, the love and joy John, Anthony, Dominic, and Benedict give when they smile, hug, or invite me to play with them is beyond anything I have experienced as a historian. I cherish every day we spend together.

My parents, Lois and Jim Gigantino, remain the source of endless love and encouragement. Without that love and support, I would not have made it to where I am now. I am thankful every day that I came from such a loving home that provided me the tools to succeed. However, while my parents have helped get me to where I am today, Stephanie Heath helps me see where I am going next. I learn something new about myself each day with her as we explore our new life together and make plans for the future. Living with her and Bosco (our best four-legged friend) has been an adventure that I never want to end. I cannot wait to see where it goes. It is to her that I dedicate this book because, as Livingston thought about his Susannah, my life would not be the same without Stephanie.

www.ingramcontent.com/pod-product-compliance
Lightning Source LLC
Chambersburg PA
CBHW030940150426
42812CB00064B/3072/J